Language and National Identity in Africa

also edited by Andrew Simpson and published by Oxford University Press
Language and National Identity in Asia

Language and National Identity in Africa

edited by

ANDREW SIMPSON

OXFORD

UNIVERSITY PRESS

*This book has been printed digitally and produced in a standard specification
in order to ensure its continuing availability*

OXFORD
UNIVERSITY PRESS

Great Clarendon Street, Oxford OX2 6DP

Oxford University Press is a department of the University of Oxford.
It furthers the University's objective of excellence in research, scholarship,
and education by publishing worldwide in

Oxford New York

Auckland Cape Town Dar es Salaam Hong Kong Karachi
Kuala Lumpur Madrid Melbourne Mexico City Nairobi
New Delhi Shanghai Taipei Toronto
With offices in
Argentina Austria Brazil Chile Czech Republic France Greece
Guatemala Hungary Italy Japan South Korea Poland Portugal
Singapore Switzerland Thailand Turkey Ukraine Vietnam

Oxford is a registered trade mark of Oxford University Press
in the UK and in certain other countries

Published in the United States
by Oxford University Press Inc., New York

ISBN 978-0-19-928675-1

Contents

List of Maps

Notes on Contributors

AKOSUA ANYIDOHO has a PhD in Foreign Language Education from the University of Texas at Austin, and has taught for many years in the Department of Linguistics, University of Ghana, Legon, where she was the Head from 2000 to 2002. She is still associated with that institution after her retirement, supervising graduate students' dissertations. Her research interests include second language teaching and learning, language in education, and women's oral culture in Africa. She has published many articles in these fields. She currently works as the Director of New York University's study abroad programme in Ghana.

DAVID APPLEYARD is Professor Emeritus of the Languages of the Horn of Africa at SOAS (School of Oriental and African Studies) in the University of London, where he taught Amharic and a number of other Horn of Africa languages, as well as various aspects of Ethiopian Studies, from 1975 until his retirement in 2006. His research interests cover a wide range of languages and linguistic issues of the region, but focus especially on the typological, comparative, and historical linguistics of Ethiopian Semitic and Cushitic languages. He has written extensively in these fields, and his major publications include *Ethiopian Manuscripts* (1993), the textbook *Colloquial Amharic* (1995), and *A Comparative Dictionary of the Agaw Languages* (2006). He is currently a member of the international advisory and editorial board of the Encyclopaedia Aethiopica.

EDMOND BILOA is Professor and Chair of the Department of African Languages and Linguistics in the University of Yaoundé I in Cameroon. His teaching interests include French linguistics, generative syntax, and psycholinguistics. He is the author of *Functional Categories and the Syntax of Focus in Tuki* (Munich: Lincom Europa 1995); *Syntaxe générative. La théorie des principes et des paramètres* (Munich: Lincom Europa 1998); *La langue française au Cameroun* (Bern: Peter Lang 2003); *Cours de linguistique contemporaine* (Munich: Lincom Europa 2004), *Grammaire générative. La théorie minimaliste de Noam Chomsky* (Yaoundé : Cameroon University Press 2004); *Le français en contact avec l'anglais au Cameroun* (Munich: Lincom Europa 2006). He has published articles on the linguistics and sociolinguistics of the French language in Cameroon, on the syntax of African languages, and on the acquisition of French.

EYAMBA G. BOKAMBA is Professor of Linguistics and African Languages in the Department of Linguistics at the University of Illinois at Urbana-Champaign where he has served since 1974 in a variety of administrative positions. Initially trained as a Bantu syntactician at Indiana University where he earned his PhD in 1976, he developed a secondary interest in sociolinguistics and has pursued research into multilingualism, in particular including language policies vis-à-vis education in Africa, language variation, and code-switching. He has published extensively in these areas, on Bantu syntax, and on African language pedagogical materials, with his latest publication (co-authored with his spouse) being *Tósolola na Lingála: A Multidimensional Approach to the Teaching and Learning of Lingála as a Foreign Language* (NALRC Press, University of Wisconsin-Madison, 2004). He is currently working on the production of a sociolinguistic book entitled *Multilingualism in Sub-Saharan Africa*, which will represent the culmination of his research in this area.

MARY ESTHER KROPP DAKUBU is a Professor in the Institute of African Studies of the University of Ghana, where she has been on the staff since 1964. Her research is centred on the Niger-Congo languages, especially Kwa and Gur. She is the author of *Dagaare Grammar* (Legon: Institute of African Studies 2005); *Ga Phonology* (Legon: IAS 2002); *Ga–English Dictionary with English–Ga Index* (Accra: Black Mask Publishers 2002); *Korle Meets the Sea, a Sociolinguistic History of Accra* (New York and Oxford: OUP 1997); *The Dangme Language: An Introductory Study* (London /Accra: Macmillan /Unimax 1987); and *One Voice: The Linguistic Culture of an Accra Lineage* (Leiden: African Studies Centre 1981). She edited and was a major contributor to *The Languages of Ghana* (London: Kegan Paul International Ltd. 1988).

GEORGE ECHU is Associate Professor of French and Linguistics and Head of the Department of Bilingual Studies in the University of Yaoundé I in Cameroon. His teaching interests include French linguistics, sociolinguistics, contrastive linguistics, and translation. He was Senior Fulbright Scholar at Indiana University Bloomington from August 2002 to May 2003. In the area of research, he has published several articles and co-edited the following books: *Official Bilingualism and Linguistic Communication in Cameroon* (New York: Peter Lang 1999); and *Africa Meets Europe: Language Contact in West Africa* (New York: Nova Science Publishers 2004).

MOHA ENNAJI holds a PhD from the University of Essex in Linguistics (1982). He is Full Professor at the Faculty of Letters, University of Fez, where he was Chair of the English Department from 1988 to 1994. He is currently the Director of the international journal *Languages and Linguistics*, published in Morocco under his supervision since 1998. Professor Ennaji is the author and/or editor of numerous books and articles on language, culture, and society. His most recent books are: *Multilingualism, Cultural Identity, and Education in Morocco* (Springer 2005); *A Grammar of Amazigh* (2004) co-authored with Fatima Sadiqi; and *A Grammar of Moroccan Arabic* (2004) (co-authored with A. Makhoukh, H. Saidi, M. Moubtassime, and S. Slaoui). His most recent articles are: 'The Arab World (Maghreb and Near East)', in *Handbook of Language and Ethnic Identity*, edited by Professor Joshua Fishman (OUP 1999), and 'Language Contact, Arabization Policy and Education in Morocco', in *Language Contact and Language Conflict in Arabic*, edited by Aleya Roushdy (Curzon 2002).

CHEGE GITHIORA is primarily engaged in descriptive studies of east African languages and linguistics. He has published on Gĩkũyũ morphosyntax and orthography, Swahili lexicography, and on culture and identity of the African Diaspora in Latin America. He is author of *Diccionario Swahili–Español* (El Colegio de Mexico 2002) and co-editor (with Manfredi and Littlefield) of *Trends in African Linguistics* Vol VI (Africa World Press 2004). His other interests are in the dynamics of language in society, and his most recent research and publication is on multilingualism and social stratification of language in Nairobi city. A graduate of Michigan State University, he taught Swahili at El Colegio de Mexico, and at Boston University (1998–2000). He is currently lecturer in Swahili at the University of London's School of Oriental and African Studies (SOAS).

WENDY JAMES is Professor of Social Anthropology in the University of Oxford, and a Fellow of the British Academy. She has taught in the University of Khartoum and carried out research in the Sudan and Ethiopia. Her particular interest is in the historical anthropology of the region of North East Africa and the continuing vitality of local cultural traditions. She has recently published a general book, *The Ceremonial Animal: A New Portrait of Anthropology* (2003). Her key publications on the Sudan include '*Kwanim Pa: The Making of the Uduk People* (1979) and *The Listening Ebony: Moral Knowledge, Religion, and Power among the Uduk of Sudan* (1988). She is co-editor of several volumes including *The Southern Marches of Imperial Ethiopia* (1986), *Juan Maria Schuver's Travels in North East Africa* (1996), and *Remapping Ethiopia: Socialism and After* (2002).

ANNE MOSENG KNUTSEN teaches French linguistics, West African culture, and fieldwork methodology at the University of Oslo, Norway. Her research focuses on the sociolinguistic variation of French in francophone Africa, especially in the Ivory Coast where she has conducted extended fieldwork. Her doctoral thesis, entitled 'Variation du français à Abidjan (Côte d'Ivoire). Etude d'un continuum linguistique et social', deals with linguistic and sociolinguistic aspects of the emerging variety of French spoken in Abidjan, Ivory Coast.

NANCY KULA holds a PhD from the University of Leiden in the Netherlands. Her thesis 'The Phonology of Verbal Derivation in Bemba' is published in the LOT series of the *Holland Academic Graphics* (2002). She is Lecturer in Linguistics in the Department of Language and Linguistics at the University of Essex. Her research interests centre on phonology and its interfaces with morphology and syntax, as well as comparative Bantu studies. She has published many articles in these areas.

VICTOR FASHOLE LUKE is Lecturer in Linguistics and Head of the Linguistics Unit of the Department of Language Studies, Fourah Bay College, the University of Sierra Leone. He lectures in advanced semantics and pragmatics, sociolinguistics, and applied linguistics but his major interest is in synchronic linguistic studies of Sierra Leone Krio. Previously, he worked as editor with Fyle and Jones in the production of their Krio–English Dictionary, and is now researching into the quest for dominance of Sierra Leone Krio within the context of linguistic pluralism in Sierra Leone. Between 2001 and 2004, he worked together with B. Akíntúndé Oyètádé of the Department of the Languages and Cultures of Africa, SOAS, studying the impact of the ten-year civil war in Sierra Leone on the lexicon of Sierra Leone Krio, and an article entitled 'Representation of Civil War Violence in Sierra Leone Krio' was published in 2005 as part of the research findings. Currently, he is working with Akin Oyètádé on a book that will contain more findings of this research project.

LUTZ MARTEN is Senior Lecturer in Southern African Languages at the School of Oriental and African Studies, University of London, where he received his PhD in 1999. His work focuses on theoretical and African linguistics, in particular in relation to Bantu languages. He has undertaken fieldwork in Zambia, Tanzania, Namibia, and Malawi, working mainly on Swahili, Bemba, and Herero. He is the author of *At the Syntax–Pragmatics Interface* (OUP 2002); *A Grammatical Sketch of Herero* (Köppe 2002, with Jekura Kavari and Wilhelm Möhlig); *Colloquial Swahili* (Routledge 2003, with Donovan McGrath); and *The Dynamics of Language* (Elsevier 2006, with Ronnie Cann and Ruth Kempson), and has published several journal articles and book chapters on African languages and linguistics.

FIONA MCLAUGHLIN is an Associate Professor of African Languages and Linguistics at the University of Florida where she currently heads a research project on the languages of urban Africa. Her research focuses on the sociolinguistics of language contact in Senegal as well as on the phonology and morphology of Wolof, Seereer, and Pulaar. She has published articles on noun classification, reduplication, and consonant mutation in journals such as *Phonology* and *Studies in African Linguistics*, and she has contributed chapters to several edited volumes including *Adjective Classes: A Cross-linguistic Typology* (OUP 2004) and *Linguistic Fieldwork* (CUP 2001). She is a former director of the West African Research Center in Dakar, Senegal, and has taught at the Université Gaston Berger de Saint-Louis in Senegal.

RAJEND MESTHRIE is Professor of Linguistics at the University of Cape Town. He is currently President of the Linguistics Society of Southern Africa. His work focuses mainly on sociolinguistics in the Southern African context. His early research on Indian migrants in South Africa was published as *Language in Indenture* (Routledge 1992) and *English in Language Shift* (CUP 1992). He has edited, *inter alia*, *Language in South Africa* (CUP 2002), the *Concise Encyclopedia of Sociolinguistics* (Elsevier 2001) and is co-author of *Introducing Sociolinguistics* (Edinburgh University Press 2000). He is on the board of numerous academic journals including *African Studies, Journal of Sociolinguistics*, and the *Journal of Multilingual and Multicultural Development*, and is series editor for CUP's *Key Topics in Sociolinguistics*.

MARTIN ORWIN is Lecturer in Somali and Amharic at SOAS (School of Oriental and African Studies) in the University of London where he teaches both languages. His research concentrates on language use in Somali poetry, in particular the metrical system, and how this and other aspects of language are used creatively by poets. He has published a number of articles on these topics and is at present in the final stages of writing a book on Somali metre. He is also involved in the translation of Somali poetry of which he has published some examples.

BENJAMIN AKÍNTÚNDÉ OYÈTÁDÉ is Lecturer in Yorùbá at SOAS (School of Oriental and African Studies) in the University of London where he teaches Yorùbá language and culture. His research concentrates on Yorùbá linguistics, language, and culture in the homeland and in the diaspora, and he has published several articles on these topics. Between 2001 and 2004, he worked together with Victor Fashole Luke of Fourah Bay College, University of Sierra Leone, studying the impact of the ten-year civil war in Sierra Leone on the lexicon of Sierra Leone Krio. This DIFD-funded and British Council-administered research project has opened up an opportunity for a further research interest on the historical and current significance of Yorùbá language and culture to Sierra Leone Krio. He is currently working on a book entitled *Yorùbá – The Making of a Language*, and is the Head of Department of the Languages and Cultures of Africa at SOAS.

FATIMA SADIQI received her PhD in Theoretical Linguistics from the University or Essex in 1982. Since that time she has published extensively on Moroccan languages and women/gender issues. She is Editor-in-Chief of *Languages and Linguistics*, an international journal, and serves on the editorial board of *Language and Gender*, the first international journal in the discipline. Professor Sadiqi was President and Founder of the Centre for Studies and Research on Women, and Director of the first graduate unit 'Gender Studies' and has served on a wide variety of national and international committees such as the Language Based Area Studies Initiative for China, Japan, Eastern Europe, and the Arabic Speaking World. In 2006, Fatima Sadiqi was awarded a Fellowship at Harvard University to lecture and write on language, gender, and Islam in North Africa.

ANDREW SIMPSON is Professor of Linguistics in the Department of Linguistics, University of Southern California, and has research interests in both comparative linguistic description and sociolinguistics. Having studied as an undergraduate at the University of Abidjan, Ivory Coast, Andrew Simpson completed his M.A. and PhD in linguistics in the School of Oriental and African Studies (SOAS), and then went on to teach in SOAS as a lecturer, senior lecturer and finally reader in linguistics between 1998 and 2006. He has travelled extensively in over twenty countries of Africa, and is particularly interested in the dynamics of post-colonial language development in West Africa. He is also the editor of the Oxford University Press volume *Language and National Identity in Asia*.

INGSE SKATTUM is professor of Francophone Studies at the Department of Culture Studies and Oriental Languages and head of the African Studies Programme at the University of Oslo. Her research interests lie in the fields of sociolinguistics, language in education, orality–literacy, and oral and written literature in Francophone Africa. She is the Norwegian coordinator of a joint project with the University of Bamako: 'Research concerning the integration of national languages into the educational system of Mali' (1996–2006). She has contributed to a number of books and journals in Norway, France, and England, edited a special issue of the *Nordic Journal of African Studies*, 'L'école et les langues nationales au Mali' (Helsinki University Press 2000), translated Ahmadou Kourouma's novel *Les soleils des indépendances* into Norwegian (*Uavhengighetens soler*, Cappelen 2005), and written *La francophonie: Une introduction critique* (Oslo: Unipub 2006, with J. K. Sanaker and K. Holter).

YASIR SULEIMAN is His Majesty Sultan Qaboos Bin Sa'id Professor of Modern Arabic Studies at the University of Cambridge, a Fellow of the Royal Society of Edinburgh, and Professorial fellow of King's College, Cambridge. He was until recently the Iraq Professor of Islamic and Arabic Studies at the University of Edinburgh where he served as Director of the Edinburgh Institute for the Study of the Arab World and Islam and as Head of the School of Literatures, Languages and Cultures. He has worked as leading consultant on Arabic language policy and reforms in the Arabian Gulf region and is interested in research on identity in the Middle East through language, literature, and translation. He has published numerous articles and books on these topics including *The Arabic Grammatical Tradition: A Study in Ta'lil* (1999), *The Arabic Language and National Identity: A Study in Ideology* (2003), and *A War of Words: Language and Conflict in the Middle East* (2004). He is also the editor of a number of books including *Arabic Sociolinguistics: Issues and Perspectives* (1994), *Language and Identity in the Middle East and North Africa* (1996), *Arabic Grammar and Linguistics* (1998), *Language and Society in the Middle East and North Africa* (1999), and editor (with Ibrahim Muhawi) of *Literature and Nation in the Middle East*. From 2003 to 2006 he held a Leverhulme Major Research Fellowship and drew on research conducted during that fellowship for the chapter in the present volume.

FAROUK TOPAN was a founding member of the Department of Swahili, University of Dar es Salaam in 1970. He introduced the teaching of Swahili literature at the University of Dar es Salaam and also at the University of Nairobi. His publications are on various aspects of Swahili literature, spirit possession, religion, and identity in East Africa. His latest volume is a co-edited book, with Pat Caplan: *Swahili Modernities. Culture, Politics and Identity on the East Coast of Africa* (2004). Topan is also a playwright: one of his plays (*Mfalme Juha*, 'The Idiot King') is a set text on the Tanzanian school curriculum. He was Senior Lecturer and Chair of the Department of Africa at the School of Oriental and African Studies until 2006, when he retired.

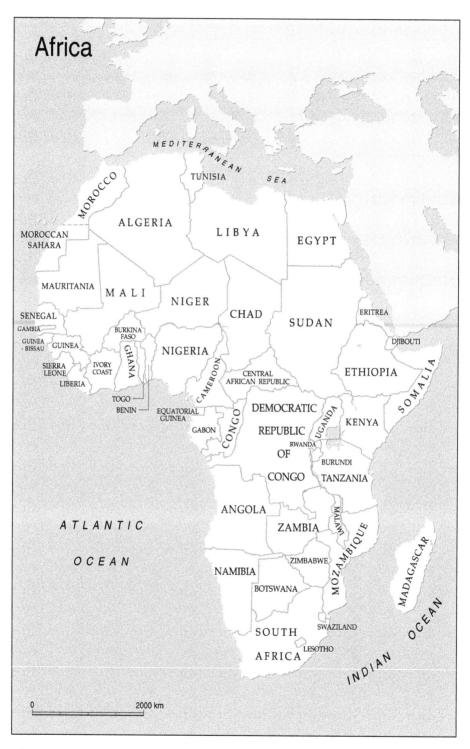

Africa

1
Introduction

Andrew Simpson

1.1 Language and the Challenge of Nation-Building in Modern African States

This book sets out to chart the role that language plays, and has played, both positively and also negatively, in the attempted construction, maintenance, and strengthening of national cohesion and identity in a broad range of states in modern Africa. Language as a communicative system varying among different populations is commonly acknowledged to function as an important symbol of group identity, often stimulating a natural sense of solidarity among communities sharing a single variety of speech, and is sometimes deliberately manipulated to create feelings of belonging to populations larger than the local or the regional, and the significant establishment of fully extensive national identities in independent states. In the African context, with the highly complex set of ethno-linguistic configurations presented by many of the continent's states, the need for careful, conscious attention to the process of 'national integration' (Alexandre 1968, Bamgbose 1991) and nation-building has been recognized as having a particularly special importance. A considerable majority of Africa's modern states exist in their current territorial shapes as the result of earlier Western colonial expansion in Africa, and the imposition of borders on contiguous bodies of land with almost no concern for creating homogeneous or coherent populations. In very many cases a wide range of quite distinct ethnic groups became artificially assembled as the demographic co-constituents of European protectorates and colonies, while other groups found themselves divided by new borders and separated into two or more Western-administered territories. In the second half of the twentieth century, when independence from colonial rule was finally achieved across Africa, the inheritance of these externally imposed, largely arbitrary borders consequently led to the sudden emergence of a great number of states with extremely mixed populations often having little in common save the sharing of a single officially recognized territory and the hopes of a better post-colonial future. This has led to a massive challenge for the leaderships of Africa's emerging independent states: how to bring together the wide array of ethno-linguistic groups cohabiting many of the continent's new states and create an over-arching sense of belonging and loyalty to a collective 'national' whole.[1] In the general attempt to build stable, integrated new states in heavily multilingual and multi-ethnic sub-Saharan Africa, language has, not surprisingly, proved to be an important and contested force intimately connected both with citizens' individual access to education, employment, and political participation and with the broader growth of a shared sense of national community, and has often given rise to perceptions of multilingualism (in the sense of the occurrence of many languages within a single population) as a principally negative complication for national development rather than as an asset to be exploited.

How issues of national-level language have affected the ongoing evolution and character of various countries in Africa is the principal, common focus of the range of chapters written for this volume, each of which also provides readers with a contextualization of language patterns in the countries concerned in the form of relevant sociolinguistic and historical information. In terms of scope of coverage, the volume offers discussion of nineteen states located in different parts of Africa and has been deliberately selective and restrictive in its contents, not attempting to be exhaustive or include detail on all of Africa's fifty-four states (which would require a volume well over twice the size of the present book), but instead aiming to provide a varied sampling of countries with clear, representative illustrations of themes that frequently reoccur in similar form in other states in Africa. In addition to sub-Saharan states where the challenges of nation-building facing multi-ethnic, multilingual states may appear to be most acute, the volume includes coverage of language and national identity issues in two North African countries, Egypt and Morocco, where it is seen that highly interesting issues in the construction of national identity also arise in the context of a much more restricted number of languages and the interaction of different varieties of Arabic (and also Berber and French, in the case of Morocco). As an introduction to these chapters focused on individual countries, the present chapter now presents an overview of some of the central issues that arise during the course of the book, highlighting significant patterns of development both in earlier periods and in more recent decades leading into the twenty-first century.

1.2 Language Promotion in Pre- and Post-colonial Africa

For many states, important influences on the prominence, extension, and functional use of languages in post-colonial times were already established during the experience of colonial occupation, not only as the result of the creation of borders which put

---

[1] Prime examples of the strikingly heterogeneous ethno-linguistic nature of many states in Africa discussed in this volume are Cameroon, with over 250 languages spoken among a population of just 16 million; Sudan, with 140 languages spread among 28 million inhabitants; Nigeria, with over 400 languages present in its population of 140 million; and Tanzania, with over 200 languages spoken by a population of 60 million.

together various ethno-linguistic groups as members of future states, but also through specific language-related activities and policies. In the area of education, a common approach adopted by colonial administrations was to provide a minimal amount of Western-language medium schooling, sufficient to train up a necessary number of junior-level civil servants with a proficiency in English or French, and to leave any education of the remaining majority of local African populations to the sporadic initiatives of missionary groups. Such a two-tiered treatment of the provision of education had two particularly significant consequences. On the one hand, missionary involvement in the spread of Christianity and the linking of such a process to education frequently resulted in the use of indigenous African languages for such purposes, which in turn required that various languages be standardized and formally described for the first time. Dictionaries, grammars, and orthographies of many African languages were consequently produced, alongside teaching materials, and those varieties of language selected for such formal promotion acquired a higher status which in many cases assisted in their diffusion as lingua francas and may have also solidified ethnic identities that were previously less clearly defined (see, for example, chapters 8, 12, and 16 on Ghana, DRC, and Zambia). On the other hand, although mother-tongue education may have made the process of learning more effective for those who received it, the use of African languages in schooling was not always openly welcomed. The fact that knowledge of a Western language often resulted in access to better jobs, due to English and French commonly being the official languages of colonial bureaucracy, created a resistance on the part of many to the use of indigenous languages rather than English/French as mediums of education, and there were sometimes even feelings that indigenous language education was a practice which Europeans introduced to deliberately withhold the linguistic means of advancement for Africans (i.e. knowledge of English, French, etc.) (Adegbija 2000).

The restriction of education through the medium of a European language to a relatively small proportion of the population in colonies in Africa, and the advantage accrued by obtaining a proficiency in such a language resulted in the creation of classes of indigenous elites in many countries, who frequently understood that a wider popular availability of Western-language education would generate greater competition for government jobs, and so was not in their own economic interests (McLaughlin, chapter 5). As many colonized territories approached independence in the middle of the twentieth century, colonial languages had therefore become positioned as the languages of economic success, higher levels of education, and (by association) social prestige, known by a relatively small percentage of the indigenous population, and sometimes jealously guarded by those who had obtained access to their learning. In contrast to this, African languages were for the most part confined to informal domains of use and had less overtly recognized prestige, even where occurring as regional lingua francas among larger populations.

When independence from foreign rule was eventually achieved by many colonies and protectorates in Africa in the late 1950s and 1960s, the new governments which took over from the previous colonial administrations needed to formulate and agree on national-level policies in a wide range of areas, including language. Ideas inherited from Western thinking suggested that newly independent states in Africa should ideally identify and promote a single indigenous language in the function of a 'national language', as a linguistic means to help draw their populations together and build a sense of belonging to a single people united in a sovereign territory and cooperating in the goal of developing a better future for all. There was also a clear need for the determination of a language (or possibly a set of languages) for practical use in government, state administration, and the wider development of education. In a maximally economic system and where the opportunity is present, countries may often hope to employ a single language (or possibly set of languages) to carry out both the former, more emotive, nation-building function and the latter, more official, functions, in order to reduce the number of languages an individual need be familiar with and to have the official use of language reinforce the presence of the national language. However, such a doubling of function is not absolutely necessary and in theory it is possible for the more formal aspects of life to be dealt with in one variety of language, while a different variety is promoted as a country's national language and used to develop sentiments of collective identity and loyalty to the state.

In much of Africa what ultimately happened in an overwhelming majority of cases was that the governments of newly independent states opted for a simple continuation of the basic language policy of pre-independence colonial times, with minor modifications in the form of declarations of intent to revisit issues of national language in the future, as and when opportunity and resources became available and presented themselves. Effectively this meant that in most cases, the colonial language which had become entrenched in administration and known among the better-educated was accepted and recognized as the official language of the state, for use in administration, government, and in the planned expansion of education for the masses, while little was undertaken with regard to the selection and promotion of national languages dedicated to the shaping of overarching new national identities. While the leaders and governments of a number of states did make affirmations that certain languages should be considered as national languages, this often appeared to be a principally symbolic gesture not supported by concrete moves to give such languages new positions of authority and heightened use. In a number of cases, all (or a numerous subset of) the indigenous languages present in a country were symbolically referred to and labelled as the 'national languages' of the state, to be respected and treasured by its citizens, resulting in a situation where realistic promotion of a single national language would not be possible without simultaneous promotion of the others, which might be practically impossible (as, for example, in the instance of Cameroon, where all 250 indigenous languages were recognized as 'national languages' in 1974, and Sudan, where a similar declaration was made with regard to the 140 indigenous languages present there).

The reasons for such a basic acceptance of the existing, pre-independence language situation, and the common reluctance to innovate and discard colonial languages for new policies substituting African languages in their place, were various and occurred in similar forms in many states at independence. A first, major problem for the elevation of an indigenous language to the status of national and/or official language status (in a meaningful rather than purely symbolic way) was that most colonized territories simply did not have any single indigenous language known by a clear majority of the population, and instead there was a common occurrence of scattered multilingualism and many languages being spoken by groups which constituted small proportions of the total population of a country. In most cases, because of the unnatural way in which colonization had grouped highly heterogeneous populations within a common set of borders, there were no natural choices of (single) national official language from the stock of languages present in countries gaining their independence in the 1950s and 1960s. Large numbers of the territories created as colonies and which subsequently achieved independence had no widely dominant ethnic majorities, and often no language known by over 50 per cent of the population. Where there were sizeable ethnic groups which might have a regional importance (as, for example, in Nigeria, with the Hausa, Igbo, and Yoruba groups, chapter 10), there was also a clear, strong fear among other ethnic minorities of being dominated by the larger groups, undermining the immediate possibility of selecting a combination of larger languages as official replacements for the ex-colonial language. Instead, smaller groups, which collectively might make up a significant amount of a nation's total population, frequently saw the ex-colonial language as a welcome guarantee of ethno-linguistic neutrality favouring no group over another and minimizing the potential of larger groups to accrue advantages for themselves through the superior control of official and national languages. In many instances, the ex-colonial languages were therefore perceived as the only languages that could impartially hold an ethnically mixed population together and maintain the often rather fragile stability of newly independent states.

Further relevant issues favouring the retention of European languages in their function as official languages involved worries about the state of development of indigenous languages and their potential for use in the same range of domains as European languages. While orthographic systems had been developed for a number of African languages, there was often no fully uniform practice of representation across dialects or agreement on which of many competing forms should be recognized as the standard form of a language.[2] Combined with the lack of expansion of the lexicon of most African languages in domains relevant to the more formal functions of life, there existed a general under-confidence in the ability of indigenous languages to

---

[2] In the case of Somalia, where a single language form was spoken by almost all the population in mutually intelligible ways, the lack of an agreed form of orthographic representation resulted in the continuation of English, Italian, and Arabic in official domains until 1972, when a uniform writing system was adopted and Somali was declared the national language for use in all official functions (chapter 15).

successfully replace Western languages in all domains of officialdom and education. It was also stressed by many that a continued proficiency in languages such as English and French was necessary for African countries to maintain access to developing science and technology, and assist in their modernization, keeping open a 'window into the rest of the world' and beneficial contact with other countries (Adegbija 1994).[3] Finally, there are also hints that the educated elites of various African countries may have favoured the retention of European languages over the promotion of African languages as a way to ensure their continued economic success and privileged status (for example in the Ivory Coast, chapter 9).

The end result of such attitudes and demographic complexities was that little significant linguistic change effectively occurred in many sub-Saharan states as they became independent nations in the 1960s, and European languages continued to occur in dominant roles in a wide range of official domains, occasioning criticism from certain intellectuals and observers who argued that foreign languages known by just a small proportion of the population did not have the real potential to unite aspiring new African nations and that other indigenous national language options had to be explored. Section 1.3 now examines what developments have in fact taken place in the decades separating the 1960s from the present and what trends have emerged with regard to the strengthening of both African and European (and also hybrid) languages in Africa.

1.3 Domains of Language Expansion and Growth: 1960s to Present

In the period that has elapsed since the initial achievement of independence from colonial rule in the 1950s and 1960s many countries in Africa have witnessed an expansion in the knowledge and use of various languages, both as the result of deliberate acts of promotion such as the development of literacy programmes, use in the educational system, the media, and public address by prominent figures, as well as via less planned and directed growth, as certain languages of inter-ethnic communication have become more widespread as unofficial lingua francas.

With regard to the field of education, the provision of schooling in a particular language to the growing youth of a nation regularly offers one of the most effective ways of spreading knowledge of a language through the population of a state where a system of mass public education is established. The choice of language as medium of instruction in schools and colleges therefore has a significant effect on the embedding of possible national and official languages in developing new states and on the creation of important, general attitudes towards

---

[3] In a related way, chapter 2 notes that Egyptian nationalists underlined the importance of maintaining an internationally shared form of Arabic as an instrument of modernization for the country, pointing to this as an advantage of 'fusha' over the local form of Arabic which did not have the same capacity to link Egypt with developments in the outside world.

languages, for example, as being instrumentally valuable, and/or potentially associated with prestige. In the second half of the twentieth century, Africa's newly independent states made efforts to increase the availability of public education and in so doing faced difficult questions concerning the selection of mediums of instruction.

The most common practice has been to utilize European languages as the mainstay of education, almost universally at the secondary level, and very widely within primary schools. Operationally, this represents the easiest choice for governments in many ways, requiring the preparation of a uniform set of teaching materials in a single language for an entire population, with many such materials being easily adaptable from outside sources. However, for the young school-going population the use of unfamiliar languages such as English and French as initial mediums of instruction is well-documented as not being optimal, and instruction through the mother tongue in (at least) the early years of education is known to be considerably more effective as a teaching strategy. With the growing acceptance of evidence of the value of mother-tongue education, and the political wish to introduce indigenous languages into education to help stimulate national coherence and pride, many African states have made attempts to provide early primary education through local languages, the mother tongue of schoolchildren wherever possible, and some other major regional language where not. Such attempts have met with varying degrees of success, continuing to grow steadily in certain cases (for example, Mali, Zambia, South Africa), but faltering or being discontinued for resource-related reasons in other states (for example, Nigeria, Ghana).

Concerning the attitude of the general public towards language use in education, studies carried out in a range of countries suggest that parents are actually most keen for their offspring to be schooled in two languages – their mother tongue and a European language of wider communication – the former as a way to facilitate learning in general and strengthen cultural knowledge, and the latter as a way to later achieve access to better employment. However, relative to the use of mother tongues as medium of instruction, there are very frequent observations that there are simply not enough appropriate resources available to make across-the-board education in mother tongues successful. It is regularly pointed out first of all that there are not enough teaching materials in the numerous languages present in many countries to facilitate learning in children's first-acquired languages, secondly that mixed classes of students with different language backgrounds often make attempts to provide mother-tongue education extremely difficult even when relevant textbooks may be available, and thirdly that there are insufficient numbers of teachers trained with the necessary linguistic skills to properly implement teaching through indigenous languages. In addition to such challenges, the delivery of education in African languages is further impeded by common attitudes that there is little practical use for the formal learning of indigenous languages, and that preference should therefore be accorded to the acquisition of European languages, which do enhance an individual's employment potential.[4] Consequently, wherever a choice has to be made between indigenous language education and instruction through European languages of wider communication, the latter is almost universally found to be preferred by parents for their children.[5]

Generally, then, while recent post-independence decades have seen the extension of education further in most countries than in colonial times, and the attempt to introduce African languages more frequently into the classroom as mediums of instruction in primary education, it is still much more common for students to receive the majority of their schooling in a European language, and the potential for the educational system to spread knowledge of African languages as a way to strengthen national unity has not yet been fully realized. Coupled with the fact that the rates of school attendance may be low even in areas where schools are provided (for example, 26% in Mali, chapter 6), it can be said that the educational system in many countries is currently still reinforcing the presence of European languages among a reduced proportion of the school-going-age younger generation, and is not yet having a really major impact on the spread of African languages in formal areas, despite many promising initiatives.

In the area of politics and government administration, two broad patterns of language use can be observed. The day-to-day paperwork and formal mechanisms of state bureaucracy are effected in ex-colonial languages, as is, most commonly, political debate in parliamentary circles, even where the use of indigenous languages in such domains may have been approved (as, for example, in Nigeria, chapter 10). However, outside such formal and elite-dominated areas of interaction, it would seem that African languages are being used significantly more by politicians, to address and woo audiences both in face-to-face public gatherings and in television interviews (see, for example, chapters 5, 6, 13, and 16). This may occur particularly with well-known lingua francas such as Wolof, Bambara, and Swahili, but is also reported with smaller, local languages where known by politicians, and is a trend that is relatively new in various countries, but clearly noticeable and apparently increasing.

Within the domain of the media, there are also two rather different patterns that can be discerned. With regard to written forms of the media, it is still European languages which are heavily dominant in sub-Saharan Africa, and though there are newspapers published in certain indigenous languages, the very clear majority of print journalism is carried out in English and French, and readers who otherwise may have strong loyalties to African languages may nevertheless prefer (and find it easier) to read in European languages (Igboanusi and Peter 2004). Consequently, although there

---

[4] Within higher education, the relatively low (and sometimes declining) rate of enrolment in undergraduate degree programmes focused on African languages in various countries is a further indication of the low economic value often attached to knowledge of indigenous languages as academic subjects. In contrast to this, degrees in West European languages attract a much higher rate of enrolment.

[5] It is relevant to note that the economic pressure to learn languages associated with better employment opportunities is not restricted to European languages alone. In Ethiopia, where Amharic is seen as the linguistic key to obtaining better paid work, education through the medium of Amharic is preferred to mother tongue schooling among many minority language groups (chapter 15).

are signs of progress in the development of African language newspapers, this is still rather slow at present. In the area of television, there is a similar tendency for African languages to have an increasing presence, though again still proportionately small in comparison to that of European languages. African-language television broadcasting is commonly sponsored by state broadcasting organizations and typically involves periodic short transmissions of news bulletins in selected regional languages. Far outstripping the use of indigenous languages in newspapers and television, however, is the presence of African languages in radio broadcasting, which in many countries has grown significantly in recent years, with more local languages being used to broadcast a range of programme types to larger listening audiences, including informal chat shows and phone-in discussions (chapter 16). As noted by Anyidoho and Dakubu in chapter 8, this expansion of indigenous languages in radio programming in contrast to their relatively weak presence in education, government bureaucracy, and newspapers may be attributed to the maintenance of a traditional view strongly associating African languages with oral communication on the one hand, and European languages with reading and writing and other forms of formal communication on the other. Indeed, the general patterns of development observed in the paragraphs above are all arguably consistent with inherited preconceptions concerning the 'proper' or 'natural' domains for use of European and African languages, and expansion of the latter is found to occur most clearly in the more informal, oral use of language.[6]

Quite generally, as the result of governmental language-planning decisions and also less obviously manipulated forces of development, various languages in Africa, both European and African, can be noted to have experienced clear growth during the second half of the twentieth century. Firmly embedded in the educational system, administration, and higher level commercial activities of many countries, the ex-colonial languages English and French have become known by an increasing percentage of Africans as general participation in these domains has expanded steadily, though unevenly and with a greater concentration in urban environments. Although broad comparative surveys of levels of language proficiency have thus far not been carried out in sub-Saharan Africa, Adegbija (2000) estimates that not more than 30 per cent of West Africans are generally able to understand and speak one of the ex-colonial languages, and in many countries the percentage may be significantly less, with knowledge of such languages gained from periods of formal education atrophying in the absence of regular use. In comparison to earlier colonial times, however, it is clear that exposure to Western languages has increased and that English and French are known

---

[6] In such a view, television programming with its heavier Western language domination would seem to have inherited the designation of a more formal media domain akin to the production of newspaper journalism (or else to employ European languages primarily to reach a 'national' audience rather than viewers proficient in one or other regional language). One can imagine that with a future increase in the ownership of television sets and a possible lowering of technical production costs, television broadcasting in African countries might become more localized and privatized, as in parts of Asia, and lead to a wider use of indigenous languages in programming.

by a broader educated cross-section of the population than in the early twentieth century. English and French (and to a lesser extent Portuguese) are therefore growing as linguistic forces rather than retreating, and continue to maintain a firm hold on specific areas of life in many states.

A number of African languages have also undergone expansion in recent decades, in various cases in a proportionately more impressive way and with a greater across-the-board application than in the case of the growth of English, French, and Portuguese. With regard to deliberate attempts at promotion in both formal and informal areas of life and the creation of a true national and official language, the post-independence spread of Swahili among the population of Tanzania is regularly noted to be a remarkably successful example of African national language planning in a multi-ethnic context. Now, following considerable extended efforts from the 1960s onwards, Swahili is extremely widely known in Tanzania and used in education, government administration, and inter-ethnic communication throughout the country. In other states lesser degrees of explicit planning have combined with 'natural' undirected forces of growth to give rise to the knowledge of a particular language among very sizeable populations: Wolof in Senegal, being the mother tongue of 40 per cent of Senegalese and used as a second language by a further 50 per cent of the population; Bambara in Mali, spoken as a first language by 40 per cent and as a second language by another 40 per cent; Swahili in Kenya, known by approximately two-thirds of the population as either a first or second language; and Akan in its different forms in Ghana, known by over 50 per cent of Ghanaians. In all these instances of multi-ethnic states, there are consequently indigenous languages now known by a majority of the population, with this reaching strikingly high levels (for Africa) in the case of Tanzania, Senegal and Mali.[7]

In addition to the growth of languages such as the above, perceived as having a specific and 'pure' identity (perhaps erroneously), in the sense of having first arisen among a particular ethnic group, either in Africa or in Europe, and then been spread among wider populations, there are also 'mixed', newer language forms in various African states which have either undergone further expansion in recent times and become understood and used by significant numbers of speakers, or alternatively come into existence for the first time over the past few decades and then achieved an immediate and growing popularity. The first set of cases are the various pidgin

---

[7] Within distinct regions of certain states, there have also been significant post-independence expansions. For example, partly as the result of an explicit policy of Hausa-centred 'northernization', knowledge of Hausa has spread throughout the north of Nigeria, continuing an earlier pattern of growth and making it the most widely known of the country's languages (though still not understood by anywhere near a majority of the entire population).

A further example of an African language known by a clear majority of the population of a multi-ethnic country but where the expansion causing this knowledge mostly occurred at an earlier time is Amharic, which became widespread in Ethiopia over a period of centuries (from the thirteenth century onwards), and was boosted in its occurrence by a deliberate policy of 'amharization' from the end of the nineteenth century.

languages formed from the combination of European and African languages as languages of inter-ethnic communication and trade. Although pidgins may be negatively classed by some as corrupted forms of other languages, in countries such as Cameroon and Nigeria English-based pidgins are now known and spoken by large and increasing numbers of speakers, most commonly as second languages and in informal contexts, where they seem to acquire covert prestige. In Sierra Leone, an original pidgin developed into a creole language with a substantial population of native speakers in the late nineteenth century, and knowledge of 'Krio' has now spread from the 10 per cent of mother-tongue speakers to the rest of the population, with the result that currently around 95 per cent of Sierra Leoneans may know and use Krio on a regular basis. Pidgins (and associated creolized varieties) are therefore important, growing language forces in a number of African states and expanding among ethnically varied populations as popular lingua francas. A second set of mixed language forms which has spontaneously emerged in recent years is a collection of new, predominantly urban slangs which have developed among the sometimes disaffected younger generation in the towns and cities of various countries. Examples of these increasingly popular codes formed from a mixture of local and foreign languages and frequently stigmatized by more conservative and older sections of society are Sheng in Kenya (formed with a heavy Swahili base), Camfranglais in Cameroon (largely resulting from a mixture of English, French, and Cameroonian languages), Tsotsisaal and Isicamtho in South Africa, and Savisman Krio in Sierra Leone (being a form of Krio adopted primarily by marginalized elements of Sierra Leonean youth). Certain of these urban slangs are already observed to be used as new symbols of ethnically neutral local identity, and with further growth may become significant linguistic elements in the expression of a broader national identity alongside longer established pidgins and creoles.

Finally, it is important to note that between standard forms of European languages and pidgins with a primary base in a European language, there are many non-standard, localized forms of English and French which have developed and stabilized in former colonial territories during the post-independence era in particular: for example, Nigerian English, Cameroonian English and French, Senegalese French, and Ghanaian English. These regularly adopt lexical items and sometimes aspects of the pronunciation and grammar of other African languages present in the country concerned, and may become known and used by more than just those with formal education in English and French, as in the case of French in Ivory Coast, where 'le français populaire d'Abidjan' has spread throughout the country and is understood and used by a wide range of the population, especially in towns and cities (chapter 9). As well as resulting in a wider socio-economic spread of 'English' and 'French' and breaking down previous barriers which made European languages the sole preserve of educated elites, spoken only in standard European ways, the importance of non-standard, localized forms of English and French is that: (a) they are each distinct in various ways, both from standard European English and French and also from other regional African varieties of these languages, hence more readily available for the projection of a differentiated identity; (b) they are generally well appreciated due to their less formal character and their ability to refer to and capture particularized aspects of daily life in the countries where they occur; and (c) their individual, localized nature serves to reduce the automatic association of European languages with earlier colonial rule. The non-standardization of these varieties also encourages innovation and spontaneity among speakers and the occurrence of healthy variation and development.

Having sketched out the ways that languages have been moving in very broad terms in post-colonial Africa, we can now turn to consider the interaction of language with national integration and identity and how a variety of different pressures is leading to the favouring and prominence of certain languages over others in the present.

1.4 Language and National Identity

With regard to the effects of language use on nation-building in Africa, three general points can be made before identifying more specific issues bearing on language choice and its effects on identity construction. First of all, with a small number of exceptions, it can be noted that Africa has not witnessed the kind of language nationalism that strikingly characterized the growth of various nations in Europe from the nineteenth century onwards, adopting Herderian views that a (single) language is the soul of a nation and a central symbolic rallying point for the championing of nationhood. This is perhaps, rather naturally, due to the practical constraints placed on nation-building by the establishment of multi-ethnic colonial territories. As in much of Asia, independence movements in Africa largely accepted the geographical shapes and ethnic composition of the territories they inhabited and commonly fought for independence from foreign rule rather than any radical redefinition of national boundaries to mirror the physical distribution of ethnic groups. Consequently, the varied ethno-linguistic character of the majority of colonies did not readily allow for a single language to be used as a fully representative symbol of an emerging nation in the way that, for example, German or Polish did in nationalist movements in Europe. Instances where specific languages did become associated with independence and post-independence nationalist movements have occurred in certain countries where a lingua franca or common language is present, such as the Arabic-speaking countries of North Africa (see for example, Morocco, chapter 3), and the Swahili area of East Africa (particularly Kenya and Tanzania, chapters 13 and 14), but elsewhere language has not figured as the central spiritual driving force of nationalism, except perhaps in the case of Afrikaner nationalism which presented Afrikaans as a unique, defining property of the Afrikaner nation in its struggle against British rule (chapter 17).

Second, there are various other indexes of identity which may have a stronger binding force for populations than language, when promoted in a vigorous way, and these may sometimes either override or alternatively obscure the potential language has to establish cohesion and loyalty across large populations. Religious adherence is particularly important in many African states and may complicate the establishment of national identities through language and other means when there is tension or conflict between members of different religious groups.[8] Similarly, loyalty to (sub-) ethnic group or clan may be a stronger force than identification with other speakers of the same essential language. Hence in Somalia (chapter 15), clan loyalties are noted to interfere in the construction of a broader national identity among speakers of Somali, and in pre-independence times in Nigeria, speakers of mutually intelligible forms of languages such as Igbo and Yoruba were not united by any single ethno-linguistic identity, and often competed against each other as bitter rivals (Gordon 2003). Elsewhere the cultivation of a national identity linked primarily to territory and the sense of belonging to a certain land may put the importance of linguistic cohesion in a backgrounded position, as discussed in chapter 2 on early territorial nationalism in Egypt. Other socio-political and economic forms of national identity construction which have not accorded any central role to language are also found in the development of African states at certain times, as for example in Zambia, where in the immediate post-independence period the country's foreign policy initiatives directed towards other unliberated parts of southern Africa together with its attention to domestic economic issues essentially defined its early national identity (chapter 16). A combative political position on the international stage, especially with regard to general African interactions with the West was also a feature of Nigerian identity politics for a period of its post-independence development (Falola 1999).

Thirdly, as pointed out well by McLaughlin in chapter 5, the notion of national identity may be relativized to internal and external image projection and identification. McLaughlin observes that the term national identity therefore may have two different meanings: 'the first of these is a population's relationship and sense of belonging to a nation-state, and the second is the identity of an individual nation-state within the international world order. Based on the first meaning, Senegal can best be described as a predominantly Wolof-speaking nation, while on the international scene it is a francophone state.' It is consequently useful to bear in mind the potential difference between the identification ordinary individuals may make with other co-members of the population of a state, and the external imagery of a state, as it may be deliberately constructed by the leadership of a country.

In what follows, a number of salient forces bearing on current individual and group use of major languages are identified, relating to observations made in the chapters of the volume. It is also noted why support is given for the occurrence of languages in prominent positions which can influence the identity of nations and their populations.

---

[8] The relation of language to religion and national identity has a particularly interesting discussion in chapters 2 and 3 on Egypt and Morocco, and has a clear relevance for states such as Nigeria, Ethiopia, Ghana, and other countries with significant populations of both Christians and Muslims.

1.4.1 Prestige, Self-advancement, Self-empowerment

The preference given to use of a particular language by multilingual individuals na-turally has the power to affect language selection in other individuals, and can lead to the increased domination of certain languages among groups of speakers. One factor which clearly draws individuals and groups towards the favouring of one language over another is the prestige value potentially associated with a language. In this regard, the proficient use of an ex-colonial, European language is still seen as a significant and pres-tigious mark of education and modernity in many countries in Africa, and is cultivated by many as a means to acquire status in society. Together with the fact that an ability to speak a Western language continues to be an important key for economic self-advancement and access to higher levels of employment, this ensures that languages such as English and French are maintaining a strong buoyancy among influential and ambitious sections of society in a majority of modern African states. Prestige-related effects on language choice also occur with other non-European languages, and poten-tially whenever there is a sociologically determined hierarchical structure of languages within a single population. Among Arabic-speaking populations, for example, there may frequently be a significant tension between the respect given to classical and modern standard Arabic on the one hand and the status of regional, colloquial forms of Arabic on the other. While the latter may be the forms of Arabic most individuals learn in the home, they are regularly characterized as having low prestige, and seen as inferior to the former. Chapter 2 observes that attempts to promote the locally developed Egyptian variety of Arabic as a supporting linguistic symbol of Egyptian ter-ritorial nationalism failed because of deeply embedded perceptions that local forms of Arabic are inferior to classical and modern standard Arabic. A similar long-established difference in the status accorded classical as opposed to the local, colloquial form of Arabic is noted in chapter 3 on Morocco, where it is added that the perception of the latter as a corrupted form of classical Arabic is held not only by the educated elite but also by the masses who may know and use only Moroccan Arabic on a regular basis.

Chapter 3 also presents an interesting discussion of the way that gender interacts with language and prestige in Morocco, with consequent effects for the question of national language. It is pointed out that the traditional position of men in patriarchal Moroccan society may be linguistically maintained by their control of Standard Arabic, and that 'many women feel that they are not welcome to participate as equal partners in the use of Standard Arabic'. As a result, women may seek self-empowerment and social prestige through other linguistic strategies, for those with education through the use of French, with its associations of modernity and civilization, as well as French–Moroccan Arabic code-switching, and for those in rural areas with no access to French through the use of female oral literature in Berber and Moroccan Arabic. Such patterns are creating and developing loyalties to different languages among the male and female population and may impede the successful promotion of a single language as a symbol of national unity for both men and women.

1.4.2 Reactionary Language Choice; Worries of Minorities

The development of a favouring of and an allegiance to a particular language among part of a country's population may sometimes occur as a response to the perception of attempted dominance by more powerful or more numerous Others within the country. Several examples of this phenomenon and the linguistic divisions it can establish are described in the present volume. In chapter 11 on Cameroon, it is observed that a growing, strong Anglophone identity with English and Pidgin English as its primary symbols of shared ethnicity has emerged among the approximately 20 per cent of the population inhabiting the southwest and northwest provinces of the country, which corresponds to an earlier British-administered part of Cameroon (and is otherwise ethno-linguistically very mixed, like the rest of Cameroon). This has been triggered, primarily, by feelings that there is an unfair and unequal governmental emphasis on the French language in Cameroon despite both English and French being formally recognized as co-official languages of the state. Perceptions of being discriminated against by a Francophone majority (although only a small proportion of such 'Francophones' are actually able to speak French) have consequently caused those in the southwest and northwest to close ranks and rally behind a hardened English-centred Anglophone identity which did not exist in such a form before, and have led to the formation of Anglophone nationalist movements calling for secession of the two 'Anglophone' provinces.

Two other cases of European languages being taken up and used by speakers of African languages in circumstances of defiance are described in chapters 6 and 17. In South Africa, English became associated with the anti-apartheid movement and perceived as the language of unity and freedom from Afrikaner rule among the Black population of the country. Following the eventual successful elimination of the apartheid system, English has emerged in South Africa with strongly positive connotations stemming from its earlier role in an opposition function and its representation of future hopes. Elsewhere, in Mali, French is noted to be used by speakers of the Songhay and Tamachek languages in instances of inter-ethnic communication as a way to avoid using Bambara, which is otherwise widely spread as a lingua franca in Mali but which, for the Songhay and Tamachek, is a representation of unwelcome domination by the Bambara.

In many other countries, European languages may be favoured as national-level official languages where ethno-linguistic minorities are concerned about the power of larger groups and how this might expand if the languages of these groups were to be given prominent official roles of authority. As noted in section 1.2, the general worry among minorities of being dominated by larger groups was widespread in different countries during the 1960s at the time of independence, and still remains as a major preoccupation in many states. In such contexts, European languages are positively valued as ethnically neutral and theoretically able to integrate and unite mixed populations in a way which appears to be even and fair for all ethnic groups. This therefore continues to provide important public support for the position of English and French in countries such as Nigeria and the Ivory Coast and many others with sizeable minority populations.

1.4.3 Further Related Issues: the Portal Function of Language; Questions of Linguistic Origin and Distinctiveness

A further pressure to retain English and French in the educational system and other prominent areas of (formal) life is the continued need for access to ongoing developments in science and technology which is enabled by materials published in these languages. The direct connection to the modern world regularly facilitated by European languages, which may be referred to as their 'portal function', has not yet been successfully replicated by African languages, which generally remain without the necessary resources in the area of technical vocabulary and embedding of use in formal domains. Even in countries where a single non-European language may have become adopted widely in public life and be known by a majority of the population and used in official roles, as for example in Swahili-speaking East Africa, Arabic-speaking countries of North Africa, and Somalia in the Horn of Africa, it is commonly found that higher education remains dominated by English or French, and a lack of teaching materials and relevant terminology in other languages is regularly blamed for the difficulty in replacing European languages in this area. Such a situation is furthermore likely to continue for the foreseeable future in most countries, due to widely held preconceptions that African languages may be inherently incapable of being adapted for use in advanced technical description: what Githiora in chapter 13 refers to as speakers' 'deeply entrenched psychic disbelief in African languages' as vehicles of modern formal communication. Such a chronic lack of confidence in the suitability of African languages for scientific purposes may therefore result in a significant gap in the otherwise broad application of an indigenous national language, in Kenya serving 'to thwart the aspirations of Swahili as a fully across-the-board linguistic vehicle for national integration in all domains'.

This occupation of prominent formal positions frequently still found with English and French in Africa is often seen as either simply unavoidable or sometimes even welcome in heavily multi-ethnic countries with imbalanced populations, but still comes in for criticism in other states where a resistance to the further spread of European languages may be urged with exhortations to develop the use of languages with higher local authenticity. A clear example of this can be seen in the policy of Arabization implemented in Morocco which sets out to spread the use of Standard Arabic across all domains of life, and gradually replace French in its occurrence in higher education and other formal areas through the modernization of Arabic. The rationale given for Arabization is that it will help ensure the continuation of cultural authenticity in Morocco and build unity and coherence in the country, not only eliminating the presence of French, which is seen by conservative elements as a linguistic threat to

Morocco's national identity, but also bringing the sizeable Berber population more firmly into an Arabic-centred national cohesion.

Quite generally, the deliberate promotion of a language as a symbol of national unity frequently needs to consider not only issues of local authenticity, and whether a language is sufficiently associated with prestige to be accepted as linguistically representative of a nation, but also the question of whether a selected national language is able to positively distinguish its speakers from those of other nations. This issue arises wherever languages which have large first or second language speaker populations spread across different states become used for national language functions in one or more countries, as occurs, for example, with Swahili in East and Central Africa, and Modern Standard Arabic in North Africa and the Middle East. With regard to the former, it is noted (chapter 13, and elsewhere) that there is a significant range of variation in the forms of Swahili cultivated and spoken in the states of East and Central Africa, and such differences are sufficient to distinguish Swahili as an (unofficially recognized) national language in Tanzania from Swahili in Kenya, Uganda, and the Democratic Republic of Congo. One essential language form can therefore be developed in different ways to produce significantly distinctive national languages.

In the case of Arabic as a national language in countries of North Africa and the Middle East, the situation is interestingly complex, and discussed both in chapters 2 and 3. Localized 'colloquial' forms of Arabic such as Moroccan Arabic and Egyptian Arabic are clearly distinctive and separate their speakers from those of other states, but are very often considered too lacking in prestige to serve as national languages. Modern Standard Arabic, more closely linked with Classical Arabic, and not mentally separated from the latter in any significant way in the minds of many speakers (Suleiman, chapter 2), is a very widely shared form of Arabic, and does not have the obvious potential to serve as a clearly distinctive national language in multiple states, though it does enjoy high prestige. This complicated situation has led to various responses among nationalists in Arabic-speaking states. In Egypt, early 'territorial' nationalists either unsuccessfully promoted the localized colloquial variety of Arabic as Egypt's distinctive national language, or alternatively denied the linking of national identity to the use of a particular language. The latter position was an attempt to sidestep the conclusion that use of shared forms of Arabic left Egypt without an individual national identity and simply part of a wider Arab nation. By way of contrast, later Egyptian Arab nationalists openly embraced pan-Arabism and the importance of Classical and Standard Arabic as markers of a shared Arab identity, but at the same time emphasized the centrality of Egypt and its culture within the wider Arab world, arguing that Egypt's close association with other Arab states did not result in any lessening of Egypt's own identity but rather a positive enhancement (Suleiman, chapter 2). The issue of linguistic and general cultural distinctiveness is therefore one which necessitates clear attention from nationalist leaders in states which appear to share their national and official languages with others, and may lead to different responses and interpretations, some better accepted than others.

1.4.4 Outcomes

The considerations and pressures on language selection noted in previous sections of this chapter have led to the establishment of a range of different patterns of language emphasis which have the power to influence the growth of national identity. A first, generally less common outcome is the deliberate promotion of a single indigenous language as the most prominent language of a state and its population, for use in both national and official functions, whether such promotion and ensuing status is accompanied by explicit formal (constitutional) recognition or not.[9] Examples of such a dominantly monolingual national language policy discussed in the present volume are Tanzania, Somalia, and Ethiopia.[10] As observed in the chapters addressing these countries, the broad, national promotion of an indigenous language in both official and informal roles across a population may be met with varying degrees of success in terms of national integration and the creation of a positively valued national identity. In Tanzania, the development and spread of Swahili in national and official language roles is generally regarded as having had very positive effects on nation-building in the post-independence era, and was extremely important for the creation of a sense of allegiance and belonging to a single, new Tanzanian nation. However, elsewhere, in Ethiopia, the more gradual growth of Amharic as the dominant language of the state, culminating in recognition as the official language of Ethiopia in 1955, has been less obviously successful in 'winning the hearts and minds' of the varied population of the country, and there have regularly been non-Amhara groups which have viewed the Amharic-centred expansion of the Ethiopian empire and its development into a modern state as quite unwelcome and akin to colonization (chapter 15). Since the Marxist revolution of 1974 and ensuing moves towards greater tolerance of other languages, there has been a regrowth of regional languages such as Tigrinya and Oromo, indicating that the long-established, high instrumental value of Amharic within Ethiopia has not been sufficient to eliminate strong loyalties to other ethnic identities. Somalia is a third state which has a single indigenous language promoted into the functions of national and official language (replacing English, Italian, and Arabic in official domains in the 1970s). It is also a state which has a largely homogeneous population, which is considerably rare in sub-Saharan Africa. Such potential advantages

[9] Hence, while Swahili is clearly accepted as Tanzania's national language and widely referred to as such, it is not officially recognized as having this status in the constitution.

[10] To these countries one might also add dominantly Arabic-speaking states such as Egypt. However, given that Arabic is a language which was brought into Africa from the Middle East, it cannot be straightforwardly classified as an 'indigenous' language in the states where it is spoken, despite its long presence in certain parts of Africa. For the purposes of nationalism, Classical/Standard Arabic has in fact sometimes been presented as a foreign language (for example, by the Egyptian nationalist Salama Musa – see chapter 2). As noted in chapter 13, Kenya is a further country which is now in the process of recognizing an African language, Swahili, as a national and official language.

have nevertheless been unable to secure long-term peace and stability within the country, which has experienced significant unrest in recent decades. As noted by Bokamba (chapter 12) and various others, the existence of official and widespread monolingualism in an indigenous language is hence not an automatic guarantee of national strength and the creation of an identity that will inseparably bind a population together.[11]

A second linguistic outcome which is far more common than the attempted promotion of a single indigenous language in all (or most) prominent national functions is the situation in which a European language has been approved as the official language of a state, and there is no indigenous language (or languages) meaningfully filling the role of national language. Such a widespread situation is generally the continuation of decisions made at independence which maintain ex-colonial languages in formal domains and do not make any clear or vigorous attempt to use indigenous languages for the construction of national identity, frequently concluding that such a task may be too complicated and also possibly dangerous. If one reflects on the level of 'success' achieved in the area of nation-building by this kind of sociolinguistic configuration, this is generally measured more in terms of the maintenance of stability, political unity, and a climate in which a gradual process of national integration can occur, rather than in terms of the deliberate, accelerated creation of a national identity with specific, clearly targeted properties. Assessed in such a less obviously ambitious way, official monolingualism in a non-indigenous language is frequently described as a policy which often does seem to help and succeed in the easing of inter-ethnic relations and the reduction of conflict in states with complex populations. It is noted as providing a means of communication in a range of areas which favours no particular ethnic group over another, so reducing the potential for language differences to heighten tensions in a country. However, as with the promotion of a single indigenous language in a strongly prominent position, the embedding of a non-indigenous language in an important nationwide role may sometimes seem to fail to achieve its primary 'peace-keeping' objective in the process of nation-building. Chapter 9 observes that the continual cultivation and spread of French in the Ivory Coast over a period of decades during the post-independence Houphouët-Boigny era gave rise to a popular impression that French (or the range of varieties of French in Ivory Coast) expressed an Ivorian identity and so had come to function in the way of a national language. The conflict-ridden decade following the death of Houphouët-Boigny in 1993 however demonstrated that the image of national unity projected by symbols such as French may have merely been a mask concealing deeper-ridden ethnic disunity, and hence the promotion of French had actually not facilitated the growth of a sense of collective belonging necessary to triumph over ethnic discord.

---

[11] The tragic warring in heavily monolingual Rwanda and Burundi is a further reminder of this, as is, in Asia, the separation of countries such as North and South Korea, and the self-inflicted genocide in Cambodia in the late 1970s.

Chapter 11 on Cameroon describes a variation of the above, second kind of configuration of language prominence and a situation in which two European languages, French and English, occur as the co-official languages of the state, with clear effects on the attempted establishment of national identity in the country. Due to an imbalance in public emphasis and individual knowledge of French and English, despite constitutional commitment to a policy of official bilingualism, the population of Cameroon is effectively divided into two major multi-ethnic groups whose higher level allegiance and identities are determined by feelings of belonging to either the Anglophone bloc or the larger Francophone part of the population. English (and the important associated form Pidgin English) and French have thus become linguistic beacons which serve to polarize and separate the population, and the uneven implementation of official bilingualism is creating serious problems for national integration, even triggering calls for secession among sections of the Anglophone community.

A third general type of 'emphasis' and presence of language in African states, both in official terms and in popular levels of consciousness where national identity is potentially established, is the occurrence of national multilingualism and the identification of ethno-linguistic pluralism as a welcome and definitive property of a state. Lying at the other end of the linguistic spectrum from the promotion of a single national or official language, 'national multilingualism' generally involves the shared perception that a range of prominent indigenous languages (often officially recognized as national languages) collectively project the national identity of a country. Such an elevated linguistic grouping is commonly given active government support and promotion in areas of education and the media, and often a European language of wider communication is also included in an official instrumental role, and sometimes as an additional component of the plurilingual national identity. In the present volume, four interesting examples of the centrality of multiple languages in forming and being perceived to form the core identity of a nation-state are Mali, Democratic Republic of Congo (DRC), Zambia, and South Africa. Chapter 6 observes that in Mali there have been sustained national efforts in the defence of cultural and linguistic pluralism, with the support of thirteen national languages in various official domains, and that the defence of pluralism has itself 'taken on symbolic value as a mark of national identity'. Chapter 12 similarly identifies DRC as a state with an essentially multilingual national identity, and argues that the development of a strong national identity in DRC is a clear counter-example to ideas that plurilingualism is necessarily divisive in nature. While it is noted that the existence of a single, broadly shared language certainly may help unite the population of a state, the case of DRC indicates significantly that it is also possible to develop a sense of national identity among speakers of a range of different languages with no commonly shared single national language. The discussion of Zambia in chapter 16 further confirms such a general view, observing that the particular patterns of multilingualism present in the country, involving use of a number of indigenous national languages and English, sometimes mixed, are together seen as establishing the national identity of Zambia. This positive acceptance of multilingualism in Zambia, where the variety of languages present in the country is perceived to be an asset rather than an obstacle to nation-building, represents a comparatively recent change in public thinking from the 1990s onwards. Prior to this the role of official monolingualism as a means to unite the country was heavily emphasized, and the change is characterized as mirroring an emerging new regional 'philosophy of plurality, of "multi" as opposed to "single" ', which is also showing itself as a force further to the south, in post-apartheid, pluralist South Africa, where eleven official languages are now recognized and supported by the government in various ways.

In between the above kind of celebrated plurilingualism and the heavy presence of single national and official languages in a state, there are other mid-way linguistic points represented by countries described in chapters of the book, each of which adds something further to a broader understanding of language and its relation to processes of nation-building. Before closing the current overview chapter with certain general remarks on patterns highlighted in the book, one final configuration of linguistic prominence deserves brief comment and inclusion in the broad description of outcomes and hierarchies presented here – the case of unofficial expanding national lingua francas. Two examples of this phenomenon are Wolof in Senegal, and Bambara in Mali. Chapter 5 remarks that the increasingly widespread, high-frequency use of the former language has embedded it in Senegal to such a degree that it is 'clearly functioning as a de facto national language', and is indeed frequently referred to as the national language of the country. However, despite the striking growth of Wolof and its spread into semi-formal domains such as parliamentary discussion, Wolof officially has no greater status than various other indigenous languages which have been recognized as 'national languages'. Furthermore, when there have been proposals to elevate the status of Wolof above the other 'national languages' and give it a formal standing in the country more on a par with French, these have met with strong resistance from certain quarters. Chapter 5 suggests that the remarkable development and spread of Wolof until the present, described as 'the creeping Wolofization of the state', is due in significant part to the fact that the language has no official status greater than that of the other recognized national languages, and has never been privileged with official support that has not also been given to the other national languages. Because of this lack of special official treatment, there are no legal grounds for disputing the increased use of Wolof, and the language has remained free to continue its natural growth throughout the country. Wolof therefore is an interesting example of a language in the process of becoming a considerably successful national language and symbol of collective Senegalese identity without the assistance of any targeted official promotion, and might even seem to be benefiting from the absence of explicit attempts at promotion. In Mali, a related situation occurs, but with certain clear and important differences. As in Senegal, a single indigenous language spoken by a sizeable minority (40%) as first language has become widespread and known and used by a large majority (80%) without this being driven by any official initiatives or unique formal status – Bambara, like Wolof in Senegal, is just one of a wider group of named national languages. Similar to the situation in Senegal, the general public will to see Bambara formally promoted to a higher official role is also not present, and in fact is much less broadly present than with Wolof, Bambara commonly not being viewed as having any special national symbolic position in Mali. Both languages are however dominant and continuing to expand in a 'natural', largely undirected way, both in terms of numbers of speakers and domains of use. Though at present these national lingua francas are unlikely to be converted into co-official or unique national languages, it will be interesting to see how they develop in future years and whether their utilization in many national linking functions later leads to a different formal status or whether their current categorization as just one of many national language will remain the most appropriate way to make use of these languages in nation-building in Mali and Senegal.[12]

1.5 Closing Remarks

Despite the majority of independent, modern African states being comparatively young and without long traditions of collective identity, the testimonies of the chapters which follow this introduction suggest that there are indeed emerging national identities among the populations of many countries on the continent, commonly stimulated by the sharing of a bordered territory and frequent histories of earlier colonial domination, along with other national symbols where these are naturally available or can be plausibly constructed, such as national football teams, forms of popular music, representation and participation in international affairs, and so on. With regard to the role of language in the development of national identity in Africa, in many cases, though not all, the heterogeneous, ethno-linguistically mixed nature of national populations has hindered the use of a single language to impart a sense of uniqueness and even destiny as a nation in the way that language has at times been used in West European nationalism (or in Asian nations such as Japan and Korea). Instead of this, the dominant role of language in nation-building in many states, at least in the early post-independence era, has been one of maintaining social harmony and preserving the territorial integrity and political unity of new nation-states, hence a focus on containment, conflict reduction, and increased cohesion – pragmatic nationism rather than aggressive nationalism. Frequently such primary concerns have led to European languages being employed as official languages and continuing to maintain a prominence which affects the creation of national identity through more indigenous linguistic means. In other states, where multilingualism is

---

[12] In this regard, one other language which has similar properties to Wolof and Bambara and which might conceivably develop an official nationwide status in the future is Krio in Sierra Leone, known by almost all the country's population, but as yet still without a formally recognized role in the country (chapter 7).

not so pronounced or has been approached in a more positively pluralistic way, indigenous languages have figured more centrally and obviously in the shaping of national identities.

Concerning the continued 'foreign' presence of European languages in many countries, and the effects of this on the general development of national identity, positive valuation of the peace-keeping, integrative roles these languages have been involved in has led to an increasing acceptance of the former colonial languages as a useful part of the linguistic landscape in many countries, it is often reported (Adegbija 1994). As a result of their instrumental value in a number of important domains, languages such as English and French may consequently seem to be becoming a permanent feature of many states, and representing at least a part of these states' national character and identity. Assisting in such a process of embedding has been the development of distinctive local varieties of English and French in many states, and the general globalization of English in particular, with English being increasingly used by large populations of first and second language users spread throughout the world. Both such developments are serving to decrease automatic associations of European languages with their countries of origin and the memory of earlier colonial occupation, and are leading to English and French being domesticated as components of national identity in certain states, as in Ghana, where chapter 8 reports that English may now even be perceived to be a Ghanaian language and occur as a (partial) marker of Ghanaian identity.

In connection with such patterns, it is useful to emphasize again a point from section 1.3, relating to observations made by Anyidoho and Dakubu in chapter 8, that in many African states which have experienced colonial rule there may be the perception of an important linguistic division between oral and written communication and that indigenous and European languages may be seen to be best suited for use in different domains, the latter in more formal areas (including reading and writing), and the former in informal interactions associated with higher degrees of solidarity. This perceived separation of languages in terms of primary communicative function may follow a tradition present in African societies and elsewhere for different languages and registers or varieties of a single language to be seen as appropriate for different activities and general areas of life. To the extent that an individual regularly engages in a range of formally distinguished activities and with varied social groups, there may be a need for multiple registers and varieties of a single language or alternatively for a proficiency in different languages. Though clearly being non-indigenous in origin and only acquired through access to education, English and French (and Portuguese) may fit into such a multi-variety system in terms of instantiating the more formal varieties of language deemed necessary in written and official communication and felt to be less appropriate for informal communication where indigenous languages commonly enjoy greater covert prestige. Such a structured organization of levels and varieties of language according to activity and domain is also found in technically monolingual populations, hence, for example, in Great Britain the more formal registers of standard English used in writing and parliamentary debate are clearly different from tokens of colloquial, spontaneous speech heard in most parts of the country. In terms of language-centred identity, it is perhaps natural to expect that the full range of language(s) which make up an individual's linguistic inventory has an influence on the creation of self-image and the way that an individual sees him/herself as relating to others, including the national population and the construct of the nation-state, and hence that languages used for formal purposes also form part of speakers' sense of national identity. This now leads us on to a final interesting observation present in various chapters of the volume (and deducible as a conclusion from the content of others), that language-formed national identities in Africa may be complex and established by a collectivity of languages in many instances, as a property both of populations and of individuals.

In section 1.4.4 we have already seen that national identity in various African states (for example, Mali, DRC, Zambia) is felt to be formed in a pluralistic way by a body of national languages present in the country rather than any single indigenous or non-indigenous language. Chapters 8 and 17 add that national identity in Ghana and South Africa are similarly composed in a complex way, frequently through knowledge and use of multiple linguistic systems. In Ghana, where English may be one rising component of national identity, it is emphasized that proficiency in an indigenous language is a further and a highly important part of belonging to the nation. Anyi-doho and Dakubu write: 'it seems that for most people Ghanaian identity entails a recognized ethnic identity, so that no matter what the status and role of English, ability to speak a Ghanaian language is also a necessary feature of the national identity'. And in South Africa, Mesthrie observes that national identity for much of the population is conveyed by balancing the use of different languages spoken in the country – English, the indigenous national languages, and (for some) the emerging urban codes Tsotsisaal and Isicamtho: 'Too much emphasis upon the traditional African languages in certain contexts appears – ironically – to many people a reminder of the apartheid era with its denial of racial dignity. Too much use of English by Black South Africans is seen (by Blacks) as inappropriate and "being too White" (Slabbert and Finlayson 2000)'. National identities in a range of African populations may consequently be linguistically based on the regular manipulation of multiple languages (which may also include non-indigenous languages) and be less clearly isolated by reference to a single prominent variety, unlike the situation in certain European contexts. In chapter 8 it is added that heavily funded, well-directed language planning initiatives might have the ability to push the mixture of languages underpinning current national identity in Ghana in one particular direction, either towards a greater cross-population embedding of English, or an expansion of indigenous languages into domains presently dominated by English. However, for the time being this seems unlikely to occur for financial and other reasons, both in Ghana and in various other African states with similar sociolinguistic situations. The 'multi', mixed linguistic foundations of national identity therefore seem set to remain as a significant characteristic of a number of national populations in Africa, adding to the general complexity of language and its interaction with the growth of nations in the modern era.

With such final remarks, the reader is now invited to continue to the main chapters of the volume for much more detail on the past and ongoing development of individual countries. It is hoped that the collection of studies here from different parts of the continent will provide a useful first base for comparative research into language and national identity in Africa and stimulate further investigation and thinking on the topic.

2

Egypt: From Egyptian to Pan-Arab Nationalism

Yasir Suleiman

2.1 Introduction: Terminology and its Consequences

The language–national identity link is a recurrent theme in nationalism studies. However, both this link and its constituent members (language and nation) are a matter of *construction*, what I have elsewhere called a discursive project (Suleiman 2006), that is amenable to formulation and counter-formulation. It is, therefore, not surprising that for much of the twentieth century the link between language and national identity in Egypt has been the subject of debate which sought to argue either for an Egypt-bound form of identity, revolving around the territory of Egypt (Egyptian nationalism), or for forms of supra-Egyptian nationalism that sought to define this identity extra-territorially by reference to dominant religion (Islam), some vague notion of a Western versus Eastern culture, or language (Gershoni and Jankowski 1995). This chapter deals with the two most important formulations of national identity in Egypt: Egyptian nationalism and Pan-Arab nationalism.

The nexus of language and national identity in Egypt is a vexed one terminologically. Although Egypt is largely a monolingual country, having Arabic as its official language, there is disagreement in the literature on how to deal with the variability of the language. The diglossic model, inspired by Ferguson (1959), would posit two varieties, a 'high' variety that is restricted to writing and other formal sociolinguistic domains, and a 'low' variety represented by the spoken language in its myriad manifestations, although Ferguson moved away from this model in his later research (1996). Other models have posited three varieties, adding what is called Educated Spoken Arabic between Ferguson's high and low varieties, a hybrid and not so fully codified code partaking of the characteristics of these two varieties (Mitchell 1978, 1986; Hary 1996). Badawi (1973) posits five *levels* (not varieties) of the language, covering the continuum between Ferguson's high and low varieties. This multiplicity of categories, regardless of their empirical validity, raises the question as to which of the above varieties or levels one talks about when dealing with the language–national identity link in Egypt. Some

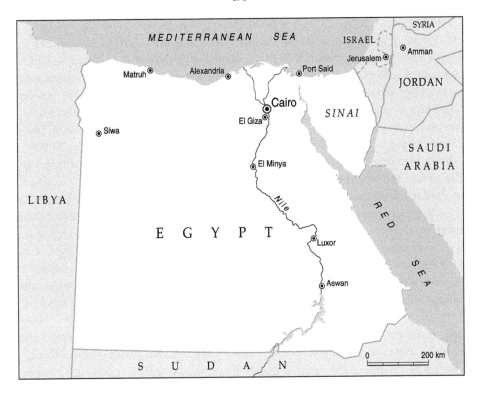

Egypt

clearing of the terminological and conceptual ground is, therefore, in order before we proceed further.

Discourse on language in national identity in Egypt has been framed in relation to the standard and colloquial varieties of Arabic, thus adhering to a view of the language situation that is essentially diglossic in character (Gershoni and Jankowski 1986, 1995; Suleiman 1996, 2003, 2004a). The terms 'standard'[1] and 'colloquial' are used in the preceding sentence to designate respectively what is referred to in the native linguistic and socio-political discourse as *al-lugha al-'arabiyya al-fusha* (eloquent Arabic language) and *al-'ammiyya* (the colloquial).[2] To eschew the pitfalls of translation and the attendant misconceptions translated terms may create for a non-Egyptian and non-Arab readership, for example the problematic use of the terms 'Classical Arabic' and 'Egyptian language' to refer to these two varieties of the language respectively

---

[1] It should be noted that the term 'standard' does not preclude variability within this category. See Bentahila and Davies (1991) for an interesting discussion of this issue

[2] I do not share Haeri's (1997) reservations about the use of the term 'colloquial' to refer to *'ammiyya* in Egypt. Most linguists writing in English use this term routinely and, in my view, unproblematically without implying that *'ammiyya* is a monolith or that it is incapable of socio-culturally sensitive style shifts, contrary to what Haeri asserts (1997: 12).

(Haeri 2003; van Gelder 2004), I will use the terms *fusha* and *'ammiyya* throughout this chapter. This approach has the virtue of discussing the language–identity link in Egyptian nationalism in terms that are consistent with the native tradition, in which these two dichotomous categories resonate with how most Egyptians conceptualize the language situation in their country, thus adopting what may be called an insider perspective in this study. As I have discussed elsewhere, resonance is an important element in constructing national identities because of the limits it sets on invention, fabrication, and myth-making in nation-building (Suleiman 2003, 2006 and Schöpflin 1997).

Paying attention to this insider perspective privileges folk beliefs about language (Niedzielski and Preston 2000) in a way which allows us to come closer to the covert orientations, assumptions, and hidden ideologies of the community and how it relates to its language repertoire. As Eid rightly observes (2002: 204), the 'perceived [and therefore, constructed] dichotomy [between *'ammiyya* and *fusha*] is deeply engrained in the collective consciousness of Arabic speakers/writers', whether in Egypt or in other Arabic-speaking countries. Thus, in spite of the criticisms levelled against the empirical validity of Ferguson's concept of Arabic diglossia, there is no doubt that this concept has a great socio-psychological and cultural validity for most Arabic speakers. From this perspective, referring to the *'ammiyya* as 'the Egyptian language' (Haeri 2003) reflects a minority view of this variety to which most Egyptians would not subscribe. For most Egyptians, *'ammiyya* is not a language but a kind of *lahja* (dialect), a variety that is denied the status of language in common parlance, although it can be legitimately ascribed the status of a 'language system' when considered empirically using the tools and theoretical frameworks of modern linguistics. In addition, for many Egyptians, *'ammiyya* is a stigmatized variety (when compared with *fusha*), often described as 'having no grammar' in the native non-technical discourse on language (an incorrect view empirically, of course), even though it is the mother tongue of Egyptians and the one through which they are socialized.

The use of *fusha* in this research, in preference to any of its English equivalents, is further motivated by the strong connotations of historical and cultural continuity it carries. For Egyptian speakers, *fusha* designates a construct which, in spite of its evolution over the centuries from its pre-Islamic days, is perceived as essentially the same language, a view that many modern linguists would argue is objectively not correct (Versteegh 1997). These connotations of continuity are important in constructing Egyptian national identity, for it is a general feature of all nationalisms to emphasize continuities with the past, and to use these continuities to endow themselves and those whom they 'nationize' with pedigree and authenticity.

To recap, the study of language in nationalism need not conform to the categories of modern linguistics which, in the case in hand, would create a distinction between *fusha* in its pre-modern and modern forms; in fact, it sometimes proceeds with little regard to these categories, buttressed by the view in nationalism studies that both languages and national identities are a matter of construction, of manipulation and counter-manipulation to suit different historical and political contingencies, orientations, and ideological positions (see Suleiman 2006). I wish to emphasize this point here because most Arabic linguists and sociolinguists, particularly in the West, have been reluctant to take this perspective on board in the name of formalistic empiricism and, in my view, misplaced objectivity (see also Ibrahim 1989). As a result, they have been unable to embrace the important distinction between *linguistic* communities and *speech* communities where 'the former are groups professing adherence to the normatively constructed, ideologically articulated "standard" language . . . and the latter are groups characterized by the actual use of a specific speech form' (Blommaert 2006: 243, following Silverstein 1996, 1998). Blommaert perceptively comments on this distinction, stating that the 'two . . . are not isomorphic, and the distance between the sociolinguistically definable community and the linguistic-ideologically definable community reveals the degree of hegemony of language ideologies [what has been referred to as folk linguistics above], often resulting in blind spots for sociolinguistic phenomena' (ibid.). Arabic sociolinguistics is full of such 'blind spots' which we seek to obviate here by referring to Egypt in the context of nation-building as a *linguistic community* with strong ideological orientations that coalesce around *fusha*, whether accepting or rejecting it, as the main and most abiding index of national identity in the linguistic domain. Exploiting *'ammiyya* as such an index is the exception to a general rule in Egypt.

Referring to Egypt as a linguistic community in the above sense enables us to adopt an insider perspective of the language–national identity link. John Eisele (2002) identifies four motifs which can be easily transferred to this link: unity, purity, continuity, and competition. As we shall see below, these motifs or topoi, especially unity and continuity, are subjected to continuous manipulation in constructions of Egyptian national identity. Competition is important in that it describes the often tense relationship between *fusha* and *'ammiyya*, whereas purity comes to the fore in discussions aiming at protecting the *fusha* against the 'corrosive' influences of the *'ammiyya* and the 'onslaught' of foreign languages, particularly under the influence of globalization, as we shall see below.

The insider perspective may also be usefully developed further by certain elaboration. This concerns the use of the pair of terms 'mother tongue' and 'native language' which I propose to customize to describe the language situation in Egypt. I believe it is necessary for our purposes here to tie these two terms respectively to the distinction between 'speech community' and 'linguistic community', on the one hand, and to that between *'ammiyya* and *fusha*, on the other, to create the following conceptual chains: (1) *'ammiyya*, mother tongue, and speech community, and (2) *fusha*, native language, and linguistic community. The former nexus of terms is anchored to the 'low' form of the language as conceptualized by Ferguson. The latter is consistent with his notion of the 'high' variety.

I am aware that the above terminological chains are new in discussing the language–national identity link in Egypt, but they are in my view necessary to forge a rapprochement between the findings of empirical linguistics and the deep-rooted beliefs of folk linguistics as ideological articulations embodying the insider perspective. The use of mother tongue to link 'ammiyya to speech community captures the nature of this form of Arabic as a spoken variety that is informally acquired and as a site of cultural intimacy. The use of 'native language' to link *fusha* to linguistic community is intended to express the ideological meanings of 'nativeness', the fact that although *fusha* is not a mother tongue to the Egyptians (due to being acquired formally through instruction in school), it still is a site of belonging and intimacy to them in socio-psychological terms. I believe that these chains allow us access to a more nuanced concept of language in discussing national identity construction in Egypt. In particular, they allow us to excavate layers of meaning that go beyond the instrumental role of language as a means of communication that dominates so much of Arabic sociolinguistics, thus stunting its ability to engage symbiotically with politics, sociology, and anthropology. The above terms and concepts lay the foundation for the discussion below.

2.2 Language and Egyptian Nationalism

Egyptian nationalism has been an important force in Egypt for many decades. Although its heyday was in the 1920s, its actual roots go back to the first half of the nineteenth century when Egypt was still nominally part of the Ottoman Empire, in particular to the effort of Muhammad Ali, Egypt's new ruler from 1805 to 1848, to build a modern state. Relying on translation as the gateway to European education and science, Muhammad Ali inadvertently underlined the importance of *fusha* as an instrument of modernization which, in the words of the famous Shaykh Hasan al-'Attar (c. 1766–1835) had the capacity to '[awaken] the mind of Egypt' (Ahmed 1960: 5). Led by Shaykh Rifa'a al-Tahtawi (1801–73), an extremely able and politically astute cleric and 'civil servant', the translation movement expanded the functional domains of *fusha*, thus invigorating it as a vehicle for modernization and preparing it to be the language of education and official government communication. An index of this is the writing of new language books for educational purposes and the use of *fusha*, alongside Turkish – the language of the political class, as in most Arabic-speaking parts of the Ottoman Empire – in the official *Egyptian Gazette*. It was not long in fact before *fusha* replaced Turkish completely as the language of this publication. The symbolic meaning of this erasure is as important in the trajectory of the language–national identity link in Egypt as the confirmation of *fusha* as the instrumental means of state communication. It should not, however, be thought from this that *fusha* lacked champions among the educated class before the rise of Muhammad Ali in Egypt. The response of al-Jabarti (famous chronicler, 1754–1825) to Napoleon's proclamation to the Egyptians during his invasion of Egypt in 1798 illustrates the symbolic importance of language as a means of textual 'resistance'. Mitchell's (1998: 133) account of this is worth quoting in full:

Landing at Alexandria and advancing upon Cairo, Napoleon's first act had been to use a printed proclamation to the Egyptian people, prepared in Arabic by French Orientalists. Jabarti's response to this strange innovation, in a chronicle written in the midst of the crisis, was an interesting one. He began his account by copying the text of the proclamation, and followed it for several pages with a detailed list of its grammatical errors. Phrase by phrase he pointed out the colloquialisms, misspellings, ellipses, inconsistencies, morphological inaccuracies and errors of syntax of the French Orientalists, drawing from these incorrect usages a picture of the corruptions, deceptions, misunderstandings and ignorance of the French authorities.

However, in spite of his interest in *fusha*, in which he composed grammar books along European lines for educational purposes, al-Tahtawi showed little interest in positing an identity for Egypt which privileged language (*fusha*) or religion (Islam) over territory. In fact, al-Tahtawi believed that one of the tasks of education was to promote the idea that the 'brotherhood of country' is different from the 'brotherhood of religion', and that one of the highest values to which the Egyptians could aspire was 'the love of the fatherland' (*hubb al-watan*) as a form of 'territorial patriotism in the modern sense' (Hourani 1983: 78–9; Zroukhi 1999). Al-Tahtawi understood the fatherland as a socialized geography in which bonds of association between individuals are forged through the instrumentality of language rather than through its capacity as an index with symbolic meanings. By privileging the fatherland as a principle of group definition, al-Tahtawi was, in effect, offering his countrymen a new way of conceptualizing themselves and their bonds of collective association in the modern world. Pursuing the distinction between the bonds of country and those of religion, al-Tahtawi displayed a keen interest in the history of Egypt in its pre-Islamic Pharaonic past – prior to the arrival of the Arabs in Egypt in the seventh century – which he believed was capable of motivating the modern Egyptians to recapture their ancient glory. At least at the level of aspirations and for reasons of task orientation, al-Tahtawi conceived of the history of Egypt as one seamless trajectory that spanned ancient Egypt to the modern period, without privileging the Arab component of this past, but without also ignoring Islam as an important component in the fabric of society. By emphasizing territory and historical continuity, and by underplaying the bonds of language and religion without, however, neglecting the need to modernize the former, al-Tahtawi laid down some of the most abiding tenets for Egyptian nationalism.

The above ideas were picked up and developed in the first two decades of the twentieth century by Ahmad Lutfi al-Sayyid (1872–1963). As one of the country's most important educators, al-Sayyid believed that Egypt, as a distinct nation, was not defined by its language (*fusha*) or majority religion (Islam) – as constructs linking it to other nations sharing these markers – but by its continuous existence in a well-defined territory that indelibly marked the character of those who lived in it, although it is not clear how this act of environmental/ecological marking was performed, what mechanisms it used, or what its causal outcomes were. Al-Sayyid promoted his ideas on the impact of ecology and the environment on people and their language through the newspaper al-Jarida which he edited between 1908 and 1914.

Yet, in spite of his interest in geography and the environment, al-Sayyid was also very interested in the role of language in modernization, and it is through this prism that he approached *fusha* in his writings. Writing many articles on language, al-Sayyid was aware that *fusha* was in need of lexical and stylistic modernization, a task he tackled from the perspective of an Egyptian nationalist who believed in the Egyptianization of *fusha* (*tamsir al-lugha*), perhaps to make it fit for defining Egyptian national identity at some future date. As a language policy platform, Egyptianizing the *fusha* consisted of creating a rapprochement, a kind of middle space, between this variety of Arabic and the *'ammiyya*, which al-Sayyid dubbed in some of his articles as the Egyptian language (*al-lugha al-misriyya*). More specifically, Egyptianizing the *fusha* consisted of simplifying it stylistically and injecting it with some of the lexical resources of the *'ammiyya* to give it a distinct Egyptian flavour.

There is no doubt that al-Tahtawi and al-Sayyid had a seminal influence on the flowering of Egyptian nationalism in the 1920s, which was given an enormous boost as a result of the pride the country felt in the 1919 revolution against British colonial rule, the establishment of a parliamentary democracy in 1922–3, the excitement following the discovery of the tomb of Tut-Ank-Amon in 1923 and the success of Mustafa Kemal Atatürk in promoting Turkish nationalism with its keen interest in language reform, which the Egyptian territorial nationalists looked to as a model. The insistence of these early advocates on territorial integrity, historical continuity with ancient Egypt, linguistic ecology, and language modernization formed the bedrock of further elaborations and developments in Egyptian nationalism of the 1920s. In particular, the territorial nationalists of this period insisted that *fusha* could not form the basis of a supra-Egyptian national identity with other Arabic-speaking countries, arguing implicitly against the Arab nationalists of the Levant who believed that Egypt was Arab by virtue of the *fusha* link. Being, however, aware that such a bond could never be expunged from Egyptian political life completely as long as *fusha* continued to be the language of Egypt's dominant religion, culture, and literature, the territorial nationalists embarked on a vernacularization campaign the essence of which was promoting the *'ammiyya* as the only authentic and legitimate voice of Egypt. This political platform was succinctly expressed by Tawfiq 'Awwan in *al-Siyasa al-Usbu'iyya*, the mouthpiece of the territorial nationalists, in 1929 (cited in Gershoni and Jankowski 1986: 220):

> Egypt has an Egyptian language; Lebanon has a Lebanese language; the Hijaz has a Hijazi language; and so forth – and all of these languages are by no means Arabic languages. Each of our countries has a language which is its own possession: so why do we not write as we converse in it? For the language in which the people speak is the language in which they also write.

To underline the above argument, the territorial nationalists emphasized the influence of the Coptic substratum[3] on 'ammiyya, pointing to the existence of some lexical items and other features in it from this substratum (see Bishai 1960; Youssef 2003). Some territorial nationalists went so far as to claim that to be true to their history, the Egyptian Copts, as the legitimate heirs of ancient Egypt, must abandon Arabic and revert to Coptic, a dead language (Suleiman 2003). Other territorial nationalists advocated the wholesale use of 'ammiyya in literature, invoking as their argument the mimetic principles of realism and naturalness in encoding the voice of Egypt and Egyptians in writing, particularly that of the peasant (*fellah*) in his countryside as the living proof of continuity with the past (see Selim 2004 for the use of 'ammiyya in literature). These strategies demanded that the introduction of Arabic into Egypt be explained in new terms. To do that, some territorial nationalists projected the seventh-century conquest of Egypt as an Arab invasion or occupation, and Arabic as the foreign language of that invader or occupier. Some of these nationalists painted Arabic as an imperial language, equating it symbolically with English as the language of British colonial rule which started in 1882 and, through various mutations, came to an effective end in 1952.

Although the ideology of these territorial nationalists continues the founding impulses of their predecessors, it was nevertheless different in some very important respects. On the one hand, there is a strong move among these nationalists in favour of the 'ammiyya as the language of Egypt, which al-Tahtawi and al-Sayyid did not support at all. In spite of his accommodating views towards some features of the 'ammiyya, for example its lexical flexibility and ability to innovate, al-Sayyid in fact displayed real contempt towards this variety (Wendell 1972). Furthermore, neither al-Tahtawi nor al-Sayyid advocated the use of 'ammiyya as the medium of literary production, as some 1920s territorial nationalists did. On the other hand, while the early nationalists emphasized the continuity of modern Egypt with its Pharaonic past without treating the Arab component of their past as rupture, the new nationalists did treat the Arab component of their past as historical rupture, which Egypt repaired through its 'historically proven' assimilatory powers. Thus, for their brand of nationalism to be true to itself, in particular in so far as they believed in the environmental/ecological base of this nationalism and its assimilating powers, the new nationalists had to somehow incorporate the Arabs and their language into the full sweep of Egyptian history. This they did by talking about the power of the Nile Valley as a demographic melting pot

---

[3] Coptic is the demotic form of ancient Egyptian as encoded in the hieroglyphics. The transition from Coptic to Arabic as the dominant language of Egypt was accomplished in the last decades of the eleventh century. This process was aided by a number of factors, including (1) the prominence of Greek in Egypt at the time of the introduction of Islam into Egypt in the seventh century; (2) limited use of Coptic in the written literature in subsequent centuries; (3) the establishment of Arabic as the language of the state apparatus, aided by the initial compact patterns of settlement of the Arabs in Egypt. For further information on the transition from Coptic to Arabic see al-Sharkawi (2002), Bishai (1963), and Rubenson (1996).

which throughout Egypt's known history could mould its inhabitants into its abiding spirit.

2.3 Egyptian Nationalism: Further Elaborations

Although the tide started to turn away from Egyptian nationalism towards supra-Egyptian forms of identity construction from the 1930s onwards, as we shall see later, the former ideology continued to have its articulate advocates in the decades that ensued. One such figure is Salama Musa (1887–1958) who continued to write on the topic in a popularizing mode well into the 1950s. Salama Musa maintained the territorial nationalist position that Egypt is not Arab in national identity terms and that *fusha* does not make all the countries sharing it a single nation in spite of the commonalities of culture and shared feelings it creates between them. In addition, he strongly promoted the Pharaonic theme in the nationalist ideology, considering this theme as the major authenticating and motivating force for Egypt. However, his thinking on Egyptian national identity shows some subtle differences from the young nationalists of the 1920s. First, he places Egypt's cultural identity in the European cultural sphere on the grounds that Egypt was under Byzantine rule before the Arab 'invasion' and 'occupation' of the country in the seventh century had subjugated it to Arab and Muslim rule. Second, he mounted a sustained critique of the language issue in this nationalism, which is remarkable considering that he believed that language is not a basis for national self-definition. His interest in this topic sprang from another agenda of his, namely the view that the modernization of Egypt could not proceed without overhauling its language situation (Suleiman 2003: 180–90). It is to this issue that I will turn next.

In his book *al-Balagha al-ʿasriyya wa-l-lugha al-ʿarabiyya* (*Contemporary Rhetoric and the Arabic Language*, 1947), Salama Musa constructed a dire picture of *fusha*, painting it as lexically defective in dealing with the exigencies of science, industry, and modernity at large owing to its origins in a desert ecology and culture from which it has been unable to break completely free. Owing to its desert origin, Arabic is said to embody values that are dangerously at variance with those of the modern world. *Fusha* is described as an unduly grammatically complex language, requiring years of learning and formal instruction without the guarantee that one would ever be able to have full mastery of it. Arabic rhetoric is condemned as a cultural site of sentimentality, emotionalism, artificiality, linguistic arrogance, outlandish metaphors, and ornate figures of speech. The Arabic script is attacked as too unwieldy to serve as the medium for a modern education system. Salama Musa concluded that these handicaps of *fusha* made it unfit to serve as an instrument of modernization for Egypt.

Fusha, furthermore, was said to have fossilized to the point where it could be declared (almost) a dead language. One way out of this dire situation for Salama Musa consisted in opening the language to the currents of grammatical and stylistic simplification, lexical borrowing from the European languages, and the use of the

Roman script in place of the defective and outmoded Arabic script. The latter reform would improve the communicative efficiency of the language, aid in its acquisition and symbolically signal the modernity of *fusha* in its new garb, thus replicating aspects of the Turkish reform experience under Atatürk. Alternatively, Egypt could divest itself of *fusha* in favour of *'ammiyya*, the true mother tongue of Egyptians and a language form over which they had complete control in competence terms. Allied to these two proposed solutions, Salama Musa called for a revival of the Coptic language, the demotic form of ancient Egyptian, which he stated was still alive in the monasteries of the Coptic Church. Salama Musa most probably realized that this was an impractical objective but put it forward for symbolic reasons, to boost the Pharaonic theme in Egyptian nationalism. Salama Musa must have calculated that by orienting the Egyptians linguistically towards a different and deeper past than that offered by the Arabs and Arabic, he could appeal to countervailing nationalist impulses of a non-Arab kind.

So, how do Salama Musa's views on language fit into his ideology of Egyptian nationalism? Is there any inbuilt contradiction between his rejection of language as an ingredient or marker of national identity and his sustained interest in it as the object and means of modernization? Does he favour a simplified form of *fusha* or *'ammiyya* as the language of/for Egypt? And how did he set about trying to promote his views on these issues?

Salama Musa's interest in language in Egyptian nationalism was essentially utilitarian in nature. He approached the topic not from the point of view of national self-definition *per se*, but from that of modernization as a socio-economic aspiration. In principle, therefore, it mattered little for him whether this modernization could be achieved through a simplified form of *fusha* or via the adoption of *'ammiyya* in its place. His preference for one or the other was not a matter of pure ideological choice, but one of reception and practicality, of judging what could or could not be achieved. His, therefore, was an eclectic approach that shunned consistency and logical rigour in favour of pragmatism. As a consummate campaigner on behalf of Egyptian nationalism, Salama Musa used print media, mainly journalism, to full effect. He wrote in an engaging, hard-hitting and clear style, almost to say to his readers 'this is the kind of modernized *fusha* I am advocating'. However, as the 1930s progressed his ideas were increasingly seen as anachronistic and harking back to a past age of Egyptian political thinking that had been deserted by those who were once its champions. As we shall see later, as a territorial nationalist, Salama Musa was left stranded as the currents of political thinking towards supra-forms of national identification started to engulf him and others in the country.

The idea that language is not sufficient to define Egypt's national identity and that Egypt is culturally more akin to Europe than the surrounding Arab countries characterizes the thinking of another territorial nationalist, Taha Hussein (1889–1973). Taha Hussein's book *Mustaqbal al-thaqafa fi misr* (*The Future of Culture in Egypt*, 1938) is a major landmark in the history of Egyptian nationalism. Unlike other nationalists, Taha

Hussein emphasized the full integrity of *fusha* as the language of culture in Egypt. He acknowledged that the formal grammar of *fusha* needed urgent simplification, but he argued vehemently that in his scheme of things this in no way infringed the 'inner' grammar of the language. Putting the modernization of *fusha* at the heart of his programme of educational reform in Egypt, Taha Hussein premised the self-regeneration of Egypt as a nation in its own right on, *mutatis mutandis*, (1) weakening the institutional hold of the ancient Al-Azhar University, Egypt's bastion of religious education, on *fusha* by allowing other agents to participate in the provision of teacher training and institutional assessment and evaluation; (2) the elimination of foreign language teaching from the state sector in the early school years to free *fusha* from the lure and competition posed by these languages; and (3) the compulsory teaching of Arabic as a school subject in all private schools where most non-Egyptians and the Egyptian upper classes sent their children.

Believing in the power of language to mould and unite members of the nation, Taha Hussein hammered the point that *fusha* was the language of the Muslims and non-Muslims in Egypt alike,[4] basing himself on the premise that religion is one thing and culture and politics are another. Starting from this perspective, he called on the Coptic Church to improve the standing of *fusha* in its sphere by ensuring that (1) its ministers were competent in the language, a standard that was not always upheld; (2) members of the Church had access to materials that were free from grammatical errors; (3) these materials were written in an elegant style; and (4) the Arabic translation of the Bible was as distinguished linguistically as the English, French, or German versions of the Bible. To this end, Taha Hussein is reported 'to have offered to help in rewriting [the liturgies] so that the Arab Christians could worship in good Arabic' (Hourani 1983: 334).

There is no doubt that *Mustaqbal al-thaqafa fi misr* was produced to counter the strong trends in 1930s Egypt in favour of supra-Egyptian forms of national self-definition, although there is in fact some evidence that, in the late forties and early fifties of the twentieth century, Taha Hussein's thinking started to take on a pan-Arab nationalist flavour, albeit of a faint kind. Before dealing with these emerging forms of nationalism, however, I will briefly examine the views of one further Egyptian nationalist to show the range of ideas that these nationalists deployed in promoting their ideology.

Luis 'Awad wrote two books, separated by over thirty years, in which he expounded his views on the language–national identity link in Egypt. The first, *Plutoland*, was published in 1947. The second, *Muqaddima fi fiqh al-lugha al-'arabiyya* (*Prolegomenon to the Foundations of the Arabic Language*) was published in 1980. In spite of the chronological distance between them, and in spite of the different ways in which they handled the language–national identity link, these two works display impulses of continuity

---

[4] Approximately 10 per cent of the population of Egypt is estimated to be Christian, mostly Coptic Christian.

and change in articulating Egyptian nationalism, but without ever compromising the principle that *fusha* does not define Egypt's national identity. In *Plutoland*, 'Awad compares the Arab conquest of Egypt in AD 640 to the British occupation of Egypt in 1882. This comparison enabled him to present *fusha* as a foreign language and as the language of occupation which needed to be resisted and ousted from Egypt if Egypt was to achieve its full independence. What was held to be necessary, therefore, was a linguistic revolution which would elevate the 'base' and 'vulgar' *'ammiyya* (as 'Awad referred to it) to the status of Egypt's national language, a language that would be fit for writing and literary production. 'Awad believed that Egyptian creativity was permanently handicapped by the outmoded and unwieldy *fusha* and that by nurturing the *'ammiyya* the Egyptians could launch themselves and their nation into a future unfettered by the linguistic shackles of the past, a view advocated by William Wilcocks (1893) before him and, it seems, Haeri in recent times (2003). Disregarding the linguistic affinities of the Egyptian *'ammiyya* to *fusha*, 'Awad asserted that Egyptian *'ammiyya* has developed its own phonology, morphology, syntax, lexicon, and prosody, and that it had done so under the influence of an Egyptian substratum (Coptic) that made it distinct from other *'ammiyya* varieties outside the borders of Egypt. That much is broadly consistent with earlier expressions of Egyptian nationalism, particularly those that were in vogue in the 1920s.

In the *Muqaddima* – written against the background of President Sadat's 'Egypt first' policy in the wake of the Arab boycott of Egypt following the peace treaty with Israel in 1979 – 'Awad argued, sometimes directly but at other times obliquely, that the Arabs originated outside the Arabian Peninsula, and that they and their language cannot, as a result, claim to be indigenous to the lands where *fusha* is the dominant language. He also argued that *fusha* cannot sustain the claims of uniqueness made about it by Arab grammarians and the cultural elite, and that it cannot act as a bond of national identity tying Egyptians to communities outside the borders of Egypt. But 'Awad offered his boldest argument when he claimed that the uniqueness of the Egyptian *'ammiyya* was in fact an outcome of the special physiology of the Egyptian vocal tract. Being physiologically determined, in his view, Egyptian *'ammiyya* therefore separated Egyptians from non-Egyptians in a genetically coded manner, and yet, he maintained, this variety is not sufficient to define the Egyptians as a national group. Like earlier nationalists, 'Awad continued to privilege geography and the environment over language in national self-definition, but like them he also felt the need to engage the language issue in national self-definition – only to dismiss it – because of the ubiquity of this factor in the ideological discourse on the topic.

There are two major attitudes to language in Egyptian nationalism. First, *fusha* was not seen to be invested with the power to define Egypt's national identity. This view was as characteristic of the proto-Egyptian nationalists of the nineteenth century, in particular al-Tahtawi, as it was of the advocates of Egyptian nationalism throughout the twentieth century. The issue is less clear-cut when it comes to *'ammiyya*, simply because it can be constructed as more specifically Egyptian than *fusha*. Egyptian nationalists understood that giving *fusha* a definitional role in their ideology would compromise their claims about the distinctiveness of Egypt as a separate nation. If *fusha* defined Egypt's national identity, then Egypt must be an Arab country, a conclusion the Egyptian nationalists would not countenance under any circumstances. The interest of most Egyptian nationalists in the definitional power of *fusha* therefore had to take the form of denying, or at least challenging, the principle that language is a marker of the nation. But some of these nationalists were also hoist by their own petard because they were willing to entertain such a definitional role for *'ammiyya*. Both of these impulses in Egyptian nationalism spring in my view from an acute application of the principle of *alterity* in national self-definition: the greater the substantive linguistic similarities between national Self and significant Other, the greater the desire to deny or explain away these similarities as a basis for a shared national identity between this Self and the Other.

Second, Egyptian nationalists evinced a strong and sustained interest in language reform and linked this to the socio-economic modernization of their country. In the *fusha* domain, reforms were called for in all areas of the language, but in varying degrees of intensity. For those who felt that *fusha* was beyond reforming, or that it did not offer the best option for nation-building and the concomitant modernization, *'ammiyya* was promoted as the only viable alternative. The difference between these two strands of Egyptian nationalism was a source of weakness in this ideology. Reading Taha Hussein's *Mustaqbal al-thaqafa fi misr*, one forms the impression that, if he was forced to choose between Egyptian nationalism and *fusha* he would actually choose the latter, even though this might in fact bring him closer to the Arab nationalists ideologically. The same could not be said with the same certainty about Ahmad Lutfi al-Sayyid who was not a supporter of *'ammiyya*, in spite of his interest in Egyptianizing *fusha* by bringing it closer to *'ammiyya*.

Egyptian nationalism, with some exceptions, stressed the role of the environment or the Nile ecology in defining the Egyptian character. This is an extremely interesting topic, particularly in the way some Egyptian nationalists have suggested it could be linked to language, but it is left unexplored in articulations of this nationalism. Apart from the influence of the Coptic substratum on *'ammiyya* in particular, especially in the lexical domain, it is not very clear how ecology imparts its definitional function through language. There is a hint, therefore, in 'Awad of a link between ecology, biology, and language, but this link is vague and not very useful in advancing our understanding of the nature of the language–identity link.

2.4 From Egyptian Nationalism to Pan-Arabism

In the 1930s Egypt witnessed a shift in its national identity orientations. Gershoni and Jankowski (1995) studied this topic at length, and they have identified the following orientations and ideologies during this period, dubbing them supra-Egyptian nationalisms:[5] (1) Egyptian Easternism (*al-rabita al-sharqiyya*), which sought to emphasize Egypt's 'Eastern' character against the claims of those who sought to ally Egypt with the West culturally; (2) Egyptian Islamic nationalism (*al-rabita al-islamiyya*), which emphasized the Muslim heritage of Egypt and its ties of faith and brotherhood to other Muslim nations; (3) integral Egyptian nationalism, which emphasized Egypt's unique character and status as a nation in its own right, while at the same time emphasizing the strong cultural ties the country has with other Arab and Muslim countries/nations; and (4) Egyptian Arab nationalism, which sought to define Egypt as an Arab country with strong cultural and political bonds with other Arabic-speaking countries. In the fullness of time, this nationalism developed into a form of pan-Arab nationalism under Nasser in the 1950s and 60s. From the point of view of language in nationalism in Egypt, none of these ideologies championed '*ammiyya* whether for communicative purposes or for the purposes of symbolic national self-definition. By taking '*ammiyya* out of the equation in these emergent nationalisms, the position of *fusha* was given greater visibility in Egypt. This is particularly the case for Egyptian Islamic nationalism and Egyptian Arab nationalism. In other words, in these nationalisms the emphasis is on the linguistic community not the speech community, and on the native language not the mother tongue.

With its emphasis on the bonds of faith, and in view of the special importance of Arabic in Islam as the language of the Qur'an,[6] it is natural that *fusha* would be accorded a special status in Egyptian Islamic nationalism. Interest in the revival of *fusha* in this nationalism was therefore treated as a precondition for the revival of the Islamic community as a whole. Wittingly or unwittingly, therefore, by emphasizing the special place of Arabic in Islam, Egyptian Islamic nationalists turned the language into an identity emblem of the Egyptians as Arabic speakers within Islam. Being always

---

[5] It is important to note that Egypt in each of these supra-nationalisms is constructed at the centre of the nationalism concerned. This is even true of Arab nationalism, which the Egyptian Arab nationalists constructed as radiating out of Egypt politically and culturally to include all the Arabic-speaking countries in a pan-Arab nation; hence, the use of the epithet 'Egyptian' in the name of these supra-nationalisms. It is also important to note that the 'nation' across these supra-nationalisms is not a construct with constant meaning. In integral Egyptian nationalism, Egypt is a nation but with strong non-national links with the Arabic-speaking countries. In Egyptian Arab nationalism, Egypt is at the centre of a pan-Arab nation that spans the Arabic-speaking countries. Egyptian Islamic nationalism postulates a separate identity for Egypt with very strong links to the countries with Muslim majorities. Egyptian Eastern nationalism emphasizes Egypt's separate national identity but highlights its similarity of culture with nations such as China and Japan. Thus, taking Egypt as the centre of a series of concentric nationalist circles, we can imagine these circles to be arranged as follows from the centre to the periphery in the nationalist discourse: Egyptian nationalism, integral Egyptian nationalism, Egyptian Arab nationalism, Egyptian Islamic nationalism, and Egyptian Eastern nationalism.

[6] Haeri (2003) has suggested at some length that *fusha* in Egypt (what she calls 'Classical Arabic') is a sacred or 'semi-sacred' language (this is my term, but it accurately reflects aspects of her discussion). This view of the language is out of kilter with one of the major trends in Egyptian nationalism: pan-Arabism with its definite secular flavour. Furthermore, this view is largely absent from supra-Egyptian national identity in the first half of the twentieth century (Gershoni and Jankowski 1995). Haeri's views on sacredness are in fact an exception to a very general view of *fusha* that, on the whole, ascribes sacredness to the 'Qur'an as revelation in the language' but not to the language as a whole, whatever this means. See Mansour (2004) and Suleiman (2004b) on this topic.

interested in carving out for Egypt a leading role in any form of supra-nationalism, the Islamic nationalists instinctively recognized the political capital afforded them by committing themselves to *fusha* as a means of symbolic identification. The logic of associating Islamic nationalism with Arabic, therefore, had the unintended consequence of premising the realization of this nationalism on some form of Arab unity, the very goal of pan-Arab nationalism. In intellectual, if not political terms, Islamic nationalism could imperceptibly fade into pan-Arabism without subscribing to its secularism, thus underpinning the move towards the strongest expression of the *fusha*–national identity link that is so characteristic of pan-Arabism.

Pan-Arab nationalism in Egypt found its strongest political and cultural expression under Nasser in the 1950s and 60s, but the impetus for this emerged in the preceding decades. Ralph Coury (1982) identifies a number of factors that have aided this process in its early stages, including (1) increased contact between Egyptians and other Arabs during the interwar years, whether in Egypt or in other Arab countries through the employment of Egyptian graduates, mainly as teachers; (2) the export of Egyptian newspapers, magazines, books, and films to other Arab countries in a way which aided the 'Egyptianization of Arab culture' and the 'Arabization of . . . Egyptian literary and cultural production' (ibid.: 460); (3) increased trade and financial links between Egypt and the Arab countries; and (4) the effect of the Palestine question and the strong feeling it generated that Egypt's political destiny and that of her Arab neighbours are intertwined. Improved transport links and electronic channels of communication, for example radio broadcasting, created greater opportunities for contact and the exchange of news and information. Pan-Arab nationalism in Egypt was not, therefore, a completely ideological creation, but one that is also rooted in objective material conditions with discernible social and cultural consequences. Furthermore, it was a movement with a broad range of supporters. Commenting on this, Gershoni and Jankowski tell us (1995: 118):

> The range of social and political strata participating in Egyptian Arab nationalist discourse was equally broad. Native Egyptians and Arab émigrés living in Egypt; Christians and Muslims; established politicians and radicals from the new extraparliamentary movements; older figures and the new effendiya emerging in the 1930s and 1940s; Wafdists and Liberals [members of two Egyptian parties]; Palace and *'ulama'*: members of all these social groups and political persuasions were involved in the intellectual construction and social dissemination of Egyptian Arab nationalism.

Egyptian Arab nationalism considered *fusha* as the most important bond that unites the Egyptians internally and as the one most capable of uniting them externally with other Arabs for whom the language is a shared code. For these nationalists, language replaced the environment in Egyptian nationalism as the most important criterion of identity. Language was thought to be supremely qualified to deliver this function because of its ability to mould the character of its people and to transmit the values of society from one generation to another. In this respect, language is Janus-like: it looks back to the past and it looks forward to the future, linking the one with the other through the present. A nation must therefore take care of its language. It must protect it against decay and external attack, but it must also nurture and develop it. Ibrahim 'Abd al-Qadir al-Mazini (1890–1949) summed this up by equating nationalism with language (Gershoni and Jankowski 1995: 118–19): 'Nationalism . . . is nothing but language. Whatever the nature of a country may be, and however deeply embedded in antiquity its origins may be, as long as people have one language, they are one people . . . the sons of each language conform to and resemble each other and are distinguished from the sons of every other language' (see also Hijazi 1979: 327–32). According to this, by attending to its language a nation attends to its sense of unique identity, that which makes it a nation *sui generis*.

The relationship between Arab nationalism and Islam is an interesting one. For some Egyptian Arab nationalists, Islam and the Arabic language are equally important in defining the Egyptian nation. However, the majority view holds that Arabic is more important than Islam in defining Egyptian national identity, on the grounds that *fusha* predates Islam and that it has the capacity to unite Muslims and non-Muslims in and outside Egypt through a common bond. In their enthusiasm for *fusha*, some nationalists construct Islam as an Arab religion, a religion embued with the spirit and values of the Arabs through Arabic. Espousing this vision of *fusha* as the criterion par excellence in defining Egyptian national identity, Arab nationalists insisted on the exclusive use of this language in literary production. Thus, the short-story writer Mahmoud Taymour (1894–1973) recast those stories of his in which he employed *'ammiyya* in new versions in *fusha* to reflect his new conversion to Arab nationalism. Arab nationalists in Egypt did not suddenly drop the idea that Egypt was a nation in its own right, but they believed Egypt was an Arab nation with strong ties to other Arab nations for whom *fusha* is a common language. Egyptian nationalists found it easy to reconcile these two positions because they thought of Egypt as the lynchpin of Arab culture, literature, and political organization. For these nationalists, Arabism represented an enhancement for Egypt in terms of cultural and political influence, not a matter of identity subtraction or a diminution in its political significance. Pan-Arab nationalism in Egypt was not therefore a completely ideological construction, but one that is also laced with a healthy degree of political calculation and enlightened pragmatism.

2.5 Final Remarks

Regardless of their ideological orientations, nationalist trends in Egypt engaged Arabic on two fronts: its fitness to serve as an index or marker of national self-definition and its role in modernization. As far as the former front is concerned, Egyptian nationalists denied *fusha* any definitional role of the national self, even when they supported this variety as a vehicle of cultural expression, as is the case with Taha Hussein who was one of its most ardent advocates. I have offered alterity, the need to differentiate Self (Egypt) from significant Other (other Arab countries/territories), as the major explanation for this phenomenon in Egyptian nationalism. Attempts to promote *'ammiyya* as such a principle of definition never gained sustained currency, owing to the strong attachment to *fusha* in Egypt, not least in the domains of religion and culture. In some cases, those who used *'ammiyya* in their writings, for example 'Abdalla al-Nadim (1845–96), did so for utilitarian purposes, coupling this practice with strong support for *fusha* as the only form of Arabic capable of serving as Egypt's 'national language' (Selim 2004). The attempts of some Egyptian nationalists to endow *'ammiyya* with ideologically impregnated symbolic meanings, to make it a durable marker of a territorial national identity, failed because of the historically sanctioned position of *fusha* in Egyptian society, the lack of political will to go down this nationalist route, and the lack of resources – for example dictionaries, grammars and school curricula – that could carry this nationalism forward institutionally. As a result, Egypt remains the locus of two communities in the language arena: a speech community centred on *'ammiyya* as mother tongue, and a linguistic community centred on *fusha* as native language, with most ideological articulations of the national self, whether Islamist or Arabist in character, continuing to be angled in relation to the latter chain of concepts.

Modernization is a two-pronged phenomenon vis-à-vis *fusha* in Egypt. On the one hand, modernization needs *fusha* instrumentally to import the fruits of progress in the west, whether processes or their products, and to help in their localization in Egypt. Here *fusha* serves as a vehicle or instrument. On the other hand, *fusha* itself has to be modernized not only to make it an instrument fit for this enterprise, but also to make its modernization symbolic of the modernization of society at large. Here, the instrumental and symbolic in *fusha* coalesce. In the linguistic sphere, modernization was proposed mainly in the form of lexical enrichment, orthographic reforms, and grammatical simplifications in the pedagogic domain (Eliraz 1986). But proposals of this kind have always been implicated in conflicts involving ideologies of tradition and change or authenticity and foreignization/Westernization (*taghrib*). Nationalism in Egypt engages language in a secondary capacity through these conflicts, thus exploiting the motifs of unity, continuity, and purity which, as I have suggested above, are central in conceptualizing the language–national identity link in Egypt.

In recent years, *fusha* in Egypt has been perceived to be under attack from the forces of globalization in a way that compromises its purity and undermines its ability to serve as an emblem of the nation (Warschauer 2002). For some, the use of Western, mainly English names, in preference to Arabic ones in shop signs has been so endemic that one scholar, Wafa' Kamil (n.d.), describes it as 'mental disturbance' (p. 44) and 'cancerous growth' (p. 94) in her empirically extensive and longitudinal studies of this linguistic landscaping phenomenon (Landry and Bourhis 1997) in Cairo over the past thirty years. Kamil (n.d.: 135–6) lists the titles of newspaper articles that deal with this phenomenon, some of which I will translate here to give the reader the flavour of how this phenomenon is conceptualized in Egypt: 'Arabic in the Valley of Neglect', 'The Winds of Foreignization Sweep the Egyptian Street', '[Foreignization]: The Defeat of a Nation, not a Crisis of Language', 'Woe to a Nation whose Tongue is Raped!', 'Before Arabenglish Spreads', and 'They [those who use foreign shop signs] Distort the Consciousness of our Nation'.

Kamil, who is Head of Arabic at Cairo University, describes the use of foreign names in shop signs as follows (n.d.: 12): 'This phenomenon deforms the face of the Egyptian street and endows it with a foreign look that is not part of its original character. And it disfigures our mother tongue in a way that harms the authentic Egyptian self.' A study of the impact of globalization on the continued ability of *fusha* to provide a robust definition of the national self in Egypt and other parts of the Arabic-speaking world would offer valuable insights into the modern political situation in the Middle East and the state of relations between this part of the world and the West.

3
Morocco: Language, Nationalism, and Gender

Moha Ennaji and Fatima Sadiqi

3.1 Introduction

This chapter is concerned with the issues of language, nationalism, and cultural identity in Morocco. It highlights the language–nationalism interface and stresses the fact that while mother tongues are fundamentally important for identity and gender-building, learned languages contribute to state-building and modernization.

Before embarking on issues relevant to language and national identity, it is useful to consider some of the terms frequently employed in discussions of nationalism and what these are used to refer to. In purely political terms, the three concepts of 'nation', 'state', and 'country' all designate unified, independent territories recognized as such by other sovereign states.[1] A cultural group is an autonomous speech community which may be socio-economically and politically dependent on a dominant group. As for the term nationalism itself, this refers to a socio-political movement aiming to achieve political and socio-economic independence. Finally, the concept of nationism is sometimes invoked to indicate efforts focused on establishing a modern and efficient administration (see in particular Fishman 1968, 1971 for details on the distinction between nationalism and nationism).

The topic of language and national identity is a controversial one. Broadly, there exist two quite opposite theoretical orientations. The first suggests that there is no direct relationship between language and national or cultural identity, and if, in some cases, there appears to be a relation between language and identity, it is only accidental (see Appel and Muysken 1987: 15). The second, more common trend states that language is a major vehicle of identity, along with cultural heritage, assumptions, values, and beliefs. According to Fishman (1999), language and national identity are closely linked, especially when the linguistic community has a favourable attitude

[1] The term 'nation' also has a somewhat different use whose precise definition is much argued over but generally involves a population that (a) is ethnically homogeneous, (b) occupies a distinct but not necessarily independent territory, (c) has a shared history. See Guibernau (1996) and Kellas (1998) for further discussion.

toward their own identity. For the many who subscribe to this latter view, language has often been a primary criterion defining and determining nationality and national identity. Each nation associates with a language, and conversely, a language is a means of identifying a nationality. For example, Arabic is used in the Arab nations, French is (largely) associated with France, Greek with Greece, Italian with Italy, and so on. Given the socio-cultural meanings that the use of languages carries in countries such as Morocco, language also has significant ramifications relating to gender, as we shall show in the last section. As argued in Charrad (2001) and Sadiqi (2003), gender has participated clearly in the interaction of language and nation, state and cultural identity-building, and may be defined as the way masculinity and femininity are projected and understood in the overall national setting.

The remainder of this chapter is divided into five sections. Section 3.2 provides a brief historical background of Morocco. Section 3.3 deals with the multilingual context in the country. Section 3.4 is concerned with Arabization and its ramifications for education. Section 3.5 reflects on the changes that have occurred in the domain of language and nationalism since the 1960s. Finally, section 3.6 deals with the extent to which language and gender are affected by and interact with nationalism and cultural revival in Morocco.

3.2 Historical Background

Morocco was colonized by France and Spain from 1912 to 1956 (Spain in the north and the south, France in the centre). During the period of French rule, Moroccans had limited access to French language education. However, after obtaining independence, the number of French speakers increased, and various other changes occurred on the linguistic and cultural levels, in particular cultural revival and the revitalization of the Arabic language and Islamic culture, and recently also the revitalization of Berber.

Having occupied much of the territory of Morocco in the early twentieth century, the so-called '*mission civilisatrice*' of the French colonial project did very little to educate the general Moroccan population, and only 1.7 per cent of Moroccans had access to French schools (Ennaji 2005: Chapter 5). During this period, nationalists set up privately funded Free Schools in which a range of traditional and modern subjects were taught in Arabic. With independence, these schools were merged into the national system, in which much larger numbers of students were educated in both French and Arabic.

Throughout the colonial period, the French colonizers made great efforts to dissociate Moroccan society from its indigenous languages and cultures, and there was an attempt to divide the country into two ethnic groups (Arabs and Berbers) to facilitate the colonization process, materializing in what came to be known as the 'Berber Decree' (le Dahir Berbère) in 1930. The Berber Decree was strongly criticized by berberophone and arabophone scholars, political leaders, and ordinary people alike,

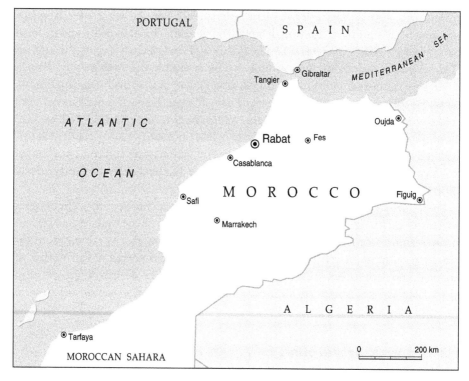

Morocco

who all expressed loyalty to Moroccan national identity and territorial integrity as well as the languages of the country, Arabic and Berber.[2]

In earlier times, it was relatively easy to differentiate Arabs from Berbers in Morocco because each linguistic community was monolingual and there were very few Arabic–Berber bilinguals. Today, however, most Berbers are bilingual and speak Moroccan Arabic as well as Berber due to increased social mobility, intermarriages, and socio-economic interactions. The general socio-cultural context therefore does not help one distinguish accurately one ethnic group from the other. Many Arabic-speaking tribes have been Berberized culturally (though not linguistically), and many Berber ones have been Arabized over the centuries (see Ayache 1956). Despite such complications, it is however possible to state that Berber speakers form an ethnic group in their own right, as non-Berbers generally speak only Arabic (see Boukous 1995; Ennaji 1995, 1999, 2005; Sadiqi 1997).

There are thus two major ethnic groups in Morocco: the Arabic-speaking group and the Berber-speaking one. Historically the latter group constituted the first inhabitants

---

[2] For example, the leader of the National Popular Movement Party, Mahjoubi Aherdan, who is well known in Morocco for his struggle for the revival of Berber, has never been either against Arabization or for the separation of the Berber and Arab ethnic groups in Morocco.

of the Maghreb (Morocco, Algeria, Mauritania, Tunisia, and Libya) whereas the former came from the Arabian Peninsula in the eighth century and brought with it a new political system, the Arabic language, and a new religion, Islam.

Following independence, Morocco adopted Classical Arabic as its official language due to its association with Islam, and its great literary tradition. Since the 1960s, in the name of state-building, Morocco has implemented a policy of Arabization, which has meant Arabizing Berbers and replacing French with Classical Arabic in all walks of life.

The Maghreb in general and Morocco in particular are characterized by multilingualism in the sense that many languages and varieties are used in different domains. In the following section, the focus will be on this multilingual aspect of Morocco.

3.3 The Multilingual Context of Morocco

Morocco presents a complex network of linguistic pluralism. This fact is not only observed by linguists and grammarians but also by speakers themselves. Due to the considerably complex and varied nature of the Moroccan speech community, the linguistic situation represents an intricate and dynamic state of multilingualism.

At least seven languages and dialects interact in this context, namely: Berber, Moroccan Arabic, Classical Arabic, Standard Arabic, French, Spanish, and English. Of the important features of multilingualism in Morocco, it is worth mentioning the phenomenon of diglossia. This notion was first discussed by Marçais (1930–31) and then by Ferguson (1959). It specifies briefly that in the Arab world there are two varieties of Arabic, a high variety (Classical Arabic) and a low one (Colloquial Spoken Arabic). Other researchers think that today there are at least three varieties of Arabic (triglossia), Classical and Standard Arabic, which are high and intermediate respectively, and colloquial Arabic (the low variety). (See Ennaji 1991 and Youssi 1995.)

Being the language of Islam in which the Qur'an was revealed, Classical Arabic (CA) is the high variety and enjoys a great literary and religious tradition. It is a written language that is learnt at school, and because of its religious connotations, it is venerated by berberophones and arabophones alike.

Standard Arabic is the middle variety, and is codified and standardized. It is used in education, the media, and administration. The main distinction between Classical and Standard Arabic resides in the fact that Standard Arabic (SA) is more flexible in its phonology, morphology, and syntax; for instance, it lacks the case marking affixes of CA, for example CA *kutubun* (books) → SA *kutub* (books); unlike Classical Arabic, Standard Arabic also exhibits an alternative new word order of Subject–Verb–Object in addition to the Verb–Subject–Object word order of CA, which might seem to be an influence of French morphosyntax. Standard Arabic has also borrowed a host of words and phrases from French (Ennaji 1988). Standard Arabic is furthermore the vehicle of modern mass culture, as it is usually considered the outcome of the Arabization process, which resulted in consolidating the place of Standard Arabic in sectors like education, administration, and the media.

The 'low' status of Moroccan Arabic can be ascribed to the fact that it is neither codified nor standardized. However, it is the variety spoken by the vast majority of the population. Berbers generally speak it as their second language. It is viewed by the masses and the elite alike as a corrupt form of Classical/Standard Arabic. Linguistically, it is characterized by vowel drop and the overuse of the schwa (e.g. Standard Arabic *kataba* 'write' → *ktƏb* in Moroccan Arabic, Standard Arabic *saariq* 'has stolen' → *sarq* or *sarƏq*). Lexically, Moroccan Arabic differs from Standard Arabic, (e.g. Standard Arabic *'umma* 'nation' → *blad*, *sariqa* 'theft' → *xeTfa*), and Moroccan Arabic has borrowed tremendously from French (e.g. French *table* → *Tabla*, French *ampoule* → *bola*), as well as from Berber (e.g. Berber *tamssumant* 'effort', *tagzzart* 'being a butcher' occur as loans in Moroccan Arabic).

Moroccan Arabic can be divided into urban and rural varieties. In the north, there is the Shamali (northern) dialect, which is spoken in cities and towns like Tangiers, Chefchaoun, Tetouan, and Larache. In central Morocco, there is the Fassi variety which is spoken in the area of Fès. There is also the Moroccan dialect of Rabat and Casablanca. In the south, there are the Marrakeshi and Agadiri dialects that are much influenced by Tashelhit Berber; these are spoken in Marrakesh, Essaouira, and Agadir. Finally, in the Moroccan Sahara, there is the dialect of Hassaniya. Despite their various lexical and phonological idiosyncrasies, these regional dialects are mutually intelligible to most Moroccans.

Berber, which is the second mother tongue in Morocco, is spoken by nearly half of the population. It falls into three major varieties: Tarifit in the north, Tamazight in the Middle Atlas and Tashelhit in the south. Berbers use Moroccan Arabic as a lingua franca because the Berber varieties are not always mutually intelligible. Berber is a language used basically in rural areas. Its major domains of use are family and street. Like Moroccan Arabic, Berber is a language that has for a long time remained non-codified and non-standardized (see Sadiqi 1997), but the situation has recently changed, as we will show below.

The European languages used in Morocco are, by order of importance: French, English, and Spanish. Firstly, French is used practically as a second language. The long-standing French colonial policy to spread French language and culture in Morocco has resulted in the firm consolidation of French in vital sectors like government, education, private businesses, and the media. In spite of being a colonial language, French is nevertheless widely appreciated by both the ruling elite and the population in general (see Elbiad 1985).

Secondly, English is popular in education, international trade, and diplomacy. The prestigious status of English is ascribed to the twin fact that it has no colonial over-tones for Moroccans, and it is by far the first international language (see Ennaji 2005: chapter 6; Sadiqi 1991).

Finally, Spanish is spoken chiefly in the areas formerly occupied by Spain: the north and the Moroccan Sahara. After independence, French and Standard Arabic gradually replaced Spanish in education and administration. Because of their geographic proximity to Spain, Moroccans in the ex-Spanish zones interact with others daily in Spanish, as much of their trade is with Spain.

In the following section, we will shed light on the Arabization policy, its aims and objectives, and the various (sometimes contradictory) attitudes toward it.

3.4 Arabization and Education

There is a complex relationship between Arabization and education in Morocco. Sociolinguistic and socio-cultural problems have resulted from the implementation of an Arabization policy since the 1960s. The heterogeneous linguistic situation of Morocco has always been construed as a serious problem with ramifications for language planning and education. However, if multilingualism is an issue at the national level, the multi-dialectal nature of the mother tongues (Moroccan Arabic and Berber) compounds the problem even more.

In this section, we would like to present the different facets of and attitudes toward Arabization. We will discuss how Arabization has been used to highlight national identity and to promote Standard Arabic in primary and secondary education, but failed in Higher Education. We will show how this failure to establish Arabization at all levels of education hampers school achievement and generates interesting sociolinguistic issues.

The process of Arabization has three major objectives: (i) to promote the Arabic language by standardizing and modernizing it to meet the new needs of independent Morocco; (ii) to gradually replace French with Standard Arabic in all the formal domains of life; and (iii) to preserve cultural authenticity and Arab-Muslim values and beliefs, as well as ensure political unity and socio-cultural coherence.

Because Moroccans are in their vast majority Muslim, they are loyal to Classical/Standard Arabic as the official national language. As mentioned above, the overall Moroccan population venerates Classical/Standard Arabic because it is the language of the holy Qur'an and a symbol of cultural independence and national unity. Berber does not compete with Classical/Standard Arabic in this respect.

There are at least three types of discourse on Arabization: the purist, the governmental, and the fundamentalist discourses. The purist discourse advocates total Arabization to ensure the ultimate eradication of French from all dynamic and formal sectors of life in Morocco. This type of discourse goes back to the colonial period when Arabic was used as a crucial weapon, along with Islam, to rally the masses in the fight against colonization. The foremost advocate of total and rapid Arabization is the right-wing Istiqlal party, which has systematically used its press to denigrate and denounce the dominant place of French in administration and education (see Mouhssine 1995).

The ruling elite has a moderate and pragmatic attitude toward the Arabization policy. It supports step-by-step Arabization and French–Arabic bilingualism. The late King Hassan II declared in his 1978 Ifrane speech that while bilingualism is necessary for pragmatic reasons, Arabization is a must to safeguard the national identity.

It is necessary to point out that Classical/Standard Arabic alone cannot at the moment take over all the domains of use of French such as (in particular) science and technology because it is neither fully prepared for this task nor utterly modernized. According to the government, French–Arabic bilingualism contributes to reinforcing Arabization in the sense that it provides Arabic with new terminology, which can be translated or directly transferred from French into Arabic. This kind of bilingualism also allows more openness to the West. It is said that bilingualism and the endeavours of Moroccan writers and researchers have helped Moroccan culture, society, and literature become increasingly well-known on the international scene, and also contribute significantly to science and world knowledge. French is therefore seen as a means of opening up channels to modern culture, science, and technology, and serves as a tool to develop socio-economic and cultural exchange with the rest of the world, as well as the transfer of ideas (see Lakhdar Ghazal 1976).

As for Muslim fundamentalists, this section of the population believes that only Classical/Standard Arabic is legitimate as a language of learning and higher discourse for Moroccans; foreign languages are to be rejected together with the local vernaculars, chiefly Moroccan Arabic and Berber. French, Spanish, and English are considered as colonial or imperial languages that transfer and spread a corrupt Western lifestyle which is in opposition to Islamic precepts and guidelines. For such people, only Classical/Standard Arabic is worth teaching and learning because it reflects Muslim tradition, beliefs, and values.

Many scholars, namely Sadiqi (2003), Ennaji (1999) and Grandguillaume (1991), claim that the Arabization policy has indirectly contributed to the development of Muslim fundamentalism and has paved the way for the growth of Islamist demands. Muslim fundamentalist leaders are reluctant to speak French, and instead make use of Classical/Standard Arabic to rally the masses in their struggle for power. The Islamist discourse is in actual fact based on a linguistic problem, as well as on religious demands, both of which are used practically for political ends. Fundamentalists exploit the problem of multilingualism in Morocco and the rivalry between the languages in use in the country to push for total Arabization.

However, Arabization is not the only factor that has led to the birth and increase of fundamentalism in the region. There are also socio-economic and international factors. The economic crisis that Morocco has suffered since the 1980s has given rise to massive unemployment among educated young people. The late King Hassan II declared in Rabat on 8 July 1999 to the French writer Jean Daniel in an interview with the French magazine *Le Nouvel Observateur* that 'poverty and economic difficulties usually bring about extremism; they have produced drug addicts and delinquents in the West and Muslim fundamentalism in North Africa'.

There is also the international dimension of fundamentalism which has started to develop since the fall of the Shah of Iran and the triumph of Khomeini's revolution in 1978; it continued to increase with the end of communism, the disappearance of the

Soviet Union, the fall of the Berlin Wall, the September 11 terrorist attacks on New York, and the American occupation of Iraq.

Let us now move on to discuss the relationship between Arabization, language planning, and education in Morocco. We will see to what extent Arabization has had an impact on the system of education and the multilingual situation in the country.

Arabization has a direct connection to education and language planning. Since independence, the policy of education has been characterized by four criteria: unification of the educational system throughout the country, Arabization, generalization of education to all segments of the population, and free education for all. Many educators today question the efficiency of these criteria, however, and argue that diversification of the school programmes is preferable to unification which seeks to impose the same curriculum across the country without taking into account the sociolinguistic and geographical characteristics of each region.

Arabization is almost complete in primary and secondary public schools. All scientific subjects are taught in Standard Arabic in primary and secondary education. However, Arabization is still an issue because many educators and decision-makers are not yet fully convinced whether to opt for total or partial Arabization. Higher education is not yet Arabized, for example. The explanation for this provided by the government is that references and books on advanced science, technology, and medicine are sorely lacking in Standard Arabic, and most of the publications available are in English and French (see Mouhssine 1995).

In private schools and in the French mission, French is also predominant. Wealthy parents who are dissatisfied with the public education system send their children to private or French schools to ensure their mastery of French, and better job prospects. Indeed, students with a good Baccalaureate from the French mission have a better chance to gain access to and succeed in studies at the faculties of medicine, science, technology, management, agriculture, and engineering, than do students with a similar certificate from the country's public schools.

What this indicates is that Arabization is basically for the poor: Arabized students even with a higher degree are less likely to find jobs than their French-educated counterparts. The present education system therefore has double standards (or as they say in French 'deux poids, deux mesures') in the sense that it discriminates against the poor and benefits the well-off both pedagogically and socio-economically. If Arabization is good, it should be good for all Moroccans. Furthermore, politicians generally do not preach what they teach: in public they defend Arabization, but when it comes to the education of their own offspring they prefer French schools. It is clearly political hypocrisy and fake nationalism when Arabization is presented by such politicians as an important cause for the development of the Moroccan nation.

The contradictory attitudes present toward Arabization reveal the complexity of modern Moroccan society, its multilingual aspect, and its different social and political trends. On the whole, there seems to be a compromise concerning the linguistic options that are seen as best for the country and its future: most Moroccans today would seem to favour French–Standard Arabic bilingualism for pragmatic reasons; French is used in technical and scientific settings and for international communication, and Standard Arabic is reserved for cultural, literary, religious, and political discourses (see Ennaji 1991). Moroccan Arabic and Berber are the languages of change, reflecting the uniqueness of Morocco and the dynamism of its people, and need to be preserved as they express the daily life of Moroccans.

3.5 Changes Regarding Nationalism and Language

The most prominent change in the area of language that has occurred over the last generation is the implementation of the Arabization policy with the aim of revitalizing and modernizing Standard Arabic. The overall goal is to generalize the use of Standard Arabic to all domains of life as a language of wider communication in place of French, which is considered by conservatives a threat to the linguistic and cultural identity of the country.

The process of Arabization was intended to modernize and standardize the language in order to meet the needs of the modern state. It also aimed to replace French in many fields, particularly in education and mass media. Given the connection between Standard Arabic, Islam, and national identity, Arabization may be considered a revival of the Arabic language and national identity. One of the further purposes of Arabization is the assimilation of Berbers into Arab cultural identity.

Another major change is the evolution of the statuses of Standard Arabic and Berber. The process of Arabization has led to the modernization and revitalization of Standard Arabic. In addition to this, the official recognition of Berber as part of the national heritage and cultural authenticity of Morocco and its introduction in Moroccan primary schools are good examples of the process of 'ethno-linguistic revival' at work in the country. This revival is mainly due to the fact that both Standard Arabic and Berber play a strong symbolic role in the national identity of Morocco, and that both of them are somewhat threatened by foreign languages, chiefly French.

The attempts to revitalize Berber are motivated by the fact that Berber is the native language of about half of the Moroccan population. This language has been in retreat under the influence of French, Standard Arabic, and Moroccan Arabic. To alleviate this threat to Berber, Berber has recently been officially recognized as part and parcel of the national cultural identity. As a token of this recognition, the Royal Institute of Amazigh Culture was created in 2001, with the objective of promoting Amazigh (Berber) language and culture in education, administration, and the media.

The ethno-linguistic revival has affected the attitudes of people toward languages and varieties of language significantly before affecting the functions and domains of use of these languages and varieties. Moroccan people are generally proud of their mother tongues and national languages. Although attitudes toward the different mother tongues and languages have changed among the people, these attitudes have to a certain extent long been ignored by governments and decision-makers. As a result,

Arabization has only been partially successful after four decades of independence and struggle for the restoration of Arabic language and culture.

In Morocco, as we have had cause to mention, Classical and Standard Arabic are venerated by the population as they have religious ramifications and symbolize national unity and Arab nationalism and solidarity. Berber and Moroccan Arabic are generally only considered a means of communication in intimate contexts and transactions, but they have recently become symbols of identity and authenticity nationwide and in inter-group relations.

At the academic level, conservative thinkers and purists who are mostly educated in Arabic stress the necessity to reinforce Arab nationalism and establish Arab unity, the purpose of which is to revive Arab-Islamic values and beliefs and gradually exclude the ex-colonizer's language and culture, and Western values more generally. Aljabri (1995) and Almandjra (1996) are among the Arab academics who enthusiastically support Arab nationalism. At the level of the populace, positive values are associated with Arab-Islamic culture. However, people also wrongly assume that a necessary connection exists between Islamic beliefs and Arabic language and culture and are often largely unaware that there exist both Christian Arabic-speaking populations in the Middle East (Lebanon, Syria, Egypt, Sudan, Iraq, etc.) and also Muslim but non-Arab populations in many parts of the world, such as the Berbers in the Maghreb, the Persians in Iran, the Kurds in the Middle East, the Pakistanis, the Malays, and the Indonesians, for example.

It is considered by Berber-language activists that Berber ought to be restored and revitalized through teaching it and using it in formal and informal settings. They reject the idea of Berber becoming a language confined to past memory and are fighting to turn it into a language of active usage and everyday communication. Amongst non-Berber conservative arabophones, however, the promotion of Berber is conversely seen as constituting a potential danger for national unity and political stability. Such views are purely received ideas which aim to maintain the socio-cultural status quo and the superior position of Arabic (see Boukous 1995; Ennaji 1997, 2005). Arabic nationalists argue that only a pro-Arabic strategy can help to consolidate the political independence of the country and preserve its national unity.

Assessing the situation as a whole, it can be said that the existence of and widespread attachment to Morocco's two indigenous languages/forms of language, Moroccan Arabic and Berber, effectively reduces the enthusiasm for Arab unity and Arab nationalism. Morocco is today experiencing two sorts of revival which are sometimes seen as being in competition with each other: (1) revival of the Arabic language and Arab-Islamic culture, and (2) attempts to promote mother tongues like Berber and Moroccan Arabic, which themselves are associated with popular national culture. Today, the supporters of Berber language and culture claim that it is now indeed necessary to recognize Berber as a national official language side by side with Arabic (see Ennaji 2005: chapter 4).

Nationalism in its broad sense of referring to the self-promotional activities of culturally long-established ethno-linguistic groups has thus had a great impact on embedding language attitudes, as well as language use and choice in Morocco. The stronger the feelings of belonging to a certain group, the stronger the desire of promoting the language of that particular group. In Morocco, nationalism and recent 'ethno-linguistic revival' have affected the mother tongues (Moroccan Arabic and Berber), Classical and Standard Arabic, and the foreign languages in use in the country in different ways, and have given rise to active public support for each of these four varieties for differing motivations. Concerning Moroccan Arabic, for example, it is now found that educated people mix Standard and Moroccan Arabic in their speech to show increased support for the latter, and various prominent writers such as Mohamed Choukry and Amine El Alami have come to use Moroccan Arabic in their writings for the reason that it is felt to more truly reveal authentic aspects of Moroccan daily life and cultural identity.

In the following section, we now turn to consider a further dimension of the multilingual context of Morocco – gender – and how this interacts in interesting ways with language choice and the projection and perception of national identity and state-building in Morocco. This will be done first through a brief description of some of the ways that non-linguistic gender-related activities have been moulded in the interests of national image, by way of general background, and then through a more specific focusing on factors determining language selection and usage among women and men in Morocco.

3.6 Gender and Nationalism

Gender issues have been linked to the national development of Morocco and its character as a nation from colonial times onwards. Colonialism itself was indeed largely perceived as a direct threat to Moroccan national and cultural identities, and as primary symbols of such identities, women were doubly disadvantaged as they often found themselves caught between the nationalists' endeavours to protect them from the occupiers and the latter's quest to 'emancipate' them as their most efficient way to 'civilize' the entire Moroccan society.

During the time of the French Protectorate and as part of their struggle for independence, the two nationalist icons, Allal al-Fassi and Mohamed Hassan Ouazzani, called for the emancipation of women for the purpose of quite different, nationalistic projects of society. Being a Salafist (religious reformist) who studied and lived in Egypt, Allal al-Fassi called for women's education in Arabic and dismissed polygamy, not because it harmed women as individuals but because it was a practice that 'tarnished' the image of 'modern' Islam. On the other hand, Mohamed Hassan Ouazzani, a modernist intellectual who studied and lived in France, called for women's education in both Arabic and French and equitable inheritance laws, not only because the existing laws were harmful to women as women but also because equitable inheritance laws were 'tokens' of a modern egalitarian society. The two men sought the 'emancipation' of women for the purpose of their different societal projects: an 'enlightened' Islamic state (al-Fassi) and a European-style state (Ouazzani). Both aims, which produced a number of what can here be referred to as 'male feminist' ideas (i.e. proposals for the apparent development of women put forward by men), were rather abstract, and were intended to be 'remedies' reforming the 'backwardness' of Morocco. In interesting ways, the two men used language to promote women as 'ideal' citizens in specific projects of society.

After independence, the new decision-makers continued to espouse the Protectorate-era male feminist views for more or less the same reasons. In 1957, for example, King Mohamed V unveiled his eldest daughter in public and stressed the need to emancipate women in order to develop society. These and similar views subsequently came to be known as 'state feminism'.

State feminism, which ultimately sprang from nationalism and the drive to project an image of Morocco as a modern state to the outside world, had a significant effect on the shaping of gender identity both before and after Morocco's independence. For example, following King Mohamed V's symbolic 'unveiling' gesture, thousands of women in cities also unveiled themselves, and religious preachers in mosques associated unveiling with job-taking and, hence, nation-building. The political parties (conservative and otherwise) followed suit and included 'feminist' ideas in their electoral campaigns, proclaiming that Morocco could not progress without educating and training women, though the more one went into their core priorities, the less 'feminist' these ideas became, as is attested in the structures and orientations of these parties that bluntly reproduced the same patriarchal visions they claimed to fight (Sadiqi, to appear).

In what follows, we consider more closely how gender factors clearly bias language choice in Morocco today, further complicating the multilingual situation of the country, and adding to the unlikelihood that a single language form may be able to serve as the unique vehicle of national identity and daily communication for all the nation's population.

3.6.1 Language Choice and the Gendered Expression of Identity

Although male feminism did not specifically aim to bring about the empowerment of women as individuals, middle- and upper-class women nevertheless did gain improved education and job opportunities, hence the means of entering the public sphere, and it was the new post-independence bourgeois class that produced the first women pharmacists, jurists, medical doctors, and university professors in Morocco. The general feminist trend of these women was liberal in the sense that they readily embraced 'modern' ideas and practices without rejecting their local specificities, including being Muslim. This liberal trend was accompanied by changes in dress, as well as other social practices such as the adoption of certain aspects of a French style and way of life, though such innovations never succeeded in significantly displacing traditional Moroccan practices and ways of life.

One of the languages present in Morocco whose use is now very clearly affected by gender factors, and in particular increases in literacy among middle- and upper-class women, is French. French is an urban, superordinate second language which is closely linked to education. It has, over the years, become very useful in the private sector. French is also necessary for obtaining better-paid forms of employment and is, thus, positively perceived as a symbol of 'social mobility', 'modernity', 'enlightenment', and 'openness to the Western world'. In general, attitudes to French in Morocco are positive. Like Moroccan Arabic, French is used by both men and women, but this use differs according to gender: whereas men use French in the higher administrative and military positions, thus exploiting the domineering, masculine aspect that usually accompanies colonial languages, women benefit more from the social prestige of the language. They derive social power from being considered 'civilized' and 'modern'. Even in conservative families, a woman speaking French to her children is perceived in a positive way.

In spite of the fact that the majority of Moroccan women do not have very easy access to French, French is in general more favoured by women than by men. Furthermore, women also tend to display proficiency in French more frequently than they do proficiency in Standard Arabic. This behaviour is linked to the fact that men are generally more favourable to women's proficiency in French than to their proficiency in Standard Arabic. The reason for this is that French is less related to cultural identity in Morocco than Standard Arabic is, and is thus less threatening to the male-anchored status quo and maintenance of men's position in Moroccan society effected through the use and control of Standard Arabic. It should also be noted that men are more favourable to women 'speaking' French than they are to women 'behaving' in a 'French' (Westernized) way because women's use of French is a guarantee that they will speak it (and teach it) to their children. Behaving in a French way is generally perceived as stripping women of their 'authenticity' as members of their own community. It is also regarded as a sign of excessive emancipation, clashing with Moroccan cultural values. This assessment has its base in Moroccan patriarchal and male-dominated culture. Women are aware of this and react by using French to gain, use, and maintain social power.

Comparing French and Standard Arabic, both can in fact be said to exert social power, but each power carries a specific symbolic meaning in the Moroccan context: French is crucial in Moroccan post-colonial administration and politics, while Standard Arabic is a symbol of a glorious past and cultural identity. The two symbolic powers ultimately serve men more than women: men appropriate the symbolic powers of both French and Standard Arabic (men hold the highest positions in politics, administration, and business) and women are more associated with the 'modern' (but 'alien') aspects of the two languages. Their use of French is socially perceived in a positive way only in relation to the fostering of the young as 'good' citizens.

Considering the full range of the four most prominent language forms in Morocco – Berber, Moroccan Arabic, Standard/Classical Arabic, and French – at one end of this language spectrum, women can be noted to be closer to Berber and Moroccan Arabic than men because Moroccan society clings to its indigenous traditions (symbolically encoded in the local languages Berber and Moroccan Arabic), but assigns the responsibility for guarding those traditions to women. At the other end of the spectrum, the majority of women are distanced from the literate languages Standard Arabic and French because they less commonly have access to schooling.

As citizens of a patriarchal multilingual nation, women are not passive; they 'fight back' by developing empowering strategies of communication according to their socio-economic status, as well as the linguistic choices that are available to them. Moroccan women's communicative strategies are primarily dictated by their geographical origin and level of education. Rural women are predominantly illiterate and use female oral literature in Berber and/or Moroccan Arabic to empower themselves. It is through self-expression in the two mediums of story-telling and the singing of folk songs that illiterate women mark their presence in the community and it is also through these mediums that they sometimes subvert the roles that patriarchy assigns them.

As for those Moroccan women who are educated and literate, they use Berber and/or Moroccan Arabic, Standard Arabic, and French. Some may even use English and/or Spanish. Their strategies of communication are different from those used by illiterate women. The most important such strategy among educated bilingual women in urban areas is code-switching, which most commonly involves the controlled alternation and mixing of Moroccan Arabic and French (see Sadiqi 2003: chapter 4). As code-switching requires competence not only in two linguistic codes, but also in the ability to appropriately manipulate these codes in real life contexts, it is generally associated with positive social attributes in Moroccan society, and is a phenomenon that is more prevalent in the speech of women than in that of men.[3]

The observation that gender plays an important role in language choice and the use of particular forms of language has consequences for the involvement of language in the construction of national identity. If attachment to Berber and Moroccan Arabic is strengthened through their habitual employment in oral literature forms used to empower the position of women in rural areas, and if French–Moroccan Arabic

---

[3] Code-switching involving Moroccan Arabic and Berber is also often present in the speech of Berber bilinguals, but this type of code-switching is not gender-sensitive as both female and male speakers engage in it, unlike French–Moroccan Arabic code-switching, which is more frequently carried out by women speakers and identified as a typically female linguistic activity. Switching between Berber and French has so far not established itself as a regular practice.

code-switching fulfils a similar empowering role for educated urban women, this works to further embed the existence of multilingualism in Morocco and deepen its complexity and diversity, generating and strengthening loyalties to different forms of language rather than focusing loyalty on a single form of speech and communication that might be the unique linguistic vehicle of Moroccan national identity. Though multilingualism is not considered to be a necessary barrier to the creation of a successful, unified nation, it is nevertheless commonly thought of as presenting an additional challenge to the process of nation-building. Consequently, insofar as the dimension of gender triggers multilingual behaviour for the variety of reasons outlined above, this adds an interesting further level of complexity to the general sociolinguistic situation in Morocco and the way that language may relate to a single national identity in the country.

In addition to this, a second way in which gender may be seen to be interacting with language and national identity is in the occurrence of new (or perhaps 'refocused') gender-related oppositions in Morocco. The rise in calls for the recognition of women's rights in recent years paired with increased attempts by women to assert themselves in the country's rigidly patriarchal society (this being linguistically manifested in phenomena such as code-switching and other self-empowerment strategies noted here) puts many women in potential conflict with aspects of Islamic fundamentalism as presented in recent years. The latter movement is associated with the projection of an Arabic-Islamic national identity which takes Classical/Standard Arabic as the appropriate linguistic emblem for Morocco. However, as observed above, many women feel that they are not welcome to participate as equal partners in the use of Standard Arabic and that this language remains the primary reserve of men. In their reaction to such a situation, assertive women are therefore taking up and developing or strengthening loyalties to other modes of language which then may keep them at some distance from embracing Standard Arabic as an all-inclusive national language embodying both men's and women's involvement in the nation. As long as such gender-related competition continues to exist, the result may be the perpetuation of partial linguistic fragmentation in the country rather than the achievement of any targeted form of unity.

3.7 Conclusion

Language and cultural identity in Morocco are marked by four important ingredients: Berber, Arabic, French, and Islam. Berber and colloquial Arabic embody popular culture, while Classical Arabic, French, and Islam represent learned culture. In this multilingual and multicultural context, the legitimacy of the state is broadly based on written culture which is closely linked to and also dependent on power for its continued promotion.

Since independence, Morocco has been wavering between modernity and conservatism. In the 1960s, 1970s, and 1980s, Morocco was inclined to the first in view of the fact that it was still under the strong influence of French culture, but since the 1990s, the pendulum has swung to conservatism under the rise of Muslim fundamentalism.

In post-independence years, the ruling elite adopted French–Arabic bilingualism as a political option in their efforts to modernize the country. Specifically, nationalism and state-building in the 1960s and 1970s gave priority to Standard Arabic as the official language and the language of religion and to French as the language of business and administration. As for Arabic dialects and Berber, these were generally relegated to informal and private domains. Today, however, tension exists not only between French/Western values and Arabic/Islamic beliefs, but also within the Moroccan context, between Berber and Arabic languages and cultures. This language situation highlights a clash of interests and ideological tensions which themselves mirror the struggle for power at various levels. In many issues, the interaction between the languages and cultures of Morocco is characterized by contrasts and paradoxes.

The multilingual situation in Morocco is not static either, and one of its newest developments is the emergence of gender as an important dimension on the present-day sociolinguistic scene. The post-independence conscious marginalization of the typically oral mother tongues, Berber and local Arabic dialects, was accompanied by a marginalization of women who, because of illiteracy and the massive migration of men to cities, spoke only these languages in the overwhelming majority of cases. Now, with the advent of calls for the improvement of human rights from the mid-1980s onwards, new demands relating to language (rights), laicization, and culture are being accompanied by serious demands for women's emancipation, an improved position for women in the family and in society and more active participation of women as political agents. Linguistically the consequences of this are an increased use of French–Arabic code-switching in urban environments and continued embedding of Berber and Moroccan Arabic as languages of female empowerment in rural areas. Quite generally, an ethno-linguistic cultural revival in the country has further revitalized the use of the mother tongues, and Moroccan Arabic and Berber are now positively valued as symbols of ethnic identity, inter-group relations, and cultural authenticity, as they reflect the most typical cultural aspects of the country. In this sense they are indeed perceived as genuine linguistic representations of the identity of Morocco, and attempts are being made by scholars and cultural associations to codify, standardize, and promote these mother tongues to the level of recognized national or regional languages.

In contrast to such liberal developments, Morocco is also witnessing the vigorous rise of Islamic fundamentalism, vehicled by Classical/Standard Arabic and emphasizing the need for a 'shy' and 'veiled' presence of women in public domains and heavily frowning on female assertiveness. The Arabization policy of post-independence years has furthermore strengthened the position of Classical and Standard Arabic in various public areas of Moroccan life and aided the growth of Arab-Islamic Moroccan nationalism, resulting in the heavy entrenchment of a traditional Arabic conservatism opposed to modernism and Western influence. How these different forces present in Moroccan society will ultimately be reconciled over the coming decades and what kind of national identity will emerge as dominant is currently far from clear, but it is certain that language will continue to be a major player involved in the determination of the character of the nation, and intricately associated with different political viewpoints on national identity.

4
Sudan: Majorities, Minorities, and Language Interactions

Wendy James

4.1 Introduction

It is commonly taken for granted in today's writing and discussion about the Sudan that it consists of very different northern and southern parts – fierce desert in the north and shady pasture in the south, occupied by 'ethnic' Arabs on the one hand and 'Black Africans' on the other, Islam in the north and a variety of Christian denominations and African traditional religions in the south. But we should treat these oppositions with great care; they are not primordial facts of geography and ethnology. The concept of north and south *as territories*, as against relative positioning along the Nile corridor, has always been a matter of contested political definition by the powers that be. The north/south opposition in much of today's discourse about the Sudan, and indeed within it, is a product of very recent political history, including some decades of civil war. In considering aspects of language and language use in the Sudan, however, and especially in noting how language issues have become caught up in politics, we can find a different approach and escape the stereotypes with profit.

Why is it important to do this? First, 'Arabs', however defined, are not indigenous to the Sudan. The old continuities of physical population history and cultural tradition in the central Nile link the Sudanese both northwards and southwards, predating the appearance of immigrants from Arabia or the spread of Arabic (which of course has its own separate momentum). There are well-known connections with the populations and civilizations of Egypt and North Africa; less known is the fact that the Nubian languages still spoken in the extreme north of the Sudan, bordering Egypt, belong to the Nilo-Saharan family, which points to an ancient southward connection. In linguistic and racial terms, the southern as well as northern reaches of the Nile valley are very diverse, this having been a corridor of movement literally since the dawn of human history. Modern efforts to define a line on the ground between north and south on ethnic or cultural grounds always come up against glaring anomalies. There certainly have always been *distinctions of status* in the Sudan, because the main centres of state-building have been on the course of the Nile itself, and these centres have tended to exploit their own peripheries for their resources, including labour. In the form of slave-trading this has helped produce today's racial stereotypes. From the sixteenth century or so elite status was linked with the Arabic language and the Islamic religion as far south as political control could reach (a process then complicated by twentieth-century policies of British imperial rule which promoted English in regions beyond the reach of the historic Sudanese kingdoms).

Claims to 'Arab' identity in the country as a whole still depend very much on an individual's ability to connect their personal genealogy to a prominent family that has already established a paternal line linking them back to mythico-historical immigrant Arab groups, preferably to the family or companions of the Prophet himself. But while elite families throughout Muslim society in the Sudan aim to consolidate their position through endogamous marriage, there has always been a high rate of intermarriage and informal unions with 'local' communities, across any social or racial lines. The result is that many people in 'the north' are able to trace an 'Arab' genealogy through the father, while the personal links on the mother's or grandmother's side may well be with a Nuba, Dinka, or Fur family. In the historic kingdoms social distinctions were certainly made on the basis of family connection with significant elites or powerful ruling groups, such as the 'Funj' of Sennar, itself a 'colour-blind' term.[1] It is only very recently that a harsh Arab/African racial divide has been introduced, as in the common portrayal of the Darfur conflict. It is not often noted that at the core of the former sultanate and its elite were the Fur, in today's journalistic terms a 'Black African' people, to whom the surrounding nomadic 'Arabs' had variable relationships, including economic cooperation and intermarriage.

For much of the half-century since its independence in 1956, Sudan has been embroiled in civil wars sparked by discontent and a sense of injustice in the remoter regions of this vast country, whether in the south, east, or west (for an overview, see Johnson 2006). There was a decade of peace following the Addis Ababa Agreement of 1972 between the central government of Gaafar Nimeiry in Khartoum and the southern-based Anyanya movement. The renewed insurgency of the Sudan People's Liberation Movement/Army (SPLM/A) from 1983 also stemmed from the south but aimed at a secular, democratic reform of the Sudanese state as a whole, and it gained some significant support, and some military success, in the northern as well as south-ern provinces. Preliminary peace talks were under way by 1988 but their conclusion was pre-empted by the military coup of Omer el Beshir in 1989, backed by the militant National Islamic Front. The war intensified, until a Comprehensive Peace Agreement (CPA) was signed on 9 January 2005, between the government of Omer el Beshir and

---

[1] In the colonial era there used to be arguments among the British as to whether the Funj, who ruled the former Kingdom of Sennar, were originally Arabs or Shilluk – a 'southern' traditional kingdom, with clear links nevertheless to the pre-Arab historical polities further north; but to Sudanese, this has never been an 'ethnic' as much as a status term (see James 1977).

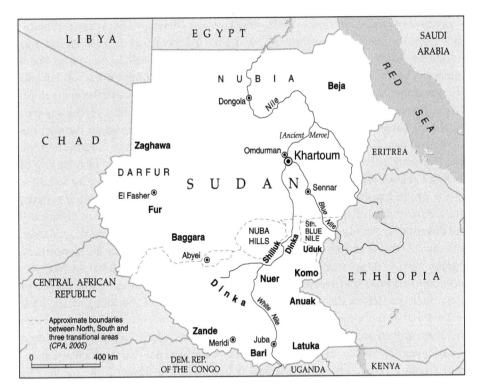

Sudan

the SPLM/A, recognizing new political rights for the South and special provisions for some adjacent areas of the North.[2] The sultanate of Darfur to the west, since its annexation in 1916, had always been a 'northern' region. As negotiations towards the agreement were under way, however, armed resistance that had been simmering for many years in Darfur suddenly escalated in early 2003. The government then mounted extremely heavy counter-insurgency measures that shocked international opinion and have led to tragic outcomes for the civilian population. In mid-2007 there is still no satisfactory conclusion to the war in Darfur. Indeed the situation there is undermining the political will and draining the resources that otherwise might have been directed towards timely implementation of the CPA.

Debates over the status and use of languages have been integral to the story of modern political struggle in the Sudan. With the advent of the Anglo-Egyptian Condominium government in 1898, Arabic and English had equal status as languages of national administration, but by 1930 English became the official language

---

[2] Henceforth, this chapter will use capital initials (North, South, Northern, Southern) to refer to these political divisions of the country as delimited by the CPA, or the 1972–83 politically defined Southern Region as against the North of that period. Lower case (north, south, etc.) will be used for more general reference and earlier historical periods, when boundaries were of less consequence.

of government and education in the south. This was challenged by nationalist politicians from the northern-based parties, and after independence in 1956 Arabic was proclaimed as the key national language, in the south as well as the north. For a number of years Arabic became the language of tuition in southern schools but this policy was then abandoned. Rows over the language question in education in the south fed directly into the rise of southern nationalism, and practice on the ground was very variable as between government-held and rebel-held areas of the south through the subsequent decades of war. Agreement was finally reached for parity of status over the whole country as between Arabic and English, on paper, in the peace negotiations of 2005 (see below). A brief summary of the position of languages as spoken by Sudanese on the ground would be as follows. While Arabic is the majority mother tongue, and lingua franca, of the whole country, this statement conceals great complexity and diversity. Linguists estimate today that among nearly 40 million people, Sudanese colloquial Arabic is spoken as the main tongue by 15 million, mainly in the northern regions; and 20,000 speak a Sudanese Arabic creole, 'Southern' or 'Juba' Arabic.[3] It is sometimes assumed that everyone in the north of the country, at least, where perhaps some three-quarters of the population are based, is an Arabic speaker; it is not often realized that at the same time there are many indigenous Sudanese languages there which are spoken as a mother tongue, alongside Arabic, which itself may be acquired at a later age. The vernacular languages of the north have not had as much attention, from linguists, politicians, or educational policy-makers, as those in the south. The tremendous linguistic richness of the south has been much studied (by comparison) and has been woven into the history of arguments over cultural and educational policy in the modern era. Education in the south was initially entrusted to missionary organizations, and eventually English became the lingua franca of the educated. At the same time, Southern Arabic has flourished as a convenient common spoken form during the years of war, even being used in many Christian churches.

The complicated situation behind this thumbnail sketch will be indicated below, but it is important to recognize at the start of this chapter that the provisions of the CPA of 2005 mark a new era for the Sudan, in immediately providing for a substantial degree of autonomy for the South (as defined by the provincial borders of 1956) and in promising a referendum six years on in which the Southerners will have the opportunity to opt for secession. From the language point of view this represents a victory for southern arguments that English should be the main language of administration and education in their region. However it is important to note here that the CPA marks a historical change in official language policy for the whole country, and not only the South, in the name of the new Government of National Unity established by the agreement. The text of the CPA establishes a quite new recognition of the linguistic diversity of the Sudan and the language rights of all the Sudanese peoples. The relevant passage is worth quoting:

---

[3] www.ethnologue.com/show_country.asp?name=SD, consulted 27 July 2006.

2.8 Language

2.8.1 All the indigenous languages are national languages which shall be respected, developed and promoted.

2.8.2 Arabic language is the widely spoken national language in the Sudan.

2.8.3 Arabic, as a major language at the national level, and English shall be the official working languages of the National Government business and languages of instruction for higher education.

2.8.4 In addition to Arabic and English, the legislature of any sub-national level of government may adopt any other national language(s) as additional official working language(s) at its level.

2.8.5 The use of either language at any level of government or education shall not be discriminated against. (CPA of 2005: 27–8)

This formulation and its provisions are more 'democratic' with respect to indigenous languages than had ever before been enacted in the Sudan. Moreover the document refers to the country as a whole, and not merely to the Southern regions where Arabic has been less influential and the issue of recognizing indigenous languages has been a focus of sharp debate for many decades. It outlines an ideal which however is very far from being easy to put into effect on the ground. On the other hand, while 'top-down' language policies are notoriously difficult to implement, there is at present a groundswell of support for the role of indigenous languages in the Sudan, not only in the present South but also in the North, and this rising sympathy for local languages from the grassroots makes the ideal prospects outlined in the CPA look more realistic.

In the rest of this chapter I first indicate something of the rich range of languages found in the territory of the modern Sudan. I then sketch the flourishing industry of language discovery and linguistic analysis which it has sustained, and how this has been linked with educational developments, especially in the mainly non-Muslim areas; how Arabic and English have come to be the main national languages and how their rivalry has developed; and finally suggest that instead of focusing on specific languages as such, and the public competition between them, we can learn much by considering how they co-exist, in practice, in all their plurality. Typical everyday contexts reveal bilingual fluency in surprising places; typical social interchange involves switching not only between, say, Arabic dialects but also cross-cutting between languages. The typical Sudanese community includes a surprising number of people who can manage 'simultaneous translation', surfacing when needed to act as interpreters, as I illustrate below. This widespread capacity of communities to overcome language difference, across the south as across the north, helps in my view to explain the resilience of Sudanese languages over time, and the ability of minority languages to persist alongside the multiple channels of public discourse. Catherine Miller and her colleagues have recently shown how complex is the relation between language and regional history in the eastern Sudan (Miller 2005), and she has pointed to the key ways in which the last generations of urbanization, war, and displacement have begun to transform the landscape of language use right across the country (Miller 2006). In many cases there has been a widening gap between affiliation to a particular 'ethnic' community and the ability to speak its language, but at the same time there is a distinct trend towards the greater cultural appreciation of indigenous languages, and I shall return to this issue in my conclusion. The upheavals of recent times have also, inevitably, meant a lull in the kind of patient enquiry that any language study entails. However, a large panel on this topic at the 7th International Sudan Studies Conference, held in Bergen in April 2006, showed that language studies are now flourishing again, and in this chapter I am indebted to several papers presented there.[4]

4.2 Language Heritage in the Middle Nile Region

The central Nile valley has always been a zone of human contact. The peripheral regions of rich grasslands, forests, and hills to the west, south, and east have fed into its patterns of trade and human movement, and turned it into an arena for linguistic interaction of all kinds. The expansion and contraction of settlement for ecological reasons, towards and away from the fertile strip of the Nile and its tributaries over the millennia, has been complemented by the waxing and waning of economic exchange links and political rivalry along a north/south axis since at least the days of pre-dynastic Egypt.

It is sometimes asked how many languages there are in the Sudan today. Answers have varied, as have figures for the country's population and its regions. Those concerned with minority rights have offered very high figures – a survey of 1995 suggested that the 28 million people of the Sudan spoke some 400 languages between them (Verney 1995: 5). More sober figures have been given by the linguists. For example the *Linguistic Survey of the Sudan* of the 1970s worked with 136 languages (Bell 1976, 1978–80). This seems well founded when we look at the current estimates on the Ethnologue website of the Summer Institute of Linguistics: there, we find, for an estimated national population today of nearly 40 million, 142 languages listed with brief descriptions, of which eight have become extinct in relatively recent times (see note 3). Of course it is often a matter of opinion as to whether two tongues are properly different 'languages' or merely variant dialects of one, and reclassification is an ongoing academic industry. But in addition to their large number, Sudan's languages are known to have diverse beginnings, belonging as they do to several historically deep language families. Three of Africa's primary large language families are well represented here: Afro-Asiatic, extending northwards and eastwards; Nilo-Saharan, found in a belt extending mainly to the west but also in the other regions of the Sudan;

---

[4] I am particularly grateful to Professor Herman Bell for commenting very helpfully on an earlier draft of this chapter.

and Niger-Congo, extending both westwards and southwards. The middle Nile Basin was quite possibly a key region in which processes of differentiation, and also of inter-language borrowing, fed into the language map and social history of a much larger area of the African continent (Ehret 2002). Scholarly interest in the languages of the upper Nile began very early, with travellers making enquiries of slaves they encountered in Cairo in the very early nineteenth century, and by the later years of the century both explorers and missionaries undertook field investigations on a surprisingly large scale (Köhler 1970, 1971). Unexpected nineteenth-century sources are still turning up: for example, several word lists from the upper Blue Nile hills in the recently published writings of the Dutch traveller Schuver (James, Baumann, and Johnson, 1996: 329–46).

The collection of word lists and grammars proceeded apace during the twentieth century, and some far-reaching decisions about the educational promotion of certain languages were made at the Rejaf Conference of 1927 (Sanderson and Sanderson 1981). The role of missionary scholars continued to be prominent, along with studies undertaken by administrators, as well as professional scholars (see Stevenson 1971). In the course of the 1970s, language research shifted from a main concern with words and grammar as such towards the way that speakers used language, the ways that Arabic was spreading, and the historical, educational, and creative potential of indigenous tongues. This was a productive period (see, for example, Thelwall 1978), and these themes are now being taken up again.

By mid-century scholars had plenty of material for comparison, and a variety of classifications of the languages of this part of Africa began to appear. An influential framework was offered by Tucker and Bryan (1955, 1966; Tucker 1978), in which clusters of related languages were identified on the ground (such as Cushitic, Nilotic) without attempts at their systematic inclusion in a global classification. Many languages were left as 'isolated units', while the framework was unduly influenced by the very facts of geographical closeness and historical assumptions of an ethno-racial kind (for example, the 'Hamitic' and 'Nilo-Hamitic' groupings). The next key stage in approaching classification was that of Joseph Greenberg (1963). He argued for a stricter 'linguistic approach' to language, setting aside any presuppositions about ethnic or cultural identities for the sake of comparison between languages as such. He transformed the accepted frameworks of classification, for example doing away with 'Hamitic' and its variants. One effect of his work was to assign languages of the central and upper Nile basin to positions within extensive super-families. The closest affinities of certain languages were with tongues found far away, in groupings extending east, south, or west. Greenberg proposed a wide 'Nilo-Saharan' family, for example, including many languages in western Africa which had not previously been linked with those in northeastern Africa. He extended the old 'Nilotic' subgroup of this family well to the south, for example, beyond its original 'geographical' locus, to include the former 'Nilo-Hamitic' languages of East Africa such as the well-known case of Masai. Subsequent work, including fresh field data, has confirmed the overall viability of the Nilo-Saharan grouping (see for example Bender 1983, 2003).[5]

Current research in applying tools of language comparison for reconstructing history has returned to a quest for the transmission of cultural meaning, that is of semantic as well as obviously 'linguistic' connections and innovations. For example, Ehret's reconstruction of the levels of historical connection in the Nilo-Saharan family emphasizes semantic associations and innovations as well as abstract shifts of sound and syntax (Ehret 2001), and points to a source region for the whole language family somewhere in the heartlands of today's Sudan. It also raises questions concerning the kinds of social and political context in which languages have waxed and waned, remained stable or shifted, and thus contribute to issues of long-term survival or change.

Indigenous languages of the Sudan have sometimes attained great importance as the medium of political ascendancy, for example in the case of the ancient kingdom of Meroe (approximately sixth century BC to fourth century AD) which controlled a good part of the territory of the modern country that we know. The two written scripts of the Meroitic language do use characters derived from Ancient Egyptian, but in a strictly phonological system that does not incorporate the large number of Ancient Egyptian ideograms. Meroitic provides a wonderful puzzle for linguists and historians: as yet little deciphered, but assumed to belong to the Nilo-Saharan family (Haycock 1971, 1978; Rilly 2004). From the region of Aswan in Egypt southwards along the Nile into Sudan as far as the Dongola Reach are the Nubian languages (the main two distinct languages being Nobíin [Fadiccha-Mahas] and Kenuzi-Dongola), still flourishing in their spoken form.[6] Their immediate ancestor of the medieval period, Old Nubian, had its own script, using characters from Coptic, Egyptian, and Meroitic (Bell and Haashim 2006), and the memory of this past is valued by Nubians today. Moreover, historical traces of Nubian are found today in the place names of a wider region than that of today's spoken tongue (Bell 1970). It has been

---

[5] Some of the original claims by Greenberg have been challenged, for example the position of Kadugli-Krongo, originally classified as Niger-Kongo, but now more generally considered Nilo-Saharan.

[6] Three distinct 'ethnic' and linguistic terms have grown up in Sudanese usage around the core syllable 'nub'. This has sometimes been claimed to be associated with the ancient Egyptian word for gold, with derivations applied to peoples of the 'land of gold'. Nubia is a region straddling the Egyptian-Sudanese border, and 'Nubian' has long applied to its people and indigenous languages (cognates, e.g. 'Nobadae', also appear in ancient Greek and Ethiopian sources). 'Nuba' has been applied since at least the late eighteenth century to the Nuba Hills in the centre of the Sudan, but also occasionally (e.g. by James Bruce) to people stationed around Sennar who derived from the upper Blue Nile. Today, the term 'Nuba' refers only to the Nuba Hills, and in a blanket sense to their people, and their languages. (The Arabic expression *bilad al-Nuba*, however, refers to the Nubian Nile.) In the far south of the Sudan, some of the military and economic adventurers who arrived in the Ottoman period were from the far northern region of Nubia, and this is thought to be the source of the label 'Nubi' which has since been applied to Sudanese soldier/merchants (and their civilian entourage) who were recruited locally and played a role in the making of British colonial East Africa. As discussed below in this chapter, the variety of southern Arabic developed in this community is known as Ki-Nubi, while the term Nubi is freely used in many parts of the southern Sudan to indicate traders, military recruits, and 'detribalized' persons in general. One can even alternate between being, say, Bari or Dinka in one's home village, and Nubi in town, using one's Arabic name.

argued that Nubian languages were still important in the successor Funj Kingdom of Sennar (early sixteenth to nineteenth centuries) though during this period Arabic secured a dominant position along with the Muslim religion (James 1977; Spaulding 1985). In the far west, the contemporaneous sultanate of Darfur presided over a local political culture couched in the Fur tongue, though also using Arabic for long-distance connections (O'Fahey and Spaulding 1974; O'Fahey 1980). Southwards on the Nile, the Shilluk kingdom, again based upon a political system operating through the indigenous language, had regional interconnections along the river and across it (Evans-Pritchard 1962 (1948); Mercer 1971) and in the far south, the realm of the Azande constituted an empire, run by a Zande-speaking elite, built up over two centuries through political and military ascendancy over many other peoples living in a wide region straddling the Congo-Nile watershed (Evans-Pritchard 1971). Other southern groups have extended their influence, including linguistic influence, over large regions: for example, in the case of the Dinka, through the accumulation of wealth in cattle and the associated patterns of regular and sometimes exploratory movement across the land. As with the northern Sudanese Arabic-speaking herders of camels and cattle, Nilotic-speaking pastoral peoples like the Dinka and the Nuer also have wide contacts and need to keep their social and economic exchange links and diplomatic ties in good order. There is substantial evidence of Nilotic influence on some of the Koman languages of the eastern Sudanese border hills, for example.

In addition to the robust role of indigenous languages in the political and economic history of the Sudan, local elites have typically used and promoted languages introduced from outside. Such 'foreign' languages have usually arrived along with trade, or as a result of conquest. Ancient evidence has been found not only of Egyptian but also of Greek and Latin contacts in the region, for example; Coptic was used in medieval Christian Nubia as one of the languages of liturgy and learning; and Turkish became the language of government during the Ottoman imperial rule (1821–85). The most lasting impact of an 'introduced' language, however, has been the case of Arabic. Although Arabs are attested in Nubia from the first century of the Islamic era, the language spread widely in the Nile Basin only some five centuries ago, in the Funj period. This happened not simply as a result of the immigration of 'Arabs' however that might be understood as an 'ethnic' term, but largely as a result of the settlement and local intermarriage of Arabic-speaking traders, along with the associated spread of itinerant Muslim teachers. The traders, and the holy men, while helping spread the networks of Arabic language communication, might themselves come from diverse backgrounds of family, descent, and original homeland. The immigration of some Arabic-speaking herding peoples, both from the lower Nile and across the Red Sea, was also a factor, especially in those cases where again there was a substantial rate of economic interaction and intermarriage (for example, by the recruitment of herders or servants from local populations, as with many of the Baggara cattle nomads) (Cunnison 1971).

4.3 Genesis of the Modern Political Framework

Turkish, as Sudan's first language of colonial administration, has left many traces in the discourse of local government, police, and military institutions. Certain Turkish elements such as *bash-* (chief) have survived into the twenty-first century, for example *bashkatib*, 'head clerk', and *bashmuhandis*, 'chief engineer'. But Turkish has disappeared as a language in everyday use, and regrettably only a handful of Sudanese or Sudanist scholars have ever had the competence to study the Ottoman archives bearing on Sudanese history. The successful rebellion of the Mahdist movement against the Ottoman Empire led to an independent Sudanese state in 1885 with a heavily Islamic and nationalist agenda, along with the re-establishment of Arabic as the language of state administration. The 'reconquest' of the Sudan by Britain and Egypt in 1898 established English as the dominant language of government, and gradually through the fifty-plus years of the Anglo-Egyptian Condominium (often today dubbed the 'British colonial' period) English spread in a variety of ways into the educational, social, and cultural life of the country's elite. It was during this time that Sudanese nationalists began to challenge the spread of English, especially through Christian mission education in the south, and to champion the cause of Arabic; and since independence of the country in 1956 the Arabic/English debate has remained at the top of the political and educational agenda.

However, the language question has not been a simple matter of rivalry between these two. It has been, rather, a triangular debate about the proper relationship between Arabic, English, and the vernacular languages of the country. The role here of the political struggle of the peoples of the southern Sudan for recognition became a key factor, especially with the first outbreak of civil war in 1955 as the country was on the brink of independence. The Arabic language and Muslim ways had been discouraged among the southern peoples during the Condominium. Following efforts to stamp out slavery, the aim was to protect southerners from further exploitation by unscrupulous traders. There was also a certain romantic thinking about saving the south from the evils of rapid urbanization, detribalization, and consequent loss of morality and discipline, which might follow from an uncontrolled immigration of Arabic-speaking northern Sudanese into the south. Administrative structures, though based on 'Indirect Rule' all over the country, were more 'direct' in the case of the three southern provinces than in the north, where enormous powers were entrusted to the key tribal leaders. It was felt that the destiny of the southerners should be more in line with the pattern of the East African colonies. According to the 'Southern Policy' of 1930, which prevailed until 1947, these principles were formalized: immigration from the north was monitored carefully in the southern provinces, and education was entrusted exclusively to the Christian mission organizations. The English language was promoted not only in education but also administration, while the missions were encouraged also to pursue the use of vernacular languages both in church and in school (Sanderson and Sanderson 1981). British officials of the Sudan Political Service were required to become proficient in Arabic if they were posted in the north, but also rewarded for studying a select number of southern languages if they were based there (Deng and Daly 1989). Some of the contradictions built into the policies of the day are revealed very clearly if we consider the case of the Nuba Hills, a region of the geographical north which displays a wonderful diversity of vernacular languages (a total of forty-three according to the Ethnologue website). This area came to be seen as an anomalous 'enclave' in the north although its peoples had long played a part in the regional workings of trade, had long supplied labour to the Nile Valley, and indeed had been a vital source of recruitment into the armies of the Sudanese state at whatever period. The Condominium government tended to emphasize the 'separateness' of the Nuba Hills, however, and allowed missionary organizations to work there and take responsibility for early education, though children had to move on to higher-level schools elsewhere in the north. The policy inevitably came up against criticism and and has been described as a failure (Elzailaee 2006). Language issues and their implication in religious matters inevitably fed into the rising nationalist politics of the (northern-based) Sudanese elite (Beshir 1969) and post-independence struggles have to some extent intensified these issues.

The gradual intensification of the first civil war from the late 1950s led to heightened criticism of British colonial policies for having played a part in the genesis of southern discontent, and all the foreign missionaries working in the south were deported by 1963, along with those in the Nuba Hills and southern Blue Nile by 1964. The case for embracing Arabic as the language of public life and education across the country was pressed by many individuals and political parties in the north, along with a rising tide of voices claiming that the Islamic religion was the true destiny of all Sudanese.

In 1969, Arabic was substituted for English as the main teaching language in northern secondary schools. By the early 1980s Arabic had taken over as the main teaching language in much of Khartoum University, while supplementary English courses were also offered to students. We should note that in more recent years, competence in English has been increasingly valued in the universities, for the sake of international relations and the reputation of Sudanese scientific research.

The secular, left-wing coup of Nimeiry in 1969 had made possible a new alignment of interests, and laid the foundations for the Addis Ababa Peace Agreement of 1972 which recognized a unitary authority for the south. However, by 1983 the basis of this agreement was being undermined by Nimeiry himself, even as he adopted a more religious personal stance and decreed the abolition of the Southern Regional Government along with the imposition of strict sharia law for the nation; and civil war again reared its head. Islamic politics has since dominated the Sudanese story, especially following the Islamist-backed coup of Omer el Beshir in 1989 which certainly set back the prospects for peace at that time. Over the whole period, the successive movements for regional autonomy, largely based in the south, have championed the cause of the vernacular tongues for initial primary education and an early introduction to English. On the ground, in the south and in the refugee camps where Sudanese lived in Ethiopia, Uganda, and Kenya, primary schooling struggled on in a remarkable way, often with voluntary teachers taking classes in broken-down buildings and under trees, while secondary education had to be sought elsewhere.

There have been major social and political transformations as a result of war, especially the most recent strife of 1983–2005. A whole range of new factors affecting the use of language by Sudanese have come into play. Specifically, we should note that the massive displacement of people from both the north and south of the country to East Africa, Egypt and the Middle Eastern countries, and Western countries, has created a complex set of diasporas in which Sudanese are now bringing up their children. Sudanese living in the West are now fluent in English, and in East Africa, typically in Swahili too – a language which is now heard in the southern Sudan. There are others transplanted to French-speaking countries, and even to such countries as Norway, Sweden, and Denmark where they are expected to learn national languages. Dress, family, and many personal areas of life have been transformed for Sudanese in the West, along with language, and especially so for women. In the Middle East many Sudanese have clearly found a 'home from home', and while the Arabic language and Muslim ways are reinforced for many individuals, the national context and international cultural exchanges made possible are rather different from those they have typically left. There are also many displaced Sudanese living in large cities such as Cairo where their position can be extremely ambivalent, even though they may speak Arabic, not only for some people from the southern regions but also some refugees from Darfur, for example.

Other complications for the language situation resulting from the years of war include the growing importance and use of communication technologies. Radio took on a highly influential role during the recent war, with the SPLA radio station (operating from Ethiopia 1985–91) itself using English, standard and southern Arabic, and a variety of indigenous languages for instruction, propaganda, and entertainment. In the early years the station urged local communities (in several languages) to support the movement, sometimes advising them in languages such as Bari or Latuka on how to join up, or instructing them to flee specific towns in advance of an attack (some of these broadcasts were monitored and translated by the BBC; see James 2000). In later years, the SPLA radio seemed to aim rather over the heads of local communities, and at rival propaganda voices emanating from Omdurman radio – often explicitly urging *jihad* – or other stations in the Middle East. Transistor radios spread very widely across the country during these years, and people both at home and in refugee camps outside the Sudan were keenly tuning in to different stations, increasingly able to follow broadcasts in both Arabic and English, as well as the occasional programme in a familiar vernacular. On the ground, the language debate shifted to and fro, and over the period of the war the position of English was consolidated in the south. Schools became dependent on teachers trained in East Africa, and using East African syllabuses, and though Arabic was typically taught as a subject, the vernacular languages tended to disappear from the syllabus (Breidlid 2006; Steven 2006).

4.4 Languages in Everyday Life

4.4.1 Arabic

While Arabic is widely spoken in the Sudan, this statement has to be qualified. There are many levels and qualities of Arabic, as well as a number of regional dialects. The religious language of the Qur'an and other ancient texts, taught in the mosques and *khalwas* (religious schools), has something of the social distance from ordinary life that Latin had in the medieval religious life of Europe. In formal public life, written communications, and on national radio and TV programmes, Modern Standard Arabic is used in the Sudan as in Egypt and other Middle Eastern countries (though there are now a number of regional radio and TV stations which take a more flexible approach; see Bell and Haashim 2006). Sudanese Colloquial Arabic, the spoken dialect of the central and northern parts of the country, occasionally finds its way into informal kinds of writing but is predominant in the ordinary round of everyday life (Trimingham 1946; Persson and Persson 1979). Even within this speech network, there are levels of sophistication marking status, education, and background: some accents, with clipped vowels tending towards Egyptian colloquial, carry an elite air, while broader vowels seem to mark the language of the street. In the far west, a regional dialect has developed its own distinctive character, while in the south a variety of Arabic has developed which has dropped a good number of 'difficult' consonants and grammatical rules (such as gender in pronouns and verbs) while picking up both lexical items and modes of expression from a variety of southern languages.

'Southern Arabic' has quite a long history, going back at least to the period of military recruitment and trade expansion during Ottoman rule (Meldon 1913; Mahmud 1983), when it served as an informal lingua franca. It easily became the common tongue of the ordinary soldiers of the southern-based guerrilla movements, and probably the commonest language used on Radio SPLA when it was functioning. One of its variants is known today as 'Juba Arabic' (Smith and Morris 2005), and even farther south is the tongue known today in Uganda and Kenya as 'Kinubi', spread by the population of various Sudanese garrisons stationed in East Africa since the 1890s (Soghayroun 1981; Luffin 2004). The soldiers gathered at these posts typically engaged in trade with local communities, and moreover took wives and partners from them. Each garrison thus tended to attract a civilian settlement around it, termed a *malakiya*. At the heart of nearly all towns in the southern Sudan even today you will find a district known as the *malakiya*, where southern Arabic has become the first language of a rising generation, who now tend to marry among themselves, thus consolidating the speech community. In major towns of East Africa there are distinctive Nubi communities whose language is perhaps so far removed from the colloquial Arabic of the northern Sudan as to be mutually unintelligible.

Arabic itself, however, of whatever variety, has prestige value in relation to other languages of the Sudan and its bordering zones. Within Sudanese Colloquial Arabic, there are long-established 'snobbish' attitudes to the merely spoken vernaculars of the illiterate 'yokels' in the rural areas. While written, enlightened languages of the world, those one studies in school such as English or French, are grouped with Arabic as *lugha*, or respected proper languages, the local tongues are dubbed *rutana*, a dismissive term invoking a limited, local, primitive way of talking inherited from the dark ages. The general attitude goes together with other difficulties: for example, within colloquial Arabic there are many terms of a derogatory sort applied to the healers and diviners of 'pagan' peoples, which makes cultural inter-translation almost impossible. A common word in Sudanese Colloquial for example is the Nuba-derived *kujur*, given the meaning of 'occult magician' and evoking the evil *jinn* of Islamic theology. To call indigenous respected ritual and religious figures by this term is to impugn and mock whatever moral and spiritual authority they might have in their own communities. Anthropologists and historians have learned to use the term 'prophet' of the religious leaders of peoples like the Nuer and the Dinka, but how can we reconcile this high-minded universalist usage with the prejudicial term *kujur* applied to them by many Sudanese? (Evans-Pritchard 1956; Lienhardt 1961; Johnson 1994). English-language anthropology itself has an overwhelming number of terms which do not easily translate, as was discovered in the University of Khartoum when attempts were made to produce a glossary; 'clan' and 'matriliny' were bad enough, but consider 'religion' and 'ritual' as *general technical terms*, whether in Arabic or indeed in Dinka. Liberal-thinking Sudanese today recognize, as do the provisions of the recent Comprehensive Peace Agreement, that the image of the country's vernacular tongues as some kind of backward past, and the way that vernacular cultures are often dismissed, will need to be transformed if there is to be a real political change.

4.4.2 Indigenous Languages of the North

Hasty journalists sometimes represent the north as uniformly Arabic-speaking, Muslim, and even 'Arab' in the 'ethnic' sense. But as I have briefly indicated above, the north is home to many languages: the Beja (Bedawi) tongues do at least belong to the Afro-Asiatic major family as Arabic does, but the Nubian languages discussed briefly above are part of the Nilo-Saharan category, along with a dozen or so minority languages in the southeastern and southern extremities of the old Blue Nile Province, in addition to many representatives in the Nuba Hills and in Darfur. Many of the languages in the Nuba Hills, by contrast, belong to the Niger-Congo category. People living in these regions of the northern Sudan are by and large comfortable living with the widespread use of Arabic while regarding their own regional language as part of an ancient Sudanese heritage. While Arabic is commonly used as the lingua franca in the Nuba Hills (as noted above), as well as in the southern Blue Nile, the indigenous peoples of these regions occupy an ambivalent position in relation to mainstream northern Sudanese society. They currently have a high political profile, some areas having been drawn into the civil war in the 1980s, which led to the recognition of the special status of the new regional states of Southern Kordofan and Blue Nile in the Comprehensive Peace Agreement of 2005.

Recent and ongoing new fieldwork is revealing interesting evidence on the ground with respect to the place of vernacular languages in regions where Arabic is spreading as a lingua franca and through education. Surveys of the 1970s demonstrated the spread of Arabic in the north, among people who had a vernacular mother tongue in regions such as Darfur and the Nuba Hills. However, there are indications even in this work that the adoption of Arabic, through education especially but also in everyday life, did not necessarily mean the loss of one's vernacular (Thelwall 1971; Bell 1978–80). Recent work seems to confirm the continuing resilience of many of Sudan's indigenous languages. Catherine Miller has emphasized not only how the spread of Arabic is not a monolithic matter, but how processes of urbanization and education can themselves stimulate fresh awareness of, and activities in, the vernaculars. More-over, identification with a recognized 'ethnic' community such as Beja, or Nuba, or Fur, is becoming a rather different matter from actually speaking a relevant language as mother tongue (Miller 2006). A particularly interesting argument has recently been made about Arabic use among the Beja of the eastern Sudan; the Beja language(s) are supposed to enshrine traditional ethics and morality, and men consequently frown on hearing their womenfolk speak in Arabic. This is of course a region where Arabic has been in general use for centuries, and so the 'ring-fencing' here of Arabic against its incursion into the morally valued domain of family life raises potential questions for other cases too (Vanhove 2006).

4.4.3 Indigenous Languages of the South

The greatest diversity of languages in the Sudan is concentrated in the south, where as explained above, indigenous languages have acquired a relatively high profile in national affairs. Linguists have found deep patterns of branching between subgroups of Nilo-Saharan and also a number of Niger-Congo tongues. The anthropologists and students of folklore have also made a significant contribution not only to the understanding of Sudan's languages as such but to their cultural expression and social role (see for example Deng 1973). Modern professional work has flourished under the auspices of the Summer Institute of Linguistics, who cooperated with the Southern Region in the late 1970s in developing educational materials for local languages. Since the return of conflict in the south they have continued to pursue Sudanese language projects even outside the country, with persons living in the diaspora in East Africa, for example. There is an astonishing range of publications available today in the languages of the south, consisting of primers, story books, and so forth, as well as scriptures. Many booklets were brought out during the years of peace in the 1970s, with the collaboration of the regional Ministry of Education in Juba and the Institute of Regional Languages in Maridi. In some of the modern refugee camps, such materials are used in the initial stages of literacy education, for which there is a large demand, and a good deal of new production goes on in both Khartoum and East Africa.[7]

The sheer demographic predominance of Dinka speakers in the south has helped shape modern politics. Dinka is the most widespread of the Nilotic languages, and Sudan's largest ethno-linguistic group if we set aside Arabic (with a population very conservatively estimated at rather more than 1 million). Dinka speakers have played a key role in political and military leadership of the southern movement over half a century, and this has led to certain tensions within the political arena (Johnson 2006). In Juba, which was the capital of the former Southern Region during the decade of peace (1972–83), rivalry became explicit between Nilotic and non-Nilotic speaking groups (the problem being seen by some Equatorians, for example, as 'Dinka Domination'). No doubt encouraged by Khartoum at the time, this rivalry fed into the decision of Nimeiry's government to abolish the Regional Government, and thus directly into the resurgence of war in 1983.

4.4.4 English Usage Today

Sudan's international contacts in diplomacy, politics, military and business partnerships, and humanitarian and development affairs have been increasing in recent years, partly due to new investment in the oil fields. These affairs are conducted in English not only with Western countries but also an increasing range of African countries such as Kenya and South Africa, and Asian countries such as China, Malaysia, and India. Standards of English teaching in the schools and universities of the northern regions have risen very markedly over the last twenty years, and this has been helped by the continuing recruitment of modest numbers of expatriate staff. During the successive periods of war, many southern Sudanese have sought education outside the country, whether as individual migrants to East Africa, refugees in official camps of the UNHCR where some education is provided, or as migrants or settlers in Western countries. Many northern Sudanese have also moved to the West. All the displaced have tried to maintain family links with their home areas, and the peace settlement means that there are now strong calls upon the diasporas to return. This can only strengthen the place of English in Sudanese life. There are for example current demands from returnees to the new Blue Nile State, part of the North but with special local provisions to recognize their connections with the cause of the South, for English teaching to be included in their plans for the development of education.

In summary, the current situation is that constitutionally both Arabic and English are national languages, but that the South is free, for the first time, to give English priority in both administration and education. In practice, formal education has scarcely existed in the South for decades, but informal teaching has continued in broken-down premises and under trees, often supported by the churches, and in the medium of local vernaculars, southern Arabic, and elementary English. In the North, Arabic is the

---

[7] For an example of the latter, see the *Mödö–English Dictionary with Grammar* (Persson and Persson 1991).

language which has long been used for internal affairs, religious studies, and primary education, while English is introduced as a subject in secondary schools and higher education, and dominates external relations.

4.5 Conclusion: Bilingualism, and the Life of the Sudanese Vernaculars

Inhabitants of the modern country of the Republic of Sudan inherit a complex history of competing languages, language divergence, and inter-borrowing, and while there are some examples of language death, there are multiple remarkable stories of language survival even among quite small speaking communities. In particular, the persistence of languages in the Sudan, over time, must always have had a good deal to do with the capacity of people to manage in more than one tongue: to cope with at least one language of trade and regional public life alongside a mother tongue, and in not a few cases to achieve some fluency in several tongues. In any given local community today, and probably at earlier times too, interpreters can be found to make communication possible across several languages. Fluid patterns of language competence are even typical of Sudan's border regions; its borders are open, not closed, to linguistic exchange.

One example from my own experience in the 1970s illustrates this. I was sitting in what I regarded as a Komo village, on the Ethiopian side of the Sudan border, trying to learn something of the Komo language (spoken on both sides, and similar to the Sudanese language Uduk I had some idea of from earlier fieldwork – see for example James 1988). My interpreter was an Anuak who had learned Komo and also knew some English. We recorded tapes in Komo and he helped me transcribe and translate them. Many people in the area expected me to know Oromo, as many foreigners in western Ethiopia did. I only had the most basic expressions in Oromo, because I had come to Ethiopia equipped with six months' classes in Amharic, which I hoped to use; I didn't realize that it was not a preferred language in the western regions of Ethiopia at that time. When the villagers really wanted to get something over to me, they would address me firmly in southern Arabic, the one language we could all manage in! Between us we could operate through various cross-over links in at least seven languages. My experience was a little un-English, perhaps, but not in itself so peculiar; Sudanese travellers must regularly face these sorts of mixed-lingual communities and diverse overlapping threads of communication. It dawned on me that this was not an unusual situation for a border village, and possibly not for villages in general over large swathes of a country like Sudan – not to mention the towns and cities. It also seemed very clear that a minority language like Komo could maintain a degree of intimacy, even privacy among its speakers, while at the same time communicating through various channels with the 'outside' world.

Despite the lively currents of inter-language exchange and the familiar everyday practices of oral translation, we should remember the depths of significance that one's mother tongue carries with it – jokes and slang and songs and realms of unspoken things. The Sudan's vernaculars are now getting fresh attention from their own communities, both through academic enquiries and the setting up of cultural projects even in towns.[8] Meanwhile, many of Sudan's vernaculars now have an electronic life of their own: not only local but also international phone calls now take place in dozens of them (for example Uduk conversations take place between Africa, North America, and Australia); song tapes in local languages like Dinka are in circulation (Miller 2006); and email communications and internet chat sites are burgeoning.

Bell and Haashim (2006) have proclaimed the need for a united Sudanese nation to build respect for its own languages; to recognize the input from those languages into Sudanese Colloquial Arabic itself; and to recognize the importance of multilingual elements in education and cultural activities. These arguments can only be reinforced when we remember the growing significance of the Sudanese diasporas and their influence on events inside the country, alongside the impact of international aid programmes. Definitions of the Sudanese as a people, with a distinct way of life and language, have often been rather restricted in the past – sometimes merely evoking the Arabic-speaking Muslims of the geographical heartland of the state, sometimes opposing these to a stereotype of Christian or culturally traditional 'southerners' which I have also criticized in this chapter. Even if this picture had some plausibility in the past, today we have to modify it. Dialects of Arabic are flourishing in the South, while some millions of people originally from the southern regions, or western regions, have now found survival only in the heartland cities of the North. The realities of the situation demand that the role of plural language use, and the stimulus of languages in movement, in exchange, be built in to any conception of its future cultural development. Such a conception would be in line with the very 'democratic' provisions of the Comprehensive Peace Agreement, as outlined at the start of this chapter; and in my view, it would also not be out of line with the 'real-world' social history of language use in the country over many centuries.

---

[8] For the setting up of Fur cultural projects in Khartoum, see Idris (2006); for recent attention to Zaghawa proverbs from the north-west, see Osman (2006); and for the academic study and language advocacy on behalf of Yulu, of the south-west, see Gabjanda (1976) and Hamid (2006).

5

Senegal: The Emergence of a National Lingua Franca

Fiona McLaughlin

5.1 National Identity in Africa

In addressing the relationship between language and national identity in the African context I take the term national identity to have two different meanings: the first of these is a population's relationship and sense of belonging to a nation-state, and the second is the identity of an individual nation-state within the international world order.[1] Based on the first meaning, Senegal can best be described as a predominantly Wolof-speaking nation, while on the international scene it is a francophone state. The African nation-state is in itself a relatively recent phenomenon, dating in most cases from the early 1960s when African colonies were granted independence from European colonial powers. Clearly, contemporary African states did not grow out of pre-existing indigenous political structures: their boundaries are artefacts of rivalries and negotiations between the European powers who eventually exerted political and economic hegemony over their respective colonies in the nineteenth and twentieth centuries. How, then, can a sense of national identity develop within the political and geographic boundaries of a state which is the artefact of European history and expansionism, and which from an African perspective is little more than an arbitrary construct?

Writing twenty or so years ago, Hannerz (1987: 548) makes the point that the accumulation of a shared post-colonial history has played an important role in the construction of nationhood, however incomplete that process might be. He writes:

> the creation of a State tends, to some degree at least, to be a self-fulfilling prophecy of the development of a nation. Even if it has been an uphill struggle in many cases ... and in the end an unsuccessful one in some of them, the former [African] colonies have continuously accumulated more common history, and each one of them now has an overarching apparatus of administration, education and media power. Gradually, if still quite incompletely,

---

[1] Political scientists who study the African state have produced a complex and sophisticated body of work on these issues against which these two definitions will seem quite elementary and even simplistic. I do not attempt to engage with that literature, but am merely using this dual definition as a tool to get at two salient aspects of the relationship between language and national identity.

they have become more nation-like, and at least some of the varied currents of meaning flowing through their social structures, and hardly insignificant ones, can now well be described as national, rather than local, regional or ethnic in their circumscription. One could only ignore this by bracketing a century or more of history.

In light of Hannerz's perspective, then, the accumulation of a common post-colonial history provides a context within which a sense of nationalism – however weak or robust – can potentially be developed. In the case of Senegal, which is the topic of this chapter, to the almost half-century of common history as a nation can be added what some scholars have viewed, although not unproblematically, as a certain cultural homogeneity attributable to the population's widespread adherence to Sufi Islam (Crowder 1962a; Cruise O'Brien 1971, 1975) and to harmony in relations between ethnic groups (UNESCO 1974). To these two important factors we can also add the emergence and spread of Wolof as the unofficial national language of Senegal which has contributed to both the semblance of homogeneity (Harney 2004: 35) and to the future emergence of a 'more viable nationhood within the territorial frontiers of the Senegalese state' (Cruise O'Brien 2003: 121). On the international scene, however, and in its official policies, the state remains overwhelmingly francophone. Thus, insofar as they are related to a linguistic identity, the two primary aspects of national identity – namely a population's sense of belonging to a nation and the identity of a nation within the world order – are at odds with each other since Wolof dominates in the former domain and French in the latter.

In this chapter I look at the relationship between language and national identity in one of Africa's most politically successful and stable states. The focus is primarily on national identity as reflected in the Senegalese population's multi-faceted sense of belonging to the nation-state, a process in which the emergence of Wolof as a national lingua franca has played a central role, but in section 5.5 I also address the way in which the state views itself and perpetuates its institutions through the use of French as the sole official language. I begin with an overview of Senegal and its history in section 5.2, moving on to a discussion of the complex relationship between language and ethnicity and the role of both in the construction or contestation of a national identity in section 5.3; section 5.4 examines the process of Wolofization as a predominantly urban phenomenon, dating from as early as the seventeenth century; and in section 5.5 I examine the role of French as Senegal's official language. As will become clear, what is so striking about Senegal as compared to other West African francophone states is that an African language has emerged as the national lingua franca, and the former colonial language, albeit the official one, has never become a language of popular communication.[2]

[2] I thank Abdoulaye Barry, Mamadou Cissé, Judith Irvine, Caroline Juillard, Abdoulaye Kane, and Leonardo Villalón for many interesting conversations on language and nationalism in Senegal, all of which have greatly enriched my understanding of the topic. I am particularly grateful to Caroline Juillard for reading and commenting extensively on an earlier version of this chapter and pointing out, quite rightly, that many of the generalizations I make for Senegal as a whole apply essentially to the northern part of the country, and that they may often have to be qualified for Casamance in particular. I regret that space

5.2 An Introduction to Senegal

Senegal is a country of ten million or so inhabitants situated on the West African coast. It shares a border with Mauritania to the north, Mali to the east, and Guinea and Guinea Bissau to the south. Dakar, Senegal's bustling capital city of more than one and a half million, situated at the end of the Cap Vert peninsula,[3] occupies the westernmost point on the African continent. Senegal is a Sahelian country located in the semi-arid savannah belt south of the Sahara desert. Its rural population consists primarily of peanut or millet farmers (Pélissier 1966) and a small minority of pastoralists from among the Pulaar-speaking population. The Senegalese population is approximately 94 per cent Muslim in the West African Sufi tradition that revolves around several Sufi orders such as the Tijaniyya and the Qadiriyya found elsewhere in the Muslim world as well as two indigenous orders: the Muridiyya or Murids, and the Layene. The remaining population is predominantly Christian, the majority of whom are Roman Catholic, while a very small minority of the population adheres to animist religions, reflexes of which are also found in local practices associated with Islam and Christianity. Since independence in 1960 Senegal has been a relatively stable multiparty democracy with very little political mobilization along the lines of ethnicity or religion,[4] and Senegal's first president, Léopold Sédar Senghor, was himself a Catholic in this majority Muslim country.

As an artefact of European colonial expansion, the northern part of Senegal is largely separated from the southern part by the small, narrow country of the Gambia through which the Gambia River runs: the Gambia was a British colony while Senegal was a French one. Although the origins of these two states are colonial in nature, the geographical division between north and south is also mirrored by a cultural divide. Senegal's noted cultural homogeneity holds true more accurately of the area north of Gambia which is dominated by societies with similar hierarchical social structures. These consist of roughly two to four main endogamous groups which, depending on the specific society, could include (1) slaves; (2) artisan castes comprised of blacksmiths, leatherworkers, woodworkers, weavers, potters, musicians, and other griots or verbal artists; (3) free men, who are traditionally farmers; and (4) nobles, and in the case of the Haalpulaar ethnic group an Islamic clerical class, the torooɓe.[5] This highly stratified social structure is not shared by most societies in the Lower Casamance region of Senegal, the more tropical, less arid, and more multilingual area south of the Gambia, and Casamançais groups such as the Joola and the Bainunk share many

constraints here prevent me from providing a more nuanced discussion of Casamance, a region that poses the most significant obstacle to national integration in Senegal, but I refer the reader to Juillard's extensive work on the topic, especially Dreyfus & Juillard (2004) and Juillard (1995).

[3] Cap Vert refers to this peninsula and is not to be confused with Cape Verde or Cabo Verde, the island nation off the west coast of Africa where a Portuguese-based Cape Verdean creole is spoken.

[4] The main exception to this generalization is the unprecedented outbreak of ethnic violence against the Moorish population in Senegal in April of 1989 that escalated from a border dispute between Senegal and Mauritania into an international crisis, and was fuelled largely by political disenchantment.

[5] There is a substantial body of scholarly literature that provides varying perspectives on these societies and their social structures, including: Diop (1981), Conrad and Frank (1995), and Tamari (1997).

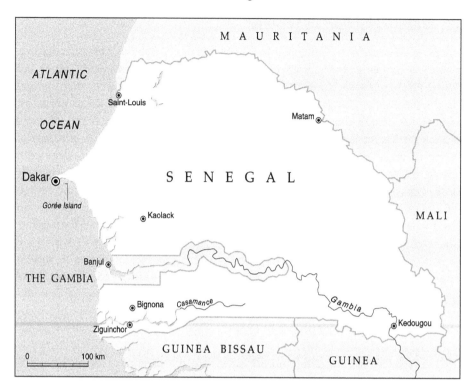

Senegal

more cultural traits with their neighbours to the south in Guinea-Bissau and Guinea than with their Sahelian compatriots to the north. In addition, the population of Lower Casamance is more heavily Catholic than the Muslim north, and until fairly recently the lingua franca of Ziguinchor, the regional capital, was a Portuguese creole which has now been partially eclipsed by Wolof (Dreyfus and Juillard 2004; Juillard 1995), although not without resistance. There has been much internal migration within Senegal so neither area is culturally, linguistically, or ethnically homogeneous, but what is important in the history of the Senegalese state is a sense of difference, distance, and even alienation from the dominant north that is felt by many Casamançais. These sentiments have given rise to a regionalist separatist movement, formed in the early 1980s as the *Mouvement des Forces Démocratiques de la Casamance*, spawning periodic bouts of violence that escalated into war in the 1980s and 1990s. Notwithstanding, these problems have rarely been cast in ethnic or linguistic terms, and the Joola, the predominant ethnic group of Casamance, enjoy a formal joking relationship, known as *kal* in Wolof, with ethnic groups north of Gambia, which involves the playful exchange of insults and claims of domination.

In spite of the fact that Wolof has emerged as a national lingua franca in Senegal for a variety of historical and social reasons discussed below, Senegal is far from being a linguistically or ethnically homogeneous nation. Like most African countries, Senegal is characterized by ethnic and linguistic diversity, although not to the same extent as countries like Nigeria or Ivory Coast. There are approximately twenty-five African languages spoken in Senegal, almost all of which belong to the Atlantic and Mande families of the Niger-Congo phylum. The relationship between language and ethnicity differs from group to group and the phenomenon of urbanization is changing both the linguistic and, to a certain extent, ethnic landscape of the country. These and related issues are discussed in section 5.3.

5.2.1 A Brief History of Senegal to Independence

Before European maritime contact the political makeup of the geographic area that now comprises Senegal consisted of a series of small kingdoms that came under the influence of both the Kingdom of Ghana from the eighth to eleventh centuries AD, and the Mali Empire in the thirteenth century. Under the influence of the Berber Almoravids, populations of settled Pulaar speakers in the northern part of the country converted to Islam by the eleventh century. They subsequently established a theocracy in Tekrur from where many West African proselytizing missions and jihads originated, especially during the latter part of the eighteenth century. The main trade routes throughout this period of history were the trans-Saharan caravan routes of the interior through which gold, salt, and slaves passed.

Early European contact came about through maritime exploration by the Portuguese and Dutch. Linguistic traces of this contact are found in place names,[6] and a Portuguese creole is still spoken in Casamance, particularly in the town of Ziguinchor. But the most significant European contact was with the French, beginning in the early 1600s. In 1638 the French made their first claim on the Senegalese coast by establishing a *comptoir* or commercial outpost on Bocos Island in the Senegal River. In 1659 the *comptoir* was moved to the larger island of Ndar, which they named Saint-Louis after King Louis IX of France, and a fort was built there. In 1678 the French established another *comptoir* on the island of Gorée which had previously been held by the Dutch. The establishment of these two small *comptoirs* on the Atlantic coast marks the beginning of a shift in trade away from the trans-Saharan routes of the interior and westward to the coast, as well as the beginnings of Senegalese urbanism and the ascent of Wolof as an urban language (McLaughlin, forthcoming, a).

The Atlantic port cities, including Saint-Louis, Gorée, and Rufisque, continued to grow and prosper in the eighteenth and nineteenth centuries, largely because of the trans-Atlantic slave trade as well as other types of commerce. For about a decade at the beginning of the nineteenth century the British occupied Gorée and Saint-Louis but they were returned to France just after the European countries had agreed to abolish slavery.

---

[6] Examples include Rufisque, a coastal city on the Cap Vert peninsula, from Portuguese *rio fresco* 'cool river', and the island of Gorée, porportedly from the Dutch *goede rade*, 'good harbour'.

By the early 1870s the coastal cities of Saint-Louis and Gorée, followed later by Rufisque and then Dakar, had been granted the status of commune, which meant that their inhabitants were French citizens with all the rights, such as voting, that citizenship afforded them, while the rest of the population were merely subjects. The inhabitants of the four communes were able to create a cosmopolitan urban African culture while claiming their legal and political rights as French citizens (Diouf 1998). At the height of the colonial period, in the late nineteenth and early twentieth centuries, France controlled vast territories on the African continent. These included Afrique Occidentale Française (AOF) or French West Africa, of which Saint-Louis served as the first capital from 1895 to 1902, when it was moved to the newer city of Dakar, founded in 1857.

5.2.2 Independence and Senghor's Legacy

Senegal gained independence from France in 1960, and Dakar became the capital of the new nation. At independence, poet, philosopher, and statesman Léopold Sédar Senghor became president and stayed in power until 1980 when his protégé Abdou Diouf acceded to the presidency. In 2000, opposition leader Abdoulaye Wade of the Parti Démocratique Sénégalais (PDS) defeated Diouf in a democratic election, ending forty years of rule by the Parti Socialiste (PS). Senghor was a French-educated intellectual and founder, along with Martinican poet Aimé Césaire, of the philosophy of *Négritude* which Harney (2004: 19) describes as both 'a theory of racial belonging for black people worldwide . . . (and) a cultural rallying point with which to begin the crucial post-colonial process of nationalist affirmation.'[7] While this process was carried out by another founding father of a post-colonial African state, namely Tanzania's Julius Nyerere, by promoting the official use of an African language – in this case Swahili – over and above the colonial language, Senghor took a radically different path, promoting the use of French in all aspects of Senegalese institutional life. From the 1950s to the 1970s a pro-Wolof movement emerged from among members of the intellectual class. The most vocal proponents for Wolof included philosopher Cheikh Anta Diop, and later the linguist Pathé Diagne, filmmaker Sembène Ousmane, and writer and mathematician Sakhir Thiam.[8] In 1971, obliged to make some concession to the status of indigenous languages, Senghor had six languages officially designated national languages. An ideological and political struggle between Senghor and his detractors ensued, based on the official orthography of the national languages. For whatever reason, Senghor would not admit the use of double letters to represent geminates, so the opposition provocatively produced magazines, films, etc. whose

---

[7] Readers interested in Senghor's life are referred to Vaillant's (1990) biography.

[8] A small group of intellectuals continue to write in Wolof. They include Sakhir Thiam, playwright and novelist Cheikh Aliou Ndao, and most recently the established novelist Boubacar Boris Diop published a first novel in Wolof.

titles included geminates written as double letters, all of which were then banned.[9] The issue, at least from Senghor's perspective, was not a linguistic one but rather one of state authority and control over language. As a final act of defiance, although double letters have long been accepted into the official spelling of Senegalese languages, Sembène Ousmane named his house *Galle Ceddo*, House of the Warrior. In reality, the designation of those six languages as official national languages was little more than a pre-emptive measure so that language would not become a political issue, and it opened the door to a long-lasting policy of neglect.

The culmination of Senghor's francophone career was his election, as poet and linguist in addition to philosopher and statesman, to the Académie Française, becoming the first black member of the elite watchdog institution of the French language. This legacy of involvement with the French language can be seen in the prominence of Senegalese writers, from Cheikh Hamidou Kane to Fatou Diome, on the literary scene in francophone Africa, and also in the 2002 accession of former president Abdou Diouf to the position of Secretary General of the *Organisation Internationale de la Francophonie*.

While the country's colonial history and Senghor's intellectual legacy might seem to predispose Senegal towards widespread use of French, this is not the case: the use of French in private and public life is considerably restricted. Instead, the northern Atlantic language, Wolof, has become the nation's lingua franca. Estimates indicate that while approximately 40 per cent of the Senegalese population are ethnically Wolof, close to 90 per cent of the population use Wolof as a first or second language. Although it enjoys only co-equal official status as a national language with several other languages, Wolof is commonly, albeit informally, referred to as the national language of Senegal. In subsequent sections we will examine the central role that Wolofization has had both on the construction of a national identity and in circumscribing the influence of the francophone elite in Senegalese nation-building.

5.2.3 Change at the Millennium

In February 2000 perennial opposition leader Abdoulaye Wade won the presidential elections, ending forty years of rule by Senghor's *Parti Socialiste*. Wade's accession to the presidency heralded a climate of change in Senegalese politics and a more dynamic approach to the situation of national languages within the country. But the president's initiatives also revealed a strong resistance to any implementation of Wolof as a co-official language with French on the part of speakers of other languages.

From 1971 until 2001 no languages had been added to the list of six officially recognized national languages designated as such by Senghor as lip-service to defuse the national language movement, whose proponents he considered 'irresponsible

---

[9] There are two hypotheses as to why Senghor forbade the use of double letters to represent geminates. The first is that there are no geminates in French, which Senghor took as a model, and the second is that there are no geminates in Seereer, Senghor's mother tongue.

romantics' (Cissé 2005: 283). The door to an increase in the number of officially
recognized national languages was opened by the 2001 constitution which named
as national languages the original six (Joola, Malinke, Pulaar, Seereer, Soninke, and
Wolof) as well as any other codified language, by which was meant a language with a
standardized writing system. Since 2001 many more languages have entered the ranks
of officially designated national languages including several of the smaller languages of
the Casamance (Balante, Mancagne, Manjak, etc.), some of the Cangin languages, and
even Hassaniyya, the Mauritanian dialect of Arabic also spoken by some small native
populations within Senegal. Presumably all Senegalese languages will be codified at
some point in the near future. Currently, there are literacy programmes in some of
the national languages, many of which are funded by foreign – primarily European
Union – non-governmental organizations, but the government has also chosen a few
primary schools as pilot sites for the introduction of national language use into the
classroom, an experiment that had been tried earlier but abandoned. Moreover, in 2004
the Ministry of Culture, in conjunction with other ministries, launched a programme
to create an academy of national languages to promote literacy in those languages
throughout the country.[10] What this actually means for the future of these languages
in real policy terms is still unclear, and large-scale implementation of the use of
national languages would take enormous resources which the Senegalese government
cannot at present afford, but the change in attitude is significant in that it marks the
opening of a space for national and minority languages on the national scene and in
national language debates.

When he was first elected, Wade's image was that of the 'can do' president – a
pragmatist who would act swiftly to solve many of Senegal's problems in innovative
ways. He adopted a populist pro-Wolof stance by using the language in tandem with
French in issuing statements to the press and in making public addresses, a practice
that other officials soon adopted. In conjunction with the liberalization of the media,
especially the privatization of radio which was already well under way during the last
years of the Diouf presidency, Wade's example paved the way for a substantial erosion
of French as the primary language of the non-print media. Today it is not uncommon
to hear a radio or television broadcast of an interview with a government official
conducted entirely in Wolof, a situation that would have been unheard of ten years
ago. The proliferation of popular Wolof-language radio stations in the last ten years has
also helped to make Wolof just as much a norm in radio broadcasting as French. There
are certain niches for programming in other national languages, especially Pulaar, but
such coverage is still quite limited.

Shortly after his accession to the presidency in 2000 Wade created a flap by proposing that all civil servants and state employees be required to know how to read and

---

[10] Literacy, to the Senegalese state, means literacy in the Roman alphabet, but it should be noted that
there is a long-standing tradition of written Wolof, Pulaar, and Malinke in the Arabic script, which includes
a literary tradition. Official Senegalese literacy rates would certainly be higher if such *ajami* writing were
taken into consideration.

write in Wolof. There was immediate objection to this proposal, most vociferously on the part of Pulaar-speaking members of the National Assembly who, along with other non-native Wolof speakers, viewed Wade's proposal as a means of furthering the creeping Wolofization of the state to the exclusion of other linguistic groups. Wade was called upon to explain himself and the proposal was never implemented. As perhaps the most telling recent incident regarding the status of Wolof as a national language, Wade's proposal and the reaction to it reveal many deep-seated beliefs about the appropriateness of language use in official settings. As it turns out, debates within the National Assembly that start off in French often end up in Wolof, and there are even some *députés* who do not speak French. Wolof is clearly functioning as a *de facto* national language in this and many other official contexts, but when it comes to discussions of legislation and the official recognition of Wolof as a national language above and beyond all other languages, there is much resistance and speakers of other languages are quick to remind the government that Senegal is a democratic multilingual society. This, too, has been played out in the National Assembly when *députés* who are speakers of other languages, thinking that the use of Wolof in an official setting has gone too far, have addressed the Assembly in Pulaar or Seereer or Joola in an act of symbolic exclusion to prove their point. Likewise, when Wade spoke to a Senegalese community living in France on an official visit to that nation in 2006, addressing them in Wolof, speakers of other Senegalese languages reacted angrily to the imposition of Wolof. Arguably, the fact that Wolof has no *de jure* status as a national language above and beyond other officially designated languages is an important factor in promoting its diffusion since there is no legal or official basis for opposition to Wolofization.

What the future holds for African languages in Senegal in terms of policy development is uncertain and depends on a variety of factors, not least of which are monetary and human resources. Cissé (2005: 306) aptly characterizes the Senegalese state's language policy up to now as one of reducing a complex multilingualism to a simplistic binary opposition (or, in his words, bilingualism) between French on one side and the national languages as an undifferentiated amalgamation on the other. He calls for a new policy that takes into account the social, economic, and political roles played by each language in order to establish a more nuanced approach to implementing their use on the national scene (2005: 306). The standardization of all Senegalese languages and their eventual designation as official national languages is a necessary first step in any comprehensive language policy, but what that policy will turn out to be is not at all clear.

5.3 Linguistic and Ethnic Identities

The relationship between language and ethnicity in Senegal is a complex and multivalent one and there are few generalizations that hold across all languages or ethnic groups. As the work of Irvine (1993), Gal and Irvine (1995) and Irvine and Gal (2000) has shown, ethnic and linguistic classification in colonial Africa – classification being the obsession of the colonial scientific project – often reflected colonial European ideologies of language and race, rather than the complexities of reality. Perhaps the most notorious case involving a Senegalese language was Meinhof's (1912) designation of Pulaar as a 'Hamitic' language, unrelated to the Atlantic languages, based on the physical appearance of its speakers. While Meinhof's classification was abandoned – although not fully until Greenberg assigned Pulaar to the Atlantic family in 1963 – other linguistic and ethnic classifications constructed through colonial ideologies have endured up to the present. Irvine and Gal (2000) show how a hierarchy of superior and inferior ethnic groups and languages in the northern part of Senegal was constructed by missionaries and colonial officials who privileged Pulaar speakers because of their long association with Islam (although this was sometimes taken as a point in their disfavour by certain missionaries) and their alleged intellectual superiority evidenced, among other things, by the subtleties of their language, meaning no doubt Pulaar's complex morpho-phonology. The lowest place in the hierarchy was accorded to those who manifested a 'primitive simplicity' (Irvine and Gal 2000: 55) through their animist practices, political organization, and language. This last group included the Seereer (whose language, in fact, has a morpho-phonology similarly complex to that of Pulaar) as well as others, notably the speakers of various Cangin languages spoken near the city of Thies, who were also designated Seereer by virtue of their same 'primitive simplicity'. Cangin speakers are still considered to be Seereer and appear as such on the Senegalese census questionnaires, and their languages are designated by compound names such as Seereer-Non, Seereer-Ndut, and Seereer-Safen.[11] What these examples clearly illustrate is that both ethnic and linguistic identities in Senegal are often constructed out of ideologies and that the resulting classification is generally a gross simplification of an ethnically and linguistically complex society where individuals are often multilingual and multi-ethnic. These caveats should be taken into account in the following discussions.

5.3.1 The Languages of Senegal

There are approximately twenty-five languages spoken in Senegal, most of which are indigenous African languages belonging to the Atlantic,[12] and to a lesser extent Mande, branches of the vast Niger-Congo phylum.[13] A full 90 per cent of the languages spoken in Senegal are Atlantic languages of which the main ones, in terms of numbers

---

[11] The history of the Cangin speakers is a complex one since they share certain cultural practices and patronyms with the Seereer, and others with the Wolof. To what extent this comes from contact or from a common origin is unclear.

[12] Because of its geographical distribution on the west coast of the continent, Atlantic was formerly known as West Atlantic, from Westermann's (1927) *Westatlantisch*, and continues to be referred to as such in some of the literature. The simplification of the name, now adopted by most scholars, dates from Doneux (1975).

[13] In the apparent absence of any shared innovation among the Atlantic languages scholars have not yet settled the question of whether it is actually a genetic family or a typological grouping.

of speakers, include Wolof, also spoken in Gambia and Mauritania; Pulaar, also known as Fula, Fulani, or Fulfulde, which is spoken across West Africa from Senegal and Mauritania to Chad; Seereer, Pulaar's closest sister language; and Joola, a cluster of languages and their respective dialects that exhibit varying degrees of mutual intelligibility. In current classification, Seereer, Pulaar, and Wolof constitute the northern branch of Atlantic, with Pulaar and Seereer quite clearly being more closely related to each other than either is to Wolof, but a clear picture of the relationship between these northern Senegalese languages has yet to emerge and awaits further research on the relationship of these three languages to the Cangin languages, discussed below.

Wolof shows remarkably little variation across dialects which, in conjunction with historical evidence, suggests its fairly widespread use as a lingua franca over time. Perhaps the major contemporary dialectal divide is between rural and urban varieties, the latter having borrowed extensively from French as the result of language contact. Several mutually intelligible varieties of Pulaar are spoken in Senegal with the dominant one being the Fuuta Tooro dialect of northern Senegal, one of the most conservative Fula dialects. Other dialects spoken in Senegal include the Casamance dialects such as Fulakunda and Fulaadu, as well as the Fuuta Jalon dialect spoken by the substantial population of Guineans living in Senegal. The Joola cluster includes several languages and dialects, including Joola Foñi or Kujamaat Joola which belong to the Bak branch of Atlantic. These northern Atlantic languages share certain typological features such as extensive noun class systems, consisting of more than twenty classes in some dialects of Pulaar; a large set of verbal extensions; and morphologically conditioned consonant mutation. They are also unusual among Niger-Congo languages in that they are not tonal. The Mande languages spoken in Senegal include Malinke or Soose and Soninke, also known as Saraxole. They are western Mande languages; they are tonal; and Soose, which plays an important role as one of the vehicular languages of northern Casamance and of Ziguinchor, in particular shows fairly typical Mande features, including only the residue of a noun class system. Soninke/Saraxole is somewhat of an outlier, with little mutual intelligibility with other Mande languages.

While the vast majority of people in Senegal are native speakers of either an Atlantic or a Mande language, there are also small populations of Arabic (Afro-Asiatic) speakers, including those who speak Hassaniyya, the Mauritanian dialect of Arabic, as well as Levantine and Moroccan dialects. Portuguese Creole is also spoken in some parts of Casamance, and in Dakar by immigrant and migrant populations from the Cape Verde islands and Casamance respectively. A certain amount of koineization has occurred between the Casamance and Cape Verde varieties, most often to the advantage of the latter.

Among the European languages spoken in Senegal, French obviously dominates as the official language and the language of education. English is gaining ground in Senegal, not only among the intellectual elite but also among members of the Senegalese trade diaspora, many of whom reside in the United States for several years at a time. Few studies have yet been conducted on the effects of migration on the

Senegalese linguistic repertoire, but many returned migrants speak several European languages quite fluently.

5.3.2 Ethnicity in Senegal

Language is often mobilized as a marker of ethnicity, not only in Africa but throughout the world, but it is not the sole component, and in many cases it is not even a particularly relevant component of ethnicity, even when it is perceived as being important. In other words, language and ethnicity are independent categories, but ones that are often closely linked to each other through language ideologies, defined by Irvine and Gal (2000: 35) as 'the ideas with which participants and observers frame their understanding of linguistic varieties and map those understandings onto people, events, and activities that are significant to them'. In contemporary Senegal, for example, there are those who would consider themselves ethnically Joola or Seereer, even though they do not speak those languages, because their parents are Joola or Seereer. Conversely, and especially in the urban context, there are those who identify themselves as ethnically Wolof because Wolof is the only language they speak, even though their parents might be Joola or Seereer. Also relevant to the complex mapping of language to ethnicity in Senegal is the fact that the categories that comprise those concepts are in many senses the artefact of the French colonial project of scientific classification, discussed in section 5.3 above. As will become clear in the following discussion, the mapping of language to ethnicity in Senegal is neither uniform not clear-cut.

The Wolof are numerically Senegal's largest ethnic group, numbering somewhat more than 40 per cent of the population. The proportional number of Senegalese who consider themselves Wolof is also increasing as a consequence of generational language shift in urban areas, and particularly Dakar. In a process that was documented as early as the 1960s, Wolof is often adopted as the primary language of the household in multilingual families. A survey of schoolchildren in towns throughout the country revealed that in households where only one spouse was Wolof, Wolof was generally the language used at home and, most interestingly, the same was also true for households where neither spouse was Wolof and they had different native languages (Wioland 1965; Wioland and Calvet 1967)[14]. Today, in similar urban situations, children in such households consider themselves to be Wolof because that is the language they speak. Linguistic Wolofization thus entails, to a certain degree, ethnic Wolofization.

A second ethnic group, the Lebu, speak a dialect of Wolof which they call Lebu and often conceive of as a different language although it is almost completely mutually intelligible with other Wolof dialects. The Lebu are primarily fishermen who live along the coast of the Cap Vert peninsula, and many are also members of a Sufi order, the Layene, founded by a member of their own ethnic group, Seydina Limamou Laye (1843–1909). Many Lebu villages, such as Yoff and Ouakam, are quickly becoming part of the greater urban area of Dakar.

---

[14] The possibility of a pro-Wolof bias in these studies is raised in Dreyfus and Juillard (2004: 8 note 8)

The Pulaar- or Fula-speaking populations of Senegal constitute approximately 23 per cent of the population and go by several different names that refer to different groups of people. The most all-encompassing ethnic term is Haalpulaar, a word that means 'speaker of Pulaar', and which can include all Pulaar speakers or only those who are also called Tukulor, depending on the specific language ideology of those using the terms. Tukulor is a term that is probably of Wolof origin and designates, roughly, the historically Muslim and settled – as opposed to pastoralist (and more recently converted to Islam) – Pulaar speakers from the northern part of the country that used to be called Tekrur, a name that gave rise to the term Tukulor. A certain number of patronyms (e.g. Ka, Kane, Pam, Athie, Agne) appear to be exclusive to this group as opposed to other patronyms (e.g. Bâ, Sow, Diallo) that are found among Pulaar-speaking populations throughout West Africa. The third term is Pullo (sg.)/Fulɓe (pl.), which is more generally used by pastoralist, or originally pastoralist, cattle-herding Pulaar-speakers throughout West Africa. Pulaar, or Fulfulde as its eastern dialects are known, is spoken throughout a vast area of West Africa by more than 12 million people but it is a minority language in every country where it is spoken. This unique position of Pulaar as a major international West African language but the dominant language of no nation has contributed to a certain vigilance on the part of its speakers who want to make sure that their language is not placed in jeopardy by large-scale language shift to dominant national languages such as Wolof. The sense of belonging to a wider, international community of Pulaar speakers is an important factor in maintaining this vigilance and legitimates the rationale and ideology of those who prefer to use the term Haalpulaar to designate all Pulaar speakers rather than just a Tukulor subset. This vigilance manifested itself particularly in a militant Haalpulaar movement that emerged among student groups in the 1980s and is still very active today.

Speakers of several mutually unintelligible languages in Senegal go by the ethnic designation of Seereer, and constitute approximately 15 per cent of the Senegalese population. These include speakers of the various major dialects of Seereer such as the designated standard variety, Seereer-Siin, as well as other regional varieties such as Nyominka, spoken in the Saloum islands, and the dialects of the Petite Côte. While these varieties are mutual intelligible, there are other small groups known as Seereer, located in the hilly area around the city of Thiès and southward, who speak five recognizably Atlantic languages that are not mutually intelligible with Seereer-Siin and have differing but not very high levels of mutual intelligibility among themselves (Williams 1994). These languages are known as the Cangin languages, so dubbed by Pichl (1966) after the local name for Thiès. They include Lehar, Palor, Safi-Safi, Non, and Ndut.

The Joola ethnic group, concentrated in Lower Casamance, also consists of speakers of a cluster of languages and dialects that have varying degrees of mutual intelligibility, with Joola Foñi or Kujamaat Joola being the lingua franca of this linguistically dense area. The Joola comprise somewhere between 5 and 6 per cent of the population of Senegal. A shared sense of Joola identity among speakers of the various languages in the Joola cluster is based on shared cultural practices, and since they are the dominant ethnic group of the Casamance, it is also based on the sense of an identity that is separate from that of the northern part of Senegal.[15]

A significant number of minority ethnic groups is also concentrated in Casmance. These include the Mancagne, Manjak, and Balante, as well as the Bassari in Upper Casamance. They contribute to the relatively high rate of multilingualism in the region, and use several vehicular languages including Malinke or Soose, Portuguese Creole, and sometimes Pulaar.

Speakers of Mande languages in Senegal constitute only 6 per cent of the population, but they belong to a much larger linguistic and ethnic area that encompasses a large part of West Africa.[16] Malinke or Soose is also used as a lingua franca in the area of Casamance north of the Casamance river. Like the Haalpulaar, the Saraxole and Soose share a great number of cultural traits with groups in the Gambia, Guinea, Mali, Ivory Coast, and even further afield, including a major West African oral tradition to which belongs the epic of Sunjata, founder of the Mali empire. There is thus a sense among them of belonging to a group that transcends national borders, although this sentiment has never been mobilized politically the way it has – with devastating results – in Ivory Coast.

In the light of Senegal's linguistic pluralism, the question of how Wolof has come to dominate on the national scene becomes a more interesting one. In the next section I discuss the phenomenon of Wolofization and the emergence of Wolof as a national lingua franca.

5.4 Wolofization

Wolofization, or the spread of Wolof as a lingua franca in Senegal, is by no means a recent phenomenon, although it has gained significant momentum with the rapid increase in urbanization that began in the mid-twentieth century. Currently, upwards of 90 per cent of the Senegalese population use Wolof as either a first or second language, and as urbanization increases this figure is likely to go up. The origins of Wolofization are to be found in pre-colonial times when the language was used as a lingua franca in the northern part of Senegal, but it gained impetus with the development of an urban coastal culture during the eighteenth and nineteenth centuries, and since that time has been associated with urbanization and modernity.

5.4.1 The History of Wolofization

Historical evidence tells us that Wolof was used as a lingua franca in the northern part of Senegal, especially between the Wolof and Seereer kingdoms, at least as early as the sixteenth century (Klein 1968), and possibly even earlier. The Wolof kingdoms of

---

[15] For a look at language and identity in Ziguinchor as compared to Dakar, see Dreyfus and Juillard's detailed 2004 study.

[16] Mansour (1993) in particular insists on the cultural unity of Mande-speaking West Africa and focuses on mutual intelligibility among the Mande languages to suggest that they are actually dialects of a single language. While Soose may fall into this category in the case of Senegal, Soninke / Saraxole does not.

Bawol and Jolof abutted the Seereer kingdom of Saalum to the south, but there were also pockets of Seereer living within the Wolof kingdoms. Wolof political, cultural, and linguistic influence on the Seereer is widely attested in the historical literature, so it is highly probable that Wolof was first used as a lingua franca in contact between these two groups. These facts help explain the widespread and long-standing bilingualism of the Seereer and the relative monolingualism of Wolof speakers who did not – and still do not – need to know other languages in order to communicate with their neighbours. It may also be one of the most important factors in explaining why there is so little dialectal diversity in Wolof and why the language is so similar from region to region – a situation that we would expect of a lingua franca since its speakers would be in frequent contact with each other.[17]

The coastal areas of northern Senegal where early sustained contact with Europeans occurred lay within the Wolof kingdoms of Waalo and Kajoor. It was here that the Atlantic cities of Saint-Louis and Gorée were first established, making of Wolof an urban language. Eighteenth-century French sources comment on the use of Wolof in these two cities, strongly advising potential traders to learn it lest they be tricked in their commercial negotiations (Searing 2005). But realistically, the French had to rely on the services of interpreters, known as *laptots*, who accompanied them on military and commercial ventures up the Senegal River from Saint-Louis. The *laptots* would certainly have played an important role in spreading Wolof along these riverine networks into the Pulaar-speaking region of Fuuta Toro.

Urban Wolof is today characterized by extensive borrowing from French, a situation that some have viewed as a post-colonial phenomenon, but there is good evidence that such was already the case by the middle of the nineteenth century, at least in Saint-Louis which was the most important city at the time (McLaughlin, forthcoming, b). It is highly unlikely that this hybrid dialect arose out of widespread societal bilingualism in Wolof and French, but rather it emerged as a prestigious urban code, modelled after the speech of a small group of bilingual elites, including the *métis* or mixed-race populations of Saint-Louis, who dominated commercial and political life at the time.

Dakar was founded in 1857, and many of those who first settled in the city came from Saint-Louis and Gorée, bringing their urban ways of speaking with them. During the first half of the twentieth century the role of Wolof as a commercial language was further strengthened by the implantation of Wolof merchants throughout the territory, including Casamance, and in particular the regional capital of Ziguinchor. The establishment of Dakar first as the capital of French West Africa and then of the newly independent nation in 1960 resulted in rapid population growth in the city. Those who arrived in the city soon learned Wolof, and today the percentage of the Dakar population that speaks the language is estimated to be higher than that of the nation as a whole, reaching a figure of approximately 96 per cent (Cissé 2005).

---

[17] That the lack of dialectal differentiation in Wolof is a research question that needs to be explained was raised by Irvine (2006).

5.4.2 The Emergence of a National Language

The history of Wolofization since the seventeenth century is intimately related to the history of urbanization in Senegal, and the language is consequently associated with urbanity and modernity, all the more so for its liberal use of French loans in the urban dialects. It is perhaps this characteristic that distinguishes it most from rural varieties and makes it recognizably urban, and since urban ways of speaking are brought back to smaller towns and villages by those who go to the city to work, it is also a variety that continues to be spread. As the Wolof language spreads and new urban immigrants start to use it on an everyday basis and in their own households, a generational linguistic shift to Wolof commonly occurs. In such contexts, when language and ethnicity become conflated, more and more people identify themselves as Wolof.

Being Wolof in an urban context can, however, mean many things since, as argued in McLaughlin (2001), Wolof is often used as a convenient term for an urban identity. A telling example comes from a Haalpulaar schoolteacher from the town of Fatick who claimed, 'When I am at home I am Haalpulaar, when I am in Dakar I am Wolof,' (McLaughlin 1995: 156), by which he meant that in Dakar he is as fully integrated an urbanite as anyone else. Paradoxically, however, the negative attributes of urban life have also been projected onto the concept of Wolof as both an ethnic group and a language. Speakers of other languages are quick to point out all the French loans in urban Wolof as a sign that Wolof speakers cannot even speak their own language well because they have been uprooted from their culture.[18] One of the reactions to these accusations of inauthenticity is the abandonment of an identity based on ethnicity in favour of an explicitly urban identity, especially among younger Dakarois who do not identify with any ethnic group, but simply say they are from Dakar. Urbanization and Wolofization are thus having a profound effect on the notion of ethnicity in Senegal. How this will eventually play out remains to be seen, but if ethnic allegiances are starting to be downplayed in the construction of identity, then the transnational allegiances based on ethnicity among Pulaar speakers and Mande speakers discussed in section 5.3.2 may also start to diminish. The de-ethnicization process that comes directly from Wolofization may eventually contribute to a stronger sense of Senegalese nationalism.

In examining how Wolof has emerged as the de facto national language of Senegal we can point to four main factors. First is the long history of the use of Wolof as a lingua franca, dating from pre-colonial times; second is the fact that Wolof was spoken in coastal areas where cities were first established and thus became an urban language; third is the intense and rapid increase in urbanization from the middle of the twentieth century; and fourth is the fact that the language has never been officially promoted through government policies, and thus there has been no real basis on which to oppose Wolofization on an official level.

---

[18] In McLaughlin (2001: 164ff) I point out that urban varieties of Pulaar and Seereer both exhibit extensive borrowing from French, but the loans are better disguised, thus not always recognized as such, because of the complex morpho-phonology of those two languages, and consonant mutation in particular.

5.4.3 From National to Global Language

The Senegalese have long participated in various transnational and global networks of trade and migration. Senegalese traders have been an important presence in various African countries, including Ivory Coast, Gabon, and South Africa, and there are also significant communities of Senegalese immigrants in France and other European countries as well as in the United States. Most recently, Senegal has been at the forefront of discussions on the illegal emigration of Africans to Europe, since a great number of the boats that leave Africa packed with would-be emigrants heading for the Canary Islands leave from Senegal. Wolof is most often the language that Senegalese of different linguistic backgrounds use as they leave home and insert themselves into Senegalese networks throughout the world. In many cases, the Senegalese traders are members of the Murid Sufi order and depend on the social and commercial networks that have been developed around this order. The Murid order has its origins in the early twentieth century in the Wolof-speaking heartlands of Senegal and its members use Wolof in both their religious activities (in conjunction with Arabic) and in their commercial activities both at home and abroad. The Wolofization process that occurs at a national level in Senegal is also being reinforced abroad as Wolof is used as the lingua franca in these trade networks, and thus it is also taking on something of a global aspect, or at least globalization is reinforcing Wolofization.[19]

5.5 A Francophone Country?

The discussion of language and national identity has, up to now, focused on the first definition of national identity, namely the population's relationship and sense of belonging to a nation-state. I turn now to the second definition of the identity of an individual nation-state within the international world order, where Senegal is quite clearly identified as a francophone state although the number of French speakers among the Senegalese population is estimated at somewhere between 10 and 24 per cent.[20]

5.5.1 Francophonie and the Senegalese State

The concept of *francophonie* is a complex one, fraught as it is with the ambivalence of the relationship between France and its former colonies, and spurred on by the spectre of English as a global language. But what exactly does francophone mean? Senegal is a francophone country not because it has a predominantly French-speaking population, but because it was a former French colony and because French is its official language. Being a francophone nation thus implies belonging to an international network of alliances at many levels. Former president Senghor recognized the value of these

---

[19] For a more in-depth discussion of issues related to Wolofization and globalization see McLaughlin (forthcoming, a).

[20] Cissé (2005: 272) reports that the 1990 report from the *Haut Conseil de la Francophonie* puts the number of 'real francophones' at 10 per cent and 'occasional francophones' at 14 per cent.

international networks and insisted on maintaining and promoting the use of French
as Senegal's official language despite his political adversaries' claims that continued
reliance and attachment to francophone networks amounted to little more than neo-
colonialism in both an economic and ideological sense. His successors, Abdou Diouf –
currently Secretary General of the *Organisation Internationale de la Francophonie* –
as well as Abdoulaye Wade, have both maintained strong ties to the international
francophone networks. With the decline of French and the rise of English as the
international language, the concept of *francophonie* has become all the more important
to France and to partially francophone Western countries like Canada and Belgium
where language policies are an important issue in domestic politics. This community
is always eager to embrace Senegal as a francophone nation and to accord it political
and economic favours by virtue of its francophone status. Whether or not Senegal
is in reality a French-speaking nation is not really relevant to its membership in the
international network of francophone states since *francophonie* is only partly about
language and mostly about politics.

5.5.2 French in Senegal

As the discussions in section 5.2 have shown, Senegal has had a long-standing official
policy of promoting French in the areas of government, bureaucracy, and education
while allowing just enough official space for indigenous languages to prevent language issues from becoming too politicized. Even initiatives that ostensibly promoted
national languages and required substantial human and financial resources such as the
1961 establishment of the Centre de Linguistique Appliquée de Dakar (CLAD) had
as their goal the promotion of French. The mandate of the linguists at CLAD was to
produce a series of studies on Senegalese languages with the primary goal of designing
better techniques to teach French to speakers of those languages.

As the official language of government and education, and other than in a small
percentage of elite French-speaking households, the French language is transmitted
through the school system in Senegal. Most schoolchildren learn French at school
from Senegalese teachers who may themselves have learned the language from other
Senegalese. Partially as a consequence of this shift in the educational system away
from native French speakers from the metropole as models – a situation that was
common up to and just after Senegalese independence from France – towards Senegalese speakers as models, a distinctive Senegalese variety of French has emerged
and has become the unmarked norm. Senegalese French incorporates many prosodic
and grammatical features from Wolof and other Senegalese languages, and its most
salient characteristics include the apical [r] as opposed to the metropolitan uvular [ʁ], a
tendency towards word-initial stress, the insertion of an epenthetic consonant such as a
glottal stop or glide at the beginning of otherwise onsetless syllables (e.g. [də.wɔɔr] for
dehors 'outside'), the breaking up of certain consonant clusters with epenthetic vowels,
and the use of the French pluperfect as a past tense without implying any anteriority
to another event.

A second way in which French has been appropriated in Senegal is through its inclusion as a lexifier language in the hybrid varieties of urban Wolof. Although the grammatical structure of Wolof remains largely intact in the urban dialects, they include large numbers of French loans. These mixed varieties have in turn led to the reinforcement of French in Senegal since migrants to the city who are first exposed to this urban way of speaking may eventually learn French. If education in Senegal continues to be in French – and there is every expectation that it will, even if eventually in tandem with education in national languages – and as school attendance increases, it is likely that proficiency in French will increase among the general population and that urban Wolof will continue to borrow liberally from French.

The effects of the global shift towards English as the main international language have also been felt in some unique ways in Senegal. An older generation of French-educated elites who held white-collar jobs was often not interested in promoting widespread proficiency in French and high standards of education among the general population because it would open the door to more competition for them and their own presumably well-educated children in a limited job market, a phenomenon that Myers-Scotton (1993) has dubbed elite closure. But the time has passed when mastery of French and a good education were the key to economic success. Senegal's economic growth, modest as it may be, and especially the building boom that is in evidence in Dakar and other parts of the country, is due in large part to the entrepreneurial efforts of emigrants and their international commercial networks and the remittances they send home. Opportunities abroad attract both those for whom formal education has not opened any doors and those who have little or no formal education and certainly do not speak French. Many emigrants find English to be a more useful language than French, and when they return to Senegal they bring with them a new and prestigious type of Wolof that incorporates a large number of English loans.

5.6 Conclusion

Although it is considered, with good reason, to be a francophone country in the international context, Senegal is in reality a multilingual but predominantly Wolof-speaking country. Wolof has emerged as the informal national language in large part because Wolofization is an informal process that has had no official backing. As Abdoulaye Wade's ill-fated proposition has shown, any official attempts to promote Wolof over and above any other Senegalese language constitute a substantial political risk, a situation that reinforces an official policy of promoting French. But even those who oppose the elevation of Wolof to any higher official status are also almost certain to use the language in their own daily interactions, and it is difficult even for those most opposed to Wolofization to resist participation in what Cruise O'Brien (2003: 140) terms 'an undirected social movement' that has played and continues to play a central role in defining the identity of the nation.

6

Mali: In Defence of Cultural and Linguistic Pluralism

Ingse Skattum

6.1 Introduction

Mali is a landlocked country bounded by seven states: Senegal in the west, Mauritania and Algeria in the north, Niger and Burkina Faso in the east, the Ivory Coast and Guinea in the south. It is one of Africa's largest countries and is divided into three climatic zones: the Sahara desert in the north, the semi-desert Sahel in the centre, and the Sudanese savannah in the south. Most of the approximately 13 million inhabitants live in the south and along the two main rivers, the Niger (which is Africa's third largest) and the Senegal. Gold and cotton are main exports, Mali being Africa's second largest cotton producer after Egypt. It is, however, one of the poorest countries in the world, coming 174th of 177 countries in the Human Development Indicator (HDI) of the United Nations Development Programme, which takes into account standard of living, life expectancy, and literacy. Statistics show that the fertility rate is high (nearly 7 children per woman), infant mortality amongst the world's highest (11.3 per cent), while life expectancy is only 48.5 years and nearly 50 per cent of the population is under 15 years of age. The literacy rate is 19 per cent and school enrolment 26 per cent.[1] Around 90 per cent of the population is Muslim, 9 per cent are animists, and 1 per cent Christian. Animism influences both Muslim and Christian practices, and religious tolerance is the rule. The capital Bamako, in the southern part of the country, has approximately 1 million inhabitants. Other important cities are Segu, Sikasso, Koutiala, Kayes, Mopti, Djenne, Timbuktu, and Gao. The country was colonized by France between 1880 and 1895 and named French Sudan in 1892. It was proclaimed an independent republic on 22 September 1960, when it took the name of the prestigious medieval Mali Empire. Since 1960, there have been three Malian republics: the first under Modibo Keita (1960–68), the second under General Moussa Traoré (1968–1991) and the third under democratically elected presidents Alpha Oumar Konaré (1992– 2002) and Amadou Toumani Touré (2002–).

[1] The above figures are all from *L'état de l'Afrique 2005* (2005) (Paris: Jeune Afrique / L'Intelligent).

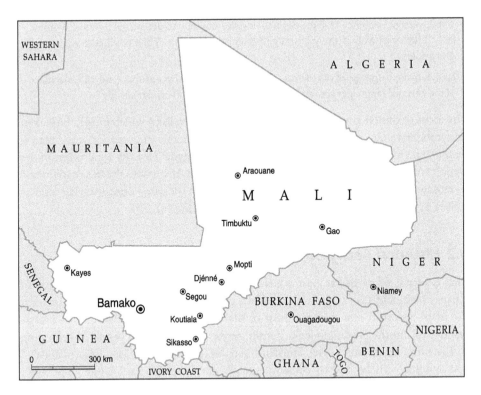

Mali

French is the official language, but mastered by only 5 to 10 per cent of the population. Mali consequently has proportionately fewer speakers of French (as either a first or second language) among its population than any other francophone state south of the Sahara.[2] This is partly because Mali is one of the few francophone countries to have an endogenous majority language, Bambara, which is spoken by around 40 per cent as mother tongue and another 40 per cent as lingua franca. Bambara has not however been granted any particular status: it is one of thirteen Malian languages recognized as 'national languages'. This status implies their codification (officially recognized alphabet and orthography) as well as their use in some domains of the public sphere, of which the most important is the educational sector. Mali is one of the few francophone sub-Saharan countries to have introduced national languages as means of instruction into its educational system. Mali is also exceptional in that it defends its cultural and linguistic pluralism in the 1992 Constitution:

---

[2] Not counting Mauritania, which has joined the *Grand Maghreb* and changed its official language to Arabic.

The Sovereign People of Mali proclaim their determination to defend the rights of Women and Children as well as the cultural and linguistic diversity of the national community. (Preamble)

French is the language of official expression. The modes of promotion and officialization of the national languages are determined by the law.   (Title II, article 25)[3]

The focus of this chapter will be on the defence of pluralism, which in Mali has taken on symbolic value as a mark of national identity. The main – though not only – reason seems to lie in the country's multi-ethnic and multilingual past. As a journalist of the weekly magazine *Jeune Afrique* put it: 'Nowhere else in Africa does the desire to unite – to reunite – which is a legacy from the past – take on the same obsessive character as it does in this north-west part of Africa' (Andriamirado 1987: 59).

6.2 Historical Background

Mali is proud of its heroic past which includes the great West African empires of Ghana, Mali, and Gao (eighth to sixteenth centuries). This 'golden age' constitutes the main historical reference for most of Mali's ethnic groups today, and to a large extent explains the prevailing feeling amongst the majority of the people of belonging to the same community. The founding peoples, the Soninke, Maninka (*Malinké*),[4] and Songhay, can be said to constitute Mali's core population (Diakité 1989: 136). The three empires however included vast territories and many populations. Hence multiculturalism and multilingualism within the state is part of the Malian legacy.

The first of these empires was Ghana (eighth to eleventh centuries), situated at the crossroads of present-day Mauritania and Mali and founded by Soninke clans who spoke the same language. They united under the pressure of nomads from the north and founded their state on the trans-Saharan trade (mostly gold from the south and salt from the north). Ruling over both black and Berber chiefdoms, they assured peace and order in the region and tolerated Islam, though they themselves were animists. The empire was however destroyed by Berber Muslims in the eleventh century (Ki-Zerbo 1978: 110).

The Mali empire (thirteenth to fifteenth centuries) was founded by Maninka clans who, in spite of a common language and culture, fought one another until they were united by Sunjata Keita in 1235. Sunjata defined the roles of the different clans and the rights and duties of the associated ethnic groups (distribution of professions and hierarchical status). This social organization lasted for centuries and still exists to some degree. The Maninka lived in the Mande mountains on the border of today's Mali and Guinea. Sunjata extended his realm mainly to the west, the empire stretching from the Atlantic Ocean to the river Niger and from the Sahara to the tropical forests in the

---

[3] All translations from French are the author's.

[4] I use the most common English names but also give French or local names where there may be doubt if we are speaking of the same language or ethnic group.

south. As Islam gained ground under this empire, the learned centres of Timbuktu and Djenne were established (Diakité 1989; Ki-Zerbo 1978).

In the middle of the fifteenth century, Mali declined and the Gao empire took over. The Songhay clans united under Sonni Ali Ber, who conquered Timbuktu and Djenne and then the Macina region (in the centre of today's Mali) as well as the Mossi kingdom (in today's Burkina Faso). One of his successors, Askia Mohammed, enforced Islam on his subjects and enlarged the empire so that it covered most of West Africa from the Atlantic Ocean to the Hausa cities of Kano and Katsina in present-day Nigeria. By the end of the sixteenth century, the capital Gao was the biggest city in West Africa, but internal feuds of succession weakened the dynasty, which in 1591 was conquered by the Moroccans (Ki-Zerbo 1978).

According to Diakité (1989), the process of state-building is the same in these three cases: clans who recognize a common cultural and linguistic heritage unite under a single political and military rule. This ethnic consolidation and homogenization is followed by an extension of the state which implies the submission of other groups. These states thus all become multi-ethnic and multilingual, and other ethnic processes are engaged, varying from mere neighbour relationships to mixing/restructuring and assimilation. The ethnic groups which found themselves united under the same political rule included, besides the founders, amongst others the Fulani (*Peul*), Serere, Berber, Arabs, Bozo, and Tuareg. The history of these groups cannot be dissociated from that of their neighbours.

Among the most important integrational factors were economy and in particular religion. The trans-Saharan trade led to the establishment of great markets and commercial cities which attracted different ethnic groups. These centres contributed to the spread of Islam, which in its turn became the most important uniting factor. The Muslims shared religious practices: prayers, mosques, and days of celebration. Islam became part of their identity and sometimes overruled ethnic relationships. The Maninka for instance considered themselves as different from the Bambara, who were ethnically and linguistically close relatives, but who for a long time refused Islam, sticking to their animist beliefs (Diakité 1989: 141–2).[5] Devisse (1989: 106) describes how, for safety reasons, both individuals and groups would sometimes change their ethnic identity and adopt that of a Muslim community. Other groups are known to posterity through Arab chroniclers only from the moment these chroniclers found them worthy of mention because they adopted Islam (ibid.: 110). Another token of the role Islam played for identity is the fact that some ethnic groups altered their myths of origin to fit in with an oriental, Muslim origin, considered more prestigious (ibid.) This is the case for instance for the Manding peoples (consisting of the closely related Maninka, Bambara, and Diula groups) (ibid.: 114).

The ethno-cultural interaction within the empires in some cases led to ethnic restructuring through mixing and/or assimilation. Diakité (1989) mentions two cases

---

[5] Even today, Bambara can be used as a synonym for 'pagan'.

where new ethnic groups seem to have emerged. The Marka, who live in the Macina region, are often said to be Soninke, but are in fact a result of Soninke migration after Ghana's downfall. The migrants married into local families of Fulani, Bambara, Bozo, and Somono origin. Though many Marka are traders like the Soninke, they also do farming, and they speak Bambara. The Arma group is another case, being the result of Moroccan conquerors marrying local Songhay women. They usually consider themselves as Arabs from Timbuktu, descendants of the Prophet, and they speak both Arabic and Songhay.

The assimilation of smaller ethnic groups or of individuals into bigger, dominating groups, with partial or total loss of proper ethnic traits, are also documented through Arab chronicles. They were the results of different migrations due to war, commerce, Islamic studies or natural catastrophes like drought. The assimilation could be natural (mixed marriages were frequent) or enforced (slave concubines), and lead to the adoption of the language, culture, and even patronym of the dominating partner (though the slave status was not forgotten). Assimilation has touched all ethnic groups in the region and probably explains why one meets the same patronymic names in most of the ethnic groups today and last, but not least, why ethnic groups in general co-exist peacefully.

During the great empires, the West African Sahel belt was thus a true melting pot where unifying forces led to ethnic consolidation (clans uniting in state structures), mixing, and/or assimilation. According to Diakité, the West African empires created a homogeneous culture, despite ethnic particularities. To this effect he cites the French anthropologist Olivier de Sardan:

> Throughout the centuries, contact between peoples and a common environment has created compatible and sometimes even homogenous social structures. But variation has not been wiped out, cultural differences and different ways of living prevail, as can be seen from the existence of distinct languages and production modes (sedentary agriculture/semi-nomadic animal breeding).   (cited in Diakité 1989: 146)

Though the unifying forces are the main characteristic of this period, centrifugal forces also existed, migrations leading some related groups to separate, in search of better living conditions. However, here I have emphasized the integrational forces in order to explain the present ethnic and linguistic situation, which, with the exception of the Tuareg rebellions, is characterized by great tolerance and peaceful cohabitation.

After the great empires followed a period of internal wars and the appearance of smaller states, most often ethnically based. In Mali, the most important of these are the Bambara kingdom of Segu and the Fulani kingdom of Macina. The Segu kingdom (eighteenth to nineteenth centuries) stretched from Mande to Timbuktu along the Niger river, including the Macina region and the cities of Djenne and Timbuktu, later also Kaarta (another Bambara kingdom to the northwest), and the lands of the Dogon and the Mossi to the east.

The Macina region, where the Fulani were dominant, was long ruled by the Bambara, but in the early nineteenth century the Fulani Cheiku Amadu defeated the Bambara, conquered Djenne and in 1825 also Timbuktu. He installed an Islamic state with mass conversion to Islam. El Hadj Umar Tall, a Tukulor (ethnically closely related to the Fulani) of Senegalese origin, launched a sacred war and attacked the pagan Bambara as well as the Muslim Fulani of Cheiku Amadu (who belonged to a different Muslim brotherhood). He founded another theocratic state on the banks of the Niger, but succumbed to the French when they arrived in Mali at the end of the nineteenth century. Under general Faidherbe, governor of Senegal, a treaty was signed between the French and El Hadj Umar Tall's son Amadu in 1866, a treaty which paved the way for the French conquest.

The French however met strong resistance from the Diula Almami Samori Touré, a chief of war who had built a Manding 'empire' on the borders of Guinea, the Ivory Coast, and Mali. He fought the French for seventeen years before he was captured in 1898 and sent into exile in Gabon, where he died in 1900. He is admired for his courage and military genius, and in particular for his resistance to the French, but at the same time hated for his brutal subjugation of other African peoples.

The French colonization, which in Mali officially lasted from 1892 till 1960, imposed French law, administration, and not least, schools and language on the region. The impact of these sixty to seventy years of French colonization is of course very important, but not as strong as in many other former French colonies in sub-Saharan Africa. The rich historical and cultural heritage as well as the long habit of ethnic co-existence and mixing are major factors in Mali's resistance to French influence and Malians' attachment to their own traditions and languages.

Since independence in 1960, there have been three Malian republics. In 1968, the first president, Modibo Keita, was overthrown in a military coup led by Lieutenant Moussa Traoré – himself overthrown in 1991 by Colonel Amadou Toumani Touré (called ATT). ATT led a transitional government until the democratic elections in 1992, which were won by Alpha Oumar Konaré. Alpha (as he is called) managed to resolve the Tuareg rebellion (1990–96), and this was marked by the burning of weapons in the 1996 'Flame of Peace'. In 1994 Moussa Traoré was taken to court in what has been considered a fair trial. Though he was sentenced to death, it was clear he would not be executed, and he was later set free in keeping with a Malian tradition of *pardon* (Skattum 1998). Konaré was re-elected in 1997 and left office in 2002 after two terms, in accordance with the Constitution (a rare event in Africa). The same year, he was appointed secretary general of the African Union's Commission, a privileged position allowing him to fight for the panafricanism he believes in:

> To keep our pledge to the peoples of Africa, we must create one great country, Africa, with African citizens, a truly African Africa of solidarity and responsibility.   (Konaré 2005: 12)

Though panafricanism embraces a wider cultural and linguistic diversity than the West African empires, it is in its way also a legacy from the past.

Konaré's predecessor ATT, who enjoyed great respect for the way he lead the transition to democracy in 1991–2, won the elections as an independent candidate in 2002. Leaning on different coalition governments, he rules according to a 'consensus' practice with roots in the African tradition of *palabre* (gatherings where everyone has the right to express their view). Since 1992, Mali has thus been recognized for its good governance.

Contemporary Mali is not however without conflicts. One of the main problems has been the strikes organized since 1992 by the AEEM (*Association des Elèves et Etudiants du Mali*), who were central in the overthrow of Moussa Traoré. The strikes as well as the riots and violence that have followed have hampered schooling and contributed to what is generally considered a degradation of the educational level of Malian students (Diakité 2000). This also goes for their linguistic competence in French.

6.3 The National Languages: an Overview

As the historical background will have shown, the boundaries between ethnic groups in Mali are uncertain, due to the mixing and assimilation of populations. Besides, their numbers are approximate, since none of the censuses (1976, 1987, 1998) have asked for ethnic or religious affiliation. The 1987 census did, however, ask for mother tongue and other languages spoken (*Recensement général de la population et de l'habitat*, 1987).

But there is no one-to-one link between ethnicity and language. As Vydrine puts it:

> It is well known in West Sudan that a person's ethnic belonging depends above all on his origin and not on his language or culture. In other words, his ethnic and linguistic profiles do not necessarily coincide, especially in urban settings, where very often the 'first' language is different from the 'father' or 'mother' tongue.   (Vydrine 1994: 200)

Estimates of the number of local languages vary greatly for reasons well known: unclear borders between language and dialect, lack of linguistic research, migrations, language shift, widespread multilingualism, and difficulties defining which are the first, second, and subsequent languages. The method adopted by linguists to distinguish between dialect and language is particularly important for the estimates. The Summer Institute of Linguistics (SIL) thus counts fifty endogenous languages in Mali (*Ethnologue* 2005: 141), while Maho (2001: 106) names twenty-seven languages. Most sources, like Canut and Dumestre (1993: 220) and Calvet (1992: 215), give estimates of around twenty languages. This is a moderate number in the African context and partly explains the fact that Mali is able to defend its multilingualism in practice, at least to some extent.

Of these languages, thirteen have been given the status of national languages. They belong to three language families: the Niger-Congo, the Nilo-Saharan, and the

Afro-Asiatic. One language, Dogon, is unclassified[6] and several others are not defini-
tively classified.[7] The Niger-Congo family is the most important in Mali as in Africa
in general. In Mali, it is represented by the Mande group, the Atlantic group, and the
Gur group (often called voltaic, from the name of the Volta river). The Mande group
is the most important of these, including the dominating Manding cluster (Bambara,
Maninka, Diula, and Xassonke)[8] and two West Mande languages: Soninke and Bozo.
The Atlantic group is represented by Fulfulde (*peul*), and the Gur group includes
Syenara (*sénoufo*), Mamara (*minyanka*), and Bomu (*bwamu, bobo*). The Nilo-Saharan
family is represented only by Songhay (whose classification is still under discussion).
The two languages of the Afro-Asiatic family are the Berber language Tamachek of the
Tuareg people and the Semitic language Hassaniyya (*maure*) of the Moores.

Ten of these languages were made national languages as early as 1967: Bambara,
Bomu, Bozo, Dogon, Fulfulde, Mamara, Syenara, Songhay, Soninke, and Tamachek,
to which were added in 1996, nearly thirty years later, Hassaniyya, Maninka, and
Xassonke. Though all thirteen languages have thus been accorded the same national
language status, they are actually very different in terms of usage (number of speakers
and domains of usage), diffusion (local, regional, national, or international), standardization (choice of dialect, development of orthographic rules) and intellectualization
(the existence of modern terminology), dynamics (usage advancing, declining, or
remaining stable), as well as their internal relationship (dialect/language).

The number of speakers of the twenty or so languages is uncertain as well, varying
from a couple of thousand to several million. The 1987 census language questions
concerned citizens over 6 years of age, totalling nearly 6 million speakers. I will refer
to this census to give an idea of the relative numerical importance of the national
languages, though it has to be realized that there are now around 13 million inhabitants
and that usage is also undergoing change.

All but Hassaniyya, which is written in Arabic script, have been given an alphabet
in Latin script.

In the following presentation of Mali's sociolinguistic profile I will limit myself to
the thirteen national languages that the state itself has indicated as the most important
by giving them official recognition. I will look first at the dominant role of the majority
language Bambara, thereafter at the situation for the other national languages. Finally
I will describe the very different roles that the two imported languages, Arabic and
French, play in the country today.

---

[6] It was formerly classified within the Gur group.

[7] For historical overviews and discussions, see Platiel and Kaboré (1998); Heine and Nurse (2000, 2004);
Maho (2001); Childs (2003); *Ethnologue* (2005). *Ethnologue*, which is often cited, is surprisingly inaccurate
with regard to the formal status of languages, stating in its 12th ed. that French is 'used for government
purposes but [is] not an official language' (1991: 300), and in its 15th ed. putting French and Malian
languages on equal footing: 'National or official languages: French, Bamanankan, [...].' (2005: 141)

[8] French linguists have suggested that the term Manding (or *mandingue*) be replaced by *mandenkan*,
based on the indigenous terms *Manden* for the area and *kan* 'language'. This term has however not yet
supplanted the well established French term *manding(ue)*.

6.4 Bambara Domination

Bambara is estimated to be spoken by around 40 per cent of the population as first language (L1) (the 1987 census, which regroups Bambara, Maninka, and Diula gives an estimate of 50 per cent: nearly 3 million out of approximately 6 million citizens). It is spoken by another 40 per cent as 'second' language (L2, L3, etc.). Though the heartland of Bambara lies in southern Mali, in Bamako and in Segu, the capital of the ancient Bambara kingdom, Bambara is advancing in all regions of Mali. This concerns its use both as first and second language, as shown by several sociolinguistic studies (Barry 1990; Calvet 1992; Vydrine 1994; Dombrowsky 1993, 1994; Canut and Keita 1994; Canut 1996). Neither its dominant position nor its dynamic character is however new. In one of the earliest scientific works on the Manding cluster, or language as he calls it, Maurice Delafosse[9] noted that it was one of the most important languages in West Africa, and that this was for historical, political, economical, administrative, and military reasons. He particularly mentioned its prestige in the middle ages and observed that it has continued to gain ground since then. Its dynamic character is even more noticeable today and is attributed by Dumestre (1994b, 2003) to several factors. First of all, there is the development of public administration and the role that civil servants coming from Bamako (who normally use Bambara, though they master French) play in spreading Bambara to the urban centres of all regions. Second, there is the improved infrastructure which allows people to travel more freely (facilitating seasonal migrations and rural exodus). Third, the spread of Islam, which often uses Bambara for preaching, also functions as a support, and even the small Catholic congregation, traditionally supportive of French (as opposed to Protestant churches, which prefer local languages), now to a certain extent uses Bambara in its services. Fourth, the homogeneous character of the language itself also facilitates communication: unlike the smaller languages Dogon, Bozo, and Mamara it is not divided into heterogeneous dialects. Between the Manding languages, the common lexical stock exceeds 85 per cent in every case and between Bambara, Maninka, and Diula syntactical variation is small as well. Bambara is furthermore, along with French, the only language that is spoken all over the national territory. The only serious resistance to Bambara domination (which is cultural, economic, and political as well as linguistic) is found in the north, far from the capital, among the Songhay and Tamachek speakers, who are culturally quite different from the southern ethnic groups (Canut 1996). In this region, Songhay has functioned as a lingua franca for centuries, while the Tuareg have been opposed to central authorities. Both of these groups in general prefer French in inter-ethnic communication.

One of the first sociolinguistic surveys in Mali (Barry 1990), conducted in the multilingual city of Djenne where nine languages are spoken, with Fulani and Songhay as the dominant ethnic groups, clearly demonstrated how Bambara had become the

---

[9] M. Delafosse, *La langue mandingue et ses dialectes (malinké, bambara, dioula)* (Paris: Geuthner), cited in Dumestre (2003: 7).

principal means of communication, gaining new territory and new domains. While only one-third of the schoolchildren taking part in the survey had Bambara as their first language, all of them could speak it, and 46 per cent of them spoke Bambara at home. The survey also revealed that the majority of marketplace transactions took place in Bambara, and that, since 1980, every play at the annual theatre festival was performed in Bambara. Kayes, Mopti, and Koutiala are further examples of towns where Bambara has become the most commonly spoken language (Dumestre 2003: 8).

As a first language, Bambara has a tendency to replace both related languages like Maninka (Canut and Keita 1994) and distinct languages like Mamara (Dombrowsky 1993, 1994) in regions where these languages have traditionally been dominant. Individuals coming to Bamako also tend to shift to Bambara as their major/first language: first generation immigrants use it as a lingua franca, the second generation as their first language while keeping up the use of the ancestral language in the family, and with the third generation, the ancestral language tends to disappear, while French makes its appearance as a second or third language amongst some of the capital's new inhabitants (Dumestre 2003).

Bambara often replaces second languages as well, for instance Fulfulde. In Djenne, Mopti, and elsewhere in the Macina, where Dogon speakers especially have traditionally picked up Fulfulde as their second language, Bambara is now the dominant means of inter-ethnic communication. As a second language, Bambara is in particular spreading in small and middle-sized towns, but also in rural areas, mostly following the establishment of some 'modern' installation such as a school, or other developments such as Islamization, the initiation of the industrial growing of crops, or simply following the return of people who have spent time away, for example in urban areas (Dumestre 2003).

As a consequence of this, the Bambaraphones, who make themselves understood nearly everywhere, tend to be monolingual, whereas minority language speakers are usually plurilingual (in African languages; we are not considering French here). As Calvet rightly notes: you learn other languages when you have the need to (1992: 199).

Bambara is slowly but steadily gaining access not only to new territories, but also to new domains. The written sphere in particular gives added prestige. An official monthly newspaper in Bambara, *Kibaru*, has been appearing regularly since 1972, and a second monthly Bambara newspaper, *Jèkabaara*, edited by the private cultural cooperative Jamana, has been coming out since 1986. Both are aimed at the rural population, and feature articles on developmental subjects like agriculture and health. A third Bambara paper, *Dibifara*, began publication in 1991. Concerning state-wide literacy campaigns, these were first conducted in French, but the authorities subsequently switched to teaching literacy in Bambara and various other national languages, this change occurring as early as 1963 (Traoré 2006: 3). As part of the literacy campaigns, a large number of booklets have been published in the national languages, especially Bambara, with the aim of developing functional literacy and giving the newly literate reading material. This has in particular been the case in the cotton zone around

Koutiala and Sikasso, where the large textile company CMDT (*Compagnie Malienne pour le Développement des Textiles*) has been very active in functional literacy campaigns. This is also an example of how Bambara comes to replace smaller languages, for though operating in a zone where Mamara is the original dominant language, the language of the literacy campaigns has in fact been Bambara (Dombrowsky 1993). In recent years, several new publishing houses (Donniya, Le Figuier, Jamana) have also begun to publish in national languages: both school books and fiction (traditional tales and other oral genres, as well as novels, poetry, and children's books, and even translations from French). The majority of these are, however, in Bambara.

In the audio-visual media, Bambara enjoys a privileged position as well. The public radio and television company ORTM (*Office de Radiodiffusion Télévision du Mali*) broadcasts television news bulletins in ten national languages,[10] ten minutes in each language twice a week. Only Bambara has an additional weekly bulletin of thirty minutes. Several other television programmes are produced in the national languages but, it would seem, always with a preference for Bambara. The titles are, for instance, all in either French or Bambara. Television publicity spots and different campaigns on development issues such as women's emancipation and vaccination are more and more frequently in Bambara, often through very popular sketches inspired by *koteba*, the traditional Malian *commedia dell'arte*.

Radio still remains the most widespread means of mass communication in the country. ORTM has two radio channels, and the sound content of the television news bulletins is also broadcast on their Channel 2. Since the democratization process of 1991–2, private radios have appeared in significant numbers throughout the country. They constitute a powerful means of support and reinforcement for all the national languages, but Bambara's dominant position is naturally reflected here as well.

Bambara also dominates the artistic world, for instance cinema production, where Mali can boast of several famous directors like Souleymane Cissé, Cheikh Oumar Cissoko and Adama Drabo. Even African cinema's grand old man, the Senegalese Sembène Ousmane, who made many films in Wolof, made his last film in Bambara. And in the domain of world music, where Mali has had a measure of international success with artists like Salif Keïta, Oumou Sangaré, and Rokia Traoré, all are found to sing in Bambara.

Lastly, the democratization process that started in 1991 has spurred politicians to give more of their speeches in national languages in order to reach their voters. Now these speeches are more and more often given in Bambara, both on television and in public meetings.

---

[10] According to the ORTM website (consulted 20 September 2006) these languages are: Bambara, Bomu, Bozo, Dogon, Fulfulde, Hassaniyya, Syenara, Soninke, Songhay, and Tamachek. The choice of these ten amongst the thirteen national languages is one of several signs that the thirteen national languages are not on equal footing in practice and that the national language status of Maninka, Xassonke, and Mamara in particular is less well supported. Hassaniyya also comes into this category, as it is still not a language of instruction.

All these domains contribute to associate Bambara with modern life, a prerogative formerly reserved for French. As Dumestre puts it (1994b, 2003), Bambara serves as a stepping-stone to French, an intermediary between the other Malian languages and French, belonging at the same time to the traditional, oral sphere and the modern, written sphere. The diglossia between French and the national languages that is common to all the former French and Belgian colonies in sub-Saharan Africa, must, in Mali, rather be seen as a triglossia consisting in French, Bambara, and the other Malian languages.

Another process worth noting is the development and diffusion of the Bamako dialect, which is spreading all the more easily as it differs little from other Manding dialects, while at the same time having prestige from its link to modern life. It is influenced by French at the lexical, phonological, and morphosyntactic levels, as described by Dumestre (2003: 10–11). Hundreds of French words have thus been introduced, most of them designating modern phenomena. Recent efforts to replace them by Bambara neologisms have had little success among ordinary people (for example *pankurunyòrò* 'jump-pirogue-place' for airport). But even French terms for father, mother, uncle, aunt, cousin, for which there are appropriate Bambara words, are frequently borrowed. At the phonological level, one finds consonant groups and closed syllables (whereas the classic syllabic structure of Bambara is CVCV), as well as unusual phonemes such as /z/, /ʃ/, and the foreign phoneme /ʋ/. Influence at the morphosyntactic level is the least noticeable but nevertheless present: one finds more plural marking (approximately twice as much in a 'modern' uttering/text as in a 'traditional' text), more nominalizations with the suffix *-li*, extended use of *ni* 'if' instead of *mana* 'if', and various other phenomena.

Despite its strikingly dominant position and dynamic nature, it is very important to note that the Malians do not acknowledge Bambara as an elevated national symbol and more of a national language than the other twelve that have this official status. On two linguistic points however, they do give way to nationalistic feelings – not creating an opposition between Bambara and the other national languages, but indicating support for Bambara/the national languages over French. The first relates to the term Bambara itself. Speakers of the language call themselves *Bamanan* and their language *bamanankan*. More and more Malians use these forms when writing French and want the French to accept them as well – which is not yet the case. The second point concerns the handful of phonetic symbols introduced into the (otherwise Latin) alphabets adopted for the national languages. These in fact cause considerable practical problems in word processing, but Malians tend to see the letters as significant symbols of cultural independence from the French language. For example, at a seminar in Segu in 2001 on the integration of national languages as means of instruction in primary school, this single point dominated the discussion at the expense of all other important pedagogical and linguistic issues concerning the bilingual education introduced by a school reform in 1994 (see below).

6.5 The Other National Languages

Four indigenous languages besides Bambara stand out in the sociolinguistic landscape of Mali: Fulfulde, Songhay, Tamachek, and Soninke. These dominate linguistically in their respective regions: Fulfulde in the centre, Songhay and Tamachek in the north, Soninke in the west. They are numerically important and their weight has been recognized in several ways: they were codified along with Bambara in 1967, and recognized as mediums of instruction in bilingual experimental schools in the early 1980s, shortly after Bambara (which was introduced in 1979). In the 1994 school reform, which generalized bilingual programmes throughout elementary schools, Bambara, Fulfulde, and Songhay were introduced from the start in 1994, Soninke, Tamachek, and Dogon in 1995. In the area of printed media, the official Bambara newspaper *Kibaru*, created in 1972, was followed by a Fulfulde version in 1983 (*Kabaaru*), a Soninke version in 1989 (*Xibaare*), and a Songhay version in 1992 (*Alhabar*) (Skattum 1994: 357).[11] The first magazine to be published in a national language was *Jama* ('Le peuple'), a magazine of popular culture and science started in 1976[12] by the *Institut des Sciences Humaines* at Bamako. The volumes are alternately in Bambara and Fulfulde (Barry 1988: 23).[13]

Two of these regional languages, Fulfulde and Songhay, function as lingua francas in their regions and are thus in an intermediate hierarchical position being 'low' languages vis-à-vis Bambara and 'high' languages vis-à-vis minor national languages (in the same way that Bambara is a 'low' language vis-à-vis French and a 'high' language vis-à-vis the other national languages).

Fulfulde is numerically the most important of these regional languages (with around 620,000 speakers, 1987[14]). Along with the Manding cluster it is one of the most widely spoken languages in its international distribution in Africa. However, though it has about 13 million speakers at the continental level (Childs 2003: 23), living across the Sahel belt from the Atlantic Ocean to Cameroon, it is everywhere a minority language, and in Mali it seems to be retreating as Bambara advances, at least as a vehicular language (lingua franca). It is principally spoken in the Niger delta in central Mali, in the Macina. However, Calvet's (1992) survey of the multi-ethnic town of Mopti, traditionally dominated by the Fulani, showed that Bambara had taken over as the dominant language in marketplace interactions (46 per cent), though Fulfulde (16 per cent) still played a significant role, followed by Songhay (13 per cent) (ibid.: 200). Fulfulde is nevertheless holding its own as a first language, as it is still passed on from one generation to the next (ibid.: 205). The Fulani are traditionally nomadic

---

[11] For some time, however, Fulfulde and Soninke versions have only appeared every three months or so for lack of journalists knowing how to write in these languages, and the Songhay version ceased production a long time ago. Only the Bambara version appears regularly every month (personal communication, Y. Diallo, editor of *Dibifara*).

[12] Until 1986 under the name of *Sankore*.

[13] *Jama* has met with the same problem as *Kabaaru* – the Fulfulde version no longer comes out because people cannot be found who are able to write in this language (personal communication, Y. Diallo).

[14] I will refer to the 1987 census by the year only when giving the number of speakers of any language.

cattle breeders and herders, but have become more and more sedentary. For cultural reasons they are reluctant to send their children to the 'French' school (for the nomads there are practical reasons as well), and few follow functional literacy classes – in both domains, rates are the lowest in the country (Canut 1996: 73–4). Their negative attitude towards literacy in their own language stands in contrast to that of the Senegalese Fulani, who are developing the writing of their language as a means to oppose Wolof domination (Fagerberg-Diallo 2001). It would be interesting to study the reasons for these diverging attitudes.

The Songhay language (c. 360,000, 1987) has the most uncertain classification within the Nilo-Saharan phylum (Heine and Nurse 2004: 69). The reason for this is its geographical isolation from the other Nilo-Saharan languages and the influence of the surrounding Mande and Berber languages. It is spoken in the north, in the Gao region near the Algerian and Niger borders, where the Songhay have mixed with Arabs to a certain extent. The Songhay are farmers and cattle breeders, two groups that often have conflicting interests. Droughts have brought many southwards along the Niger river to Lake Debo, in the Macina, and even to Bamako. It is hard to get teachers to work in this poor and isolated region, and school enrolment as well as literacy is low. The sociolinguistic survey conducted by Calvet (1992) in the regional capital Gao showed that the Songhay language plays the same role here as Bambara does in Bamako: Songhay is first language for most people and also functions as a lingua franca, with an estimated 77 per cent of market interactions taking place in Songhay. Like the Bambara, the Songhay are predominantly monolingual, while the other groups speak several languages: the Tamachek two or three, the Fulani two, three, or four. Even the Bambara are usually bilingual in this area, speaking Songhay as well as their own language (ibid.: 209). There is also a noticeable resistance to Bambara amongst the Songhay, contrary to what one finds amongst groups like the Maninka, Soninke, Bozo and Mamara. When they are in Bamako, Songhay people stick to their own language more than do other groups, and whenever possible, choose French instead of Bambara (such migrants usually have had some schooling) (Canut 1996: 116–17).

Soninke (c. 360,000, 1987) is a West Mande language. There is no mutual understanding between it and the Manding cluster, nor with the other West Mande language, Bozo. The Soninke (also called Sarakolle and, erroneously as we have seen, Marka), live in the west, in the arid region of Kayes, and are wide-roaming traders. Both facts explain why they form a significant proportion of Malian immigrants in France. Though their language is dominant in western Mali, Soninke tradesmen are known to be pragmatic and to shift very easily to Bambara (Vydrine 1994: 201).

Tamachek (c. 245,000, 1987) is also spoken in the north, around Timbuktu, by the Tuareg (sing. Targi). The Tuareg are nomads of Berber descent who live in the most desert-filled part of Mali, in the region of Adrar des Iforas. They make their livelihood from camel, cattle, and goat breeding and the trans-Saharan salt trade. There have been conflicts of interest between them and the Songhay as well as with local government authorities, whom they contest in every country they live in (Libya, Algeria, Mali, Niger, and Burkina Faso) (Bernus 1992: 24). The Tuareg have been responsible for the only uprisings in Mali in modern times, triggered by political, economic, and cultural rather than ethnic issues, and rooted in the geographical distance of the Tuareg from the central power, the extreme climatic conditions, their nomadic way of life, and their claim to independence. The Tuareg have always been opposed to external power, refusing to send their children to the 'French' school. They are the only Berber people to have their own alphabet, *tifinagh*, which is found on ancient and contemporary rock carvings in the Sahara. Though they use Songhay as a lingua franca, the Tuareg are very attached to their own language: 'The fundamental element of our identity is our language', explains one Tuareg (cited in Canut 1996: 77). Due to the 'rebellion' in the 1990s, many of these nomads migrated to neighbouring countries or southwards. In Bamako, they easily acquired Bambara, but usually prefer French (like the Songhay, Tuareg migrants often belonged to the educated elite) (Canut 1996: 129).

The Dogon dialects (c. 407,000, 1987) are spoken in a concentrated area east of the Macina, in the Bandiagara cliffs and the plains below. Their most striking characteristic is their extraordinary diversification, exceptional for the Malian context. Different sources suggest that there are twelve to fifteen dialects, while one survey indicates there may be at least twenty (Plungian and Tembiné 1994: 164). There is also discussion as to whether the different dialects are in fact dialects or actually constitute different languages: among the different varieties mutual intelligibility does not exist except for neighbouring dialects, and even then difficulties arise. No common variety has developed that permits inter-dialectal communication. This hinders the possibility of language standardization and accounts for Dogon dialects being predominantly oral and intra-ethnic. Little linguistic research has as yet been done on the Dogon language, though the people are one of the best known Malian ethnic groups through extensive ethnological research on their sophisticated cosmogony.

The other Manding national languages are much less used than Bambara. Maninka is spoken in the south, on the border with Guinea and the Ivory Coast, with a stronghold around Kita, south-west of Bamako. Though it is an important language in the neighbouring countries and has historic prestige due to association with the Mali empire, its position in Mali is quite inferior: it was amongst the last three languages to be recognized as a national language, it is one of the two national languages that have not been introduced in schools as a medium of instruction, and it is not used in the public television news bulletins. This is probably because it is so closely related to Bambara and also to some degree considered a 'peasant' language, which results in many Maninka trying to adopt the more urban Bambara (Canut and Keita 1994).

Xassonke (c. 67,000, 1987) is spoken in the western part of the country, principally in Kayes and Bafoulabé. It is less closely related to the other three languages in the Manding cluster (it has around 70 per cent lexical similarity with the Mandinka language of Senegal and the Gambia), and is influenced both by Bambara and Soninke (Vydrine 1994). Like Maninka it was one of the last three languages to be declared a national language and it is also one of the three national languages which do not feature in television news bulletins. It is used as medium of instruction, but was one of the last languages to obtain this privilege, in 2001. Protestant missionaries have, however, been successful in extending its written use.

The West Mande language Bozo (c. 114,000, 1987) is spoken by fishermen along the river Niger, particularly in the Mopti region, which they inhabited before other groups arrived in the area (Gardi 1989: 91). The Bozo follow the rise and fall of the river, some spending all year in their boats. A sociolinguistic survey in Mopti showed that today, only 5 per cent of marketplace interactions take place in Bozo, though the Bozo themselves claim that they make use of it. L.-J. Calvet (1992: 200–5) suggests that the Bozo may worry that their language is threatened and try to convince themselves that it is not. The death of the Bozo language would not seem to be imminent, however, as Bozo still is passed on from one generation to the next. Furthermore, the Bozo language benefits from public support: it was introduced as a medium of school instruction in 2001, and is one of the ten national languages used in television news bulletins.

The Gur languages Syenara (*sénoufo*) (c. 141,000, 1987) and Mamara (*minyanka*) (c. 228,000, 1987) are spoken in southeast Mali around Sikasso and Koutiala, on the Ivory Coast border, where rains are fairly generous and cotton crops provide a livelihood for most of the population. These languages are more loosely related to Bomu (*bwamu, bobo*) (c. 136,000), also spoken in the south. Mamara has often been considered a branch of Syenara (Dombrowsky 1994: 16), and in several overviews they are grouped together as one language community (CONFEMEN 1986, Cissé 1992). Contemporary ethnologues however define the Mamara as an independent people with their own language (Dombrowsky: 1994). Mamara dialects are internally fairly different from one another. Both this fact and Mamara's close relationship to Syenara may explain why sociolinguistically, Mamara seems to have an inferior position compared to Syenara and Bomu. The two latter are used in public news bulletins, which is not the case with Mamara, and they were introduced as mediums of instruction in schools in 1997, while Mamara had to wait until 2001 for this status. Perhaps the most remarkable sociolinguistic fact relating to Mamara, however, is the way that Bambara is invading the region, without much opposition it would seem (ibid.).

The final member of the national language group, Hassaniyya (c. 22,000 speakers, 1987) belongs to the Arabic branch of Semitic, and is otherwise known as Moor (*maure*) which is the name given to the speakers of the language. The Moors constitute a small minority near the Mauritanian border in the northwest. Generally, they are nomads breeding cattle, sheep, and camels, but they also deal in transport, trade, and sometimes settle as farmers. Their language is not used as a medium of instruction, but does appear in the ORTM television news.

6.6 Arabic[15]

Except for the Hassaniyya dialect which is spoken by a small minority, Arabic is not a native language in Mali. The literate varieties of Classical and Modern Standard Arabic are however important, historically and for religious reasons. Arabic was the first written language in the region and for six centuries remained the written language of Islamic scholars. Most written sources on early history are in Arabic, and some Malian languages have also been represented in Arabic script. Under the Mali and Gao empires Timbuktu and Djenne were internationally well-known centres of Islamic, Arabic learning, and in the recently created Ahmed Baba Centre in Timbuktu, named after the renowned scholar from the seventeenth century, an extremely interesting collection of ancient Arabic manuscripts is attracting the attention of international scholars.

Today, the modernizing Islamic schools, madrasas, where Arabic is used as means and subject of instruction, are contributing to a wider use of the language. The madrasas teach both religious and secular subject matter (French included), and use modern methods to teach Arabic as a living foreign language, with good results. They are very popular with parents, and some 30 per cent of schoolchildren attend these schools (Bouwman 2005: 1), the madrasas being recognized as part of the formal educational system. This is not the case with the traditional Qur'anic schools, which come under the jurisdiction of the Ministry of the Interior together with the country's mosques. A large but unknown number attend the traditional schools, where the children memorize parts of the Qur'an without actually learning Arabic. Many parents prefer the Islamic schools, both traditional and modern, to 'French' schools, because their teaching is closer to traditional values (Dumestre 1997, 2000), and because they 'increase the chances for paradise for their children and themselves' (Bouwman 2005: 189). Such schools cost less as well, as they receive substantial financial support from Arab countries.

The Malian government offers no funding for the Islamic schools and 'tries to control, francophonize and secularize them' (Bouwman 2005: 189). This is because Mali is a secular state where a Sufi orientation of Islam has prevailed, while the Arab countries, especially Saudi Arabia, use their financial support to disseminate the Wahhabi orientation of Islam. This fundamentalist orientation 'propagates the interpretation of law-giving Islamic sources in their most literal form' and 'condemns much of the traditional Islamic practice in West Africa' (ibid.: 9).

As a madrasa education leads to few career options and government policy tends to make students exiting such schools feel marginalized in Mali, many continue their studies in Egypt, where the salafiyya orientation is dominant, and in Saudi Arabia, returning to Mali to further disseminate these forms of Islam (which in the Malian context blend and both go by the name of Wahhabi). The students also come back with a much better proficiency in Arabic:

---

[15] Information provided in this section is to a significant extent sourced from Bouwman (2005).

While traditionally educated marabouts, imams, preachers and ulema make only limited use of Arabic in their work and rely on Islamic knowledge transmitted in Malian languages, arabisants and ulema of modern Arabic education employ Arabic much more than often assumed.   (Bouwman 2005: 190)

So, while Arabic is neither a national language nor an official one, like French, it is gaining ground in contemporary Mali.

6.7 French

More than a century after the first Christian missions were established (in the town of Kita in 1888), the first French administrators came to the country (creating the colony of French Soudan in 1892), and the first railway was built (Kayes–Niger in 1904), the percentage of Malians with 'real'[16] competence in French is estimated to be only 5 per cent of the population (Dumestre 1993: 219), with an additional 5 per cent having a more restrictive knowledge of and ability in French (Rossillon 1995: 86). This is partly explained by the geographical location of the country: being landlocked, Mali has been less exposed to French influence than the coastal states of Africa. A second important factor contributing to the low degree of proficiency in French amongst the population is the existence of an indigenous majority language that functions as means of inter-ethnic communication in place of French. Thirdly, one can note that low literacy rates (19 per cent) may also play a role, as French is acquired mainly at school (where the enrolment rate is only around 26 per cent). What is more, the 'real' Francophones are probably even fewer than suggested by the figures above, as those who have been to school easily forget what they have learned for lack of practice. Calvet (1992: 197) records that only 4 per cent of the interactions in the marketplaces in Bamako, for instance, take place in French. The contrast in knowledge and use of French is therefore great when set in comparison with the occurrence of French in the neighbouring Ivory Coast and its capital Abidjan.

In Mali, French is spoken mainly among the upper class, and mainly at work – outside work, people with an ability in French most often speak one of the Malian languages. Parents' social position and mastery of French make a great difference for the children and tend to result in the reproduction of social differences. The francophone elite regularly try to expose their children to French through private lessons, private schools, schools abroad, and so on. (Dumestre 1997, 2000). Very few, however, choose to speak French at home to help their children. French is not used for identity purposes, but as an instrument of social promotion. For the Songhay and Tamachek who use it to avoid Bambara domination, French has an instrumental role as well.

[16] Defined as those who have completed six years of primary school. This criterion is used in the absence of a more reliable alternative way to ascertain linguistic competence in French.

Though absent from everyday use, French is nevertheless an extremely important language in Mali, as in the neighbouring countries. Its prestige and association with modern life clearly surpass those of Bambara. All laws are written in French and most of the country's administrative texts. State affairs are conducted in French, as are public matters, and the president and government ministers regularly address the people in French – though there has been an evolution towards more use of national languages in this domain. Most children in primary school still receive all instruction in French (Traoré 2006), and so do all children from the seventh grade on. At the University of Bamako, French is taught in the *Département des Lettres*, like in France, while other languages are taught in foreign language departments of English, German, etc.[17]

The French that is spoken and written in Mali in administrative matters, National Assembly, court, public speeches, newpapers, radio, and television is fairly close to standard, metropolitan French. French is 'protected' from developing into a local variety by being used almost exclusively in formal settings. There are, of course, certain terms and expressions that distinguish Malian French from metropolitan French. Malians themselves hardly notice them, since they more or less all use them (for example: *absenter* 'to find someone absent', *et consort* 'along with others', *au niveau de* used for several shorter prepositions like *à*, *dans*, *chez*, or intransitive use of the transitive verb *échanger* 'talk together', etc.). There are also signs that the general competence in French is deteriorating, though no study known to the author has actually quantified or proved the degradation. Some studies do however show that French is very far from being mastered in primary and secondary school (Opheim 1999; Skattum 2000b; Thyness 2003).

The contact between French, Arabic, and Malian languages necessarily leads to language mixing either through the incorporation of loans or through code-switching. In the past, Malian languages have borrowed extensively from Arabic (religious terms, days of the week, etc.), but these loans are now so well integrated that they are hardly noticeable. The most important mixing today takes place between French and African languages, more than between the African languages themselves. As part of this process, the Bambara spoken in Bamako would seem to be the most mixed variety of all, many people referring to it as hybrid and impoverished by French. Loans also take place in the other direction, with French borrowing from Bambara, but very rarely from Songhay, Fulfulde, or Tamachek. Mixing is typical of urban contexts, where French is mainly spoken.

As yet, French does not seem threatened either as the official language of the country, or as the foremost language of social promotion and prestige. However, it is significant to note that the national languages and Bambara in particular are gaining ground in actual use and to some degree in public recognition, especially in the media and the educational sector.

---

[17] A proposal to develop a department of African languages was officially approved in 2007.

6.8 National Languages in Education

Since independence, the authorities have time and again expressed the desire to see all the national languages revalued, developed, and introduced into the schools of Mali (decrees of 1962, 1968, 1970, and the report from the National Seminar on Education of 1978) (CONFEMEN 1986: 207). Though it must be said that concrete action has followed on from speech only partly, and rather slowly, Mali has nevertheless made stronger efforts than any other sub-Saharan francophone country to support mother-tongue education.[18]

The first experiment took place nearly twenty years after independence, in 1979, with a French–Bambara programme in four primary schools. The same type of bilingual programme was applied to Fulfulde, Songhay, and Tamachek and around 100 schools adopted this 'first generation experiment', which to begin with showed good results, but later ultimately failed due to a lack of pedagogical materials and appropriate teacher training (Skattum 1997).

In 1987, a second bilingual experiment called Convergent Teaching (CT) began in Segu, in Bambara. Positive results convinced the authorities to adopt it at a national level. In 1994, a school reform making use of CT was successfully voted for and in 1998, a more ambitious reform (also using CT) took its place, the PRODEC (*Programme Décennal de Développement de l'Education*). The policy has been to proceed slowly, in order to avoid failures like those in Guinea and Madagascar, where national languages replaced French as means of instruction without sufficient preparation, and where the reforms were abandoned after some years. In Mali, eleven national languages have been progressively introduced as means of instruction along with French: Bambara, Fulfulde, and Songhay (1994); Dogon, Soninke, and Tamachek (1995); Bomu and Syenara (1997); Bozo, Mamara, and Xassonke (2001). Only Maninka and Hassaniyya have not been granted this recognition. Bilingual education was given a legal status in 1999: 'Education is provided in the official language and in the national languages' (Traoré 2006: 3). A third phase started in 2002, with the introduction of a bilingual curriculum according to competency. This curriculum is intended to ameliorate the weak points of PRODEC (it is as yet too early to see if this will be the case). By 2005–2006, bilingual education had reached 2,550 primary schools (out of 8,063), which corresponds to 31.62 per cent of the total number of schools in the country (Traoré 2006: 5) There are plans to introduce the national languages in teacher training colleges as well. This would be a major improvement since at present, teachers are only trained in French as means and subject of instruction, with short summer courses in national language transcription, without any teaching of their grammar or of mother-tongue didactics.

---

[18] It may be in recognition of this fact that the headquarters of the pan-African African Academy of Languages (ACALAN), created in 2001 by the African Union, was located in Bamako (though this may of course also be due to or aided by the influence of former Mali president Alpha Oumar Konaré).

The Ministry of Education is responsible for both formal and non-formal education, with a relatively strong accent on the informal sector, which consists of functional literacy centres, women's centres, and the so-called CED (*Centres d'Education pour le Développement*), which educate drop-outs or young people who have never attended school. The instruction in such centres is given in national languages. Though laudable as a general enterprise, the quality of this education has been questioned in a recent doctoral dissertation (Haïdara 2005). The author points to the low level of instruction of the instructors themselves (who very often lack pedagogical training as well as knowledge of the orthography and grammar of the national language) and also to the almost complete lack of a written environment, making it difficult for those exiting these informal educational institutions to maintain their newly acquired literacy skills.

The formal sector includes four types of school: state, community (collectively owned), private (owned by individuals), and confessional, both Christian and Muslim. The bilingual programme is mainly used in state schools, while community, private, and Christian schools almost exclusively use French. The madrasas officially teach in Arabic, but are in practice bilingual, translating the Arabic texts into national languages as well as giving explanations in the vernacular, as several studies have shown (Kane 1991; Dombrowsky 1994; Bouwman 2005, all cited in Tamari 2006: 1–2).

Extremely multilingual communities like Mopti and Djenne present a special challenge to the bilingual CT programme. Choosing a national language as co-medium of instruction here is far from easy. According to the Malian minister of education, the authorities will propose that the communities choose the language spoken amongst children in the school when they play (Traoré 2006: 6). This bottom-up approach seems pedagogically sound and in keeping with the view of Mali linguist A. Barry (1988: 26): 'There can be no question of imposing one of these languages on other people, because that would simply mean moving the problem. The French language represents a disadvantage to the Bamanan child, but the Bamanan language would be just as much of a disadvantage to a Fulani child.' However, the reality is that as most children pick up Bambara in these multilingual towns, the Ministry's proposal is actually likely to further strengthen the position of Bambara.

6.9 Language Attitudes

Parents' attitudes towards the introduction of national languages as means of instruction are of course of the utmost importance to the success of the bilingual teaching reform. It is generally supposed that parents are against teaching in national languages, as French is the way to social promotion. A common objection in Mali as in other African countries is that there is no use in learning a language one already knows. As a village teacher in the Segu region explained:

At first, when we were told that it was to going be Bambara [during a public awareness campaign], the peasants did not at all like the idea, because to them, going to school means learning something, trying to have something that you don't know. – But we already know Bambara! Are you telling us tales?   (Opheim 1999: 155)

The deterioration of school results was another motif of opposition, with parents putting the blame on the time used to learn Bambara, as in the following criticism from a father:

Before, after three or four years of school, you were able to write letters. But that changed a long time ago. School has become very complicated these days. Now you do literacy [in Bambara] and school [in French] at the same time. What we know is this: *our children no longer know how to write letters in the 4th grade.*   (A.C., cited in Opheim 1999: 156; italics in the text)

The parents clearly prefer French because of the socio-economic advantages it gives their children:

Your language is the language of money and regular salary. If a person has success, is it not a question of money? If you know French, you can travel and know the world, and nobody can fool you. With our language, you don't know anything.   (N.M., ibid.: 155)

It's French that's useful, that's what we've seen here in Dugukuna, because those of our children who have learnt it have become important people. But to this day, we haven't seen that any pupil who has studied Bambara has gained anything from it.   (O.C., ibid.)

However, language attitudes amongst parents are not always as negative as in this little village, which had very poor school results compared to other schools in the region. A survey conducted amongst seven schools of the same region gives a more positive picture (Haïdara 2005: 253–84). The region and especially the city of Segu have hosted most of the bilingual experimental schools, and M. L. Haïdara shows that 41.8 per cent of the parents had had at least one child in a bilingual school, and that 39.3 per cent of these parents were satisfied with the teaching, while only 26 per cent were dissatisfied, 34.6 per cent having no opinion (ibid.: 253). Amongst all the parents of the survey, 63 per cent were in favour of bilingual teaching, only 6 per cent against it, while 31 per cent gave unclear answers (ibid.: 257). However, more than half the parents felt that the means to teach in national languages were insufficient (ibid.: 255–6). Questioned at a more general level, 86.6 per cent of the parents agreed that mother-tongue teaching would contribute to better learning (ibid.: 255), while 68 per cent also agreed that any language could be developed into a language of scientific communication, such a feeling being in contrast to the common prejudice that national languages are unfit for scientific purposes. Several factors influence the parents' attitude to national language teaching. Parents without schooling in particular, but also those with higher education, tended to be positive, while those with just some schooling were rather negative (they may have wished they had a better command of French). The people of Segu city, where the CT experiment was conducted, were most positive, presumably because their experience had reassured them that school results were good (ibid.: 260). Age also played a role: older parents tended to reject national language teaching (as might be anticipated given that older people may be more prone to fear change; furthermore, colonial attitudes towards French as the only legitimate language of instruction may linger on, as well as respect for the official language). The majority of younger parents were favourably disposed towards national language teaching, which certainly gives hope for the future (ibid.: 263). Teachers' attitudes were also investigated in a survey,[19] revealing that as may as 74.2 per cent were favourable to national language instruction.

Haïdara's 2005 survey however shows that here as elsewhere, speech and behaviour do not necessarily go hand in hand. When observing the parents' registration of their children in these seven schools, Haïdara found that the monolingual French ('classic') schools all filled up first. Deprecatory remarks were overheard: 'I'm not enrolling my child in a Bambara school!' or 'We have avoided the use of national languages once more this year' (a school director reassuring a parent) (ibid.: 283). In real life, the more education a parent had, the more it turned out he preferred French for his children, and this included the teachers themselves.

What this shows is that though people may be in favour of national languages, they may not wish to gamble with the future of their own children in national language education. To make national language instruction attractive, it must be made truly useful. The government would have to introduce such instruction beyond the first cycle of elementary school and also make writing skills in one of the national languages a prerequisite for getting jobs in the public sector. NGOs often ask for such a skill, and this has prompted many adults to follow literacy courses in addition to their French studies.

6.10 Conclusion

In this chapter, we have seen that Mali is a country that has consistently invested effort in what amounts to a broad defence of cultural and linguistic pluralism, rather than the narrower targeted promotion of a single language such as the official language French or the dominant language Bambara. Of the twenty or so languages that make up the linguistic landscape, thirteen have been granted the status of 'national language'. In Mali, this is more than mere nomination. Not only does the 1992 Constitution of the Third Republic state their equal rights according to the law, but language policy has followed up by introducing them into the educational system, the audio-visual media, and the written press. This policy, which started on a modest scale after 1960, has been more noticeable following the democratization process of 1991–1992.

---

[19] A. Diarra and Y. Haïdara (1999), 'Etude sociolinguistique sur l'identification des langues nationales dominantes par zone et du potentiel enseignant par langue', cited in Haïdara (2005: 284).

However, it has to be admitted that the national languages are advancing only slowly: only around 30 per cent of schoolchildren in primary school attend bilingual classes in French plus a national language, only five monthly newspapers and one magazine are published in the national languages, and the national television company only reserves ten minutes of news bulletins for ten of them twice a week. The authorities explain this slowness as caution, aimed at avoiding the failures of francophone countries such as Guinea and Madagascar. The education sector in particular needs the support of parents and teachers, who are traditionally in favour of French. These two groups are now more readily accepting national languages as suitable means of instruction.

The expression of attitudes about language and actual behaviour do not seem to correspond well, however, and most parents still prefer to send their children to monolingual French schools, especially if they themselves have had some schooling. Around one-third of schoolchildren are also registered in the madrasas, where Modern Standard Arabic is the language of instruction. Arabic competence is thus improving and spreading, but the language has no formal status in the country.

In spite of the limitations in language policy and behaviour mentioned here, there does appear to be a wide consensus amongst ordinary people as well as with the authorities that the national languages should be defended – and this means all of them. The striking domination of Bambara as first language and lingua franca finds no related aggressive expression in language attitudes. Very few Malians seem to want to make Bambara an official language – either alone or along with French, even though it is spoken by around 80 per cent of the population, while French is spoken by only 5–10 per cent, making Mali the least francophone of the earlier French colonies.

The explanation for this lies mainly in the tradition of cultural, religious, and linguistic tolerance that is a legacy from the medieval empires Ghana, Mali, and Gao. Mali is a rare case in sub-Saharan Africa: a country that existed prior to the making of the modern state. History has given the Malian peoples a common identity and the conviction that they belong to a very old and prestigious nation. Multilingualism is part of this nation's identity and is the main reason for the state's language policy in defence of cultural and linguistic pluralism.

7

Sierra Leone: Krio and the Quest for National Integration

B. Akíntúndé Oyètádé and Victor Fashole Luke

7.1 Introduction

The Republic of Sierra Leone is a smaller country in size, population, and the number of its languages than many other countries on the West African coast such as Ghana, Ivory Coast, and Nigeria. A particularly interesting phenomenon is however present in the configuration of the languages present and used in the country, and how language links up the general population. Though there are two proportionately large indigenous languages spoken in the country, Temne and Mende, it is found that the language which has spread and serves as a universal lingua franca known by as much as 95 per cent of the population of Sierra Leone is in fact an English-based creole known as Krio, which is the mother tongue of a much smaller group of speakers primarily located in and near the capital city Freetown. This chapter examines the growing significance of Krio in Sierra Leone and how it originally developed as a contact language among different groups of resettled emancipated slaves and other indigenous inhabitants of the Freetown area. The implications of the growth of Krio for national language policy and the position of English as the official language are examined, as well as the existence of ambivalent and changing attitudes towards the Krio language. Section 7.2 begins with a brief historical outline of the emergence of Sierra Leone and its special population in Freetown. Section 7.3 then provides an overview of the variety of different languages present in the country and their role in everyday life in Sierra Leone. Section 7.4 focuses heavily on both the Krio people and their language during the colonial period and after independence, and how Krio has come to spread as a common, inter-ethnic language among almost all of the population of Sierra Leone. Section 7.5 concludes the chapter with a re-examination of the issues surrounding language and national identity in the country and whether and how national language(s) might be planned for Sierra Leone.[1]

[1] The writers wish to gratefully acknowledge the role of the following institutions, bodies, and organizations in the accomplishment of this work: The British Council in Sierra Leone, the University of Sierra Leone, the Government of Sierra Leone, and SOAS.

7.2 The Formation of Sierra Leone

The name Sierra Leone is a derivative of the Portuguese name Sierra Leoya given to the country by the Portuguese navigator Pedro da Cintra when he discovered the land in 1462. Regularized European contacts with Sierra Leone were among the first in West Africa, and in the seventeenth century slaves began to be brought to North America from the area of Sierra Leone to work on the various plantations established in the southern states such as Georgia and South Carolina, this developing into a thriving trade during the course of the eighteenth century. Somewhat later on, when the tide of British public opinion turned strongly against the slave trade, there were various attempts to resettle emancipated slaves in the coastal area which became Freetown. The first group of these 'Liberated Africans' were known as the 'Black Poor' and were brought in 1787 from London to land purchased from local Temne people. However, after just a single year the majority of this initial group of 400 had perished from disease and conflict with the Temne. Five years later in 1792, a second group of 1,100 slaves who had received their freedom in return for agreeing to fight for the British in the American War of Independence was transported to the Freetown area from Nova Scotia, where they had been emancipated but lived in very poor conditions. Protected by the British in Sierra Leone, the 'Nova Scotians' were joined in 1800 by a third group of 500 freed slaves from Jamaica known as the 'Maroons' who brought with them an English pidgin. In 1808 the British Abolition Act outlawed the participation of British citizens in the trans-Atlantic slave trade and the British navy was used to intercept the slave ships of other nations plying between West Africa and the Americas (Cole 2006: 36), resulting in the resettlement of as many as 50,000 slaves in the Freetown area between 1808 and 1864 (Wyse 1989: 1–2; Sengova 2006: 170). These had originally been seized from a wide variety of regions and ethnic groups in West Africa, though they included a significant concentration of Yoruba people and also slaves who originated from the territory of Sierra Leone itself. Formed into a new community and shielded by the British, during the nineteenth century the 'Creoles' or 'Krio', as they became known, established a prosperous trade in Sierra Leone and a new shared identity, while Freetown itself became increasingly important in regional terms, the territories of the Gold Coast (modern Ghana) and the Gambia being administered by the British governor in Freetown, and Freetown also having the only English-language university-level institute of education in all of West Africa for many years, Fourah Bay College, opened in 1827.

In the twentieth century, Sierra Leone gained its independence peaceably in 1961. The new nation was formed from the combination of the comparatively small Crown Colony centred in Freetown, and the much larger hinterland areas which had been made into a British Protectorate in 1896. The result is a territory of approximately 30,000 square miles, bounded to the north by Guinea, to the southeast by Liberia, and to the southwest by the Atlantic ocean, with a coastline of some 265 miles. There are four administrative divisions in the country: the Western Area consisting in the urban area of Freetown and its surrounding countryside, and three (northern, southern,

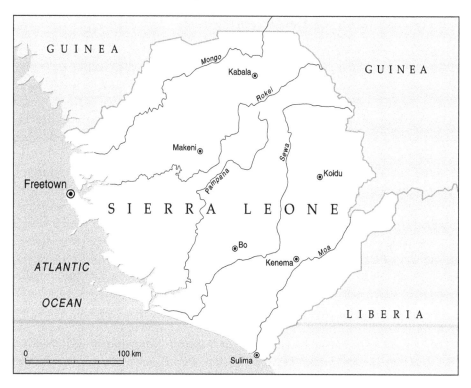

Sierra Leone

and eastern) provinces. Currently the population of the country is estimated to be around six million and is made up of eighteen indigenous ethnic groups, with no group constituting more than a third of the total population. Several thousand Europeans, Indians, and Lebanese are also present in the country and active in the economy, along with a sizeable number of Nigerians, and a mixture of Gambians, Liberians, and Africans from other regional states.

Between 1991 and 2000, Sierra Leone experienced a destructive decade of civil war in which large-scale loss of life and damage to the country's infrastructure occurred, as well as much internal displacement of people fleeing from the fighting. The population of Freetown in particular was greatly swelled and diversified during this period by refugees arriving from rural areas. Since peace has been restored with the involvement of the United Nations, a considerable amount of foreign assistance and aid has helped in the rebuilding of the country and its shattered economy, which is heavily based on mining. Though clear and encouraging progress has already been made, there is much left to do, and the reconstruction of Sierra Leone will require the positive cooperation of all sectors of society and the nation's ethnic groups.

7.3 The Languages of Sierra Leone

7.3.1 Overview

Sierra Leone is a multilingual country and most of the population is either bilingual or multilingual. English is the official language of the country and is the primary, dominant language in education, government administration, law, written communication, and all other formal domains of life. It is also the language of status and prestige, being a symbol of high education. In addition to English, and though the country is witnessing a gradual dying out of certain of its less spoken languages, no less than sixteen Sierra Leonean languages are regularly used by their L1 (i.e. mother tongue / first language) speakers:[2]

Krio	Mende	Temne	Limba
Kono	Susu	Sherbro	Fula
Yalunka	Krim	Vai	Kissi
Kru	Madingo	Loko	Gola

All of these languages with the exception of Krio belong to the same family, the Niger-Kordofanian family of African languages, which as a family is divided into two groups: (a) the Niger-Congo Branch, and (b) the Kordofanian Branch. The Niger-Congo branch sub-divides into two other groups, one of which is the Mande Group to which Kono, Susu, Yalunka, Vai, and Mende belong. The remaining ones, Temne, Sherbro, Krim, Kissi, Gola, and Limba belong to the West Atlantic (or Atlantic Congo) subfamily. To date, no language or set of languages has been officially declared the national language(s) of Sierra Leone, though four of the sixteen Sierra Leonean languages listed above are seen as more prominent than the others and consequently figure more in the media and recent attempts to introduce mother-tongue education: Mende, Temne, Limba, and Krio, discussed below.

7.3.2 Mende, Temne, and Limba

The Mendes are one of the largest speech communities in Sierra Leone, estimated to be approximately 30 per cent of the population, and as a group wield considerable ethnic political power. The speakers of this language occupy an area of 12,000 square miles in the southern and eastern provinces stretching over major districts such as Bo, Kenema, Kailahun Pujehun, and Moyamba. The Mendes originally arrived in Sierra Leone from Lofa in Liberia and from Guinea. The language evolved from the South

---

[2] Quite a few languages that were used in Sierra Leone in the past no longer productively exist as mediums of meaningful and viable communication. Among these are Loma, Fante, Bassa, and Yoruba. Mayinka has been absorbed by Mende and the majority of its speakers now live in Liberia. Loma is essentially now a Liberian language and is hardly spoken in Sierra Leone any more. Fante, Bassa, and Yoruba no longer have a viable speech community in Sierra Leone and the languages are hardly used in regular interpersonal communication, though Yoruba does still exist as a ritualistic language in secret societies and in cultural legacies such as in first or second names (but not regularly in last or family names), names of events, and indigenous associations.

Western family of Mande languages, which also includes the Loko, Gbandi, Kpelle and Loma languages. Currently there are four principal dialects of Mende, all of which are mutually intelligible: Kappa Mende, Sewama Mende, Kɔɔ Mende, and Wanjama Mende. With regards to their culture and society, the Mendes are largely Muslims, who practise polygamy, and rule according to clans. Their traditional societies are the Poro, Wande, and Kobo for men and the Bondo for women. These traditional societies also serve as final courts of appeal in their communities. The Mendes, like the Temnes and the Limbas, are a people who show strong ethnic loyalty and bonding to each other.

The Temnes, according to history, are also not originally from Sierra Leone, but are believed to have migrated into Sierra Leone from the area of the Futa Jallon Mountains in Guinea. On their initial arrival in Sierra Leone around the fourteenth century, they clashed with the Sosos in the coastal area and were actually driven back to Guinea. Ultimately they entered successfully through the interior of the northern segment of Sierra Leone and settled there, coming to dominate the northern part of the country over time. Quite similar to the Mendes in population size, they are now estimated to make up around 31 per cent of Sierra Leone's population, and occupy a very large area of the country, predominantly in the Kambia, Port Loko, Bombali, and Tonkolili districts. Spread over this broad area there are five mutually intelligible dialects of Temne: the Western, Yoni, Eastern Koninke, Western Koninke and Bombali dialects. In terms of culture and lifestyle, the Temnes are largely Muslims and divided into different clans. The traditional societies in which their culture and tradition are preserved are the Poro for men and the Ragbenle for women. Young Temne girls and boys are initiated into adulthood through these societies.

The third major indigenous (or 'long-present') ethnic group in Sierra Leone is that of the Limbas. The Limbas figure as an important ethnic group of Sierra Leone mainly because of the role of some members of this group in politics, business, and education. The Limbas represent about 8.7 per cent of the population and occupy an area of 19,000 square miles, predominantly in the north of the country, where there are five dialects: Tonko, Safroko, Biriwa, Sella, and Warawara. Like the Mendes and the Temnes, they rule by clans and have secret societies in which their culture and tradition are preserved and passed on to the younger generation: the Gbangbani, Kofo, and Poro for males, and the Bondo for female Limbas.

Concerning the actual degree to which the above three groups numerically domi-nate the areas in which they are concentrated, in largely Mende areas of the south and east such as Kailahun, Kono, Bo, Bonthe, and Pujehun, the percentage of L1 speakers of Mende is as high as 74.5, 80.5, 78.6, 87.5 and 94.8 respectively. In Temne areas of the north such as Kambia, Port Loko, and Tonkolili, the percentage of L1 Temne speakers is now estimated to be 54.7, 87.2, and 79 per cent respectively (data from the Statistics Department of Sierra Leone, 2003). In major Limba areas of the north such as Bombali and Koinadugu, the figures are 24 per cent and 20 per cent respectively. From this it can be seen that Bombali is now more dominated by Temne than Limba suggesting that Limba is gradually coming to be overshadowed by Temne. Quite generally, Temne and

Mende are also learned and used by L2 (i.e. second language) speakers for interaction with the Temnes and Mendes in the south and east and in the north, whereas smaller languages such as Soso, Sherbro, Kono, Madingo, Fula, and also Limba are not learned by outsiders and are only heard in interactions among members of these specific ethnic groups. In addition to their presence in predominantly Temne areas, L1 Temne speakers are also found in significant numbers in the Western Area, where the Krio are actually dominant. The following is a breakdown of the ethnic composition of the important Western Urban Area: 39.5 per cent Krio, 37.1 per cent Temne, 7.1 per cent Mende, 8 per cent Madingo, and 3 per cent Limba.[3] Despite the occurrence of many Temne and also other groups in Freetown and its urban environs, the dominant language which seems to be spoken everywhere in the Western Urban Area is very clearly Krio. In the Western Rural Area, the picture is almost the same: 40.6 per cent Krio, 9.4 per cent Mende, 27.3 per cent Temne, and 6.4 per cent Limba, and Krio is again heavily dominant here.

Temne, Mende, Krio, and to a lesser extent Limba also now have a (limited) presence in education. Following a UNESCO report on the potential use of indigenous languages in education published in 1981, Temne, Mende, Krio, and Limba were selected for standardization and the development of orthographies so that they could be used as mediums of education in primary schools and taught as subjects in later years. This is now taking place, and there are also attempts to produce literature in the four languages, with particularly helpful support in the creation of educational materials from the Lekon Consultancies formed by (the late) Professor Clifford Fyle.

7.3.3 Krio

While Temne and Mende are important languages in Sierra Leone with significant populations of L1 speakers forming approximately 60 per cent of the population, as well as certain L2 speakers, the use of Temne and Mende is predominantly local and restricted to the regions where these languages are dominant, and there has been no extension of either Temne or Mende across a broader national domain. Krio, by way of considerable contrast, is a language which is the mother tongue of just 10 per cent of the population (World Bank data, 2004),[4] largely confined to the comparatively

---

[3] The versatility of the Temnes can be detected here: more of the Temnes than any of the other ethnic groups have left their original area to live in the city. Concerning the occurrence of ethnic mobility in general, it should be noted that the percentages quoted in the text were taken after the war and contrast with the more homogeneous population of the Western Area prior to 1990. There has consequently been a marked increase in urban relocation as an outcome of the war.

[4] Sengova (1987: 523) suggests that the population and proportion of L1 Krio speakers is considerably less than this, estimating it to be just 100,000 in 1987. The 1993 Ethnologue report for Sierra Leone, by way of contrast, notes a figure of 472,600, which would be around 13 per cent of today's population if correct. As many Krio left for other countries during the course of the civil war in the 1990s, the more recent, post-war, 2004 World Bank estimate of 10 per cent seems quite compatible with the 1993 Ethnologue figure once Krio emigration is taken into account. Whatever the exact percentage of the population made up by L1 Krio speakers actually is, it is clearly small when compared to the extent that Krio is known as an L2 (by almost all of the population).

small, (though economically very important) Western Area, but which has developed dramatically into the lingua franca of the whole country, known by members of every ethnic group in Sierra Leone and used for inter-ethnic communication by as much as 95 per cent of the population, in trading, local business, and a wide variety of other, informal contexts in everyday life. Krio has now become so popular and commands such importance and significance in Sierra Leone that even foreign nationals regularly attempt to learn it.

Concerning the actual origins of this enormously successful English-based creole, there are three theories that have regularly been put forward and defended in the literature.

The Americo-Caribbean Origin Theory   This theory claims that Krio originated in the Americas as a result of the Atlantic Slave Trade and was transplanted into Freetown when the colony was declared a haven for freed slaves at the end of the eighteenth century. It is suggested that the Maroons in particular may have developed a pidgin form of English during the period when they developed as a community in Jamaica, prior to being resettled in Sierra Leone, and that their pidgin subsequently developed further into Krio. In support of such a theory, it is pointed out that there are creoles with striking similarities to Krio elsewhere in the Caribbean today.

The Domestic Pre-settlement Theory   This theory suggests that there existed an English-based pidgin along the African coast before the settlement of the colonies, and that such a contact language was taken with slaves to the new world and developed into Krio, prior to being reimported to Sierra Leone. It is believed that the earliest form of Krio was therefore a lingua franca spoken along the Guinea coast between the first European traders and local Africans.

The Domestic Post-settlement Theory   The most commonly held theory of the evolution of Krio suggests that it came into being in Freetown between the late eighteenth century and the early nineteenth century following the founding of the settlement. It is held that Krio arose first as a pidgin, then as a fully-fledged creole with mother-tongue speakers due to the pressing need for a common means of communication among the diverse groups of settlers in the colony (as described in section 7.2): the Nova Scotians, the survivors of the Black Poor, the Maroons, the tens of thousands of Liberated Africans, the British colonists, and the Sierra Leonean inhabitants of the Freetown peninsula at the time of the slave resettlements in Freetown. Each of these groups had their peculiar linguistic and socio-cultural identities, and the Liberated Africans in particular were of heterogeneous origin, speaking many different African languages (Spitzer 1974: 11). Krio is suggested to have emerged from this conglomeration of languages due to the necessity for the settlers to interact with each other for simple survival needs.

Certainly, when one considers the Krio lexicon today and in records of the past, one finds borrowings and input from an extremely wide range of sources, with English and Yoruba being most present, then Hausa, Wolof, Portuguese, Jamaican Creole, Arabic, Fanti, French, Fula, Mende, Temne, and other African languages. With such a tremendously mixed lexical background and the situation present in Freetown at the turn of the nineteenth century, it seems most likely that Krio did evolve in Freetown among its mixed population, first as a simple pidgin, and then as a more complete creole as it came to be used by the settlers' children as their mother tongue, eventually metamorphosing into the Krio language that is known today.

In more recent years, efforts have been made conservatively within academic circles to identify a standard form of Krio, which can be used in education and as a model for L2 learners. Though there has been certain success in the description of standard L1 Krio, the properties of standard Krio have at present not been fully adopted by the huge L2 speaking population, and there are actually many different variant L2 forms of Krio which have emerged as a result of the massive spread of the language throughout the country among speakers for whom Krio is a second language. Amongst the Mendes, the Temnes, the Limbas and other groups there are clearly variant forms in syntax, phonology, and the lexicon, and the systematic production of 'dialects' quite different from the variety used at home by L1 speakers. Examples of some of the variation found in non-standard Krio are provided in Table 7.1 where the regional varieties are compared with Standard English and Standard Krio varieties.

Table 7.1 Comparison of regional varieties of Krio with Standard Krio and Standard English.

Regional Varieties	Standard Krio	Standard English
We tu ɛn in na padi.	In na mi padi.	He is my friend.
Na mi de stɔdi am.	Na mi de tek an lɛsin.	I am his/her tutor.
Mi pɛn dɔn kɔt ink.	Mi pɛn dɔn tap fɔ rayt.	There is no more ink in my pen.
Sɛn fɔ mi rɛs, ya.	Briŋ rɛs fɔ mi, ya.	Bring me some rice, OK.
Di chɔp dɔn rɛdi mek wi chɔp.	Di it dɔn redi, lɛ wi it.	The food is ready let's eat.

It is relevant to note that the vast majority of L2 speakers of Krio in Sierra Leone learn it not from L1 speakers, who are in the minority, but from L2 speakers, who essentially dominate the Krio-speaking environment. Most L2 speakers also do not learn the language primarily to communicate with L1 speakers, but rather to communicate with other L2 speakers who have different mother tongues. Many L2 speakers have become extremely confident in their forms of Krio, and ironically are now exerting an influence on the Krio spoken by the L1 population, with various previously non-standard forms creeping into the speech of native speakers of Krio.

In terms of how Krio is added to the linguistic inventory commanded by multilingual Sierra Leoneans, patterns of bi- and multilingualism vary considerably from area to area and person to person. In Freetown where the percentage of the educated and literate is highest, people are frequently bilingual in Krio and English and possibly also know a third language such as Temne, Limba, or Fula (or Lebanese, Arabic,

French, etc. in the case of those with ancestry in other countries). As one progresses into the interior of the country and away from Freetown, English quickly becomes much less commonly known, and Krio becomes the dominant vehicle of inter-ethnic communication functioning with one or two other local languages.

As Krio has come to be used so extensively by multilingual speakers in different situations, the vocabulary has been enriched and considerably expanded, allowing Krio to be used in almost all of the contexts of everyday life that Sierra Leoneans encounter on a regular basis, outside the very formal, where English still dominates and is spoken by those who have a good level of education (approximately 10 per cent). Given this widespread use of Krio in a broad array of domains and the fact that Krio is known by almost all of the country's population, the question naturally arises whether Krio should be considered for formal elevation to the status of official or national language of Sierra Leone. In order to examine the feasibility of such a potential increase in the official status of Krio in the country, it is necessary to take into account general attitudes towards the language held among both L2 and L1 speakers, along with aspects of the social history of the Krio people and their interactions with the rest of the country's population. A brief description of the sociolinguistic relation of Krio and its speakers to the population of Sierra Leone past and present is now provided in section 7.4.

7.4 The Krios and their Language: Attitudes and History

7.4.1 Negative Issues Concerning the Krios and their Language

Spencer-Walters (2006: 236) points out that the resettlement of emancipated slaves in Sierra Leone was originally conceived of as a 'civilizing project', which it was intended would demonstrate to both Europeans and other African nations the possibility of creating a 'civilized' African society. The 'Sierra Leone Experiment' therefore placed considerable emphasis on providing Western education for the mixed population of resettled Africans, and encouraged the adoption of various aspects of Western culture, including Christian religion. Significant numbers of the Krio took advantage of this opportunity to gain a formal education, and from the mid nineteenth century onwards many used their qualifications to obtain positions as doctors, lawyers, and other professional and clerical appointments in the colonial bureaucracy, out-competing other Sierra Leonean Africans who had not been given access to education by the British (Dixon-Fyle and Cole 2006: 16). The successful and educated among the Krios often chose to adopt western names and keenly absorbed and manifested many trappings of Western culture, to the extent that 'many were proud to call themselves not just Christians but "Black Englishmen" '(ibid: 3). Such a positive response to the exposure to education and Western civilization offered to the Krios was then frequently rewarded in the form of privileged access to a range of resources controlled by the colonial authorities, allowing the Krios to establish themselves with many advantages not readily available to other Sierra Leoneans.

During the course of the nineteenth century, the variety of groups resettled by the British in Freetown increasingly coalesced and came to share an emergent, new identity, cultivated by the common experience and special conditions of life present under direct British rule, and developed as a community with properties distinct from those of other indigenous African groups, including now a largely stabilized creole language used as a means of in-group communication in domains where standard English was not utilized. Importantly, it is reported that the accelerated educational and economic advancement of the Krios, combined with their particular path of development and separation from other groups, also resulted in perceptions of superiority among the Krios, at least among those who strove to imitate a European style of life and considered themselves cultured, educated, and successful. Attitudes of prejudice and contempt from the educated Krios towards other local, indigenous groups seen as backward and uncultured consequently created a significant ethnic division between the Krios and other indigenous peoples in British-administered Sierra Leone. The latter, for their part, felt that the Krios received an unfair share of resources administered and distributed by the British, and in doing so severely inhibited the development of the non-Krio population, hence negative feelings between portions of the Krio and non-Krio population came into existence from the nineteenth century onwards.[5]

A perception that the Krios and other Sierra Leonean groups were quite different in nature and origin grew and was shared by Krio and non-Krios alike through the colonial period, deepening the divide between the two parts of the population. As Cole (2006: 49) notes, as independence approached Sierra Leone in the 1950s: 'Both sides had been socialized into thinking of each other as different and separate', and the potential value that a shared experience of British occupation might have brought to the growth and promotion of an all-inclusive Sierra Leonean national identity was not exploited at independence. Quite the contrary occurred, in fact, and ethnic divisions were manipulated for political ends by extremists on both Krio and non-Krio sides, causing a general increase in mistrust and a negative hardening of ethnic boundaries. In the period since the achievement of independence, Krio relations with other groups have frequently remained less than optimal, with continued economic inequality in the country still being attributed to earlier British favouring of the Krio and stimulating 'animosities [which] have gravely threatened national unity since independence' (Dixon-Fyle and Cole 2006: 15).

Linguistically, it can be noted that Krio as a language was for long perceived as a non-indigenous language, primarily a reduced variety of English, this further embedding the distinct foreign-origin status of its native speakers, the Krios, in the eyes of other Sierra Leoneans. As a 'mixed' language lacking the authority and purity of either English or other indigenous languages, Krio has been viewed by some as less genuine and less worthy of respect than Sierra Leone's larger languages or English, and was

---

[5] A violent physical manifestation of anti-Krio feeling surfaced in the Hut Tax War in 1898 when hundreds of Krios were killed by other groups in the (mistaken) belief that the Krios supported a new tax introduced by the British, which threatened to be a major burden for other Sierra Leoneans.

actually banned from use in schools and official domains until quite recently, when 'rehabilitated' along with Temne, Mende, and Limba in the development of indigenous languages in education from the early 1980s (Sengova 2006: 184). Negative attitudes held towards Krio on the grounds of its being a mixed language of foreign origin (or at least perceived as such) may have also translated into prejudices against its native speakers, according to Bangura (2006: 163), and it is often remarked that the phrase 'Krio nɔto neshɔn' (lit. '(the) Krio (are) not a nation') has been used to disparage the Krios as a mixed collection of people not having the authenticity of a real ethnic group ('neshɔn/nation' here being used in the sense of a distinct ethnic group of Sierra Leone; Spencer-Walters 2006: 226). Both the Krio themselves and their language have therefore occasioned negative reactions from other parts of the population in Sierra Leone, on the grounds of unfair past economic advantage, perceptions of contempt held towards uneducated non-Krios by the Krios, and a language portrayed as impure and foreign in basic origin.

Furthermore, it is not only non-Krios who have voiced criticisms of the Krio language in some form or another. The fact that the Krios were the first to obtain access to (English-medium) education during colonial times may have had negative effects on their own attitude towards Krio, increasing the intensity of an already low estimation of the language. When many Krios availed themselves of education, they neglected their own native language, and passed this legacy of negation on to their children, preferring to use standard English wherever possible. In the 1980s, when there were proposals to formally introduce Krio as a language in schooling alongside Temne, Mende, and Limba, elements of the Krio population were the most vocal in their opposition to the use of Krio as a medium of instruction (Spencer-Walters 2006: 240). Krio as a language can therefore be said to have experienced an 'embarrassing past'. Unlike the situation with other Sierra Leonean languages, whose communities did not inhibit or denigrate use of their native languages, the children of the Krios were in many instances made to feel ashamed of their mother tongue, and even today there are some among the educated Krios who still see the use of Krio as having an essentially negative impact on the cultivation of standard English and so being potentially harmful to the academic development of the young. With this kind of negative inbuilt attitude towards Krio in parts of the Krio community, the present educated generation of Krios have not had much to gain linguistically from their parents, many of whom scarcely used the language at home. Because of this, the average educated native speaker of Krio today may actually have a smaller Krio lexicon than second-language speakers of Krio from the Mende, Temne, or Limba groups, an odd situation indeed.[6]

---

[6] In very recent years, further prejudice against Krio in general has been triggered among certain educated elites by the growth of a form of Krio known as 'Savisman Krio' (lit. 'service-man Krio'), which has become particularly popular among drug-taking youths and other elements on the fringe of society, and which is marked by the use of vulgar and violent language. The worry has been expressed that this variety may be coming to displace the use of more mainstream Krio. However, it is actually very unlikely that this form of Krio will somehow replace more commonly spoken Krio, as Savisman Krio is only used by a very restricted section of the population. Nevertheless, concern over the emergence of Savisman Krio

In highlighting the complications for the future development of Krio that the socio-linguistic dynamics of the past may bring with it, we should also add the more purely linguistic issue of the lack of a standardized orthography during much of the history of Krio prior to 1980, when a widely accepted writing system for the language was finally established in Fyle and Jones' Krio–English Dictionary. Spencer-Walters (2006: 239) notes that variation in the way that Krio has been written in the past has hindered the creation of a well-respected literature, and even today a good knowledge of stan-dardized Krio orthography may still be poorly spread, even among those engaged in the creation of literature. Furthermore, as this system makes use of various symbols which do not occur in the Roman alphabet, difficulties for its use in typesetting and word processing may sometimes also occur.

7.4.2 Positive Issues Concerning Krio–non-Krio Ethnic Relations and Krio Language

From the discussion above in section 7.4.1, it is clear that various aspects of the history of Krio and its native speakers might be seen as potential obstacles to the elevation of Krio into a higher official capacity, this stemming principally from negative attitudes to the Krio people on the one hand and Krio as a creolized language on the other. Although such attitudes may exist among segments of the population, a fuller picture of the situation of Krio in Sierra Leone today and in the recent past also reveals many more positive perceptions of Krio and its usefulness for the maintenance of inter-ethnic relations in the country.

First of all, though the most strident dismissal of Krio as a 'broken' or 'bastardized' form of standard English has frequently come from within the Krio elite itself (Spencer-Walters 2006: 240), there are also members of the educated Krio elite who have demonstrated more enlightened views of Krio. A prime example of a quite different attitude to Krio is noted in Spencer-Walters (2006: 247) in the case of the prominent Krio journalist Thomas Decker, who engaged in a wide range of activities designed to promote a more positive awareness of Krio as a valuable and 'genuine' language able to express complex thoughts just as any other language may. This included the writing of plays in Krio, the sustained use of newspaper columns and radio interviews to promote respect for Krio, and the translation of Shakespeare's *Julius Caesar* into the language (here recalling Joseph Nyerere's translation of Shakespeare into Swahili to promote Swahili as a national language in Tanzania: see Topan, this volume). Decker's actions prompted others to follow suit and resulted in a wave of plays written in Krio through the 1970s and 1980s.

Secondly, just as the Krio elite were not necessarily all negative in their perceptions of Krio, Bangura (2006), Cole (2006), and others stress that the Krio population as a whole was not nearly as monolithic as is sometimes understood, and that in addition

has strengthened the attachment that certain L1 Krio speakers have to English and increased their negative views of Krio.

to the educated elites who may have been largely absorbed in adopting aspects of Western language and culture, there were (and are) also very many among the Krio population who were less educated and belonged to the working-class, and who did not assimilate or attempt to copy British ways of life, often remaining Muslim or animist in religious belief despite strong encouragements to convert to Christianity. This less vocal but numerically significant section of the Krios is not associated with any overt stigmatization of Krio parallel to that exhibited by (many of) the elites.

Third, it is important to recognize that negative attitudes to Krio as a creolized language form may not exist widely outside the Krio elite and certain other educated non-Krios. Among the many in Sierra Leone who have not established an ability to speak standard English, a proficiency in Krio, with its heavily English-sourced lexicon, is in fact considered to be a desirable index of civil exposure, moving an individual closer to being able to speak English at some point, if additional effort is applied to 'convert' knowledge of Krio into knowledge of standard English. Krio is thus seen by many as a positive stepping-stone to education, with the ultimate indicator of having acquired a recognizable standard of education being the ability to understand, speak, and manipulate standard English. An ability to learn and speak Krio, therefore, brings those who aspire to learn English a step further along the path to their intended goal, and the regular use of Krio is not perceived to be an impediment to the proper acquisition of English (quite the contrary, in fact).

A fourth, major point is the simple observation that knowledge and use of Krio has spread massively throughout Sierra Leone among speakers of other languages and is thriving and developing in a strikingly vibrant way. Ironically, while Krio was being stifled in the homes of educated native speakers in Freetown and a rather decayed form of the language was being passed on to their offspring, those in the provinces have expanded Krio considerably and moulded the language further with forms and patterns from their own native languages, resulting in the creation of a number of different sub-varieties: Mende-Krio, Temne-Krio, and other regional forms (Sengova 2006: 180). The widespread adoption and use of Krio as a means of wider communication is a testament to the high degree to which the language is felt to be acceptable as well as practical, and would certainly not have occurred in such an unforced and spontaneous way had there been deeply entrenched negative attitudes to Krio present in the population. Krio is now also taught formally in the educational system, and much popularity is recorded for Krio classes, both in schools and at the teacher training and university levels.

As a further significant part of the ongoing development of Krio in Sierra Leone, a recent research project carried out by one of the authors among various categories of L1 and L2 Krio speakers in the Freetown area observed that there seems to be an interesting increase in the domains in which Krio is coming to be used, and Krio is now beginning to compete with English in certain formal contexts hitherto fully monopolized by English. The study, yet to be published, revealed that Krio is being increasingly used in certain circles and formal settings where previously only English would have occurred to deliberately facilitate a more informal atmosphere and break down stiff social barriers. Such an innovation again underlines a broad current acceptance of Krio and importantly suggests that use of the language may no longer be seen as restricted to purely informal contexts.

Finally, the uncoerced, extensive adoption of Krio as a lingua franca which is ethnically neutral among the majority non-Krio population has meant that Krio has come to play a highly important role in the negotiation of inter-ethnic relations in Sierra Leone, and it is widely acknowledged that the availability of Krio as a common language has been a major factor helping ease situations of ethnic conflict in the country. Sengova (2006: 172) highlights this critical, binding function of Krio in recent times:

> Many would agree that Krio has not only successfully bridged differences in ethnicity, language, culture, and so forth among Sierra Leone's many groups, it has also become a vital communicative tool creating social harmony, cohesion and collaboration among the population.... the *lingua franca* status of Krio in Sierra Leone has also narrowed considerably many socio-cultural and linguistic barriers that might otherwise have created greater political discord than that recently witnessed in our decade-old internecine war and carnage in the country.

Krio is therefore seen by many as having helped lessen conflict and divisions in multi-ethnic Sierra Leone, hence while it may not (yet) occur as a strongly positive national symbol which Sierra Leoneans would overtly express pride about and categorize as prestigious, covertly the language has been of much importance in helping maintain the integrity of the nation. Sengova goes on to express a cautious optimism about the future of Sierra Leone, noting the presence of a new attitude of ethnic accommodation in the nation, and again emphasizes the pivotal role that Krio has played in facilitating this:

> 20th century social and political relations in Sierra Leone, especially that between the Krio and the rest of our putative aborigine population appear to be sometimes marred by tension and mistrust, but more recently, conditions also appear to have improved considerably. In one significant respect, Sierra Leoneans have moved from a myth created and held denying nationhood (indigenous ethnicity) to the Krio and commonly spelled in the widely used expression, 'Krio noto nation', to full acceptance of the nation's global multilingualism and ethnic pluralism. The principal vehicle that has brought this about was language and the use of Krio as a unifying vehicle of communication ... The nation now appears to have adopted the Krio language and perhaps many aspects of the Krio social lifestyle and practice that were once held in disdain thanks to a familiar package of colonial stigmas inherited from the European progenitor.   (Sengova 2006: 176–7)

Given such developments and the range of other positive properties associated with Krio here, this now leads us back to Krio and the national/official language question, reapproached in section 7.5.

7.5 Krio: A National Language for Sierra Leone?

Sierra Leone, like many African countries south of the Sahara, is a multilingual, multi-ethnic state which needs to cultivate a notion of national unity in order to assist its future survival as a single territorial entity. As in many other West African states, feelings of national identity were not stimulated during the period of colonial occupation, and Sierra Leone attained independence without having established the clear foundations of a distinct and coherent nation. In recent years, the country has experienced much internal ethnic strife which has threatened the continued stability of Sierra Leone as a country. It is therefore of much concern that all means possible be found to re-establish inter-ethnic harmony and create a feeling of belonging to a single nation among the various groups present in the country. In such a general context, the identification and promotion of a national language for Sierra Leone, which could be used to build up feelings of positive cohesion in the country, would certainly be an important forward step in the pursuit of establishing a broad national identity and encouraging unity among Sierra Leoneans.

In (re)considering the potential options available for such a purpose, these realistically reduce to a choice from the following set of languages spoken in the country: (a) one or more of the major indigenous languages, (b) English, or (c) Krio. With regard to the first possibility, although Sierra Leone possesses regional languages such as Temne and Mende which have long enabled different communities to communicate and do business, these languages do not have the obvious potential to enhance national cohesiveness and form the basis of a true national identity. In fact, such languages have a greater potential to become a source of political divisiveness and social fragmentation if ethnicity is made use of for political means, as has often sadly been the case in Sierra Leone, as in other African countries. This is not to say that there should be any repression of the major indigenous languages as prominent symbols of the ethnic identities they are associated with. Such sub-national identities should not be interfered with and should be allowed to continue to function as useful bonds among different groups in Sierra Leone. However, on top of regional and ethnic identities, there is a need to construct a higher-level national cohesion to enhance Sierra Leonean nationhood and development of the country. What Sierra Leone therefore needs is a language that can hold the people together in a nationalistic bond, one which they can identify and relate to in a safe way, without losing their ethnicity, jeopardizing their cultural heritage, and endangering their traditional values.

Considering the possibility of English being used to fulfil such a role, in Africa in general, there is a common view (which many would call a misconception) that national integration can be achieved through the use of ex-colonial languages such as English, French, and Portuguese to facilitate inter-ethnic communication. In the case of Sierra Leone, English has become entrenched as the only official language of the country and the primary index of higher education. However, many would argue that real integration can never be achieved in this manner. Bamgbose (1991:

18) summarizes the potential weakness in the use of colonial languages as national languages in African states in the following way:

> The point which is often missed in this approach is that the kind of integration made possible in this way is only horizontal integration which involves a combination of the segment of the educated elites from each of the different ethnic or linguistic groups in the country.

In a situation such as that in Sierra Leone where only 10 per cent of the population is proficient in English, ethnic diversity rather than ethnic integration will be the fundamental outcome. The dangers here are very clear, and a nation that intends to foster true nationalism and ethnic cohesiveness must look for a more inclusive and more embracing approach. This kind of targeted national integration needs to cut across ethnic borders and should result in what Bamgbose (1991) calls genuine 'vertical integration'. In Sierra Leone, current prognoses suggest that it is quite unlikely that English will become known by a much greater percentage of the population in the near future, and therefore English is not a good candidate for selection as national language.

In many sub-Saharan African states, once major indigenous languages and ex-colonial languages are discounted as possible choices for promotion as national languages this often exhausts the linguistic inventory present in a country and languages conceivable as nationwide means of communication. However, in the case of Sierra Leone, the widely known creole and pidgin language Krio is clearly a further plausible alternative for consideration as the selected national language of the country, and has many positive attributes to support its candidacy in such a role.

As noted earlier, an extremely important property of Krio is the simple fact that it is known by as much as 95 per cent of the population, giving it a combined first and second language population that is proportionately greater in Sierra Leone than that enjoyed by major languages in most other countries of sub-Saharan Africa. This very extensive spread of Krio puts it in a position where promotion of Krio to the status of a national language would result in Sierra Leone having a national language known by almost all of its population, and able to achieve the kind of vertical integration Bamgbose highlights as essential for both the development of democracy and an inclusive national identity. Today Krio is not just a language of the Krio population of Freetown, who have frequently disparaged and rejected it, but a language of the whole country, spoken with enthusiasm by people in all parts of Sierra Leone. It is furthermore a language which most non-Krio Sierra Leoneans have come in contact with almost simultaneously with their mother tongue or very shortly thereafter, making it an intimate and very familiar linguistic system.

Concerning the broad spread of Krio among different groups in Sierra Leone, this has had the effect, already noted in part, that Krio has absorbed various phonological, lexical, and syntactic features of other languages in the country, giving it a vibrant multi-ethnic and nationalistic flavour, and resulting in it being a preferred language in situations of inter-ethnic communication where socio-cultural boundaries are transcended, and differences between Sierra Leoneans are no longer emphasized. Although Krio may in origin be a creole language with a strong English lexical base, it can now be suggested to qualify as Sierra Leonean and at least semi-indigenous due to having been continually developed in the country under the clear influence of local languages, rendering it less obviously foreign and unauthentic. Variation and deviation from the Krio of L1 speakers can therefore be seen in a positive light as having helped increase the acceptability of Krio and feelings of identification with the language among the population as a whole.

In virtue of all of the above – the early intimate familiarity with Krio among L2 speakers, its local variation, and its highly widespread nature – Krio can now be seen as the principal cultural bond that holds the people of Sierra Leone together as a single national whole. The language has a unique potential to establish cohesiveness among the population, is the only language that can dissipate inter-ethnic tension and bring Sierra Leoneans together as a single nation, and is able to communicate meaning to (almost) the entire population. Though it may not so far be seen as overtly prestigious (in the sense that overt pride towards the language is not frequently expressed), it has perhaps already become a powerful 'covert' mark of national identity, being highly valued by much of the population in a generally unstated way. Finally, in thinking about how Krio measures up to the current official language of the country, English, it has to be conceded that the latter holds a position of unquestioned importance in many institutions and settings in Sierra Leone and is valued for its use in formal and 'elevated' domains. Krio, it can now be noted, also has a clear potential for use in more 'sober' situations and its occurrence does not necessarily result in any loss of the formality of a situation, though it certainly can be used to heighten feelings of informality. Because of such versatility and the ability to be used in both informal and formal settings, Krio can be seen as a fitting and convenient 'deputy' for English in many situations which might be thought of as requiring the use of an official-type language.

The range of positive properties reviewed here and in section 7.4.2 suggests that Sierra Leone should take advantage of the special opportunity Krio presents for helping stimulate national integration and elevate Krio to some higher nationwide status. We therefore submit the following as a practicable way forward to encourage the further growth of national identity in Sierra Leone at the same time as satisfying requirements of nationism and the maintenance of linguistic links with the outside world. We suggest that Krio be formally recognized as a co-official language of the country along with English, and that Krio also be given the status of Sierra Leone's unique national language, these new roles to be supported by the development of Krio for extended use in education and the media, as well as in contexts such as the national anthem, the military, and public address to national audiences. Promoting Krio as a co-official rather than unique official language of Sierra Leone pragmatically recognizes the fact that even with heavy promotion of Krio, English is unlikely to fully disappear from use in various formal domains of life given its long-accrued sociolinguistic clout, international integrity, and educational leverage, but is also not likely to become known by a majority of the population in the immediately foreseeable future. However, if Krio is adopted as the national and a co-official language of Sierra Leone, the vast majority of the population who currently have no access to the present official language, English, will automatically have the opportunity to become involved in important national matters, enhancing feelings of belonging to a single national unit. This kind of inclusive participation in the future development of the nation will only occur when an appropriate indigenous (or 'semi-indigenous') language is adequately empowered, which further strongly supports the case for adding Krio to English as the official languages of the country. We furthermore suggest that the major regional languages, Temne, Mende, and Limba, be recognized as official languages in the provinces in which they predominantly occur, and be similarly developed for increased use within education and the media. Finally, we support additional increased use of other Sierra Leonean languages in the media, where this is practically possible.

If Krio is promoted in this way to help the growth of Sierra Leonean national identity, it will certainly need to confront and overcome a number of obvious challenges. First of all, if Krio is elevated to the status of national and co-official language, it will be necessary to establish more precisely what is to be considered the standard form of the language, and a careful description of standard Krio will be important so as to ensure consistency in official/formal representations. Secondly, there will most probably be certain negative attitudinal reactions to the official elevation of Krio among various elite sections of the population, and these will have to be addressed if the recommended linguistic resolution is to exercise any lasting vertical effect on development.[7] Thirdly, given the small percentage of native speakers of Krio in comparison to the very large L2 population, questions are increasingly likely to arise questions relating to the legitimate 'ownership' of the language and who has the right to determine what should be accepted as the standard forms of the language – the L1 Krio population, or the majority L2-speaking population, which makes use of a wide range of variant forms. Despite such obstacles, we confidently believe that Sierra Leoneans

---

[7] Concerning the issue of how negative aspects of the image of the Krio in the past may be 'rehabilitated' in a more inclusive drive towards Sierra Leonean nationhood, previously there has been an emphasis in histories of the country on the role of non-Sierra Leonean groups in forming the Krio population, and this has clearly stressed the non-indigenous nature of the group. However, recently scholars such as Cole (2006: 33) suggest that more recognition can and should be given to the presence of locally recaptured slaves in building up the Krio group, and that there were also many Sierra Leonean slaves who were emancipated and brought to join the settlement in Freetown, ultimately forming the Krio group. Though the numbers of these locally recaptured slaves were much less than slaves resettled in Freetown from other regions of West Africa, a careful presentation and highlighting of the original local component in the Krio population may well help in further 'authenticating' the current status of the Krios as an indigenous group.

have the ability to make a success story from the promotion of Krio to national and official language status, and that if Sierra Leone shows itself able to successfully elevate a creole/pidgin language to national and official language status, this may well serve as an important inspiration for other African countries to attempt similar solutions to the problem of language and national integration where widespread pidgin/creole languages exist.

8

Ghana: Indigenous Languages, English, and an Emerging National Identity

Akosua Anyidoho and M. E. Kropp Dakubu

8.1 Introduction

Like most sub-Saharan countries, Ghana is highly multilingual and linguistically complex. But at the same time, the Akan language with its close relatives squarely occupies two-thirds of the country, and has had and continues to have a strong influence on the rest of it. Although it may well be true that the national geo-political borders were a colonial creation based more on the relations between the European colonizing powers than on the local situation, it is also a fact that today's Ghana almost exactly coincides with the territory and sphere of influence of the Akan-speaking Asante (Ashanti) empire in the nineteenth century (Wilks 1993: 203). However this does not necessarily simplify the problem of the relationships between language, ethnic identity, nationalism, and the existence and nature of Ghanaian national identity, and might even be said to complicate it.

It is sometimes doubted whether ex-colonies such as Ghana have a national identity at all, but Ghana became independent in 1957, before more than half of its present population was born. People under the age of 50 have grown up in an independent state with characteristic institutions, surrounded by states that contrast with it in many ways. We believe that there is indeed such a thing as a Ghanaian national identity, and that most of the population is conscious of it. The question then arises, what role did language play in the nationalist movement that led to the creation of the independent state of Ghana, and what place does it have in nationalist political ideologies today? Pursuing these topics we examine language policy and practice as they have developed since pre-colonial times and as they are expressed today, especially in education, in the media, and in government both local and national.

We begin with a general overview of the language geography of Ghana. This is followed by a discussion of the ideology of language and national identity as it

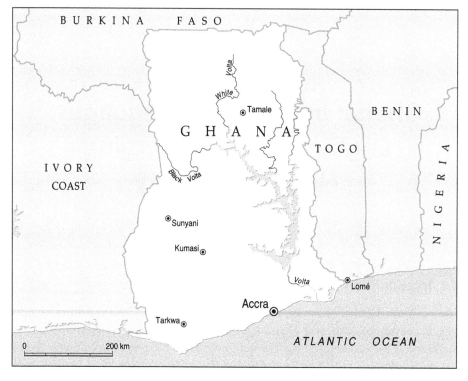

Ghana

developed up to and after the time of independence from British colonial rule in 1957, and then a section on the intimately related topic of language policy in education. We follow these overviews with sections on the relationship between language and identity both national and sub-national as displayed by various language groups in the country. We conclude with remarks on the tension between national integration and democracy as expressed in the public discourse.

8.2 Overview of Multilingualism in Ghana

In terms of the number of languages that count as 'indigenous' to its territory, Ghana has approximately fifty non-mutually intelligible languages, almost all belonging to the Gur and Kwa branches of the Niger-Congo phylum (the sole exceptions are two small languages belonging to the Mande branch, Ligby and Bisa). With a population of a little over 18 million, according to the Census held in 2000, this means that the 'average' Ghanaian language has about 360,000 speakers. But of course, very few languages are 'average'. The Akan language has more than seven million native speakers, and many more second-language speakers, while Safaliba (spoken in the far west of the Northern Region) has five thousand speakers or less. Most languages fall somewhere between these extremes. Besides the indigenous languages, two languages belonging to very different language families are used throughout the country: Hausa, a Chadic (Afro-Asiatic) language, and English, a Germanic (Indo-European) language. They are the first languages or mother tongues of extremely few, but they are very important to inter-group communication, especially in urban centres.

Linguistically and to some extent culturally, the country is divided roughly into two parts. The languages spoken south of the confluence of the White and Black Volta rivers are classified within Niger-Congo as Kwa, although the relationship among them is not a close one. Akan in its many dialect forms, Nzema and its close relatives, and the Guan (or Guang) languages are all closely and obviously related, but those to the east – Ga-Dangme, Ewe, and most of the other languages of the Volta Region – are very dissimilar and quite distantly related, to each other and to the Comoe languages. To the north, in the savannah regions, the languages belong to the Gur family, principally the Oti-Volta and the Grusi branches of Central Gur. (For further details see Dakubu 1988.)

In both north and south, certain languages have historically been the languages of expanding empires. In the south several Akan-speaking kingdoms went through expansionist phases, but by far the most powerful in recent times was Asante (Ashanti). The Asante dialect of the Akan language continues to expand as a second language in urban areas such as Accra, the capital, and to some extent throughout the country.

Ewe is the second largest language in the country and the largest to have been seriously affected by colonial boundary drawing, since perhaps half of its speakers are in the Republic of Togo, and all its close linguistic relatives are in Togo and the Republic of Benin. Within Ghana the Ewe language has spread from east to west, sometimes at the expense of languages that were already there, and is used as a second language among some of the smaller linguistic groupings in the Volta Region. Over the past three centuries several Akan-speaking communities have also established themselves east of the Volta.

In the north, there have historically been several expansionist kingdoms, notably Gonja and Dagbon. However in the eighteenth century Asante defeated both of these kingdoms (Ward 1948: 131). Their languages, Gonja and Dagbani, respectively, are securely established in their home areas, but there is no evidence that either of these, or any other Gur language, is important as a second language, either among northern communities or among northern groups in the cities of the south. An exception must be made for Wali, the language of Wa, capital of the Upper West Region. Although the Wa kingdom was never among the largest or strongest, it is and was the only commercial town of any size in its region, and its language, which is for the most part mutually intelligible with the Dagaare of the surrounding countryside, is reported to be spreading in that area as a trade language.

8.3 The English Language, the Language of Governance, and Ghanaian Identity

Currently English is the official language of Ghana, while about a dozen Ghanaian languages are recognized for certain purposes in education and information dissemination. It has never been clearly stated that all Ghanaians should necessarily become English speaking, although it could be argued that this is the implication of the current education policy, discussed later in this chapter. Certainly it has never publicly been explicitly advocated that English is or should be a marker of Ghanaian identity.[1] Nevertheless, we propose, somewhat contentiously, that the situation may well be developing in this direction.

Ghana was the first sub-Saharan British colony (the Gold Coast and Northern Territories) to achieve independence, in 1957. In line with the Pan-African ideology of the country's leadership headed by Kwame Nkrumah, the first president, the name of the country was changed from the colonial (and pre-colonial) 'Gold Coast', which signified only the European trading interest, to the name of a West African medieval empire that once existed not in the territory of present-day Ghana, but on the Mauritania–Mali border. However language reform did not go beyond this symbolic gesture. The working language of the British colonial government had of course been English, and the practice was inherited by the pre-independence Legislative Assembly and then the independent Parliament and the national Courts of Justice. All three of Ghana's neighbours, the Republics of Togo, Ivory Coast, and Burkina Faso (formerly Upper Volta) were colonies of France, and are officially 'francophone' to this day, so that 'anglophone' Ghana is surrounded by countries with a different linguistic, political, and educational history.

Nearly all legal and constitutional documents from colonial times to the present are silent on any possible role for Ghanaian languages, tacitly confining them to domestic, local, and 'traditional', non-literate domains. In 1934, the 'Standing Orders and Rules of the Legislative Council of the Gold Coast Colony' stated that 'The proceedings and debates of the Council shall be in the English language, but (ii) a Member may present a Petition in any other language if the Petition be accompanied by an English translation certified to be correct by the Member who presents it.'[2] A year later the 'Ordinances of the Gold Coast, Ashanti, Northern Territories and Togoland under British Mandate' made no mention of language except to state that, under 'Fees for Particular Duties Division 4 Interpretation in Civil Causes (c)' there should be a fee 'for interpreting any language except one in common use in

---

[1] Although Boadi's (1994: 56) statement that 'One hopes that . . . a standard Ghanaian English will emerge' is coherent only if a characteristically Ghanaian English is to be an index of Ghanaian national identity.

[2] The Standing Orders and Rules of the Legislative Council of the Gold Coast Colony. Accra: Government Printing Office, 1934. Section A1 Article 3 (1).

the district, for each day 1 to 5 shillings'.[3] Evidently, interpreting in the language in common use, which must have been a very frequent occurrence, was not worth a fee.

Documents reflecting the constitutional history of the country are also silent on the subject of language, with one notable exception. The Gold Coast Constitution of 1951 provided among the qualifications for 'Special and Elected Membership' of the Legislative Assembly that such a member must be 'able to speak and, unless incapacitated ... read the English language with a degree of proficiency sufficient to enable him to take an active part in the proceedings of the Assembly'.[4] Subsequent constitutions maintained this requirement verbatim,[5] until it was dropped in the Constitution of 1992, which is in operation today.[6] It has been pointed out that, while it has been generally felt that making English the sole official language avoids a potentially divisive issue, this omission means that the current constitutional status of English is unclear (Asante 2006: 14). In apparent contrast, at the time of independence, a person wishing to be registered as a citizen of Ghana needed to satisfy the relevant Minister 'that he ... had sufficient knowledge of a Ghanaian language',[7] and the Constitutions of 1969 (pg. 10 art. 2), 1979 (pg. 17 art. 17(2)), and 1992 (pg. 8 art. 9 (2)) all maintain knowledge of a Ghanaian language as a requirement for naturalization.

In none of these documents is there any explicit recognition that a very large proportion of the population cannot function in English at the required level. All constitutions have sections on the legal rights of citizens, but there is no constitutional right to due process in a language the accused understands. It appears that knowledge of a Ghanaian language is a necessary condition for becoming a Ghanaian citizen, but not a sufficient condition for exercising one's rights as such.

Colonial language policy is also the reason why Hausa is an inter-ethnic lingua franca. When the colonial regime established a local police force, and later an army division to fight in its wars, it recruited mainly men from the savannah regions extending from today's northern Ghana to Nigeria. Hausa was deliberately promoted as the language to be used with and within the lower ranks (Gillespie 1955). Hausa is still maintained as a language of inter-ethnic communication in towns among people originating from outside southern Ghana, especially from areas to the northeast. For Ghanaian speakers Hausa is certainly not a language of ethnic identity, any more than English is. However for many it does signify a kind of Ghanaian

---

[3] Ordinances of the Gold Coast, Ashanti, Northern Territories and Togoland under British Mandate. Accra: Government Printing Department (1935). P. 264 Appendix B Part 3.

[4] The Gold Coast Constitution, brought into operation on 1 January 1951. Accra: Government Printing Department (1951). P. 19 art. 42.

[5] Namely, *Constitution of the Republic of Ghana*, Accra-Tema: Ghana Publishing Corporation (1969) art. 57 (1)d pg. 64; *Constitution of the Republic of Ghana*, Accra-Tema: Ghana Publishing Corporation (1979) art. 76(1)c.

[6] *Constitution of the Republic of Ghana*, Tema: Ghana Publishing Corporation (1992), pg. 73 art. 94(1)c.

[7] The Proposals of the Constitutional Commission for a Constitution for Ghana (1968) p. 37, para. 145, which refers to the Ghana Nationality and Citizenship Act of 1957.

identity, or rather an urban identity related to 'Ghana' as a modern, urban idea associated with national government and the inter-regional, inter-ethnic institutions it sponsors.

The question of whether Ghana needs a national language other than English has arisen frequently in the public and academic discourses on national integration and democracy – two processes that do not necessarily reinforce each other. Many have felt that such a language is needed, whether or not it is given formal official status (Ansre 1970; Chinebuah 1977), and in 1971 a motion to this effect was passed in parliament, although it had no practical consequences (Amonoo 1989: 42–3). Apronti, reflecting the opinion of many intellectuals of the time, believed that the dominant position of English in the Ghanaian state 'calls into question the very idea of sovereignty' (Apronti 1974: 54). He regarded it as the preserve of the elite, and its use as the language of national political discourse as inherently undemocratic. Yankah (2004) argues in the same tradition, see also Boadi (1994: 61). These scholars also recognize however that selecting a single Ghanaian language is politically very difficult. Apronti and Yankah advocate a gradual approach, by encouraging learning of a second Ghanaian language in the schools and expression in Ghanaian languages in the public media. Chinebuah (1977) on the other hand strongly advocated Akan, as had such distinguished non-linguists as Ephraim Amu, K.A.B. Jones-Quartey before him and later, somewhat cautiously, Amonoo (1989: 43).

In October–November 2005 the present authors conducted two questionnaire surveys, one among people living and working in Accra, another among students of the University of Ghana.[8] The questionnaires were aimed at, among other things, eliciting attitudes on the question of a national language. The samples, consisting of 143 persons living in Accra and 108 university students (both Arts and Sciences), were small and represent mainly (but not solely) the relatively well educated, the relatively well off, and females. The results therefore are by no means definitive, but they do seem to reflect observable attitudes among the class of people likely to have an opinion on the topic. Mother-tongue speakers of Akan were the largest single linguistic group – 55.3 per cent of the people working in Accra, 38.8 per cent of the university students. English was by far the most generally spoken language – 100 per cent of the students and over 89 per cent of the Accra working group. Akan was also spoken by more than half of each group, all other languages by considerably less than half.

Respondents were asked whether they thought that there is one language that every Ghanaian should be able to speak, and if so, which; and whether this language should be declared a national language for Ghana, with additional questions intended to elicit details of attitudes to specific languages. Not all the responses were clear or quantifiable, but we conclude from them that the Accra bourgeoisie, and the future bourgeoisie as represented by university students, are generally positively

---

[8] This research was supported by the Institute of African Studies, University of Ghana through the Ghana Educational Trust Fund.

oriented to English. It also appears that while linguistic unity is perceived as desirable – 79.6 per cent of the students and 65 per cent of the others thought that there should be one language spoken by all Ghanaians – opinion was evenly split on whether multilingualism is a divisive factor in Ghanaian society, and it is not perceived as a serious problem. Although an indigenous language as national language was considered desirable by many, few held strong feelings about it, and no clear candidate emerged. Even among the Akan, while some favoured Akan as national language this was not the majority position, although many felt all Ghanaians should learn it. This is possibly because English is perceived as in some sense a Ghanaian language (as is Hausa among the relatively few who mentioned it) – some actually included it among the Ghanaian languages they spoke or that people should know.

8.4 Language Policy and Education

If there is any relationship between language and nationalism we would expect it to be reflected in language policy in education, which is a major avenue through which nationalist sensibilities are fostered. Formal education in Ghana began with the activities of European merchants and Christian missionaries on the West African coast. Europeans were active on the coast of Ghana from the end of the fifteenth century, but the history of modern education begins with the establishment of permanent Christian missions in the nineteenth.

The Wesleyan Mission started evangelistic activities along the coast of Ghana in 1838 and later opened schools in the Cape Coast area to train their converts. McWilliam and Kwamena-Poh (1975) report that this mission emphasized English in its school curriculum, not the local language. However, by the 1870s some of the ministers realized that their task of evangelizing would be easier if the children were taught to read Fante. They accordingly started to translate the gospels into Fante and to develop primers, but their efforts were questioned by their own colleagues who supported the use of English. Some of those who were against the development of Fante were Africans who had attended mission schools and/or had received higher education in Europe. These Gold Coast elites viewed English as the language of civilization and religion and did not see the importance of developing the local language (McWilliam and Kwamena-Poh 1975).

Nevertheless, by 1890 there was a nationalist reaction to the sole use of English as school language in the Fante area, expressed in the works of J. E. Caseley Hayford and John Mensah Sarbah, who tried to open their own schools to provide alternative education. Their efforts were unsuccessful because their pupils sought English-style professions, which could only be certified by examining bodies in England.

Meanwhile, the Basel mission established itself in the Akuapem and Ga areas. The first school in Akropong-Akuapem opened in 1843. Unlike the Wesleyans, the Basel Mission believed from the start that spreading the gospel would be accomplished best if the converts could read the Bible in their own language. Thus, the teaching of literacy and content subjects developed in the local language. The Bremen Mission (Norddeutsche Missionsgesellschaft) began work among the Ewe in 1847, using the Ewe language in its schools. These two missions are said to have discouraged the use of English in their schools, not only because they wanted the children to use their primary language, but also because being German, they did not want to encourage the language of their competitors. In any case, the Basel and the Bremen missions laid the foundation for indigenous language education in Twi, Ga, and Ewe. Between 1853 and 1905, they produced primers and readers for school children, grammars, dictionaries, Bibles, and many reading materials.

In 1874 when Britain appropriated the southern part of the country as a crown colony and later began establishing public schools, the medium of instruction was English, as might be expected. Boadi (1976) informs us that the Christian missions which used only local languages in their schools were forced to include English in their curriculum if they were to access government financial support. The colonial policy of instruction through English held sway till 1922, when the Phelps-Stokes Commission was set up to make recommendations towards the improvement of education in British West Africa. One of its recommendations was that the local languages be used as medium of instruction in the lower primary classes, and English at the upper levels.

In 1951, in connection with what came to be known as the Accelerated Development Plan, a committee was requested to make recommendations towards improving education in the country. Its terms of reference included investigation of the feasibility of using English as the language of instruction at all levels of education. The committee in its report agreed with the recommendation of the Phelps-Stokes Commission, and suggested the use of the local language medium in the lower classes. As in previous policies, the local language was to be taught as a subject from Primary 4 onwards.

In 1957 another committee also endorsed the local language medium for Primary 1 to 3. However, a minority report advocated use of English as the medium of instruction at all levels, including the earliest stages. This minority view was accepted and an English-only policy was implemented by government in 1957 – ironically, the very year that Ghana gained political independence, and upon the recommendation of a son of the country implemented by the Convention People's Party (CPP) government, which can certainly be described as nationalistic.

The next important landmark was in 1967, when the military government of the National Liberation Council (which ousted the administration of Dr. Kwame Nkrumah in 1966) set up an Education Review Committee, which among other things made recommendations on the language of instruction. Basically, the committee recommended a return to the local language policy. In recommending that the local language should be used as the medium of instruction in Primary 1–3, with instruction in English starting from Primary 4, and that after this level, the study of the local language should continue, the committee recognized that most Ghanaian children lived in a monolingual environment where they had little access to English. However, an exception was made for public schools in the urban centres where children had early exposure to English. They could be taught in English earlier than Primary 4. The other caveat was to take care of private institutions known as 'international schools', whose pupils spoke different languages and where lessons were taught solely in English from the first year. These were allowed to continue that practice, but in addition they were required to teach the main local language of the area as a subject throughout the six-year period. These recommendations were accepted by the NLC.

The civilian Progress Party administration (1969–1971) maintained the local language medium in the lower primary. McWilliam and Kwamena-Poh (1975: 120) quote a Ministry of Education document, entitled 'Curricula Changes in Elementary Education', confirming this:

> It is now government policy that the main Ghanaian language at present provided for in the curricula of primary and middle schools should be the medium of instruction in the first three years of the primary course and, where the subject makes it possible, in the next three years as well. In any upper primary or higher classes where English is the teaching medium, the appropriate Ghanaian language(s) will be properly taught as a school subject.

Note that this policy did not include all the fifty Ghanaian languages, but those 'at present provided for in the curricula of primary and middle schools', which in the 1960s were: Akuapem, Fante, Ewe, Ga, Dagbani, Kasem, and Nzema. By the 1980s the list had been increased to include Asante, Dangme, Gonja, Dagaare, and Wali, still a small percentage of the nation's total of languages.

The military National Redemption Council succeeded the Progress Party government in 1972 and adopted the indigenous language policy for Primary 1 only, contrary to the recommendation of the committee it set up to review education. Like all the other governments, the policy statement specified that the local language should continue to be taught as a subject after that level.

In theory rather than in practice, the military government of the Provisional National Defence Council (1982–2000) that metamorphosed into the National Democratic Congress (1993–2000) maintained the language policy it inherited. While not much changed in the early part of its rule, in 1989 when the PNDC decided on a restructuring of education, it made the local language compulsory and examinable at the end of both the Junior and Senior Secondary School levels. This policy seemed to give legitimacy to the study of Ghanaian languages, as those private 'international' schools which did not have this subject in their curriculum were forced to prepare their students for the examinations. However, in 1994 when the new education system ran into difficulties and education experts were asked to review it and suggest ways of addressing the problems, the local language fell a victim. In the opinion of the experts the number of subjects in the curriculum was too large, making in-depth teaching and learning difficult. The local language was therefore made an optional subject.

Towards the end of the NDC administration, with funding from the German Gesellschaft für Technische Zusammenarbeit, the Ministry of Education produced books for teaching literacy, mathematics, and environmental studies to Primary 1–3, in Akan, Ewe, Dagbani, Gonja and Ga. These books would have allowed some 75 per cent of school children to learn in the languages in which they were supposed to be taught. However, by the time the books were ready to be distributed to schools in 2002, the political leadership had changed, and with it, the language policy for education.

The National Patriotic Party which came to power in January 2000 was the political heir of the Progress Party; in language policy in education, however, its position was totally different. In May 2002 the NPP Minister of Education announced the government's plan to make English the only medium of instruction at all levels. He expressed the hope that the new policy would better equip students to write examinations in English and prepare them for higher education. This sparked off a nationwide debate, but the minister announced that the decision was final. Like its predecessors, the NPP government set up an education review committee when it came into office; unlike them, however, it did not wait for the committee to complete its task. The English-only education policy was announced long before the committee presented its report.

The government never publicly announced that its position on school language had changed; however, a section of a white paper on the Report of the Education Reform Review Committee published in October 2004 indicates some modification. It reads:

> Government accepts the recommendation that the children's first home language and Ghana's official language, English, should be used as the medium of instruction at the kindergarten and primary level.   (p. 27)

In the same section, it specifies the situation in which the local language may be employed as follows:

> where teachers and learning materials are available and linguistic composition of classes is fairly uniform, the children's first language must be used as the dominant medium of instruction in kindergarten and lower primary.   (p. 27–8)

The public continues to debate the issue. Ghanaian newspapers from time to time carry articles advocating either the maintenance of the policy or a change to local languages. Those who support maintenance reiterate the old arguments, that problems such as multiplicity of languages, inadequate resources to support their teaching and learning, classrooms with children from diverse linguistic backgrounds, etc., make the English medium a better option. They also never fail to mention the huge social capital that fluency in English confers on individuals. Their opponents stress that these drawbacks are the consequence of the prevailing negative attitude towards local languages and lack of attention to their development, rather than inherent to the policy.[9]

---

[9] See Anyidoho (2004) for an overview of the debate.

On the basis of this brief historical sketch, we may observe that since independence, a change in the political arena almost invariably leads to change or modification in policy on school language. Such frequent changes do not allow for any of the policies to be implemented fully, monitored, evaluated, and the weaknesses addressed. An exception is the PNDC/NDC government which ruled for nineteen years. For a long time this government was focused on protecting itself from coup plotters and legitimizing its status, and was probably not in a position to take on a sensitive subject such as language in education. Two democratically elected civilian administrations (1957 and 2000) chose an English-only education for their citizens.

At present, the powerful position that English occupies in the contemporary world has almost pushed local language out of the school environment, making it difficult for students to see how relevant its study is. For example, in June 2006, Owusu-Ansah cites the report of the Chief Examiner for one of the languages in the 2003 West African Examination Council papers as follows (p. 17): 'The policy of the teaching and learning of the Ghanaian languages, as it stands today, undermines the promotion of the development of the Ghanaian languages. Students despise the study of the Ghanaian languages.'

At the same time as the local language is relegated to the periphery in the education system, a number of Ghanaian languages are now vigorously promoted through radio and television. Many stations broadcast mainly in local languages, not primarily to promote them but to reach as many listeners as possible. These stations are very popular. This development can be suggested to support the view that many Ghanaians associate indigenous languages with oral communication, English with reading and writing. We have also noted in the previous section that perhaps among both literate and non-literate Ghanaians, English is now perceived as one of the languages of the country.

8.5 Language and Competing Identities

For the inhabitants of Ghana, language would appear to be the main marker of sub-national (or in some cases supra-national) ethnic identity. Furthermore, it seems that for most people Ghanaian identity entails a recognized ethnic identity, so that no matter what the status and role of English, ability to speak a Ghanaian language is also a necessary feature of the national identity. Language as an index of ethnic grouping was employed (quite unsatisfactorily: see Dakubu 2002/3) in the most recent census (Government of Ghana 2001: Table 4) as it was in the census of 1960. At a Symposium on National Integration held in Accra by the Ghana Academy of Arts and Sciences in 2003, a historian expressed the opinion that nationality by birth implies a language and an associated territory (Perbi 2006: 36), while Chief Justice Acquah (2006: 48) stated that language was not only a constitutional requirement for naturalization, it was the only one that could not be waived by the President or the relevant Minister. In another symposium held in 2005 that attracted considerable media interest, the chief of Juaben, one of the Akan states, reiterated the definition of ethnic group as crucially including language.[10] Ethnic identities therefore are not held in isolation from the national identity, but in parallel, and may sometimes come into conflict with it.

8.5.1 Language and Competing Identities: the Akan

'Akan' occurs in the earlier literature as an ethnographic label referring to people sharing ethnographic traits and speaking related languages found in Ghana and in the eastern part of the Ivory Coast. It is still sometimes used in this way. Since the 1960s, the name has been used in Ghana as an umbrella term for the mutually intelligible varieties of the language that a majority of those people speak. Akan in this sense includes all the varieties commonly known as 'Twi' – Asante, Akyem, Akuapem, Akwamu, Wassa, etc. – and Fante on and near the coast including Borebore, Agona, Gomoa; as well as Bono, the dialects spoken in the northern part of the linguistic area in the Brong-Ahafo Region. Before these groups became parts of a single colony and then a nation-state, each dialect coincided with an autonomous state, its members regarding themselves as linguistically as well as politically different from the others.

The Akan as a whole are perceived by others as having a strong attachment to their language and culture (which is regarded as the source of the chieftaincy system throughout the southern part of the country), but the particularism of the individual states and dialect areas has continued to have an impact. With the advent of European-style education in the area, the Akuapem-based orthography originated by the Basel Mission was spread throughout the Twi-speaking areas including Asante as a 'standard' form. The Fante-speaking areas used a different orthography. However, by the 1960s, through the efforts of several Asante linguists and writers, an Asante orthography was developed and adopted for Asante and the dialects most closely related to it. The result is that Akan, whose dialects by and large are mutually intelligible, officially exists as three languages: Fante, Asante, and Akuapem. A Unified Akan Orthography was devised by a committee set up by the Bureau of Ghana Languages, which was at that time the Ghanaian languages publishing wing of the Ministry of Education. A report embodying its recommendations was completed and presented to the Minister late in 1979, but was never implemented – partly because Ghanaian language teaching and publishing generally have declined, but also through passive resistance on the part of writers. The sole publication in the unified orthography to date appears to be a Methodist hymn book, *Kristofoɔ Ndwom Nwoma*. A pan-Akan nationalism based on language (or anything else) seems not to exist.[11]

Meanwhile, the language is indeed spreading as a lingua franca, and more than 50 per cent of the country has some degree of knowledge of it. At the same time,

---

[10] Nana Otuo Siriboe II in GAAS/FES (2005: 29), and as reported in the *Daily Graphic* of 21 June 2005, p. 9.

[11] Thanks to Florence Dolphyne (personal communication) for detailed information here.

perhaps because of their status as the largest group and perhaps also as a legacy of past expansionism, the people are often seen by other ethnic groups as too controlling, proud, and there is anecdotal evidence of individuals who passively resist using the language. Even though from time to time people have advocated the selection and development of Akan as a national language on the basis of the comparatively large number of speakers, others fear resulting domination by that ethnic group. As our survey in Accra indicated, most Akan speakers seem content to let the matter ride. We hypothesize that in the view of Akan speakers and even some other Ghanaians, this language tends to be identified with Ghanaian identity, perhaps making a specifically Akan linguistic nationalism redundant.

8.5.2 Ewe

The Ewe people, whose language is spoken by about 12.7 per cent of the population of Ghana (2000 Census Table 4) share language and history with the Ewe-speaking people on the Togo side of the border. Unlike Akan, Ewe has a standard version, developed in the nineteenth century by missionaries of the Bremen Mission. Although it was based mainly on southern varieties of the language, it is not identical with any of them, and is essentially a written, not a spoken, language. The missionaries saw to the production of much literature in this standard, and a translation of the bible that became very popular. The crucial factor, according to Lawrance (2005), was that during the time that the Ewe-speaking area was a German colony, basic education in Ewe was vigorously pursued, if only as a buffer against English, since there was a general resistance to learning German (Lawrance 2005: 223). This led to widespread literacy in and acceptance of the standard language throughout the Ewe-speaking lands, and it was the focus of an emerging Ewe nationalism.

After Togoland was divided between Britain and France in 1914, emphasis on education in Ewe declined, especially in the French mandated territory where there was a deliberate attempt to destabilize Ewe ethnic consciousness, which was viewed as a threat (Lawrance 2005: 223). In the British mandated area, which became the Volta Region of Ghana at independence, although Ewe suffered from official neglect it was still a rallying point for a (southern) regional nationalism. In 1956 there was a plebiscite to determine whether British Togoland should join the Gold Coast, soon to become Ghana, or join Togo, and although 58 per cent of the vote went in favour of union with Ghana, it is believed that most of the Ewe voted to join Togo, with the northern and non-Ewe population making the crucial difference (Amenumey 1989: 266, 267).

Many non-Ewe have perceived the Ewe as clannish, nationalist and even separatist, a perception that has led occasionally to expressed hostility, although not to violence. (See Amonoo 1989: 34–7 on ethnic stereotyping in Ghana.) Whether Ewe nationalism is now a factor in national politics is debatable, but it is not in doubt that the written as well as the spoken language is an important element in Ewe self-identification.

Particularly as the language of the Evangelical Presbyterian Church, the heir to the Bremen Mission, and of the Roman Catholic church introduced in German times by the Styler mission (Lawrance 2005: 220), the standard language remains in active use both in public and in private, to an extent not found with any other Ghanaian language.

8.5.3 Ga

The situation of Ga is entirely different. According to the 2000 census Ga is the language of less than 4 per cent of the population of the country. Like Ewe and Akan it has been a language of literacy, education and Christian (mainly Protestant) religion since the middle of the nineteenth century. However, not only is the area in which the language is spoken much smaller, its area is also the area of the national capital; indeed Accra is called 'Ga' in the Ga language.[12] Accra has been a trading centre since before the seventeenth century, and became the colonial capital in 1876 (Owusu-Ansah and McFarland 1995: 11). After World War II it started to spread, and (like many tropical cities) has recently grown immensely. This has meant a huge influx of people from other parts of the country, above all Akans, who now outnumber the Ga in Accra by a considerable margin. The presence of government has also meant the alienation of large portions of Ga land, for government and other public purposes. Farm lands are being sold (sometimes several times over) for commercial and residential building. The result has been a fair amount of Ga popular unrest. Ga people commonly complain that their language is dying, and there has been agitation, often successful, to have streets and districts renamed in Ga.[13]

It seems however that the role of the Ga language in this case is mainly symbolic. The Ga have long used other languages, particularly Akan and European languages, for communication with the wider world. There seems to be no real move to encourage other people to speak Ga. Apart from a few individuals the Ga show little interest in their language as a written medium. Although the Ga bible is still in use, in a new translation, there is anecdotal evidence that Ga churches rarely if ever hold services entirely in Ga, the preferred language being English or Twi, depending on the denomination and the social class of the congregation.

Nevertheless, and despite its cosmopolitan character, Accra is home to many people who follow a traditional way of life and speech, particularly the fishermen and their families. The following song (originally in Ga) expresses their identification with Accra as represented by the Ga language, and their feeling of alienation from distant parts of the country that speak other languages.[14] Consonant with the multilingual character of the environment, some of the words, transcribed here in italics, were in

---

[12] On language in Accra see Dakubu (1997).

[13] For an account of one such agitation see Dakubu (1997: 5ff.).

[14] Text collected, transcribed and translated by Mr. Daniel Nortey. I am grateful for his permission to use it. The song relates an incident in which the singing group having travelled to the north was stopped by police or soldiers, and felt themselves harassed in a language they did not understand.

pidgin English, exactly those lines that express frustration with an unknown language. Buko(m) is an area of downtown Accra, a centre of Ga life.

> We are going to Bukom, *talk*
>
> …
>
> *Talk to me, talk to me*
> *Talk to me in Bukom language*
> We were going to Tamale
> We went to the lorry station
> We boarded the vehicle
> We left Accra behind us
> We were going to Tamale
> We travelled for a while
> We saw a vast plain
> They have proper eagles there
> When we got to Tamale
> They did not speak *in Bukom language*
> We said we do not understand their language
> They said they are speaking Dagomba
> We are going to our home town, *brother*
> We are going straight to our home town.

8.5.4 Guan

There are ten or possibly more Guan languages, each spoken by a few thousand people and scattered in a crescent from Gonja in the Northern Region, down the Volta River valley to the coast at Senya Beraku west of Accra. Except in the northeast of their area they are isolated from each other. Although prolonged contact with different languages has produced some considerable differences among them, they are very closely related from the point of view of linguistic genesis. Only one, Gonja, which is also the furthest north, has an established orthography and recognition in the education system.

In the 1980s and early 1990s a series of Guan Delegate Conferences and Congresses were held in various locations, to foster unity among the different communities, 'for the purpose of social, political, and cultural revival of the Guan' (programme for Guan Congress 1988, p. 3). On the face of it, this was an organization for the assertion of an ethnic identity in which a number of groups too small to do so alone formed an alliance, primarily on the basis of language, or very similar languages. There was clearly an assumption that this common linguistic heritage entailed a common cultural and historical heritage, despite acknowledged differences.

However not all the participating groups in fact spoke a Guan language, a well-established genetic classification.[15] The languages considered 'Guan' (or Guang) for

---

[15] For a list of Guan-g-languages and their classification as currently accepted by linguists see Dakubu (1988: 51, 79) and Bendor-Samuel (1989: 225ff).

this essentially political purpose included several other small languages of the Volta Region, which are quite clearly related to the Comoe (or Akanic) languages of which Guan forms a branch, but are equally clearly not Guan.[16] The linguistic relationship was not exactly invented, because it is true that one exists, but it was certainly stretched, apparently to allow other groups who in fact have historically been closely associated with Guan groups in the area to participate in and strengthen by numbers the assertion of a non-Akan, non-Ewe identity in the face of these larger linguistic groups. According to Nugent (2000: 179) disputes over the status of several chieftaincies were at the heart of the matter.

8.5.5 Northern Ghana

Rather little specific information is available on the northern part of the country, which until fairly recently had little public voice. The languages of the area, especially in what are now the Upper East and Upper West Regions, were in many cases first written by Catholic missionaries ('White Fathers') who came into the area from the north, from what is now Burkina Faso. They produced mainly religious materials, but most of these were not published until recent years, or were cyclostyled at best. These were used in church-run schools, but there were very few schools of any kind before the 1960s.

The Dagaare-speaking Jirapa area of the Upper West was one of the first successful Catholic mission fields, in the 1930s, and so its language was among the first to be written extensively. This orthography as adopted by the Bureau of Ghana Languages became the version taught in schools after independence. However the language has a major dialect division, with the area north of Jirapa extending into Burkina Faso speaking a dialect (Dagara) that is sufficiently different that mutual intelligibility is rather low. In recent years there has been some dispute over the viability of the current standard, a dispute that has undercurrents related to competing nationalisms, as well as competing ethnic and linguistic loyalties.[17]

In each of the original nine administrative Regions of Ghana, the traditional language of the regional capital was among those recognized in the education system. However, after the Upper Region was divided into the Upper East and the Upper West this was not true of the language of Bolgatanga, capital of the Upper East, although Gurene (or Frafra), the language of the capital, is also the largest in the Region. There were a few Catholic religious writings, but next to nothing in print. This was recognized as a problem by the Bolgatanga District Assembly, which in the 1980s set up a Language Development Committee that sponsored the development of an orthography, a project in which one author of this chapter was involved. It happens that the speakers of this language also suffered for many years from particularly low

---

[16] See the list in the Guan Congress souvenir brochures for 1991 (p. 22), and for 1988 (p. 22). It seems in fact to be derived from Guang plus Heine's (1968) NA grouping of Central Togo languages ('Togorestsprachen'). Languages belonging to the linguistically more distant KA group do not appear.

[17] The dispute is described by Bemile (2000: 218–9).

prestige in the south, perceived as merely domestic and manual labourers. Speakers of the language both in its homeland and through regional associations in Accra have taken a keen interest in the development of written material in the language. Development of a dictionary, for example, is clearly regarded not merely as a useful tool but as a monument and a symbol that validates the community and contributes to its self-esteem and the esteem in which it is held by others.

8.6 Conclusion

Ghanaian discourse since independence has turned on the competing desires for national integration, perceived as urgent largely because of the diversity of the population, which in turn is indexed mainly by language, and democracy, which is perceived to require free access to the discourse concerning governance, and therefore to the language in which it is conducted. Thorough-going democracy is only attainable if that discourse is carried out in languages people truly understand, that is, in indigenous languages, but both democracy and integration can also be endangered by use of Ghanaian languages – although Ghana has largely escaped the ethnic and sectional violence that has plagued so many African countries, the spectre of 'tribalism' looms large in the popular consciousness.

Because of these factors, as far as identity at the national level is concerned, English and the indigenous languages are and are likely to remain inextricably intertwined. A language policy formulated and carried out through the education system with political will, and therefore with serious funding behind it, could alter the situation, towards achievement of real universal competence in English, or towards serious use of indigenous languages in formal contexts, but for the time being there is no sign that such a thing will come to pass.

9

Ivory Coast: The Supremacy of French

Anne Moseng Knutsen

9.1 Introduction

The Ivory Coast borders Liberia and Guinea in the west, Mali and Burkina Faso in the north, Ghana in the east, and the North Atlantic Ocean in the south. The country has two main topographical zones: the savannah in the north and the forest zone in the south. According to the latest census (1998), the population is 15 million inhabitants, of which 78 per cent are located in the forest zone of the south.[1] The population is mostly Muslim (39 per cent) or Christian (30 per cent). Although Yamoussoukro is the formal capital, Abidjan is the commercial and administrative centre of the country, with 3 million inhabitants. Other important cities are Bouaké, Korhogo, Daloa, Gagnoa, and San Pedro. The Ivory Coast was a French colony from 1893 to 1960, when it became *La République de Côte d'Ivoire*. The country is among the world's largest producers and exporters of coffee and cocoa and by maintaining close ties with France and encouraging foreign investments, the Ivory Coast has developed into one of the most prosperous states in sub-Saharan Africa. However, since the death of the nation's founder Félix Houphouët-Boigny in 1993, the country has faced increasingly severe ethno-political problems, which have resulted in a division of the country into a government-held south and a rebel-held north.

The Ivory Coast is one of the most linguistically diverse states in West Africa. At the same time, it is also held to be one of the most francophone states in the region. French is the only official language and Ivorian languages do not enjoy any legal status. In addition to a general sociolinguistic description of the Ivory Coast, the main focus of this chapter will be the historical, political, and linguistic reasons for the dominant position of French in the Ivory Coast today and the emergence of French as a language of consensus and potential unity between different ethnic groups, considered (by some) to express the national identity. The chapter will also consider the extent to which language plays a part in the current ethno-political conflict.

---

[1] All statistics are taken from the official census of 1998 (Institut National de la Statistique 2001).

9.2 Population

The borders of the Ivory Coast are a direct result of European colonization and the Berlin Conference (1884–5) and correspond in consequence to no 'natural' geographical borders. The country is in fact a confluence of four major ethnic groups having their cultural roots outside the boundaries of the current state. The *Kru* group, that occupies the southwest, is considered to constitute the first occupants of the Ivory Coast. Their cultural roots are probably from current Liberia. The *Kwa* (Akan) group emigrated from present-day Ghana by successive waves from the tenth to the eighteenth century, primarily as a result of feuds within the Ashanti confederation, and settled in the south-east and the centre of the current Ivory Coast. From the tenth century, the *Gur* group settled in the northern part of the territory between Odienné and Kong. From the fifteenth century the latter were pushed eastwards by the *Malinke* who had emigrated southwards as a result of the expansion of the Mali empire. Today, the four major ethnic groups cover approximately equal parts of the country but have different numeric importance. According to the latest census (1998), the Kwa (or Akan) group represents 42 per cent, north and south Mande (Malinke) 26.5 per cent, Gur 18 per cent and the Kru group 11 per cent of the Ivorian population. 26.5 per cent of the total population of the country are immigrants, mostly from neighbouring countries such as Mali, Burkina Faso, and Guinea.[2] Extensive immigration, especially towards Abidjan and regions in the south, has led to a significant blend of populations and the emerging of urban, more ethnically neutral cultures in the big cities, especially in Abidjan, which appears as a linguistic and cultural melting pot.

Even if there are numerous examples of long-term interaction between different ethnic groups in the history of the Ivory Coast, the question of a 'national Ivorian identity' is ambiguous. Zolberg (cited in Tice 1974: 211) claims that 'Africans in the Ivory Coast have not found within their past a source of myth for contemporary unity'. Bouquet (2005: 169) stresses the duality that exists between a form of French-patterned national citizenship and the power of family, village, or regional identity, often formalized in ethnic or regional associations, which have always played an important role in Ivorian civil and political life. The main ethno-cultural border of the Ivory Coast is between the Muslim north and the Christian south. However, this ethno-cultural border is no longer strictly geographical but rather based on religion. Ivorian citizens born in the south are identified as northerners on the bases of religion (Islam) and patronymic name. Important disparities have developed between the two parts of the country, a development that began during French colonization when the colonial regime intensified its policy of forced labour in the plantations in the south. After independence, the disparity was reinforced when human and capital resources

---

[2] 'Immigrant' is however a problematic term in the current political situation in the Ivory Coast. In fact, a large number of those defined as immigrants in the census of 1998 were born on Ivorian territory. According to Bouquet (2005: 184) the accurate number of immigrants would be 13.7 per cent if those who were born on Ivorian soil had been defined as Ivorians in the census.

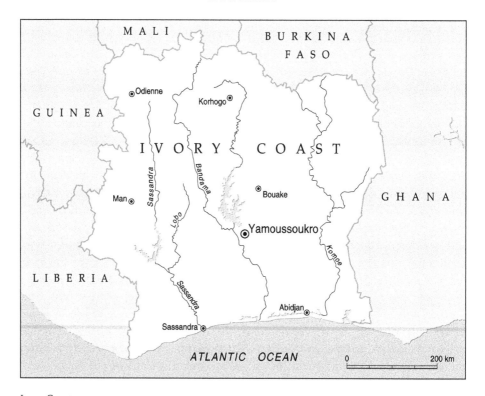

Ivory Coast

were concentrated in the south (Woods 1988: 105). As Woods points out, 'the loss of manpower to the south and the sharpening of regional inequality helped to crystallize ethnic and religious differences between the Muslim north and Christian south' (ibid.). These inequalities prevail today and are reflected in important differences in access to education and social infrastructure. As we shall see, the cultural differences and disparities that were tamed during the Houphouët area (1960–93) backfired after his death and resulted in an ethno-political crisis.

9.3 Historical Background

In 1945–46, Félix Houphouët-Boigny, who came from a rich Baule family of planters, founded the *Parti Démocratique de Côte d'Ivoire* (PDCI) and was elected deputy of the Ivory Coast in the National Assembly in France. At the same time, he took the leadership of the pan-African movement *Rassemblement Démocratique Africain* (RDA), leading the anti-colonial movement in francophone Africa. However, when the Ivory Coast gained independence from France in 1960, Houphouët opted for a privileged cooperation with the former colonial power, which has remained one of the country's most important allies until this day.

In his presidential reign, Houphoüet governed the Ivory Coast as a neo-patrimonial state (Bouquet 2005: 205). His leadership was founded on redistribution of economic and political power to both political partisans and opponents in order to assure their fidelity to the regime. By building alliances with ethnic groups and influential families, the Ivorian leadership was able to assure political stability and ethnic coherence within the one-party state. Elections were merely a formal procedure to celebrate the President's power. Positions within the public sector and national enterprises were given to party members, who emerged as a national elite. This clientelist regime was only possible because of the economic prosperity of the Ivory Coast from independence and into the 1980s. In fact, during the 1960s and 1970s, the Ivory Coast became one of the most prosperous states in Africa, mostly due to the coffee and cocoa industry, which brought the state important financial resources that could be used to develop infrastructure and assure social progress.

This African economic miracle also attracted millions of immigrants. Such immigration was welcomed by the Ivorian leadership, in need of labour to help build the country during its period of prosperous growth. Houphouët's response to critical voices opposing immigration was 'the land belongs to those who cultivate it'. The Ivory Coast thus became the land of hospitality in West Africa, integrating several million immigrants and guest workers, especially from poorer neighbouring states such as Mali, Burkina Faso, and Guinea, and extending to these arrivals the rights both to vote and to own land in the country.

In the late 1970s and 1980s, an economic depression hit the Ivory Coast as the country developed considerable foreign debt, causing the Bretton Woods institutions to impose structural adjustment programmes on the country. Such a development led to much public discontent and parts of the population, especially students, began for the first time to question Houphouët's authority. In his famous speech at the France–Africa Summit in La Baule in 1990, the French President Mitterrand stated that African countries should make efforts toward democratization in order to benefit from French aid. Confronted with certain negative public opinion and international pressure, Houphouët had no other choice than to organize multi-party elections in 1990, in which he defeated the leader of the *Front Populaire Ivoirien* (FPI), Laurent Gbagbo. When Houphouët died in 1993, after thirty-three years in power, Henri Konan Bédié, the President of Parliament, filled the office of President. This marked the beginning of a long and troubled path that would lead the country into a *coup d'état* in 1999, followed by a civil war-like situation that still prevails today. If fact, while Houphouët managed to unite all ethnic groups within his one-party state, Ivorian politics is now clearly divided up along ethnic lines. In the beginning of his presidency, Bédié developed the concept of *ivoirité* ('Ivorianess'), which evolved around three major concepts: nationality, eligibility for the presidency, and land ownership. In 1994, the Parliament approved an electoral code which excluded non-Ivorians from elections and limited the right to be elected to citizens born of Ivorian parents. In 1998, the National Assembly adopted a new land law that gave priority to traditional and ancestral land rights. The concept of *ivoirité* created ethnic tensions and led to numerous ethnic clashes, both in rural and urban areas. In 2000, a court ruled that Alassane Ouattara, former prime minister and leader of the *Rassemblement des Républicains* (RDR), the party of the northern populations, was ineligible for the presidency because his mother was from the neighbouring Burkina Faso. For the majority of the northern population the exclusion of Ouattara symbolized their own marginalization from the country's centre of power. The tension between the Christian south and the Muslim north increased considerably as xenophobic and ethnically motivated persecutions and even killings became frequent. The victims of these persecutions were mostly *Diula*, a term that does not necessarily refer to people from the Malinke-Diula group but to northerners and Muslims in general. In 1999, a mutiny within the army developed into a *coup d'état* and former Chief of Staff General Robert Gueï was presented as the new president. Gueï organized multi-party elections in October 2000 but when he proclaimed himself the winner of the elections, widespread popular demonstrations occurred. Finally his adversary, Laurent Gbagbo, was in fact proclaimed president in October 2000. Domestic conflict and disturbance reappeared in September 2002, however, when a northern rebellion attacked the cities of Abidjan and Bouaké. After several days of battle, the country was divided into a rebel-held north (ten northern *départements*) and a government-held south (forty-eight southern *départements*). In spite of peace negotiations (the most important being the French-brokered Linas-Marcoussis peace agreement of January 2003, creating a new government of national reconciliation), the country remains divided in two parts, and from being a politically stable and economically prosperous state which enjoyed considerable ethnic and religious harmony, the Ivory Coast has within ten years degenerated into being a state now clearly divided along ethnic, political, and religious lines.[3]

9.4 Sociolinguistic Profile

Although the Ivory Coast is considered to be one of the most linguistically diversified states in West Africa, the estimated sixty languages present in the country can be divided into four distinct linguistic groups, which all belong to the Niger-Congo phylum: the *Gur* languages of the northeast (Senofo, Kolango, Lobiri), the *Kru* languages of the southwest (Bete, Dida, Wobe-Guere), the *Kwa* languages of the southeast (Baule, Agni), and finally the *Mande* languages, which separate into two branches, the north Mande languages of the northwest (Maukan, Wodjenekan, and the vehicular trade language Diula) and the south Mande languages in the west of the country (Yacuba, Gagu, Goro).[4] The degree of mutual comprehension between

---

[3] It is not possible to deconstruct the concept of *ivoirité* and the current ethno-political crisis within this chapter. For a thorough analysis of the historical, political, and sociological reasons underlying this crisis, see Bouquet (2005).

[4] Only the most important languages of the respective groups are mentioned here, referred to by means of the most commonly used transcriptions in English-speaking literature.

the different dialects and languages within these four linguistic groups varies quite considerably. For instance, while the languages within the north Mande group can be characterized as different dialects of the same language, there is no intercomprehension between the different languages of the south Mande group. The relationship between language and ethnicity is also very complex. While there is an almost perfect intercomprehension between Baule and Agni of the Kwa group, the speakers of these languages consider themselves to be members of two distinct ethnic groups (Kouadio N'Guessan 2001).

Each of the sixty languages occupies different positions within the sociolinguistic configuration of the Ivory Coast. Most Ivorian languages are used strictly in intra-ethnic contexts in rural areas or within the (extended) family in urban areas. However, some languages have gained an inter-ethnic (or regional) function and are used in larger ethnic contexts. Yacuba (south Mande), Agni (Kwa), Attie (Kwa), and Guere (Kru) are examples of regional languages that are often learned as a second language by those whose first language is an intra-ethnic language. Four languages, Baule (Kwa), Diula (Mande), Bete (Kru), and Senofo (Gur), exceed the regional context and appear as the most important languages of their respective linguistic groups. They are thus often referred to as *national* languages although they do not have a particular legal status as the Ivorian Constitution of 2000 refers to the existence of 'national languages' in general without specifically naming these. However, unlike other Ivorian languages, these four larger languages enjoy some degree of institutionalization, as they are used in certain radio and television programmes and are also subject to domestic linguistic research (Lafage 1982). The Mande language Diula has gained a vehicular function and is used all over the national territory as a lingua franca between different ethnic groups, especially in the informal trade and transport sector and to a lesser extent in agriculture involving guest workers from neighbouring countries (Mali, Guinea, and Burkina Faso, in particular). Even though Diula is propagated all over the territory as a trade language, the population of the south generally associates Diula with the northern areas of the country (and thus with informal commerce, the main occupation of the northern populations) and with Islam, which accounts for their reluctance to make use of the language.

Due to the fact that the Ivory Coast is an economic centre of gravity in West Africa, a number of languages from neighbouring states also play a role in the sociolinguistic configuration of the country, for example Mande languages from Guinea and Mali, Moore from Burkina Faso, and Hausa from Niger and Nigeria. Quite generally in the country, the face of official monolingualism masks the fact that most Ivorians are indeed bilingual. The nature of this bilingualism depends largely on geographic origin. While Ivorians in rural areas often learn an inter-regional language as a second language in addition to French, the urban population only learn French in addition to their first language. In this situation of multilingualism, no Ivorian language has by popular consensus or as a result of language planning been accepted as an official or truly national language. The significant urbanization that has taken place in the

Ivory Coast has in fact led to a regression of inter-regional languages and in urban areas, and especially in Abidjan, French is becoming all the more frequently a first language of speakers as ethno-cultural ties between townspeople and their place of origin get weaker. This lack of a dominant language on a national level has led to an extended use of French in all aspects of Ivorian society. The choice of French as a language of consensus and official language has, as we shall see, historical, political, and sociological motivations.

9.5 Language Policy in the Ivory Coast: the Supremacy of French

The language policy of the Ivory Coast since independence from France in 1960 has continually been based on the privileged position of French. During the period of colonial occupation, French was the only language used in official administration, while Ivorian languages were systematically set aside. In order to communicate with local chiefs and the population in general, the French colonial regime educated their own African interpreters, a procedure that was consistent with the assimilation policy that characterized all aspects of the French colonial regime. When the Ivory Coast gained political independence from France in 1960, Houphouët and the Ivorian leadership chose French as the official language (Constitution of 1960, 1st Article). When the constitution was revised over forty years later in 2000, practically nothing had changed. French remained the official language and despite the fact that Article 29 of the new constitution contained a vague reference to 'national languages', French has in fact strengthened its position in the Ivory Coast. This language is all the more frequently used for communication in domains previously reserved for African languages and is the only language used in public administration and in school curricula. In what follows, the chapter discusses the reasons underlying the Ivorian leadership's choice of French as official language. Their reluctance to introduce any indigenous language in language-planning strategies has led to French occupying a dominant position in every aspect of the public and civil sectors of the Ivory Coast today. The position of French is in fact much stronger in the Ivory Coast than in neighbouring states such as Mali, Guinea, and Burkina Faso, which share the same colonial past as the Ivory Coast and have comparable sociolinguistic profiles.

In 1960, the Ivorian leadership was confronted with urgent matters relating to the building of a national state and to the securing of national integration of the numerous ethnic groups that constituted the new nation. To Houphouët, developing an over-riding national identity was a prerequisite for preventing potential tribalism in the multi-ethnic state, as this might pose a threat to his leadership and, in a worst case scenario, could potentially lead the new nation into civil war. Indeed, national integration and coherence became a priority against which all other matters were measured. In this context of nation-building, the choice of one or several Ivorian languages was believed to compromise the effort of nation-building and French was regarded as the only language that could prevent ethnic division. Such a view was expressed by

Philippe Yacé, the President of the National Assembly, in a speech addressed to the United Nations in 1976:

> The adoption of French ... has indubitably been one of the factors favouring the successful and rapid accomplishment of the work of national construction which [...] President Félix Houphouët-Boigny has made the primary theme of his attention and action. French, freely accepted by us, has been a factor of cohesion within the Ivory Coast where it has favoured the unity of our hundred or so ethnic groups. (cited in Turcotte 1981: 66, author's translation)

Houphouët himself in fact only mentioned the language question on one occasion, and in an indirect manner, when he referred to French as 'our national language' in his Proclamation of Independence speech in 1960. Some Ivorian linguists, such as Kouadio N'Guessan (2001) characterize the attitude of the Ivorian leadership and especially that of Houphouët towards African languages as downright hostile. Despite the efforts of various scholars attached to the University of Abidjan in the 1970s and 1980s to bring the language question up for open debate, every time the Ivorian leadership has been confronted with the subject of language planning with Ivorian languages, such issues have been systematically brushed aside.

The second argument commonly given in favour of French as official language was its international status. This argument must be seen in relation to the privileged relations between the Ivory Coast and France that prevailed from 1960 up to the political events that took place in 1999. In fact, France regarded the Ivory Coast as one of its most reliable allies in the region and had considerable economic interests to defend in the country, while the Ivory Coast profited from cultural, technical, and educational support as well as military cooperation from France. In this situation of privileged cooperation, the choice of French as official language can be interpreted as a sign of loyalty to the former colonial ruler and as a means to facilitate Franco-Ivorian relations. This was seen as particularly important in the context of the cold war, in which the Ivory Coast sided with the Western bloc through its privileged cooperation with France, as opposed to neighbouring countries like Guinea and Mali, which developed privileged relations with the Eastern bloc.

The choice of French as official language is also seen by some scholars as a strategy used by the Ivorian elite to preserve their status as a privileged class in the post-colonial context of the Ivory Coast. Politicians and other members of the elite had profited from education in French colonial schools and the choice of French as official language of the state can be interpreted as a strategy to assure social reproduction. This view is put forward by Alexandre, claiming that 'the use of French in Francophone Africa has created a new nontribal or supratribal group, which ... has frequently become a kind of oligarchy or class, because of its monopoly of this very special and powerful intellectual instrument or tool' (cited in Alidou and Jung 2002: 65). Other scholars stress more functional aspects of the choice of French as official language. Since African languages were mostly oral and non-codified, the Ivorian leadership took the only operational language that they had at hand, namely French, to begin the building of the new nation in the turmoil of independence.

In the 1970s and 1980s, scholars attached to the Institute of Applied Linguistics (ILA) at the University of Abidjan began to question the dominant position of French, particularly its role in education. Two domains were seen as particularly important: pre-school education of children (4–6 years), and devising writing systems for indigenous languages for adults in rural areas (Kokora 1983). These considerations led to various projects that received positive evaluations by the Ivorian authorities, namely pre-school education in the Adiokro language in Mopoyem (1980), in Baule and Diula in Yaokoffikro (1982), in the Yacuba language in Dompleu (1985), and most importantly the 'Projet Nord' in Diula and Senofo in Korhogo and Boundiali in the mid-eighties. These projects gave ILA precious field experience and a base on which they could develop practical solutions for the integration of Ivorian languages in the education sector. However, the lack of serious political and economic support from the authorities for these projects put an end to any broad national aspirations. Today, most of the education and alphabetization projects in Ivorian languages are conducted by NGOs and are not submitted to governmental supervision and coordination, which of course gives these projects a rather haphazard, unsystematic character.

In 1977, ILA was mandated to study the theoretical and practical conditions for the integration of national languages in state education by Article 80 of the Reform Law of 1977. This law also stated in Article 79 that 'the introduction of national languages in the official education system constitutes a factor of national unity and allows us, at the same time, to revalidate our cultural heritage' (Kouadio N'Guessan 2001, author's translation). The promotion of African languages, which had initially been seen as a serious threat to national unity by the Ivorian leadership, now came to be seen (by some) as a means to assure national unity. The most important debate on this matter took place in the *National Commission on Educational Reform*, mandated by the PDCI and the RDA (see section 9.3) to prepare for reform of the national education system. This commission brought together people from public and civil society, including teachers, parents, and members of village associations. Although those consulted agreed on the importance of integrating national languages in the school system, they did not agree as to which languages should be promoted. Some of the members of the commission advocated the promotion of one major language from each of the four main linguistic and ethnic groups of the country in order to progressively assure communication between the various ethnic groups. Others objected that because of important inter-regional migration, schools could not be considered as regional but national entities and that consequently the promotion of different regional languages would constitute a political problem (Kouadio N'Guessan 2001: 186–7). However, even if the law of 1977 stressed the importance of African languages and the necessity of their promotion in the school system, no judicial or practical solution was offered by the commission to implement these principles.

Almost twenty years later on in 1996, the issue of the use of indigenous languages in education appeared again. Some weeks before the beginning of the academic year, the Minister of Education, Pierre Kipré, quite unexpectedly announced that Ivorian languages would be introduced in the country's schools, causing substantial turmoil both among school administrators and the general public. Kouadio N'Guessan (2001: 195) points out that such precipitate action was very much representative of the Ivorian authorities' attitude towards the integration of national languages in education. Their logic appeared to be that as Ivorians spoke and understood Ivorian languages, the integration of Ivorian languages into the school system could be quite easily implemented, without any linguistic, didactic, or practical preparation. Not surprisingly, Kipré's decree was never actually implemented.

Thus in spite of sporadic debate on the language question over several decades, nothing has seriously threatened the dominant position of French in Ivorian society. Since the 1960s, French has broadened its use in everyday life throughout the country and today serves as a general lingua franca between the different ethnic groups in the Ivory Coast. A knowledge of French is now also a prerequisite for participation in urban life and as such, it is no longer the privilege of the educated elite. The symbolic line is in fact no longer drawn between those who speak French and those who do not, but between those who speak standard French and those who speak the popular variety, the *français populaire d'Abidjan*, as now discussed in section 9.6

9.6 The *français populaire d'Abidjan*

The functional expansion of French and its generalization to speakers with no (or poor) formal education has led to important structural changes in the French spoken widely in the Ivory Coast. In general terms, French in Africa can be divided into two main types. The first type is characterized by a clear discontinuity between French and local African languages, resulting in the maintenance of a relatively normative variety of French, due to the speaker's ability to keep the two (or more) linguistic systems separated, both psychologically and functionally. The second type is characterized by non-complete separation of French and local African languages, giving rise to some extent to mixing of the two (or more) linguistic systems. French in the Ivory Coast belongs to the second type and appears as one of the most restructured varieties of French in West Africa. Although Ivorian French is characterized by important variation, it is possible to isolate stable, non-standard linguistic features that have both intra-systemic and inter-systemic motivations. Described as a pidgin language by Hattiger (1983), Ivorian French has undergone linguistic stabilization and appears today as an emerging new variety of French, comparable to Canadian French or, to some extent, creole languages.[5]

---

[5] For a sociolinguistic and linguistic description of this variety, see Ploog (2002) or Knutsen (2007).

This Ivorian variety of French has received numerous labels, the most common being the *français populaire d'Abidjan*. Even though the name suggests that the variety is merely an Abidjan phenomenon, it is in fact used all over the national territory as a means of communication not only in inter-ethnic scenarios but also within ethnic groups and even within the family, especially in urban areas. This local variety occurs in opposition to standard French, and the relationship between them can best be described as a situation of diglossia. Standard French, which is principally used in education, media, and the legal system, has high inherent prestige, while the local variety of French, which is used in informal communication and to some extent in publicity and popular culture, has low inherent prestige. The local variety appears, however, to have a strong emblematic function. It is felt by the speakers to express an Ivorian identity, as opposed to standard French, which at least in some ways is associated with the colonial past, neo-colonialism, and class conflict. An educated speaker will typically use both standard French and the local variety, and the choice between the two codes will depend on the degree of formality of the situation. A speaker with no or poor education will be constrained to use the local variety, which can be inappropriate in certain formal situations. In consequence, the diglossic situation between standard French and the local variety mirrors a latent conflict between those who have benefited from a formal education and those who have not, Ivorian society being characterized by a considerable disparity in access to education.

9.7 French vs. African Languages in Ivorian Society Today

The Ivorian educational system and curricula are still, more than forty years after independence, founded on French cultural values and French is both a subject of study and the exclusive medium of instruction at all levels. The hegemony of French in education is perceived as a general problem in francophone West Africa and may account for the general failure of the African school. Because the Ivory Coast is one of the most francophone states in the region, the exclusive use of French in education may have less dramatic consequences for children's learning than in other French-speaking countries, because of the extended use of French outside of education, both in the public sector and in everyday life. Thus most Ivorian children, at least in urban or semi-urban areas, have some mastery of French when they enter school and may therefore benefit from education in French. That said, this pragmatic view does not take into account cultural alienation and the potential improvement of learning that education in indigenous languages or bilingual education would imply. In the current situation though, education in local languages or bilingual education seems out of reach, primarily because of the Ivorian leadership's reluctance to deal with language planning and the lack of national support for systematic linguistic and didactic research on Ivorian languages, which is a prerequisite for their implementation in education. Meanwhile, both the Ivorian school child and Ivorian society pay the price for an education that is not fully adapted either to the schoolchild's linguistic background or to Ivorian society's need for culturally relevant curricula, crucial for the development of a national identity.

In the media, French is dominant in radio, television, and the written press, although the National Radio and Television Company (RTI) does transmit a few hours of information in Ivorian languages every week. French is the only language used in the legal system and mastery of French is a requirement to serve on a jury. Although Diula is traditionally the main language of informal commerce, French is now increasingly frequently used in marketplaces, especially in urban areas. Religion is in fact the only institutional domain where Ivorian languages retain some importance. Ivorian languages are to some extent used in Christian services and by the Muslim population, with Diula often serving as the language of religion in speech events other than the rituals of Islam, which are conducted uniformly in Arabic. The hegemony of French in the institutional domain is indeed so great that no citizen can participate fully in society without some level of competence in the language. Illiteracy (estimated at 60 per cent of the population) and a lack of channels of communication in Ivorian languages sometimes constitute a problem for democracy. A recent example of this was the referendum on the constitution held in 2000, when the population was asked to vote on a document of thirty pages written in a language that the majority of the population could not read. Even if the consequences of official monolingualism are amplified by a high rate of illiteracy, minimal effort is expended by the authorities to ensure democratic participation for all citizens, by giving equal access to education or by creating appropriate channels of information in national languages for those who cannot read.

As a consequence of the institutional hegemony of French, the use of Ivorian languages is mostly limited to communication within the family and within the ethnic group. However, a recent study (Knutsen 2007) shows that French is now more frequently used within the family context in urban areas. Although parents may see the use of French as strengthening cultural alienation, they encourage their children to learn and speak this language because they know that mastery of French is important for access to education and employment. Ivorian languages are often seen by the population as 'traditional' and unfit for modern purposes, such as technology, science, and international communication. This traditionalist view of African languages is not merely an Ivorian phenomenon but seems to be widespread throughout West Africa and accounts for a general reluctance (or at least indifference) among the general population to consider the possibility of promoting local languages in formal domains. Such an attitude is representative of what Alexander (2002) calls the 'static maintenance syndrome', which implies that African languages are held by citizens to be suited for use in family and in communitarian and religious contexts but unfit to be developed into languages of power. In the Ivory Coast, the negative attitudes towards Ivorian languages as official languages may reside in the fact that the choice between French and Ivorian languages has always been presented to the population in either–or terms (national coherence vs. tribalism) and that no model of official multilingualism has been thoroughly discussed and presented as a possible alternative.

In the absence of any indigenous language being sufficiently developed and widely enough accepted to express Ivorian national identity, French has by official language policy and popular consensus become this language, as described very clearly by an Ivorian informant quoted in Simard (1994: 23, author's translation):

> Instead of seeing themselves as Baule, Diula, Wobe, or Senofo, [the generation born after 1955] see themselves as Ivorian, belonging to the Ivorian nation. Throughout their years in school, they had friends from the four corners of the country with whom they shared the same ideas, the same visions of the world and the same language, namely French, which had the advantage of not belonging to any specific ethnic group and in consequence had the advantage of not generating interethnic rivalry, which could have easily happened if a local language became dominant.

All things considered, however, it seems obvious that the strategies developed by the Ivorian leadership in the Houphouët era to cement national identity have not in fact been successful, given the current political crisis. In this respect, official monolingualism is representative of a policy of presenting symbols of national unity that has masked underlying ethnic antagonisms and power struggles. It is also obvious that the national identity referred to in the above quotation was in fact already highly fragile and in decay when confronted with the concept of 'ivoirité' and ethno-political power struggle in the post-Houphouët years. In the current difficult situation, ideological and practical conditions are such that the promotion of one or several Ivorian languages as official languages or languages of education still seems quite out of reach. However, when the Ivory Coast finally overcomes its current ethno-political crisis and when the time comes for the Ivorian people and leadership to redefine national identity, language planning and integration of Ivorian languages will have to be a priority in order to assure genuine ethnic integration and access to information for all citizens, instead of the continued belief in a fictive monolingualism.

9.8 Conclusion

Since 1960, Ivorian language policy has been one-sidedly based on French, a choice that has historical, political, and sociological motivations. Ivorian languages have systematically been put on the sidelines and enjoy no legal status, despite a (vague) reference to the 'national languages' in the Constitution of 2000. Official monolingualism masks the fact that the majority of the population is in fact bilingual and also constitutes an obstacle to democratization as the majority of the population is unable to read and write French. The lack of a dominant national language has favoured the use of French not only in official domains such as education but also in inter-ethnic contexts, an evolution assisted by significant domestic migration that has led to the emergence of ethno-neutral cultures in urban areas. The Ivorian variety of French, often referred to as the *français populaire d'Abidjan*, has emerged as one of the most restructured varieties of French in Africa and appears to express an Ivorian identity, as opposed to standard French, which, at least to some extent, symbolizes neo-colonialism and class-conflict between those who have benefited from formal education and those who have not. Even though French has emerged as a 'national language' and expresses an 'Ivorian identity', the current ethno-political crisis has revealed severe antagonisms and power struggles between the different ethnic groups in the Ivory Coast. The official language policy resulting in the hegemony of French must therefore be seen as one of largely external symbolism presenting an image of national unity that has failed to take into account the need to assure genuine integration of the different ethno-linguistic groups constituting the country as part of the process of building an inclusive national identity potentially shared by all Ivorians.

10

Nigeria: Ethno-linguistic Competition in the Giant of Africa

Andrew Simpson and B. Akíntúndé Oyètádé

10.1 Introduction

Nigeria is a country with an immense population of over 140 million, the largest in Africa, and several hundred languages and ethnic groups (over 400 in some estimates, 510 according to *Ethnologue* 2005), though with no single group being a majority, and the three largest ethnic groups together constituting only approximately half of the country's total population. Having been formed as a united territory by British colonial forces in 1914, with artificially created borders arbitrarily including certain ethnic groups while dividing others with neighbouring states, Nigeria and its complex ethno-linguistic situation in many ways is a prime representation of the classic set of problems faced by many newly developing states in Africa when decisions of national language policy and planning have to be made, and the potential role of language in nation-building has to be determined. When independence came to Nigeria in 1960, it was agreed that English would be the country's single official language, and there was little serious support for the possible attempted promotion of any of Nigeria's indigenous languages into the role of national official language. This chapter considers the socio-political and historical background to the establishment of English as Nigeria's official language, and the development of the country over the subsequent post-independence era, and asks the following question. After five decades of experience of life with English as the nation's sole official language, if people in Nigeria were to be given the opportunity to reformulate national language policy as they wished, might one expect a different official language structure to be requested, perhaps with one or a combination of indigenous languages as a replacement for English, or is the current English-centred structuring of officialdom felt to be satisfactory and appropriate given the ethnic configuration of the country? In approaching this question and the issues which relate to it, the chapter refers to the results of a range of revealing surveys carried out by sociolinguists in Nigeria in recent years which have attempted to probe public attitudes towards language(s) in the country and which provide useful insights into the relation of language to national identity in Nigeria. The chapter is organized in the following way. Section 10.2 first provides an overview of the broad array of languages in Nigeria, highlighting properties of the three major indigenous languages, Hausa, Yoruba, and Igbo, as well as the presence of English and Nigerian Pidgin English as significant forces in the country. Section 10.3 then describes how Nigeria came into existence historically as a British-ruled territory and what kind of administrative structures and language hierarchies were inherited and essentially accepted for the future of Nigeria at independence. Section 10.4 considers how Nigeria has developed as a country from the 1960s through to the end of the twentieth century, a period including a damaging civil war fought between the Igbos and government forces in the late 1960s and much ethnic rivalry and competition for political power and resources in the decades following that, with the population of the Hausa-speaking Muslim north of the country and that of the more heavily Christian south with its dominant Yorubas often seeing themselves as adversaries rather than as co-nationals cooperating in the construction of a better Nigeria for all those living in the country. Sections 10.5 and 10.6 subsequently return to the national language issue, discussing attitudes to language in present-day Nigeria, and consider how different sections of the population appear to express primary loyalties and support for different languages depending in part on the size of the ethnic group they belong to and their geographical location, as well as the general level of respect that is accorded to a language. The chapter is concluded with an assessment of how the ethnic configuration of the country combined with economic factors and attitudes towards language may conspire to force a particular policy on national-level language in Nigeria.

10.2 An Overview of Languages in Nigeria

Nigeria's many languages are spread broadly throughout the country's thirty-six states and have populations that vary quite considerably in size, with three particular ethno-linguistic groups making up over half of the total population, having in excess of 20 million mother tongue speakers each, a further ten languages falling in the 1 to 5 million range, sixty languages having between 100,000 and 1 million speakers, and the remaining several hundred languages being spoken by much smaller, in many cases with linguistically endangered, populations.

Although it is currently not possible to obtain fully accurate and reliable figures of the populations of all Nigeria's ethnic groups, due to the fact that groups may sometimes over-report their size as a means to access more government resources, Table 10.1, adapted from Badru (1998: 3), provides a reasonable picture of the proportional size of the larger groups present in the country.[1]

[1] Note that the figures from Badru (1998) here reflect the proportional relation of the country's population shortly after independence in the 1960s. As there have been no really significant changes in population development among the larger ethnic groups since that time (with the possible exception of

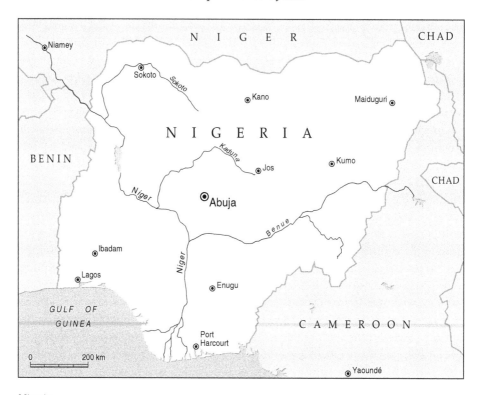

Nigeria

With a population now estimated to be between 25 and 30 million, the Hausas are the most populous of Nigeria's three major ethnic groups and numerically dominate the northern part of the country. Unlike the majority of Nigeria's languages, which are members of the Niger-Congo family, Hausa is an Afro-Asiatic language (Chadic sub-branch), and its original speakers migrated into the area of Nigeria from further east during the first millennium, settling in the fertile savannah area between the forested southern part of Nigeria and the beginnings of the Sahara further to the north. Rather than forming a unified empire, the Hausas established separate city-states which regularly competed with each other in trading with the trans-Saharan caravans which arrived from North Africa, converting to Islam in the process to facilitate relations with Arabic traders (Nelson 1982: 13). In the nineteenth century, 'Hausaland', the area primarily connected by common usage of the Hausa language, was invaded by Fulani people who successfully installed themselves as the rulers of the Hausa, but also adopted Hausa language and culture in many cases. The result of this mingling of the Fulani with the Hausa is that the Fulani are now often indistinguishable from

partial depletion of the Igbo population during the Nigerian civil war), and other statistics on individual groups have often been gathered at different times, Table 10.1 remains a good impression of the size of the three major groups relative to each other and the other larger languages.

Table 10.1 Nigerian ethnic groups

Group	% of population
Hausa-Fulani	29.5
Yoruba	20.3
Igbo	16.6
Kanuri	4.1
Ibibio	3.6
Tiv	2.5
Ijaw	2.0
Edo	1.7
Nupe	1.2
all others	17.5

the Hausa, and the term Hausa-Fulani is sometimes used to refer to the Hausa together with the assimilated Fulani.[2] Currently, Hausa is used both as a mother tongue and as a lingua franca throughout a significant amount of northern Nigeria and further afield in West Africa in Niger, Togo, Benin, Ghana, and Mali. Having been written down for many centuries in an adaptation of Arabic script known as Ajami, since colonial times the language has been commonly represented with Romanized orthography whose conventions are now fully standardized both in Nigeria and other countries where Hausa occurs. The language itself has also long been standardized, partly as the result of its use in the British colonial administration of northern Nigeria.

The second largest ethno-linguistic group in Nigeria is that of the Yorubas, who dominate the southwestern part of the country. For much of their history, the Yorubas did not exist as a politically united people with a common identity, but instead were organized in many subgroups and separate kingdoms which often fought against each other, for example the Ife, Oyo, Ijebu, Kabba, Ondo, and several others. The global referring term 'Yoruba', which originally referred to the Oyo people as the Yorubas proper, was indeed said to have been first coined and spread by outsiders, the Hausa and then Christian missionaries, as a way of referring to all those groups who spoke a related and mutually intelligible 'Yoruba' language, and it was only quite some time later that the term was also adopted by Yoruba-speakers themselves, as a genuine shared identity began to establish itself during colonial rule due to the occurrence of inter-ethnic competition (Gordon 2003: 12–13). Currently, there are populations of Yoruba speakers not only in southwestern Nigeria, but also in neighbouring Benin and also Togo, due to the way that the region was partitioned into separate territories by European colonial forces, as well as in Ghana, Ivory Coast, and Senegal as the result

---

[2] Elsewhere the Fulani, who originate from the area of modern-day Senegal, are known as the Peul (in Senegal) and as the Fula (in Mali), and their language, which is from the Western Atlantic branch of Niger-Congo may be called Fulfulde (Gordon 2003: 14).

of recent migration and settlement of Yorubas as traders. Within Nigeria itself, Yoruba is known and used by the native speakers of many other smaller languages in the 'midwest' area to the immediate east of Yorubaland, but otherwise is not as extensive in its occurrence as a lingua franca in the south of the country as Hausa is in the north. A standard orthography for Yoruba was finally agreed on in 1974 by the Yoruba Studies Association of Nigeria, and is now used to teach standard Yoruba, which is based on the Oyo dialect. There is a growing literature in the language, several newspapers, and regular use of standard Yoruba on television and the radio, though different dialects of the language are still in widespread use in Yorubaland. In terms of religious affiliation, Christianity, Islam, and traditional religious forms all exist quite peaceably among the Yorubas, with Christians being in the clear majority. Religious differences have never been the source of any major conflict amongst the Yoruba themselves (Sadiku 1996: 127).

Situated in southeastern Nigeria, the Igbos are today Nigeria's third major ethnic group. Like the Yorubas, the Igbo in pre-colonial times were not organized as a single empire or kingdom, and in fact existed in much smaller organizational units, over 200 'village groups' made up of collections of up to thirty villages apiece (Nelson 1982: 105). Despite the sharing of a common language (in various dialect forms), the Igbo like the Yoruba experienced periods of warfare between their various subgroups and only developed a clearer pan-Igbo identity during the course of the twentieth century, this becoming particularly salient in the aftermath of the civil war which resulted in much loss of Igbo life (section 10.4). The Igbo language has a standardized form and an accepted, standard orthography, though less of a long tradition of writing than that associated with Hausa, and more restricted use as an inter-ethnic lingua franca than either Hausa or Yoruba, partly as an effect of the defeat of Igbo forces in the civil war. The majority of Igbo people are now Christians, though Islam and traditional forms of religion also occur among them.

Quite generally, the most populous areas of Nigeria today are the areas where the three major languages occur – the north (and in particular the central part of the north), the southwest, and the southeast, and these highly populous areas are heavily dominated by Hausa, Yoruba, and Igbo. In terms of broader linguistic divisions, the southern two-thirds of the country is mostly composed of languages from the Niger-Congo group (including Yoruba and Igbo), while the north has a range of Afro-Asiatic languages. A much smaller number of Nilo-Saharan languages (including Kanuri, with around 3 million speakers) is also present in Nigeria.

In addition to the three major indigenous languages, Hausa, Yoruba, and Igbo, a further semi-indigenous variety of language that plays a useful, daily role in the lives of many Nigerians is Nigerian Pidgin English/NPE, which is known, understood, and used primarily as a second language lingua franca by over a third of the population, in particular in the southern parts of the country. Commonly assumed to be derived from early contact between Europeans (initially Portuguese, later British) and indigenous people living along the coast of Nigeria, NPE now occurs in two main regional varieties, Port-Harcourt and Warri-Sapele-Benin and has a mother-tongue population of approximately one million. Currently there is still no recognized standard form of NPE or fully accepted way of writing the language, but it is used in television, on the radio, and in certain forms of literature. Section 10.5 returns to consider the place of NPE and also Standard English in Nigerian society today and the attitudes that are associated with these two forms of language. First of all, however, the chapter considers the socio-political and linguistic development of colonial and post-independence Nigeria.

10.3 Colonial Rule and the Creation of Nigeria

European contact with the territory of Nigeria began in the fifteenth century with the arrival of the Portuguese, followed by the British, French, and Dutch in the sixteenth century. When the Europeans first came to Nigeria, it was the northern, savannah areas inhabited by the Hausas that were the most prosperous, with sizeable cities, having profited for many centuries from involvement in the important trans-Saharan trade in textiles, gold, salt, spices, and also slaves. As the Europeans established themselves on the coast and developed a significant new trans-Atlantic slave trade, this began a shift in the focus of commerce to the south of Nigeria, further strengthened when the slave trade was abolished in the early nineteenth century and came to be replaced by lucrative sea-borne trade in products such as palm oil, rubber, and coffee, transported to Europe in exchange for European manufactured goods, tobacco, guns, and iron (Falola 1999: 46). A monopoly over such trading from the area of southern Nigeria was then granted by the British and its naval forces to the Royal Niger Company, which received the authority to charge duties on the trade it oversaw and began to develop control over territory in the interior of Nigeria both by means of treaties negotiated with local chiefs and by force. As the southern interior was explored and subsequently exploited by British commercial interests, missionary activity made its presence felt in much of the south of Nigeria, particularly during the second half of the nineteenth century, this resulting in the study and description of many indigenous languages, with grammars of a range of languages being produced, including Yoruba, Nupe, Efik, and Kanuri (Crowder 1962b: 132–3). Contact with Europeans over a period of time also led to the development of a pidgin used in trading. Meanwhile in the north of the territory of Nigeria, the nineteenth century saw the Hausa states being overrun by the Fulani people in a major jihad set on spreading and reforming Islam in the region. Prior to the nineteenth century, Islam was largely only practised by the Hausa elites in northern Nigeria. Following the successful replacement of the Hausa leadership by the Fulani led by Sheikh Uthman dan Fodio and the establishment of the extensive Sokoto Caliphate, Islam became widely embedded as the dominant religion of the north of Nigeria.

In the latter part of the nineteenth century and the early years of the twentieth century, the British extended their control over almost all the area of modern-day

Nigeria. When the borders of this British possession were agreed upon with the other European powers competing for territory in West Africa, the French and the Germans, it resulted in the division of the Yoruba and the Hausa into different countries and the rather arbitrary incorporation of a vast number of quite distinct peoples in a single administrative structure (Falola 1999: 60). In fact, what evolved in the area of Nigeria was at first three formally separate territories: the Crown Colony of Lagos in the south-west, the Protectorate of Southern Nigeria, and the Protectorate of Northern Nigeria. The former two were quickly merged in 1906 as the Colony and Protectorate of Southern Nigeria, and then amalgamated with the north in 1914, under the governorship of Lord Frederick Lugard. Lugard saw the north of Nigeria as significantly different from the south, however, and so instituted rather different policies in north and south, hindering fully balanced integration of Nigeria and helping entrench what was set to become a long-lasting internal division in the country that would be the source of many future problems. Throughout Nigeria, the decision was taken to administer the country via indirect rule and the use of indigenous, local rulers who would collect taxes and resolve disputes on behalf of the British in return for British support and legitimization of their positions of authority. The rationale for indirect rule was that it would both minimize the administrative costs of governing the huge territory of Nigeria, and reduce the general visibility of the British colonial presence and its intrusion in the country. Indirect rule was heralded as a great success in the north, where the British allowed the Fulani rulers to continue in their role as emirs and leaders of the northern population, promising minimal interference in the daily life of those in the north and a guarantee of respect for the continued practice of Islam. Christian missionary activity in the north was consequently only permitted in those areas which were not Islamic (Akinwumi 2004: 20). Elsewhere, in the south, however, the policy of indirect rule resulted in much resentment as it often created local rulers with powers far greater than those traditionally permitted in indigenous societies such as those of the Yoruba and the Igbo. Effectively answerable only to the British and no longer needing the support of the communities they were responsible for, many of the newly established local rulers became corrupt and abused their positions of authority (Gordon 2003: 77). The 'assignment' of populations to specific rulers and new structures of governance also began to create broader connections among people now dominated in the same way and the emergence of a wider collective ethnicity that had not existed in pre-colonial times.

In terms of official language use and education, the British developed the south and the north of Nigeria in different ways. In the south, the British relied heavily on Nigerian interpreters to communicate with indigenous people, a policy which accorded much potential power to the interpreters and often resulted in abuse of this power (Falola 1999: 73). The interpreters and many other petty officials employed in the administration of southern Nigeria needed to acquire a proficiency in English in order to be able to interact with the higher level British administrators, and education in English along with other simple skills was essentially provided by missionary

schools wherever these were available, rather than by institutions of education established by the government. In the main, the British aimed to keep the indigenous people
of Nigeria largely unchanged and undeveloped as a way to ensure the continuation
of colonial rule. Consequently, as long as the missionary schools supplied enough
minor officials with a basic knowledge of English, it was felt that there was no need to
establish education on a broader basis for the masses, and most indigenous people
outside a small, increasingly privileged elite were not able to access any form of
education (Gordon 2003: 80).

In the north of the country, the situation was rather different. Due to the occurrence
of Hausa as a lingua franca in much of the north, it was decided that Hausa should
be used as the language of administration. In addition to being widely understood
by the northern population, Hausa had the advantage that it had already been standardized and successfully used to generate a tradition of literature in pre-colonial
times (Adegbija 1994: 43). The adoption of Hausa by the colonial bureaucracy had
the effect of spreading the language still further, and British administrators also
learned and used the language. A significant change that has shaped the development
of Hausa since the early colonial time is that when Hausa was officially adopted
as the language of government administration, it was decided it should be represented with Roman rather than Arabic script. This government-led pressure on the
language coupled with the clear opportunities to obtain work that a knowledge
of Romanized Hausa opened up led to a decline in the use of Ajami to represent
Hausa and an almost complete switch to Romanization over time (Igboanusi and
Peter 2005: 47).

An important linguistic difference between the north and the south resulting from
the British promise to exclude missionaries from the Islamic north and the decision
to use Hausa in government administration was that missionary schools teaching
English were not established in the north of Nigeria during the colonial period, and
it was only in the south that proficiency in English developed. This geographical
imbalance in the knowledge of English would later have harmful consequences for
north–south relations when Nigeria neared independence and southerners came to
dominate positions in the English-medium nationwide bureaucracy as well as other
professions that required a Western education (Falola 1999: 78).

The education that was available in the south of Nigeria also had the effect of
producing a new ambitious elite which often aspired to Western values and cultural habits. As this elite developed, it found itself increasingly frustrated by racial
discrimination by the British and apparent limits placed on the advancement of
Nigerians within the civil service. Further challenged by economic difficulties experienced during the worldwide depression of the 1930s, the new southern elite began
to criticize the colonial government and call for greater participation in the running of the country. A nationalist movement thus began in the 1930s and produced national, multi-ethnic organizations such as the Nigeria Youth Movement
demanding improvements in social conditions and genuine inclusion in political

decision-making. In the 1940s, the nationalist movement attained a mass follow-ing, having earlier been restricted to the educated elite, and started to call for a timetable that would lead to a full transfer of power to Nigerians and indepen-dence for the country. Though many of the political parties that were formed at the time had ethnic or regional bases, there was clear cooperation between them and open commitment to the common cause of obtaining national self-determination (Oyebade 2003: 23).

In the 1950s, as the attainment of independence seemed guaranteed and set to occur not far off in the future, the mood in Nigerian politics changed dramatically. Replacing earlier emphasis on pan-Nigerian ideals and the targeting of an ethnically unified and harmonious nation came unashamed new appeals to divisions in ethnicity, region, and religion as a way to mobilize support in political campaigns and elections. Politicians quickly found that the utilization of regional and ethnic issues was the easiest and most effective way to recruit a population that would vote for them, and political parties evolved into entities with a narrow focus on a specific ethnic group or region rather than a national agenda and the goal of winning electoral support from all parts of the country. In southwest Nigeria the Egbe Omo Oduduwa was a Yoruba party which attempted to bring together all of the subgroups present in Yorubaland with emphasis on the shared creation myth and common spiritual home of Yoruba speakers (Gordon 2003: 94). In the southeast, the Igbo State Union and the National Council of Nigeria and the Cameroons/NCNC (later renamed the National Council of Nigerian Citizens) were both Igbo-based organizations which in similar fashion from the 1950s onwards championed the cause of an Igbo nation which politicians simultaneously tried to establish in the minds of Igbo-speakers, even composing a new Igbo national anthem (Akinwumi 2004: 152). In the north, the Jamiyar Mutenan Arewa and the Northern People's Congress reacted by using Islam and reference to the past glory of the Sokoto Caliphate to attract political support (Falola 1999: 91). Many of the minorities also created political organizations to defend their particular interests, for example the Ibibio State Union, the Tiv Progressive Union, the Calabar Improvement League, and the Borno Youth Movement, among others (Akinwumi 2004: 152). In many instances, these new political organizations had to a great extent to invent the ethnicities they claimed to represent and then work at convincing local and regional populations that they collectively belonged to the same ethnic group. Although this was no easy task to begin with in various instances,[3] as historically Yoruba-speakers, Igbo-speakers, and Hausa-speakers had not formed unified groups with clear cross-group loyalties, after a certain time the rhetoric and insistence of the new breed of politicians achieved their desired results and, as observed in Gordon (2003: 83): 'It was not long before communities that had previously not identified as a people began to see themselves as tribes and to mobilize on this basis.' The activities of politicians in

---

[3] Gordon (2003: 96) describes one case where an Igbo leader conceded that an Igbo identity practically did not exist after having spent four years canvassing Igbo speakers from 1947 to 1951 and trying to convince them (with little success) that they all belonged to a single Igbo people.

the 1950s thus did much to coalesce and embed broad new ethnic identities where they had previously been weak and ill-defined. With regard to the Yoruba, Hausa, and Igbo populations, it is commonly argued that the British division of Nigeria into different regions greatly assisted the development of regional and ethnic identities. Having established separate regional administrations in the north and south of the country from an early time, in 1939 the south was further divided into separate southwest and southeast regions, in theory to improve the quality and speed of regional administration. However, such a partitioning also created a situation in which each of the three major language groups in Nigeria came to be numerically dominant in its own region, allowing for region and major ethno-linguistic group to become more closely identified with each other, heightening the potential for rivalry and competition for resources to be linked to ethnicity and official homeland. The division of Nigeria into three administrative regions was also foreseen as continuing on after independence in various constitutions that were drawn up by the British in preparation for an ultimate handover of power. The 1954 constitution furthermore permitted each region to request self-government, which the (south)western and eastern regions did in 1956, and the north in 1959, resulting in Nigeria becoming a federation of three regions each with its own legislative and executive power, and decreasing connections between the three parts of the country, outside the important competition for central resources.

With the development of powerful ethnic blocs among the Yoruba, Hausa, and Igbo and their domination of the three regions, the minorities in Nigeria became increasingly worried for their future, and called for the creation of new states where they could live without the threat of being marginalized and potentially discriminated against in access to employment and education. Differences in religion between the north and the south of the country further compounded tensions present in pre-independence Nigeria, and were added to by a general northern concern that the southern elites would dominate the country following independence. The north consequently insisted that its large population be guaranteed proportional representation in any post-independence government so as to assure itself of adequate defensive political power. Gordon (2003: 97) neatly sums up some of the principal worries that faced the country as it neared independence:

- The north feared domination by the more economically developed south. The north was determined to balance southern economic dominance with political dominance.

- The south feared domination by the north. The north's population size advantage would allow it to control the federal government and use its power to support northern interests.

- Minorities would be dominated by the biggest ethnic group in their region. Only by creating more regions, in which minorities could become majorities, could they be assured a fair deal.

When independence finally did arrive in 1960, the pan-Nigerian nationalist movement of the 1940s had been all but destroyed and replaced by self-seeking ethno-regional politics. In the words of Falola (1999: 91): 'Things would never be the same again as the leaders abandoned pan-Nigerian issues and focused more and more on regional concerns. Within one generation, nationalists became tribalists, interested in independence for narrow gains.' Having been ill-prepared for nationhood by the colonial practice of regionalism, Nigeria emerged as an independent state wracked with internal disharmony and serious question-marks hanging over the future stability and integrity of the country. Akinwumi (2004: 155) refers to 'an ethnic war [being] fought through ballot boxes' and quotes a Nigerian academic as summarizing the situation and how it would proceed in post-independence years in the following way:

> By the time of national independence in 1960, Nigerian politics had become synonymous with the inter-ethnic struggle for power. Political power was perceived as an instrument in the struggle among ethnic groups for the division of national wealth.

10.4 Language and the Development of Nigeria: 1960–2003

10.4.1 Independence

As Nigeria became an independent state in 1960 made up of three large regions each dominated by a major ethnic group, elections resulted in the Northern People's Congress gaining control of the country's new government, though with the necessary support of the Igbo-led NCNC as a junior coalition partner. Having assured itself of a significant degree of dominance of central government, largely due to the voting power of its population which equalled that of both western and eastern regions combined, the north then moved to establish greater internal cohesion in its vast region (almost three-quarters of the total territory of Nigeria), through the intensification of a policy of 'Northernization' first initiated in 1957. Concerned by the possibility that members of the better educated and economically more successful southern population would take jobs away from northerners in the civil service and come to monopolize commercial activity, the policy of Northernization required that northerners be favoured over non-northerners in the competition for government employment wherever candidates' qualifications were otherwise similar. It also introduced restrictions on the purchase of land and the awarding of contracts for public works to southerners. Such affirmative action discriminating in favour of northerners led to much discontent, especially among Igbo migrants in the north, and resulted in many southerners actually losing government jobs and positions they already had (Okeke 1998: 7). Official Northernization was also partnered by serious attempts to further coalesce the huge population of the north and develop an increased sense of loyalty to the region which would even transcend that of loyalty to specific ethnic group, under the motto 'One North, One People, irrespective of religion, rank, or tribe' (Maduka-Durunze 1998: 80). Combined with the perception that the north was now appropriating a disproportionate share of federal revenues for its own development, much of which came from oil production in the eastern region, and the occurrence of feuding in the western region among rival Yoruba groups, the initial post-independence years retained the many ethnic and regional tensions that had characterized the years approaching independence.

In such an atmosphere of mutual mistrust, suspicion, and sometimes open resentment, a range of national issues had to be agreed upon as part of the development of Nigeria as a new, independent state in charge of its own affairs and identity. One of these concerned language and the question of what language(s) should be specified for use at the national level, in parliamentary discussion and national public address. The question was whether there should be any substantive change from linguistic practices in pre-independence Nigeria, or whether existing practices should simply be permitted to continue. The constitution adopted at independence in 1960 specified English as the language of parliamentary debate, hence official at the national level, as it had been during the colonial period. In 1961, once adjustment to self-government had been made, the issue of national language was revisited in parliament and generated much heated debate. Central to the discussion was a motion to spread the learning of Hausa, Yoruba, and Igbo throughout the country with the ultimate goal of selecting one of the three major languages as the future national language of Nigeria (Elugbe 1994: 74). Parliamentary members from minority language groups put up particularly strong resistance to the idea of elevating either one or potentially all three of the major languages to the status of national language (Igboanusi and Ohia 2001: 128). With acrimonious discussion of the issue spilling out into the media, the motion to develop Hausa, Yoruba, and Igbo as candidates for consideration as future national language(s) of the country was actually carried, but then subsequently not acted upon in any concrete way (Omamor 1994: 49), it being quietly concluded that it would be wiser and indeed safer to err on the side of caution rather than experiment with the open grooming and promotion of the major three languages while there was strong public opposition to such a move and serious instability caused by poor inter-ethnic relations. Nigeria was consequently left with English as its de facto official language in most formal domains at the national level, as under British rule, and without a clear road map for the establishment of a national language. Banjo (1981, quoted in Omamor 1994: 209) neatly summarizes the linguistic consequences of the fragile political situation in the post-independence era, stating that: 'the problems of an explicitly stated national language policy have been cautiously avoided because of their explosive implications'. And so things would continue, at least until the late 1970s.

At the regional level, official institutional support was however provided in the northern region for Hausa, as part of the Northernization drive, and the 1963 regional constitution of the north named Hausa as a co-official language of the region for potential use alongside English in the regional parliament. This effectively continued and formally endorsed the practice established during the colonial period in which

Hausa was recognized as an official language of government administration in the north (Omamor 1994: 48). It also considerably assisted the wide dissemination of Hausa throughout the north during the 1960s, which helped embed the growth of a common, supra-ethnic northern identity (Bamgbose 1991: 23).

10.4.2 Rising Conflicts and Civil War

The caution and restraint exercised with regard to specification of a national language policy in the early post-independence years was motivated by worries that Nigeria was not in a stable enough condition to initiate changes that might seem to favour one ethnic or regional group or set of groups over others. Such concerns were well justified given the backdrop of ethnic troubles that increasingly afflicted the country following independence. From 1960 to 1966 a continual stream of challenges to the establishment of ethnic and inter-regional harmony occurred, including serious north–south disputes both over census results in 1962 and 1963, and over regional election results in 1962 and 1965–66, the latter of which led to the deaths of thousands of people in the western region. Though the government attempted to reduce pressure from various minority groups worried by majority group domination through the creation of a new mid-western region from part of the western region in 1963, problems and tension continued to mount until by the end of 1965 'It became increasingly clear that sooner or later there would be a fundamental and probably violent change.' (Mwakikagile 2001: 8).

This occurred in early 1966 when a group of Igbo army officers staged a coup and successfully overthrew the government, eliminating various senior political leaders, and seizing full control over the country. Claiming that the military takeover was inspired by the aim of ridding Nigeria of a corrupt leadership and restoring law and order to the country, the coup-makers and their motives soon came under question when it transpired that no Igbo politicians or key military personnel had been killed during the coup and of those newly promoted to senior positions in the army nearly 90 per cent were Igbos (Falola 1999: 117–18). The inhabitants of the northern region were then further dismayed by the declaration that the division of Nigeria into semi-autonomous regions administered by regional governments was going to be replaced by a fully unified administrative structure. Such a move threatened dangerously to dismantle the protection that Northernization and its policies offered against southern competition for jobs in the north, and confirmed suspicions in northerners' minds that the coup was simply a bid to grab power for the south and allow for Igbo commercial exploitation of the northern region. The unguarded celebration of the coup by many Igbo migrants in the north compounded tensions, and demonstrations led to riots and then to violence against Igbos in the north. A counter-coup initiated by the northerner-dominated army then wrested power away from the Igbo military leaders, and hundreds of Igbo soldiers were killed along with tens of thousands of Igbo residents of the northern region. Following a mass exodus of Igbos from the north back to the southeast and the threat from Igbo leaders that the eastern region would secede and declare itself an independent state, civil war ensued in 1967 and continued for two and a half years until 1970, when the exhausted east finally capitulated. The first decade of independence in Nigeria thus culminated in a tragedy of huge proportions which all too clearly underlined the fragility of the new nation and how easily ethno-regional rivalries could spiral out of all control.

Though massively overshadowed by the destruction and loss of life resulting from the civil war, the immediate ethno-linguistic consequences of the conflict were that those eastern minority groups which might previously have fallen closely within the Igbo orbit and spoken Igbo as an inter-ethnic lingua franca switched to use other languages for the purposes of inter-group communication, most commonly Nigerian Pidgin and to a lesser extent Hausa (Igboanusi and Peter 2005: 29, 51). Negative attitudes towards the Igbo as the result of the war combined with concern at being seen to be close to the Igbo thus led to a clear linguistic distancing of many minorities from the latter and considerable reduction in the use of Igbo as a second language. This trend was further assisted by another significant development that had occurred just before the outbreak of the war. In an attempt to address the long-term concerns of many minority groups that they were continually being dominated by the major ethnic groups in the three principal regions of Nigeria, and to prevent threats of secession by the minorities, the government under Lt. Col. Gowon radically restructured the internal administrative divisions of Nigeria and partitioned the country into twelve new states. The replacement of the previously over-powerful and fiercely competitive regions with a larger number of smaller states was intended to reduce the potential for head-on conflict between large power blocs in the country, and was maintained as a structural reorganization after the civil war finally came to an end. In the former eastern region, the reorganization had the effect that various minorities found themselves in new states out of direct Igbo influence, and so freely switched to other mediums of wider communication.

10.4.3 The 1970s: Economic Growth and the Development of National Policies

Following the conclusion of the civil war, the government emphasized appeasement and reconciliation in the country, and a general amnesty granted to the Igbos together with a 'No Victor No Vanquished' policy did much to help mend broken relations and reintegrate the Igbo population with the rest of Nigeria (Okeke 1998: 23). Nigeria in the 1970s also benefited from a significant boom in oil prices, allowing for a sustained, major programme of public spending throughout the country building roads, hospitals, schools, and other badly needed components of infrastructure. In the latter part of the 1970s, public education expanded considerably as the result of the growth in the economy, with new schools and universities providing much broader popular access to education and learning than in previous decades (Falola 1999: 139). The 1970s also proved to be a period of much less ethnic conflict and greater stability than the previous twenty years, perhaps due to the conversion of the regional structure into twelve smaller states and the elimination of the three powerful regions dominated by the Yoruba, Hausa, and Igbo groups. Further lobbying from minority groups during the 1970s led to an expansion of the state system and the creation of seven new states in 1976, bringing the total up to nineteen. On a more negative note, the oil-driven economic growth experienced in the 1970s also brought with it the spread of serious corruption among those elected into positions of political power, where decisions on the awarding of contracts for public works and the construction of new infrastructure commonly led to huge self-enrichment among those controlling the decision-making process. Furthermore, in the scramble to obtain government-allocated resources, the practice of inflating population figures became endemic with the result that census figures were regularly challenged and often suggested to be heavily exaggerated (Falola 1999: 25).

Two important events occurred relating to the status and development of language in the latter part of the 1970s. The first of these, in 1977 (revised in 1981) was the declaration of the National Policy on Education. This was the first clear set of official guidelines on the use of language in primary and secondary education. In its first major pronouncement it stated that the medium of education in the early years of primary school (and in pre-school) should be the mother tongue of children being taught or the common language of the immediate community. Thereafter, and through secondary school, English was to be the medium of instruction. The National Policy on Education also indicated that during secondary school every child should learn one of the three major languages of the country, identified as Hausa, Yoruba, and Igbo, in addition to his/her mother tongue, as a way to encourage and develop national unity. Government policy makers thus recognized the value of mother-tongue education in the early years of schooling and also saw the potential that second-language learning of Hausa, Yoruba, and Igbo might have for stimulating a greater sense of belonging to a single multilingual nation. At around this time, the effective use of mother-tongue education in primary schools had furthermore been clearly demonstrated in Nigeria in a project carried out by the University of Ife Institute of Education in which children in one primary school were taught uniquely in Yoruba for the first six years of schooling, and compared with others schooled in English during the same period. The results gathered in 1976 indicated that children taught via their mother tongue made better progress than those schooled in another, foreign medium, supporting general emerging assumptions in the international community about the importance of mother-tongue education.

The second significant government reference to the use of language in Nigeria came in the 1979 constitution. This officially approved the use of Hausa, Igbo, and Yoruba as languages of discussion in the National Assembly, alongside English. At the sub-national, state level, the constitution indicated that the languages to be made use of in the country's various Houses of Assembly were to be English and the dominant language(s) of the state, again allowing for a (localized) official status to be given to indigenous languages (Bamgbose 2000: 114). The constitution also specified the twin national goals of eliminating illiteracy in the country and making available free education for all citizens, from the primary level onwards, with primary education becoming mandatory for all Nigerian children (Bamgbose 1994: 9). Three years later a major nationwide literacy campaign was initiated to attempt to achieve the former goal within a ten-year period. In the late 1970s, language issues thus came openly onto the agenda in Nigeria, and started to gain a momentum with enthusiasm for the promotion of knowledge and wider formal use of indigenous languages in education and public affairs, stimulated by general economic prosperity in the country and the growth in educational facilities made possible by this prosperity.

10.4.4 The 1980s and 1990s: Military Rule and Economic Decline

In the 1980s and 1990s, however, the positive developments emerging in the 1970s suffered from a range of serious challenges. Oil prices dropped, the economy went into serious decline, the military took over power to eliminate major corruption and embezzlement among the political leadership, but then held on to power for well over a decade and a half, as unemployment, crime, and violent conflict relating to religion continued to rise dramatically. The economy crashed so badly during the period that the 1970s per capita income of £1,500 had dropped as low as £300 by 1998 (Falola 1999: 16), resulting in the poorest living standards experienced since independence and a large-scale collapse of many public services including education due to lack of financial support. Falola (1999: 200) remarks that: 'The media and the public began to talk of a nation in ruin, one that would require decades to rebuild', and adds that there were significant consequences for morale, with the spirit of cooperation being replaced by an 'every man for himself' attitude: 'Patriotism and nationalism were eroded – to many people Nigeria was not worth defending, it should be exploited for self-promotion' (Falola 1999: 175). Corruption and self-enrichment at the expense of the nation thus remained a major problem among the ruling elite and hindered whatever progress might have been made under the challenging circumstances.

Self-preservation and the need to struggle for resources with larger neighbours led minorities to call for the creation of more states, resulting in the establishment of two new states in 1987 and nine more in 1991, and a fragmented patchwork of self-governing administrative units that were barely economically viable in many cases and concentrated people's attention on the local rather than the national. Politically, there was disappointment and outrage when the results of general elections in 1993 were annulled by the military after being apparently won by a Yoruba candidate from the south. The fact that the military continued to be dominated by northerners led to feelings among southerners that forces loyal to the north would never relinquish political power to a southerner, worsening north–south relations.

Given the dramatic deterioration of the economy during the 1980s and 1990s it is perhaps not surprising that little real progress was made with the government's aspirations to institute nationwide mother-tongue education in primary schools. Although the ambitious intention was that children everywhere should receive their first three years of primary schooling in their mother tongue or the language of the local community, in practice this actually happened only sporadically, and more so in Yoruba, Hausa, and Igbo areas and public schools than in minority areas and private education, which was set on providing all-English education from a very early age (primarily to satisfy the wishes of fee-paying parents that their children learn English well so as to be able to find better employment at a later age). Commonly it was claimed that a chronic lack of resources was (and to a significant extent still is) to blame for schools' inability to deliver mother-tongue education, causing both a shortage of teachers trained to teach through the medium of languages other than English, and a desperate lack of teaching materials in Nigeria's many languages, particularly in the case of the non-major languages. Odumuh (2000) describes an investigation of the real situation of mother-tongue education in a randomly selected set of public and private schools near to Abuja in a minority language area. The study reveals that 64 per cent of the primary school teachers used only English in their teaching, and the remaining 36 per cent used a combination of English and Nigerian languages, though the latter were often Yoruba, Hausa, and Igbo which were not the languages of the local community or the mothertongue of the children being schooled. It is noted that even where teachers did know the minority languages of the local community, they did not use these to teach with, as relevant teaching materials were unavailable and had not been developed. Other teachers noted that they did not know the local languages of the community they taught in, having grown up elsewhere in Nigeria. The study concludes that English is likely to remain the major language of instruction in primary schools for quite some time to come, as no real practical measures to help implement mother-tongue education have been funded by the government, aside from the development of certain materials in the three major languages.[4, 5]

Significant growth in the use of Yoruba, Hausa, and Igbo in debates in the National Assembly, provided for by the 1979 constitution, has similarly not come about, with the lack of development of the major languages in high, formal domains again being

---

[4] Following the targeted three years of mother-tongue education in primary school, use of languages other than English by students in primary and secondary schools is in fact often reported as being discouraged and students may even be penalized for speaking vernacular languages (Adegbija 1994).

[5] A further, recent complication adding to the difficulties schools have in following government directives relating to language teaching came in 1998, when the military leader of the country, General Abacha, announced that French would henceforth be a co-official language of Nigeria and that all schoolchildren should begin learning the language. Finding teachers immediately able to teach French throughout Nigeria's schools was naturally an impossible task. With the death of Abacha later in the same year, the initiative to promote French as a co-official language seems to have been largely forgotten about, however, and Abacha's public support for French in 1998 was essentially just a political move, designed to win support from France at a time when the military regime in Nigeria was being isolated by other English-speaking countries in the West (Igboanusi and Peter 2004: 122).

attributed, at least partially, to a government failure to provide the necessary support for such a linguistic expansion. Although a project was initiated to create relevant new terminology for the major languages for use in a range of new domains, and there were proposals to hire translators to assist in multilingual parliamentary debates, with the end of the Second Republic in 1983 and the military takeover of government, the programme was discontinued and development came to a halt (Bamgbose 1991). Elsewhere, there is also attitudinal evidence of a strong dispreference towards the use of languages other than English in political institutions. Adegbite (2004: 94) notes that in 1991 the Lagos State House of Assembly considered whether to permit the use of Yoruba in its meetings, Yoruba being the dominant language of the state and the mother tongue of the members of the assembly, but ultimately rejected such a possibility, stating that:

> Yoruba language is not appropriate for the conduct of business of the House of Assembly since Lagos is a cosmopolitan city. Besides, its use is capable of demeaning and reducing the intellectual capacity of legislators.   (*The Guardian*, 10 December 1999, quoted in Adegbite 2004: 94)

Indeed, perhaps the only area in which the indigenous languages of Nigeria did seem to make clear progress in a relatively new domain during the 1980s and 1990s was in communication relating to agriculture, with government employees learning local languages so as to be able to interact with farmers (Oyetade 2001: 16). Meanwhile English continued to dominate the formal domains of life and showed a positive flourish in the area of literature, with Wole Soyinka becoming the first African writer to win the Nobel Prize for Literature in 1986. Nigerian authors writing in English had in general been very successful since the 1960s, and the high quality output of authors such as Soyinka, Chinua Achebe, and Amos Tutuola was maintained throughout the difficulties of the 1980s and 1990s.

10.5 Language in Nigeria Today: Patterns and Attitudes

It is now approximately half a century since Nigeria established its independence and accepted a continuation of English as the country's single official language. Since that time Nigeria has experienced much and passed through periods of civil war, great prosperity, and also great economic challenge, and military rule as well as periodic occurrences of democracy. At the turn of the twenty-first century, the well-respected Nigerian historian Toyin Falola expressed a very bleak view of the country's position:

> As Nigeria enters the next millennium, it does so as a weakened nation with its economy in a shambles, its politics unstable, its external image badly soiled, its people in great despair and agony, and violent protests and civil strife as routine occurrences. 'The giant of Africa' is now listed by the World Bank as one of the twenty poorest countries in the world. (Falola 1999: 16)

However, there are also more optimistic voices to be heard, and signs that the destructive power of ethno-regional politics might finally be changing. In 1999 a southerner was elected president for the first time, Olusegun Obasanjo, and then returned as president in elections in 2003. The fact that a Christian Yoruba was able to win more support in the Muslim north than in his ethnic homeland has been seen as an indication that voting along narrow ethnic, religious, and regional lines is no longer the near automatic occurrence it was in earlier years, and that political competition in Nigeria might be approaching a new, more open-minded maturity (Gordon 2003: 265). In this final section, the chapter asks whether, after five decades of independent development, the inherited policy of English as single official language is still the most appropriate, albeit imperfect, fit for Nigeria, or whether public opinion might support a change from the linguistic status quo and the establishment of a national language or set of national languages that would have a meaningful, widespread role in Nigeria and assist in the hitherto heavily neglected process of national integration and nation-building. In revisiting the national language issue here, we will take advantage of a range of informative surveys of attitudes towards languages in Nigeria which have been carried out in recent years, and which attempt to establish how speakers of various groups perceive their own and others' languages in both formal and informal domains. These include Oyetade (2001), Igboanusi and Peter (2005), Babajide (2001), Igboanusi and Ohia (2001), and Adegbija (1994 and 2000).[6] It should be noted that these surveys primarily investigate the views of educated speakers from the middle class, typically students, teachers, journalists, and civil servants. Although this means that the views of those with less formal education are not directly canvassed in the surveys, the educated middle class is the section of society which is arguably most likely to have clear views and opinions on language issues and to be most vocal about possibilities of change in language policy, justifying the focus on this group in the language surveys. As it turns out, there are also clear differences of opinion between the various language groups investigated (Yorubas, Hausas, Igbos, and minority language groups), hence the acquisition of education does not lead to a uniform set of attitudes towards language and still allows for revealing cross-ethnic variation to be identified.

Considering first attitudes by speakers towards their mother tongues, the broad picture that consistently emerges from the various studies is that speakers of almost all languages in Nigeria express clear and strong feelings of loyalty towards their mother tongues when asked (see, for example, Adegbija 1994 for an overview). Amongst the three major languages, Hausa has been commonly found to command the highest degree of loyalty, followed by Yoruba and Igbo (Maduka-Durunze 1998: 74). In terms of actual figures, the comprehensive survey reported in Igboanusi and Peter (2005: 141) found that 87 per cent of Hausa speakers confirmed that their preferred language

---

[6] Note that Adegbija (1994) is not a questionnaire-derived survey but an overview of general perceptions of attitudes towards languages in Nigeria made by the author.

in general was indeed Hausa, while 54 per cent of Yoruba speakers and 52 per cent of Igbo speakers specified Yoruba and Igbo respectively as their commonly preferred languages.[7] When the consumption of language in the form of television, radio, newspapers, and magazines was investigated in the same study, similar ratios of preferred language were attested among speakers of Hausa, Yoruba, and Igbo, though with percentages being lower by at least one-third in the preferred language of reading. A significant portion of Igbo speakers in particular were found to prefer their mother tongue less than speakers of Hausa and Yoruba in the media and print. As for the speakers of minority languages, studies such as Adegbija (2000) report a high degree of the expression of loyalty and positive attitudes towards speakers' mother tongues and note that most minority languages are still highly valued in traditional areas of life. However, when speakers of minority languages are asked to explicitly rank languages according to their general preference, it is found that the mother tongue, though well esteemed, is very often not specified as the language of highest preference. Igboanusi and Ohia (2001: 132) note that a survey of northern and southern minorities averaged together indicated a higher general preference for English (50 per cent) than local, minority languages (42 per cent).

Turning to what Nigerians of various groups actually now speak in informal domains (as opposed to what they may express a general preference for), the declared language of use in the home is noted in Igboanusi and Peter (2005: 142) to be Hausa for 98 per cent of mother-tongue Hausa speakers, Igbo for 81 per cent of Igbo speakers, and Yoruba for 73 per cent of Yoruba speakers, much as might be expected given the cross-linguistically common domination of mother tongues in informal and domestic environments. Amongst speakers of minority languages, however, the same study indicates surprisingly that the common language of the home is in fact now Hausa for 57 per cent of the northern minorities, followed by English used by 18 per cent of speakers. In the south, 39 per cent of minority language speakers stated that English was the common language of the home, and 24 per cent that it was Nigerian Pidgin. As the authors of the survey point out, Hausa, English, and Nigerian Pidgin are therefore coming to dominate communication in informal domains where mother tongues are expected to be used, posing a serious threat to the continued transmission of many minority languages. Various researchers make the observation that individual state governments have often done little to provide institutional support for the minority languages spoken within their borders, even where a particular minority language may be spoken by a majority of the population within a single state, and that the failure of the implementation of the mother-tongue education policy may lead to rising generations acquiring more English and Hausa (in the north) in schools and importing this into the home, possibly even encouraged by their parents. With regard to Nigerian Pidgin, this seems to be growing in use in a number of domains

[7] With both Yoruba and Igbo speakers, English was indicated as the preferred language by 42 per cent of those interviewed.

such as the media, music, commercial advertisements, political propaganda, and the world of sport, supplementing its widespread use in the army and the police. It does not, as yet, occur in more formal domains due to a lack of standardization and development, and therefore remains a threat and popular competitor to the use of minority languages only in informal interaction and mostly among those without education.

In terms of attitudes to the current and potential use of Nigerian languages in more formal domains such as education and government administration, the following has been observed through recent investigations. In the area of education, one survey reported in Adegbija (2000) noted that 77 per cent of its 600 respondents would be against the potential replacement of English as medium of school instruction with a Nigerian language, although 57 per cent conceded that students might learn more effectively if taught through the mother tongue. An earlier study, Iruafemi (1988) (referred to in Oyetade 2001: 19), which allowed its respondents a greater range of potential answers, showed that while only 6 per cent of parents approved of early education in just the mother tongue, only 24 per cent were in favour of English as the sole medium of early education, and a majority of 70 per cent supported the use of both English and the mother tongue as joint mediums of education. Concerning the government's policy for children to learn one of the major Nigerian languages as a second language subject, Igboanusi and Ohia (2001: 137) found that over 70 per cent of the minority language groups they interviewed thought the policy was a good one. However, only 25 per cent of those questioned thought the learning of the major languages in school would actually be of any obvious benefit to them or their offspring. The value of the policy may be attributed to its potential role in integration, 56 per cent of the same set of speakers stating that they thought that the increased, widespread use of the three major languages would stimulate unity among Nigerians. Relating to the perception of a relatively low instrumental value of the indigenous languages revealed in speakers' responses to the question about personal benefit resulting from the learning of the major languages, the low level of admission rates into university degree courses focused on Yoruba, Igbo, and (to a lesser extent) Hausa would seem to confirm that the major indigenous languages are generally not seen as important for success in obtaining good employment.

When asked whether the major languages might be able to cope effectively with application to science and technology, Adegbija's (2000) survey indicated that as many as 73 per cent of speakers felt this would not be possible, and similar preconceptions about the inherent unsuitability of the indigenous languages for scientific and advanced academic description are commonly reported in other works. As for current language preference in the area of official functions, Nigerian languages appear not to be highly valued and Igboanusi and Peter (2005: 101) found that the majority of speakers of all groups prefer the use of English in formal domains, with figures being around 90 per cent for Yoruba, Igbo, and minority groups, and 56 per cent for Hausa speakers (40 per cent of whom supported the use of Hausa in official functions). Finally, with an eye on the future, Igboanusi and Peter (2005: 98) attempted to probe general speaker preference for a widespread future lingua franca in Nigeria, and it was found that Hausa speakers were the only group to have a majority in favour of its own Nigerian language as the future lingua franca of the country (58 per cent), and under 25 per cent of Igbo and Yoruba speakers indicated a preference for their language to be the future lingua franca of the country. With this last, revealing observation on attitudes to the indigenous languages in different domains of life in Nigeria, it is now time to consider attitudes towards the non-indigenous competitor language which currently dominates the formal domains of life in Nigeria: English.

As mentioned earlier, English is the language of most government administration, education (apart from early mother-tongue schooling), business, most occurrences of writing, the majority of the mass media, and also serves as a means of inter-ethnic communication for those who have received some education. Before we reflect on attitudes towards English as revealed in various surveys of recent years, it is useful to note down the principal arguments both for and against the position of English as Nigeria's leading language in formal domains, as these are often direct causes of the attitudes held towards the language. Commonly, there are two main criticisms of English as the country's single official language. The first of these is that English has been inherited from the former colonial power and is therefore both a non-indigenous language and a constant linguistic reminder of the humiliation of earlier colonial occupation and exploitation that should ideally be done away with, if at all possible. Adesanoye (1994: 86) summarizes the spirit of this view, observing that 'not a few well-intentioned Nigerians are of the opinion that total independence is chimerical as long as we still conduct our "independent" affairs in the language of the erstwhile colonists.' A second oft-made negative point about the maintenance of English as the official language of Nigeria is that English is only known by a minority of the population and that those who do not know English are automatically excluded from participation in the political life of Nigeria, as election to any government position requires at least a School Certificate level of education, which in turn necessitates proficiency in English (Maduka-Durunze 1998: 95).[8] A third, related criticism that has frequently been made in recent times is that the standard of English attained by many occupying posts in government service is often poor, both at lower levels and sometimes also higher levels (Bamgbose 1994: 4). In education it is noted that a similar failure to master English well may be responsible in part for high drop-out rates in secondary schools (Ogunsiji

---

[8] Concerning the actual percentage of the population that understands and can speak English, this is not well established and various figures are given in the literature, ranging from a low of around 10 per cent to just over 30 per cent. A recent piece of research by Simire (2004: 139) estimates that approximately 33 per cent of the population can speak, read, and write English, though perhaps only 15 per cent actually make regular use of English in their professional life. In theory, everyone who has completed more than three years of education should have had exposure to English in school and attained at least a basic familiarity with the language. As the educational system has experienced difficulties relating to financing and personnel since the 1980s, it is clear that success rates in schools, and hence the adequate learning of English, are far from ideal.

2001: 153), and that primary school teachers and university students also often have a less-than-satisfactory ability in English (Abdulkadir 2000: 245).[9]

Turning now to note what are most commonly highlighted as the principal advantages of keeping English as the official language of Nigeria, there are two key functions which English provides which no other Nigerian language could obviously replicate. First of all, precisely because of its foreign-sourced nature, English is seen to be an ethnically neutral language which has the capacity to unify the many different ethno-linguistic groups in Nigeria without according an explicit advantage to one group over the others. It is widely recognized that English does indeed constitute a unifying force in Nigeria and that there might well be more conflict in the country if English were not available as a neutral language for use in inter-ethnic communication (Bamgbose 1994: 84; Igboanusi and Peter 2005: 16). Such a neutral linguistic force is particularly appreciated by the minority groups, who may otherwise feel dominated by speakers of the major three languages. The second area in which English 'scores' very heavily is in its ability to provide access and links to the wider outside world and the science and technology that is necessary for Nigeria to develop and successfully compete with other countries. Without a well-established proficiency in English (or some other language of wider international communication) among its educated elite, Nigeria would be severely disadvantaged in a wide range of areas involving access to developing knowledge.

The factors noted above have a direct influence on attitudes towards English. In all of the major studies on attitudes towards languages in Nigeria, researchers report that English consistently receives a very high rating as the language of formal domains and is regularly ranked by a clear majority of speakers as (a) the preferred language of officialdom and administration, (b) the preferred language for written communication, (c) the language most important for the development of a full education through to secondary level, and (d) the preferred general lingua franca for Nigeria in the future. For minority groups, the general preference for English within formal contexts of life extends even further, as noted earlier, and a study averaging responses from both southern and northern minorities in Igboanusi and Ohia (2001: 132) showed that the language preferred overall across all domains by the majority of speakers (50 per cent) was indeed English (as opposed to a 42 per cent preference for mother tongue). For a great many speakers from different groups, English is also valued as a language of prestige, a sign of education, and a mark of modernity (Igboanusi and Peter 2005: 131). The

---

[9] To be fair, it is not clear whether this general failure to achieve a high level of proficiency in English is due to any inherent difficulty in learning English in particular as opposed to other languages. If, for example, Hausa, an Afro-Asiatic language, were to be substituted for English in schools with speakers of minority Niger-Congo languages (as might happen if Hausa were to replace English as the medium of education in many of the northern states), it is far from evident that student achievement would be higher, and the non-indigenous nature of English should not automatically make it more difficult to learn than languages which are indigenous but which stem from different African language families. Rather, what might seem to be to blame here is either the system of such extensive use of a second language as medium of education, or the insufficient training of teachers themselves competent in English.

one obvious exception to these patterns reported in a number of surveys and works on language attitudes relates to mother-tongue speakers of Hausa, whose attitude towards English is much more ambivalent than that of other groups. The Hausas are regularly noted both to be extremely proud of their language, with such enthusiasm reportedly even leading to feelings of linguistic superiority among certain speakers, and to have much more frequent negative attitudes towards English than members of other groups, Babajide (2001: 7) estimating that approximately 62.5 per cent of Hausas may have negative feelings about English, compared to similar attitudes being held by only 15 per cent of Igbos and minority groups and 25 per cent of Yorubas. Nevertheless, Igboanusi and Peter (2005: 113) remark that even though English may generate negative feelings among Muslim Hausa speakers, the same speakers also generally recognize the high instrumental value of a knowledge of English for obtaining employment and the significant access that the language provides to outside learning. Its utility in official domains is furthermore acknowledged, receiving a 56 per cent preference from Hausa speakers in the same study. Across the broad population in Nigeria, there consequently appears to be a clear acknowledgement of the importance and value of English both for personal advancement and for the general development of the country in the area of science and technology, the economy and education. One informant, responding to the suggestion from certain quarters that Nigeria should free itself from the English language and develop a replacement for English from among the indigenous languages, expressed the following feeling, which would probably be endorsed by other Nigerians:

> You cannot just be talking about emancipation from *language*. What about emancipation from (not) being able to produce the things we need? ... produce how much food we need ... produce technology. These things are more crucial to us and more important than wasting money on developing a new language ... And they're busy thinking about how they can spend money so that I no longer talk in English.   Adegbija (1994: 61)

In addition to being rated fairly highly in positive terms with regard to many domains, particularly those connected with formal aspects of life, it is relevant to note that English is generally not the object of strongly negative feelings, with the exception of reactions from certain portions of the Hausa population. When speakers were asked to identify which language they had the greatest dislike for in Nigeria in a study carried out among northern and southern minorities, Igboanusi and Ohia (2001: 132) found that 40 per cent identified Hausa, 21 per cent Yoruba, 27 per cent Igbo, and only 3 per cent English as the most disliked language. There is also very widespread agreement on the ability English has as an ethnically neutral language to unify different groups within Nigeria, and serve as a common means of communication between speakers of different languages without encoding the linguistic dominance of either party. Ogunsiji (2001: 156, 157) suggests that 'English unites us in our diversity and guarantees our continued existence as a nation' and that 'The English language is therefore an important symbol of national unity; it is one of those things that bind the country together.' Finally, concerning the negative perception of English as a continued colonial intrusion in the life of independent Nigeria, a variety of studies note the occurrence of a change and shift in attitude here, and with the globalization of English and its increasing use as a second language by large populations of speakers throughout the world, English is coming to be seen less and less as 'the special preserve of the British people, but rather as a kind of international medium of communication' (Adesanoye 1994: 93). Earlier automatic associations of the English language with the British and colonial domination have also been further weakened by the development of a distinctly Nigerian form of English over the years, with a lexicon and pronunciation that attach the language to Nigeria, just as there are other new divergent local forms of English in West Africa, for example Ghanaian English and Cameroonian English. This being so, it is possible that the negative mental associations of English with colonial domination are no longer as strong as they might have been several decades ago, and may no longer constitute a serious and genuine reason to object to the use of English in formal domains in the eyes of the majority of the population. At the time of writing, there are no statistics available indicating the degree to which Nigerians in the twenty-first century may continue to associate English with British imperialism, and it would be an interesting area to investigate. However, one would certainly expect that the more time goes past and distances the colonial period, the fewer people there will be with negative memories of colonial rule, and currently the majority of Nigeria's population will indeed have been born at some time well after the departure of the British in 1960.

10.6 The National Language Issue Revisited

We can now take stock of the information accumulated in section 10.5 and earlier sections, and see how this bears on the issue of national language and integration. As noted during the course of the chapter, Nigeria is a country which, having received its independence, has continually had to deal with an extremely complex ethno-linguistic configuration and set of challenges to the process of nation-building, having been forged as a single territory from areas containing several hundred different groups and no clear majority language that could naturally be used to develop a national language in the way that has occurred in more monolingual countries such as Somalia, Rwanda, Burundi, and Madagascar. Instead, Nigeria contains three considerably sizeable languages spoken in total by approximately one-half to two-thirds of the population, and a vast array of other medium- and small-sized languages scattered throughout the country, whose mother-tongue speakers account for at least a third of the population. At independence in 1960, faced with a major surge in inter-ethnic and regional political competition, the pre-independence policy recognizing English as the single official language of Nigeria was simply maintained and, in the decades following on from this and up until the present, there has been an explicit lack of attention to the development of a national language in Nigeria, despite the approval of policies in the

1970s appearing to support the development of the three major languages as future potential national languages. The presence of English as an official language made use of in national-level activities may indeed have partially contributed to the avoidance of the national language issue, as noted by Ogunsiji (2001: 158): 'because English is seen as a language performing the role of a national language the Nigerian government, language planners, linguists and so on do not seem to feel the necessity for having a truly national language.' The question is, after nearly five decades of the inherited policy of English as sole official language should there perhaps now be a restructuring of the hierarchy of languages in Nigeria and an indigenization of language at the highest national/official level, and would public opinion support such a move, as far as can be ascertained?

Quite generally, there seems to be a consensus of opinion that if Nigeria is to develop a meaningful concept of national language sourced from within its borders, this might actually need to be a composite set of the three major indigenous languages, Hausa, Yoruba, and Igbo.[10] The oft-quoted words of Nida and Wonderly (1971: 65) written shortly after the end of Nigeria's civil war are as valid today as they were in 1971 when the country was nearly split apart due to ethnic conflict:

> In Nigeria there is simply no politically neutral [indigenous] language ... The political survival of Nigeria as a country would be even more seriously threatened than it is if any one of these three languages were promoted by the Government as being the one national language.

However, as time and experience since the 1970s have shown, the endeavour to promote the three indigenous languages across the nation through the educational system will require very serious long-term commitment from the government in the form of major financial support for teacher-training, the creation of teaching materials, and careful placement of teachers in suitable locations. Without such planning and resources, the necessary spread in knowledge of the three major languages will simply fail to occur, as can be seen from the generally poor results that the mother-tongue education policy has produced thus far. Any promotion of the three major languages as national official languages on a par with or replacing English in all official and formal domains will also need a massive, sustained investment of government funds, as the high costs of maintaining genuine official multilingualism in countries such as Canada, Singapore, and Switzerland have shown. At the present point in time, this kind of major expenditure might seem to be something that Nigeria unfortunately cannot

---

[10] The possible development of Nigerian Pidgin as Nigeria's national language does not seem to have much genuine support as an alternative to promotion of the three major languages. Although Nigerian Pidgin is widely spoken and understood in the south of the country, it is pointed out in Bamgbose (1994: 6) that spreading its knowledge to the rest of Nigeria would be very difficult, given that Nigerian Pidgin has not been standardized and exhibits much variation. In addition to this, as a pidgin it is typically associated with a range of negative attitudes and thought by many to be unsuitable for use outside purely informal domains. Consequently, there might be considerable resistance to any attempted elevation of Nigerian Pidgin to a higher, national/official status.

afford. Having suffered a drastic downturn in its economy since the 1980s, crippling the country's ability to innovate and develop new infrastructure on a national scale, now would not appear to be the time for experimentation with a new language policy poorly provided with financial support. Rather than see new national language policies fail or worse still intensify ethnic disharmony, it would seem that Nigeria is in fact realistically stuck with the inherited status quo for at least the immediate future, until the economy is rebuilt to a state where it could hypothetically bear the burden of a new national language initiative. Such a conclusion, to a considerable extent forced by external financial constraints, may not be so disheartening or desperately unwelcome, however. From the available evidence, gathered from a range of investigations of attitudes, it would appear that there are actually widespread, largely positive attitudes towards English in its occurrence as the linking language of officialdom and education, for a variety of reasons. Though this may not assist in nation-building in the way of directly helping construct a specifically Nigerian national identity shared by the population, there are times when the optimal role of language in national integration may not be one of attempting to actively mould new forms of identity, but rather a minimization of the conflict and national disintegration that may otherwise arise through problems relating to language. While various countries at points in their history have been presented with circumstances that help facilitate the development of a shared language as a strong symbol of the nation, Nigeria, emerging from several decades of emotionally charged ethno-regional politics and competition would currently seem to need to adopt the safest possible language strategies to help secure its future as a nation built from many nations. It can therefore be concluded that, for the time being, until better foundations are created for the strong growth of a single Nigerian nation, the retention of English as official language of the state might seem to remain the best imperfect fit for the country, and that a majority of the population polled in recent surveys appears to recognize the high pragmatic imperative and utility of such a 'nationist' rather than nationalist linguistic policy (Bamgbose 1991).[11]

---

[11] For example, the study referred to in Adegbija (1994: 66) reports that 73.5 per cent of respondents wanted English retained as the official language of Nigeria. Igboanusi and Ohia (2001: 134) found that 66 per cent of their respondents identified English as their preferred retained future lingua franca of Nigeria, and Igboanusi and Peter (2005: 98) registered an average 68 per cent approval of English for the same status, with all non-Hausa groups approving at a rate of 73 per cent or over. Other studies suggest similar conclusions.

11

Cameroon: Official Bilingualism in a Multilingual State

Edmond Biloa and George Echu

11.1 Introduction

Cameroon is a linguistic melting pot and contains over 250 languages from three of the four linguistic phyla attested on the continent. However, none of Cameroon's many autochthonous languages is spoken by a majority in the country and most of its languages have relatively small populations of speakers. As a result of colonization, English and French are the official languages of Cameroon and a policy of official bilingualism is enshrined in the state constitution. Consequently, English and French are the languages: (a) of the state (that is, all administrative documents have to be written in either French or English, or both), (b) of business, (c) of public and private education, (d) of the print media, (e) of radio and television, (f) of administration, and (g) of internal communication.

However, despite the official equality of English and French, public space is more occupied by the French language than by the English language. Thus, for example, in the media world, 90 per cent of the print media is in French; 65 per cent of radio and TV programmes are produced in French and 35 per cent in English. This is so because the largest part of Cameroon, which contains approximately 80 per cent of the population, was under French colonial rule, whereas the former British-administered territory of Cameroon comprises only 20 per cent of the overall population. While French tends to be a language of wider communication in large cities, the use of English is now threatened by the popularity of Pidgin English, with the effect that the latter is more used as a language of wider communication than the former, which remains rather the language of the well-educated and formal situations.

A policy of official language bilingualism in French and English has been adopted by the state since independence in order to foster national integration, ensure social peace, guarantee respect for constitutional rights, and favour the socio-economic development of the country, and much money has since been spent by the government in the attempted implementation of the bilingual policy. However, in the long run, contact between French-speaking and English-speaking Cameroonians has in fact been far from harmonious. The two linguistic groups have ended up identifying themselves with the two European languages so much that the relationship between the two languages has become a source of both linguistic and political conflict. The Anglophone elite feel that they are linguistically and politically dominated by their Francophone counterparts, and therefore would like to see Cameroon, now one unitary state, go back to federalism as practised between 1961 and 1972 when there existed two distinct federated states (English-speaking West Cameroon and French-speaking East Cameroon). This quest for federalism or secession in Cameroon has come to be known as 'the Anglophone problem' (Konings and Nyamnjoh 1997).[1]

The chapter starts with a survey of the sociolinguistic situation of Cameroon in section 11.2, followed by an examination of the issue of multilingualism, national identity, and language policy in 11.3. Consideration of the Anglophone problem in particular and conflict generated by contact between English and French is the focus of 11.4, and the chapter is concluded in 11.5 with some summarizing thoughts on the links between language and both national and sub-national ethnic identity in the country.

11.2 A Brief Survey of the Language Situation in Cameroon

Situated in Central Africa, Cameroon has a population of just over 16 million inhabitants (2005 estimate) and a surface area of 475,442 square kilometres. It is bounded to the west by Nigeria, to the northeast by Chad, to the east by the Central African Republic, Equatorial Guinea, and Gabon, and to the south by the Democratic Republic of Congo (Brazzaville).

According to Breton and Fohtung (1991), Cameroon has 248 indigenous languages. This estimate contrasts with figures advanced by *Ethnologue* and Bitja'a Kody (2003) which respectively credit the country with 279 and 285 indigenous languages.[2] Whatever the precise total of distinct languages currently present in Cameroon, it is certainly a heavily multilingual country with one of the highest language-to-population ratios in Africa and linguistic representation of three of Africa's four major language families. The Afro-Asiatic family is represented by 58 languages spoken in the Far North

---

[1] Note that throughout this chapter Anglophone and Francophone are written with capital initial letters as these terms have come to designate specific linguistic groups in Cameroon which are centred on the use of English and French but not fully defined by knowledge of these languages (see section 11.3). The terms therefore have an extended designation which may be different from common use of the non-capitalized terms anglophone and francophone.

[2] It is important to mention that the statistics put forth by Grimes (1996) are presently somewhat outdated given that between 1996 and 2003 several languages have either disappeared or are fast disappearing (Bitja'a Kody 2003). A majority of researchers would in fact seem to adopt the figures advanced in Breton and Fohtung (1991) due to the fact that their atlas furnishes precise details on the geographical area covered by each language.

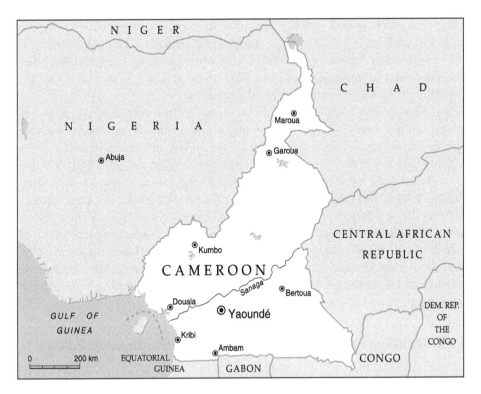

Cameroon

province, the Niger-Congo family by 188 languages located all over Cameroon, and the Nilo-Saharan group by just two languages.[3]

At the sociolinguistic level, the languages spoken in Cameroon can be classified under three categories: official languages, languages of wider communication, and other indigenous, ethnic group languages.[4] Socially, the official languages are more prestigious than the other two categories, and so occupy a higher position in society in terms of usage. They are closely followed by the languages of wider communication, among which are Basaa, Beti-Fang, Duala, Fe'fe', Fulfulde, Ghomala, Hausa, Kanuri, Mungaka, Wandala, Shuwa Arabic, and Cameroon Pidgin English. These languages are used beyond ethnic boundaries, whether at the local, regional, or national level. For instance, Beti-Fang is spoken by more than 2 million people in the Centre, South, and East provinces (*Ethnologue* 2004),[5] while Fulfulde is spoken in much of the Adamawa, North, and Far North provinces of the northern part of the country. As for Cameroon Pidgin English, this is spoken by Cameroonians spread throughout the

---

[3] The Khoisan language family is the only African language family absent from Cameroon.
[4] This classification does not take into cognizance foreign languages taught in Cameroonian schools such as Spanish, German, and Arabic.
[5] http://www.ethnologue.com/

national territory, as well as other non-native speakers from neighbouring Nigeria. Todd and Jumbam (1992: 4) estimate the potential population of pidginophones at close to 6 million. Further down the sociolinguistic hierarchy are found the other indigenous ethnic languages that enjoy little or no prestige, as they are generally limited to the various ethnic groups of their speakers.

It is important to point out from the start that in Cameroon the indigenous languages of the country have never really played any major role in issues of national identity, and the critical languages involved in the projection of major group identities in Cameroon are in fact the ex-colonial languages, English and French. This is due to the fact that the most territorially widespread languages in Cameroon are indeed English, French, and Pidgin English, and no indigenous language has a population of speakers that is a majority in the country or powerful enough to have attempted to impose its language throughout the country. Because of this lack of participation of individual Cameroonian languages in issues of broad national identity, much of the discussion in this chapter will be focused on the dynamic existing between English, French, and Pidgin English in Cameroon, as this is where the more serious issues of ethno-linguistic and national identity are contested in the country.

11.3 Multilingualism, National Identity, and Language Policy

Territorially, Cameroon was initially formed as a German colony, but later came to be divided between Britain and France as a result of settlements at the end of World War I, with two provinces being put under British administration and five under French rule. Even before the arrival of the Germans in Cameroon, Pidgin English was present in the region as a lingua franca of trade not only in coastal areas but also in inner parts of the territory. Under German rule the popularity of Pidgin English as a lingua franca further increased, although German was officially taught in certain places within the colony. Following German rule, the French colonial administration heavily promoted the learning and use of French culture, under a policy of assimilation, and the use of Pidgin English was banned in the Francophone portion of the territory. British administration was, by way of contrast, rather less intrusive and did not seek to enforce the same degree of cultural and linguistic assimilation. The use of Pidgin English was therefore not suppressed in the Anglophone provinces, though Standard English was also taught in school.

As the result of the division of Cameroon into two English- and French-administered zones, during the British and French occupation of the country two separate educational systems evolved and two different colonial languages came to be promoted in formal domains in the two parts of the country. When independence was achieved, both colonial languages were subsequently selected as official languages of Cameroon, in an attempt to unify the country as a single, multilingual nation. The choice of the two European languages as official languages was deliberately made so as not to alienate either the Anglophone or Francophone community through the preferential selection of just one language for all official purposes. As there was no obvious indigenous language (or pair/set of languages) that could realistically be selected as official languages (no indigenous language having the geographic coverage of the territory that English and French enjoyed, and most indigenous languages not being standardized at the time), the choice of English and French as joint official languages also appeared to be the most practical linguistic way forward in the circumstances Cameroon found itself in at independence. This situation and the decision to adopt a policy of official bilingualism has resulted in Cameroon being unique in Africa in having two European languages as the selected official languages of the state. As will later be seen, however, the path of official bilingualism in Cameroon has not been fully smooth, and there remains a clear division of the country into separate Anglophone and Francophone identities.

Concerning the issue of the selection of one or more *national* languages for Cameroon, given the multilingual nature of the country, and coupled with the fear of creating a situation of language conflict by designating only certain languages as national languages,[6] in 1974 adoption of the term 'national language' was unanimously supported by delegates of the National Council for Cultural Affairs as a way to refer to all of the indigenous languages of Cameroon. By giving all of Cameroon's indigenous languages this measure of recognition, it was intended that this would signal that none of the country's indigenous languages should be considered more important than any other, and that no indigenous language should be held to be inferior to other local languages. The adoption of the term 'national language' for all of Cameroon's autochthonous languages was therefore largely made for reasons of national unity and nation-building, and since 1974, linguists and non-linguists alike have used the term to refer to all of the country's indigenous languages, with the exception of Cameroon Pidgin English, which has never benefited from this measure of recognition. With the passing of time, this 'global' view of national language in Cameroon has also received the support of the state in the constitution of 1996 which for the first time in the history of Cameroon explicitly mentions the protection and promotion of national languages as part of the country's language policy. Logically, the act of raising all indigenous languages to the level of national languages and guaranteeing their protection and promotion stems from the fact that together as a group they are considered a collective symbol of national identity and the expression of Cameroonian cultural heritage.

Long before this major development in the planned promotion of indigenous languages, it can be noted that other serious initiatives relative to indigenous languages in Cameroon had in fact been carried out, especially during the colonial period. For

---

[6] Cameroonian authorities have always been haunted by the fear of creating language conflict if any form of preference is ever given to certain indigenous languages. This explains why the teaching of Duala, Basaa, Ewondo, Bulu, Fulfulde, and Fe'fe' in the Department of African Languages and Linguistics of the University of Yaoundé from 1970 to 1977 was later abolished for fear that speakers of other languages not taught might engage in protest and revolt (Echu 2003: 37).

example, certain indigenous languages such as Duala, Mungaka, Bulu, and Ewondo were widely used by missionaries both in schools and churches during the German, British, and French colonial periods. While the Basel Mission promoted Duala and Mungaka in English-speaking Cameroon, the American Presbyterian Missionaries taught Bulu in schools of the southern part of the country, and the Catholic Mission promoted the use of Ewondo around the present-day Centre province. Such private initiatives from the missionaries, although originally intended to facilitate the dissemination of Christianity, greatly contributed to the promotion of indigenous languages, creating a new awareness among the indigenous population of the utility and prestige value of their languages. Another significant initiative was that carried out by Sultan Njoya in the Bamoun region, where the Bamoun language was promoted in 1896 and taught in forty-seven schools opened for this purpose, and a special printing press created. Although these schools were eventually closed down by the French colonial administration and the printing press destroyed, the existence of this project was a clear testimony to the spirit of pride in indigenous languages that was present at the time. Equally significant is the fact that, much later in 1967, UNESCO designated indigenous languages such as Ewondo, Basaa, Duala, Ghomala, Makaa, Fulfulde, Bafia, Lamnso, and Bakweri as languages for the development of literacy.

However, although the indigenous languages have the potential to (jointly) project and express Cameroonian national identity, they are still largely non-standardized and mainly oral in nature. As such, careful language planning would seem to be the only way that their long-term preservation and value can be guaranteed. Given that 'for a language to be used in school and by government ... it requires a writing system, a spelling system, the nomenclatures and styles of academic and governmental communications, in short, the dictionaries, grammars, and style manuals' (Fishman, 1997: 339), the Cameroonian indigenous languages cannot pretend to assume any meaningful national dimension if serious planning and development is not applied to them.

Overall, language policy since independence has instead tended to favour the two official languages, English and French, through the policy of official language bilingualism instituted in the country in 1961. This policy has favoured the growth and development of English and French and brought about the existence of two distinct local varieties: Cameroon English and Cameroon French. For such new varieties to gain recognition as established regional/national forms of English and French, significant corpus planning is necessary in the area of usage, spelling, stylistic conventions and so forth. Work of this kind is indeed being carried out on Cameroon French in the continuation of a project initiated in the late 1970s under the name 'Inventaire des particularités lexicales du français du Cameroun'. Unfortunately, nothing of comparable standards has been achieved as far as Cameroon English is concerned, in spite of pockets of initiatives occurring here and there. Nevertheless, there does seem to be a measure of international recognition of the existence of both language varieties, found in reference to Cameroon English and Cameroon French on the worldwide web and in the world of information technology and also in academic studies of the two forms of language. Cameroon English and Cameroon French have furthermore become an expression of the particular national identity of the Cameroonian people and their culture through the occurrence of lexical items and phrases peculiar to the Cameroonian context, and Cameroon English and Cameroon French are viewed as being able to express aspects of life particular to Cameroon in a more vibrant and precise way than standard English and French can.

It should also be noted that both varieties have developed language expressing the shared aspirations and outlook on life of Cameroonians as a common people, especially so in French, the dominant official language. Prominent among popular coinages are, for example: 'le Cameroon c'est le Cameroon' (Cameroon has its specificity), 'l'impossible n'est pas camerounais' (there's nothing impossible in Cameroon), and 'le pays des Lions Indomptables' (the land of the Indomitable Lions).[7] Such phrases create a feeling of inclusion and a sense of oneness among Cameroonians, as they tend to reinforce the belief that Cameroonians have a common destiny as a single people.

However, despite numerous governmental efforts aimed at building a feeling of inclusion and a sense of oneness among Cameroonians through the policy of official bilingualism, bilingual knowledge of English/French remains quite uneven, and Anglophone Cameroonians generally appear to know and have an ability to communicate in French more frequently than Francophone Cameroonians know and are able to communicate in English. For example, in the French-speaking part of the country (now made up of eight provinces), civil servants in public administration structures are found to speak very little English, while in the English-speaking part of Cameroon (comprising two provinces), civil servants tend to speak the French language fluently. Regular exposure to the official languages is certainly a determining factor here, as Anglophone Cameroonians tend to be more exposed to the French language than Francophone Cameroonians are to English. It has been pointed out by Bitja'a Kody (1999) and Biloa (2003, 2006) that French is clearly more visible than English in various areas of public life, in spite of the declared equality of the two languages. Hence, currently as much as 90 per cent of the printed press operates in French, and 65 per cent of the radio and television programmes at CRTV (Cameroon Radio and Television, the national radio and television broadcasting house) are made in French, and only 35 per cent in English. Furthermore, while French (in its various forms) is the language of wider communication in all the major cities of the land in both formal and informal domains, English is mostly spoken in formal situations and is the language of intellectuals, with Pidgin English being more broadly used as the Anglophone area language of wider communication.

The dominant status of the French language and the uneven spread and distribution of French/English bilingualism may be finally showing signs of a change, however, as

---

[7] The Indomitable Lions is the name of the country's national football team, a team that symbolizes national unity and the pride of the Cameroonian people during its participation in the African Nations' Cup and World Cup competitions.

more of the younger generation receive a fuller exposure to both French and English in their education. Today, in most urban centres, more often than not, every child going to school in an English-medium school has to learn French. Similarly, every Francophone child attending a French-medium school has to learn English. In the not too distant future French/English bilingualism may therefore become more widespread in both Anglophone and Francophone urban communities than it currently is and has been. Indeed, researchers such as Ngamassu (1999) and Echu (2006) have observed that more and more Francophone parents are sending their children either to bilingual schools or to English-medium schools. Echu (2006: 184) similarly indicates that young French-speaking Cameroonians are now showing significant progress on the way to bilingualism as children learn more English and take advantage of the immersion English language programmes designed by the British and American embassies. Such increased interest in learning English among Francophone youth is quite possibly due to the ever-rising status of English as a global, international language and the associated new opportunities that a knowledge of English now brings to those with an ability in it.

In spite of this potential advance in the area of education, however, it is felt by many in the Anglophone community that much more remains to be done before an equitable balance is struck between the two official languages in Cameroon, an issue returned to in section 11.4. Apart from the two official languages, French and English, there are two other language forms in Cameroon that are frequently perceived as expressions of broad group identity – Cameroon Pidgin English and Camfranglais.

In Cameroon, Pidgin English is increasingly considered as a marker of specifically Anglophone identity, and Francophone Cameroonians generally have negative attitudes both towards Cameroon Pidgin English and also towards those who use it. Believing that Pidgin English is a corrupting influence on (standard) English, many Francophone Cameroonians have come to develop pejorative attitudes towards Anglophones mainly on grounds of their (pidgin) language use, and accordingly might not wish for their offspring to associate with Anglophones due to the danger of 'contracting' Pidgin English. Furthermore, so long as Cameroon Pidgin English continues to be strongly associated with the Anglophone community alone, it is likely that the majority Francophone ruling government will not accord it any importance and simply continue to disregard its existence as a language form despite its widespread use in many parts of the country. Cameroon Pidgin English can in fact be said to be suffering from a form of 'double marginalization' in that, unlike the indigenous languages that have of late attracted attention and sympathy from official circles and the Cameroonian elite, Pidgin English continues to be given no real attention by policy makers and little or no consideration by society. However, in spite of such disregard by the community, Cameroon Pidgin English enjoys much popularity within Anglophone circles in Cameroon (Echu, forthcoming). This lingua franca, more than standard Cameroon English, is indeed the strongest symbol of Anglophone identity in the country, being spoken and understood by an overwhelming majority of Anglophones not only in the two English-speaking provinces but also elsewhere in the nation.[8] It should also be added that among pidginophones (people who can understand a pidgin), the particular variety of Cameroon Pidgin English spoken by an individual actually has an important role in determining whether or not the speaker is considered as an Anglophone.[9] While speakers of the Grassland, Bororo, and Coastal varieties of Pidgin English are considered Anglophones, those of other varieties from Francophone areas will commonly not be classified as Anglophones, no matter what their degree of proficiency in the language. Such distinctions underline the general fact that being classed as Anglophone within the Cameroonian context is actually not directly the result of purely linguistic criteria, and may instead be partly based on other considerations having little to do with language. For example, an old woman born and bred in one of the two English-speaking provinces of the country may very often be considered Anglophone even if she cannot understand or speak either English or Pidgin English. Conversely, someone of specifically Francophone parentage born and bred in one of the two English-speaking provinces will be frequently rejected outright as belonging to the Anglophone community in spite of any mastery of English and Pidgin English that person might actually have. Such exclusion from group member-ship is clearly based more on ethnic grounds than on linguistic considerations and associates membership of an ethno-linguistic group with blood descent rather than present linguistic ability.

As for 'Camfranglais', this novel slang (Kouega 2003) that is rapidly developing in Cameroon among youths residing in major towns and cities of the French-speaking provinces of the country has come to be regarded by many as a new symbol of Cameroonian identity. Being an acronym coined from the words 'Camerounais + Français + Anglais' (Cameroonian + French + English),[10] Camfranglais is a French-based slang made up of French, English, Cameroon Pidgin English, Cameroonian indigenous languages, as well as input from other foreign languages taught or spo-ken in Cameroon such as Spanish, German, and even Latin. It is therefore a broad mixture and sampling of the wide range of languages that constitute the multilin-gual composition of the country, and in this respect a genuinely inclusive expression of Cameroon multilingualism. Created and developed in urban centres of French-speaking Cameroon by the young, including students, school dropouts, and other

---

[8] Although standard English is often considered a marker of being Anglophone, a majority of those referred to as Anglophone Cameroonians simply because they come from the South-West and North-West provinces neither speak nor understand standard English. However, such people are generally proficient in Cameroon Pidgin English to a considerable extent, having acquired this informally, unlike standard (Cameroon) English which is normally acquired formally through explicit education.

[9] According to Echu (forthcoming), there are basically four distinct varieties of Cameroon Pidgin English: the Grassland variety spoken in the North-West province, the Bororo variety spoken by the Bororo people, the Coastal variety spoken in the South-West province, and the Francophone variety spoken by Francophones.

[10] See Mbah Onana and Mbah Onana (1994: 29).

city-dwellers involved in petty trading, Camfranglais as a language form successfully creates a kind of group solidarity and identity among members of the younger generation who want to be perceived differently from the rest of the community by fostering their own secret code, one which can be properly understood only by insiders. Thus, as Carole de Féral aptly puts it, speaking Camfranglais communicates that one is a young city-dweller who has claims to a broad Cameroonian identity in an officially bilingual country (de Féral 1993: 213). In spite of its limited number of speakers and usage compared to Cameroon Pidgin English and the two official languages, Camfranglais has in fact succeeded in winning the admiration of many in Cameroon as a speech form well-suited to express the Cameroonian way of life, and light-hearted, comic situations in particular.[11]

11.4 Anglophone Nationalism and the Language Question

It is well observed that language can become a focus of loyalty for a minority community which thinks it is suppressed, persecuted, or subject to discrimination. The French language in Canada in the mid-twentieth century is a good example of this, as is the case of Tetum on East Timor, during the period of Indonesian occupation from 1975 to 2002. While language conflict in Cameroon is present in many different environments and at various different levels, the most pronounced of all is arguably that between English and French, and it is clear that English is today becoming a strong focus of loyalty for the minority Anglophone community that purports to be marginalized. This situation has led to the increased assertion of the 'Anglophoneness' or the Anglo-Saxon colonial and cultural heritage of this section of the population, with the result that broadly shared language plays a dominant role in expressing the identity of those Cameroonians who originate from the South-West and North-West provinces of the country. For the approximately 20 per cent of the national population who are Anglophones, the nationally dominant language, French, is seen as controlling administration, politics, the economy, and the media, in short all forms of public life. This situation creates a sense of frustration and a feeling of marginalization, ultimately leading to resistance and nationalism within the underprivileged group.

The ongoing situation of conflict relating to the two official languages can be traced back to the 1961 federal constitution that gave the false impression that English and French were to have equal status in independent, post-colonial Cameroon. At that time the previously British-administered area of Southern Cameroons was renamed the Federated State of West Cameroon and joined with the formerly French-administered zone, renamed the Federated State of East Cameroon, in a new two-state federation, the Federal Republic of Cameroon. Such a federal arrangement helped in masking the imbalance of English and French in the country by somehow limiting the use

---

[11] Because its speakers have created this artificial language through a somewhat voluntary pidginization process that is seen negatively by many others, Camfranglais has sometimes also been referred to as a stigmatized local pidgin (cf. Echu and Grundstrom 1999: xix).

of the two official languages. While English continued to be predominantly used in Anglophone Cameroon (West Cameroon), French was predominantly used in Francophone Cameroon (East Cameroon). However, in 1972 President Ahidjo unilaterally put an end to the federal organization of Cameroon and replaced this with a non-federal unitary state. From this time onwards, Anglophone Cameroonians began to feel very keenly the more pervasive dominance of French in the country and quickly became aware of the fact that they constituted a minority in the state of Cameroon, both demographically and linguistically.

At the linguistic level, French soon came to dominate the political and administrative landscape of the unitary state, as could be seen from the fact that most official texts such as laws, decrees, orders, decisions, circular letters, and service memos were initially conceived and written almost exclusively in French, though at times they were later translated into English. This was and is especially telling in the case of the competitive public service examinations which are often set in French and then translated into English, resulting in the English version of such examinations being almost always a poor rendition of the French texts (Shey 1989). Even today, in spite of the experience of four decades of official bilingualism, the English language is generally relegated to second place or virtually absent from some spheres of life such as the army where French remains the sole language in use (see Constable 1974; Elime 2000). Although several appeals and reminders have been made by government on different occasions,[12] the balance sheet as regards the use of the two official languages in Cameroon tilts desperately in favour of French. This state of affairs often provokes a feeling of marginalization within the Anglophone community and some Anglophone Cameroonians have the impression that French is imposed on them at all costs to the detriment of English. One of the cases often pointed to by Anglophone activists is that a state corporation such as the National Oil Refinery (SONARA) situated in Limbe in the English-speaking sector of the country employs mostly French-speaking Cameroonians and operates almost exclusively in the French language.

Such a feeling of domination, and the psychological hostility that has often characterized Anglophone–Francophone relations, has understandably resulted in a situation in which the Anglophone community in Cameroon have become strong advocates for the English language. Because they consider themselves discriminated against by the majority Francophone language community, the Anglophones feel left with no other option than to defend themselves as a historico-linguistic group, and it is this historical and linguistic motivation and sense of belonging to a common group that has been responsible for the creation of a range of socio-political organizations and groups, including Anglophone nationalist movements, which function to mobilize the

---

[12] For example, Prime Ministerial Circular letter No. 001/CAB/PM of 16 August 1991, Presidential Order No. 03/CAB/PR of 30 May 1996, as well as Prime Ministerial Circular letter No. A685/CAB/PM of 25 April 2000 in relation to the practice of official bilingualism in the public sector and the simultaneous use of English and French in the preparation of official documents.

Anglophone community whenever a threat to its interests is perceived – for example the Cameroon Anglophone Movement, the All Anglophone Conference, the Teachers' Association of Cameroon, and the Southern Cameroons National Council.[13]

In the development of actual 'Anglophone nationalism' in Cameroon, the English language stands out as a common, though not fully exclusive, denominator and symbol of identity, the other being Pidgin English, which is equally perceived as a marker of Anglophone identity in Cameroon.[14] Anglophone nationalist movements in fact originated long before the territory of Cameroon received its independence from colonial occupation, with one of the first such movements being the Cameroon Youth League created in 1941 in Lagos. Other groups such as the Bamenda Improvement Association and the Bakweri Union also strove to preserve the identity of Southern Cameroons within Nigerian political groups, and political parties like Ndeh Ntumazah's One Kamerun Movement were clearly driven by nationalistic motivations. After reunification in 1961, Anglophone nationalism became relatively silent, if not non-existent, under the political repression that characterized this era of the Ahidjo dictatorship. Even after 1972, the much-contested unitary state did not provoke overt nationalistic sentiments from Anglophones in spite of their tacit disapproval of the way in which the referendum in favour of a unitary state was conducted, and all Anglophone political activism remained essentially clandestine. However, with the introduction of political pluralism by the Biya government in the early 1990s, Anglophone nationalism resurfaced in Cameroon once again. Groups such as the Cameroon Anglophone Movement, the All Anglophone Conference, and the Southern Cameroons National Council have since occupied the political arena, calling for a return to federalism and greater autonomy and political independence within a federal state, and in some instances pushing for outright secession of Anglophone Cameroon from the Republic of Cameroon.

In March 1993, a general assembly of Anglophone Cameroonians known as the All Anglophone Conference was held in Buea in the South-West province through the initiative of a number of leading Anglophones. During this meeting, Anglophones from all corners of the country came together to discuss their common problems and for the first time openly voiced their feelings of marginalization by French-speaking compatriots in a document captioned the 'Buea Peace Initiative'. An important resolution of the conference was the need for a return to federalism as a *sine qua non* for peaceful coexistence between Anglophones and Francophones in Cameroon. Among the numerous participants at the conference were John Ngu Foncha, Vice President of Cameroon (1961–68) and Prime Minister of West Cameroon (1961–65),

---

[13] One example of such mobilization occurred in 1991–92 when the Anglophone community stood firm behind the Teachers' Association of Cameroon and the Confederation of Anglophone Parent-Teachers' Associations of Cameroon and carried out numerous protest actions throughout the country, calling for the creation of a new Cameroon General Certificate of Education Board, this being finally granted by the government in 1993 (Nyamnjoh 1996).

[14] Though not in the case of the variety of Pidgin English largely spoken in the Francophone provinces, as noted in section 11.3.

and Solomon Tandeng Muna, Vice President of Cameroon (1968–72) and Speaker of the National Assembly (1973–88). The participation of these two personalities who played a prominent role in the reunification of Southern Cameroons with French-speaking Cameroon can be seen as a clear testimony to the importance Anglophones attached to the Buea conference and the seriousness of their intentions.

While the All Anglophone Conference ultimately failed to have nationwide impact as a pressure group, the Southern Cameroons National Council (SCNC) currently maintains an important position in Cameroonian politics, though by calling for out-right secession of the two Anglophone provinces from the Republic of Cameroon, Anglophone nationalism is clearly assuming an extremist dimension. In addition to sending a number of missions abroad in order to lobby for the Anglophone cause in international circles (such as at the United Nations in New York in 1995), domesti-cally leaders of the SCNC have carried out various actions in the two Anglophone provinces aimed at attracting public attention and drawing it to the nationalist cause. In September 2005, mounting tension in the Anglophone community and plans for the proclamation of an independent Anglophone Cameroon led the government to carry out a vigorous campaign against SCNC activists in the South-West and North-West provinces. The activities of the SCNC are therefore a clear indication of the existence of an 'Anglophone problem' in Cameroon, which should best be solved through con-structive dialogue and rigorous application of the 1996 Constitution according some measure of regional autonomy to the different provinces, rather than through acts of repression and intimidation.[15]

In general, it is clear that Anglophone nationalism in Cameroon has language as its most fundamental characteristic and is united in a strong desire to preserve a common identity through the English language. This may easily be understood given that the fortunes and misfortunes of history have resulted in the destiny of Anglophone Cameroonians being inextricably linked with the status and fate of the English language, and although this received, official language may be foreign in its origin to the Cameroonian people, it is fast becoming an important, integral part of Anglophones' cultural identity. After more than four decades of coexistence with French Cameroon, Anglophone Cameroonians generally seem to be more than ever disgruntled, this dissatisfaction translating into an increasing spirit of nationalism and calls for secession from Francophone Cameroon. Such a situation of mounting language conflict can still be corrected or checked, however, if an equitable system of language planning is finally established which properly implements the constitutional equality between English and French and guarantees equal usage of the two official languages.[16] If such a reconciliation does not occur, it is likely that the fracturing of national unity will continue to be fuelled in a serious way by feelings of inequality

---

[15] See also Konings and Nyamnjoh (1997) on the Anglophone problem in Cameroon.
[16] The 1996 constitution states that: 'The official languages of the Republic of Cameroon shall be English and French, both languages having the same status. The state shall guarantee the promotion of bilingualism throughout the Country.'

spread among the sizeable Anglophone part of the population, giving further impetus to calls for independence.

11.5 Conclusion

Cameroon is a densely multilingual country where over two hundred indigenous languages coexist with English and French (the two official languages of the country), Cameroon Pidgin English (a widespread lingua franca), and Camfranglais (a pidginized French-based slang). The present linguistic situation, unique in Africa in terms of a single state having two non-indigenous, colonial languages as its official languages, is a result of the special historical conditions in which Cameroon achieved its independence. Having emerged from an extended period of colonial rule by Britain and France during which time English and French were promoted and embedded in official and other formal domains of life in separate parts of the territory of Cameroon, the decision was made at independence to select both English and French as the official languages of the state. Such a decision was prompted by the assessment that none of the autochthonous languages of Cameroon presented a realistic opportunity for promotion to official language status and might trigger civil disturbances if attempted, and that the choice of either French or English alone as the country's single official language also risked causing significant language-related conflict and possibly even civil war. It was furthermore hoped that the selection of both English and French combined with a policy of official bilingualism had the potential to link up the whole population and help progress towards the creation of a unified, multilingual Cameroonian nation. To the extent that language issues have not resulted in any major splitting apart of the country since independence, the selection of English and French as co-official languages of Cameroon might seem to have been successful and to have contained a difficult multilingual, multi-ethnic situation. If one attempts to assess progress in a rather less positive way, however, the question of whether Cameroon's policy of official bilingualism has helped harmonize its population and achieved a positive degree of unification and nation-building cannot be answered so optimistically. After five decades of independence, it would seem that the government's language policies have ultimately not helped stimulate a single, shared national identity, and instead the country is broadly divided between two major group identities that have language as a central symbol of allegiance, the Anglophone bloc and the larger Francophone population. Though English and French are imported languages originally associated with colonial rule, in the period since independence they have become so much part of Cameroonian cultural heritage that many Cameroonians now identify themselves strongly in relation to these languages as being first and foremost Anglophone or Francophone and only secondly as belonging to a single Cameroonian nation. This is perhaps most strongly so among the Anglophones who perceive the dominance of French as a threat to English and to equal Anglophone participation in Cameroonian life and who have developed a heightened loyalty to English as a direct consequence of this. Anglophones are widely dissatisfied with the current situation of English and French in Cameroon and openly complain about the unequal status of the official languages, to the point of entertaining secession or a return to federalism as a possible solution to language-generated problems for the Anglophone part of the country. Due to such polarization into distinct language-centred divisions in which English and French are viewed more in the way of national languages than simple official languages (in the sense of functioning as foci of allegiance for large competitive, territory-holding populations), it seems likely that the process of merging Anglophones and Francophones into a single Cameroonian national identity will take much more time, and whatever common links of identity have so far been established among the population of the country, these have been won despite and not in virtue of language as a potential binding force. Official bilingualism is consequently not working well as a mechanism of integration in Cameroon, though arguably not due to any inherent flaw in multilingualism as a viable national policy, but rather due to a perceived failure in the fair implementation of such a policy.

12

D. R. Congo: Language and 'Authentic Nationalism'

Eyamba G. Bokamba

12.1 Introduction

What is known today as the Democratic Republic of the Congo (DRC) represents one of the most multilingual nations in Africa with an estimated 214 living indigenous languages or ethnic groupings (*Ethnologue* 2005). To this number must be added French, the declared official language of DRC, and a few other non-indigenous languages (e.g. Lebanese Arabic, English, Greek, Hindi, Portuguese, and Wolof) that are spoken by significant communities in urban centres. What the ultimate number of languages spoken in DRC may turn out to be and how accurate such a datum may be remain open questions in the absence of census data that include a linguistic component. What is certain, however, is that DRC is a stable multilingual state with twenty-one well-known major indigenous languages with an estimated population of at least 500,000 each (*Ethnologue* 2005). Of these, four languages – Kikongo, Kiswahili,[1] Lingala, and Tshiluba – serve as national languages in selected domains, with French as the official language in most public domains (Bokamba 1976, forthcoming).

With this type of pervasive multilingualism the question that naturally arises in the context of language and national identity is whether there is a single or many competing identities based on the linguistic cleavages. This chapter examines this question and related sub-questions in an attempt to ascertain, from historical facts and linguistic practices, the factors that characterize Congolese nationalism. The study examines the role played by expressed language policy practices, Congolese music, political policies, and the invocation of the ideology of 'authenticity' under the second republic (1965–97) in shaping a Congolese identity. It will be argued below, first, that contrary to the perception that prevails in the West regarding the divisive nature of multilingualism, it is indeed possible to develop a sense of national identity in a stable multilingual

---

[1] Note that the language Kiswahili is sometimes referred to without its Ki- prefix simply as 'Swahili'. There is no difference in what these two terms refer to, though use of the prefixed form is often felt to be linguistically more correct.

nation. Second, that in the case of DRC several factors have interacted, in spite of the post-1996 crisis, to develop and maintain a Congolese identity notwithstanding the pervasiveness of individual and societal multilingualism. And third, that the failure of the international community to create an Eastern vs. Western DRC divide, portrayed in the Western press as Swahili-speaking vs. Lingala-speaking Congo, in the 2006 presidential elections constitutes the strongest evidence to date of the resilience of Congolese nationalism.

12.2 Geographical and Historical Backgrounds

DRC, known as the Republic of Zaire from 1971 to 1997, is located in the very heart of the African continent on both sides of the equator, and is bordered by a total of nine countries. It is the continent's second largest landmass after the Sudan with an area of 905,365 square miles, and the fourth most populous African country, with an estimated population of 60 million inhabitants (*Wikipedia* 2006).

The territory of DRC was first officially established as a private fiefdom of King Leopold II of Belgium in the late nineteenth century under the name the Congo

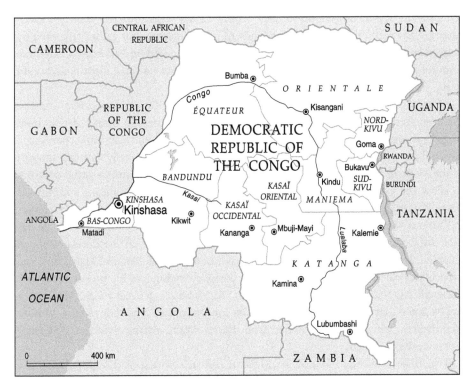

Democratic Republic of the Congo

Free State. In 1908, following international condemnation of the brutal treatment of the indigenous population of the Congo Free State which led to the deaths of about 50 per cent of its inhabitants, King Leopold was forced to relinquish his personal claim to the territory and it was bequeathed to the Kingdom of Belgium as a colony (Hochschild 1998), thereafter being referred to as the 'Belgian Congo' until it acceded to political independence on June 30, 1960. While direct Belgian rule was much less brutal than her king's, the colonial administration nonetheless practised open racial discrimination and segregation in most major spheres and domains, and denied Congolese many fundamental rights, including the rights to vote, stand for a public office, receive an equitable salary, and obtain public education (Anstey 1966; Nzongola-Ntalaja 2002).

Independence from Belgium was finally achieved in 1960. Shortly after this, however, DRC experienced a series of significant crises to its quest for liberation, including a mutiny of the *Force Publique* (the former colonial national army) in Kinshasa (5–9 July 1960), subsequent Belgian military intervention to quell the mutiny, a coup d'état led by the Congolese National Army under its chief of staff Lieutenant Colonel Joseph Mobutu (14 September 1960), assassination of DRC's popular, first elected Prime Minister, Patrice Lumumba, in Elizabethville, Katanga (17 January 1961), and Western-fomented secessions of two of the Congolese mineral-rich provinces, Katanga and Kasai, from 1960 to 1963. The Katanga secession crisis was not motivated by any aspirations for independence of its population, but rather triggered by Belgian and multinational companies so as to maintain unfettered access to Congolese resources. The crisis nevertheless gave the appearance of a national identity and unity crisis.

After two and a half years of civil war to end the Katanga secession and the first ever free and fair nationwide multi-party elections, held in May 1965, Mobutu staged a second coup d'état (24 November 1965) and established a strongly centralized national government, ruling DRC autocratically and kleptocratically with the support of the West until 24 April 1990 when he acceded to internal and external pressure to allow the establishment of multi-party politics. The most significant and historic development at this point was the convening of the 'Sovereign National Conference' in Kinshasa, a transitional deliberative body with 2,842 delegates representing all segments of Congolese society, which re-energized Congolese nationalism, and developed an practicable political programme to reintroduce accountability, multi-partyism, and participatory democracy, despite Mobutu doing everything in his power to thwart these efforts (Nzongola-Ntalaja 2002, 2006). To Mobutu's general credit, however, it can be noted that during his rule he kept the country united, and reduced the number of provinces, which had proliferated from six to twenty-one prior to the 1965 coup d'état, down to eleven.

Two major consequences of the Mobutu regime's widespread unpopularity and mismanagement of the country's resources were that a state of economic decay ensued and the regime also ultimately lost control of the national borders, especially in the country's central eastern region (the Kivu provinces). This facilitated the invasion of DRC in 1996 (and later 1998) by Rwanda and Uganda with the cooperation of Congolese nationals as facades, ostensibly to dismantle Hutu refugee camps that were being used as bases for the launching of guerrilla warfare in western Rwanda. Post-invasion analyses revealed that the main goals of the invasion were not in fact the prevention of guerrilla warfare in Rwanda, but rather a regime change in Kinshasa, the legitimization of territorial expansion by Rwanda in the Kivus, and the pillaging of Congolese resources in the eastern region of DRC by the client states Rwanda, Uganda, and their Western allies (Madsen 1999; Nzongola-Ntalaja 2002; Ngbanda 2004). The success of the 1996 invasion brought Laurent Desiré Kabila to Kinshasa where he assumed power, proclaimed himself president, and unilaterally changed the name of the country from the Republic of Zaire back to DRC on 17 May 1997. Kabila's self-proclamation as president surprised his Rwandan and Ugandan sponsors both within and outside of his immediate entourage and immediately introduced tensions between Kabila and the latter.

To begin with, Kabila was received by many of Kinshasa's inhabitants as a welcome liberator from the long-time dictator Mobutu, whom forces of the democratic movement had attempted unsuccessfully to remove from power several times. Within a few months of Kabila's inauguration, however, the people of Kinshasa began to criticize him for bringing an army of occupation, not of liberation. In 1998, the Rwandan military officers whom Kabila had dismissed from his entourage and the country turned around and re-invaded DRC with the support of Ugandan forces and their internal Congolese allies (Madsen 1999; Nzongola-Ntalaja 2002). The invaders failed to capture Kinshasa from their western entry point thanks to Kabila's quick action in soliciting Angolan, Zimbabwean, and Namibian military support. The re-invasion of DRC was intended to secure a foothold in the country's government in order to guarantee free access to DRC's immense natural resources. As a result of the conflict, the country was partitioned into four regions controlled by warlords, as well as Kabila's government, injecting a sense of balkanization that threatened the unity of DRC as a political entity, and its viability as a nation-state. Kabila's initial refusal and eventual reluctance to recognize the 'rebels' and to negotiate with them at meetings convened by the Organization of African Unity contributed to his assassination on 16 January 2001.

The open war between the Congolese army and the various rebel factions officially ended on 17 December 2002 when an inclusive agreement was signed in Pretoria, South Africa, which called for the establishment of a two-year transitional government of national unity in which there would be one president (Joseph Kabila, the adopted son of Laurent Kabila) and four vice-presidents representing the two main rebel movements, the Kabila government, and the non-armed opposition and civil societies. A sense of unitary government directed from Kinshasa resumed after this accord, and the war in the east that had claimed the lives of over 4 million people was terminated.

In 2006, new general elections resulted in Kabila being declared the presidential winner with 58.05 per cent of the vote against 41.95 per cent for Bemba, though these results have been disputed by many Congolese. The results of the presidential voting furthermore appeared to show an East–West schism: Bemba reportedly won massively in six provinces in the West, including the capital city of Kinshasa, while Kabila won similarly in five eastern provinces. This schism, which is much more complex than reported in the international mass media, has been portrayed as a 'Lingalaphone' vs. 'Swahiliphone' divide based not only on the fact that Kiswahili is the dominant national language in Eastern DRC and Lingala in the Western DRC, but also that Bemba is a Mongala (i.e. Lingala speaker) and Kabila a Muswahili (Kiswahili-speaker) who does not know Lingala. As will be seen from the description of the national languages presented in section 12.3.2 below, however, Lingala is a competing lingua franca against Kiswahili in the Orientale Province, but not against Tshiluba in the two Kasai provinces. In addition, Lingala has a strong presence in both Kivu provinces. The East–West dichotomy presented in the media is therefore over-simplistic and an attempt to create a linguistic division for political purposes where none in fact exists.

In considering political and historical developments in both pre- and post-independence DRC, a remarkable aspect of the long-term suffering endured by the Congolese people from the time of the creation of the Congo Free State right until the present can be noted to be the resilience and strong sense of unity and nation-alism they have exhibited: their *Congolité*. Political pundits in the West have long characterized DRC as the land of 'unending crises' or the epitome of a 'failed state', and have attributed this failure to several factors, including the lack of preparation for governance during the colonial period, initial lack of university-educated cadres at the time of decolonization, tribalism, mismanagement, corruption, incompetence in governing an immense and underdeveloped nation, and sheer kleptocracy (Leslie 1983; Young and Turner 1985). More recent studies have attributed the socio-economic failures in DRC to Western states' interference in DRC's internal affairs and predatory economic interests there and the deliberate undermining of democratic efforts (Pongo 1999; Madsen 1999; Nzongola-Ntalaja 2002; Braeckman 2003; French 2004; Ngbanda 2004; Kankwenda 2005). The analyses of the earlier researchers have often led to the projection of a breakdown of the state into smaller nations: balkanization or 'Somalization'. Such a prediction has remained unfulfilled, however, due to the refusal of the Congolese people to divide up their country into small nation-states, even under the heaviest of pressure as occurred following the devastating invasion and war of 1998–2002 when Rwanda openly imposed its own administrative structure in the two Kivu provinces, barred the circulation of the Congolese franc, and even required Kivutians to buy car licence plates that carried the Rwandan numbering system. The Congolese in those provinces demonstrated open resistance to this neo-colonialist behaviour,[2] and neither did a fragmentation of the state occur, nor was the idea of a loose federation ever seriously entertained in the post-war political discussions – in fact, the possibility of federalism was flatly rejected. Given such an ardent attachment to the unity of the country, it is natural to ask what factors may account for the strength of Congolese nationalism both before and after the regime changes and wars of invasion. The answers here lie in a complex of socio-historical developments which we take up and examine in sections 12.3 and 12.4.

12.3 Language Patterns in DRC, Past and Present

12.3.1 Language during the Colonial Era

In order to understand the nexus between language and nationalism in DRC, it is necessary to grasp the evolution of the Congolese language policies both prior to and after independence. To facilitate the introduction and the eventual spread of Christianity and Western education, during the colonial period, Roman Catholic and Protestant missions were authorized to enter the colony and establish basic-education schools. In this undertaking they were given considerable operational latitude in their respective domains, including the introduction and operation of school systems for which they formulated the language policies. Over time, a number of regional languages were selected, provided with orthographies, and incorporated in other forms of corpus planning and language policies vis-à-vis evangelization and education; these included Kikongo, Kiswahili, Kitetela, Lingala, Lomongo, Tshiluba, and Zande (Polomé 1968, Bokamba 1976, Yates 1981).

The colonial government is reported to have developed a few non-mission schools from 1906 to 1920 (the so-called *écoles officielles congréganistes*), but these were staffed by Roman Catholic orders (Georis and Agbiano 1965). The church missions continued to dominate the education sector, with the Roman Catholic church being given preferential consideration in subsidies until 1946 when the colonial government began to pay serious attention to and to exercise control over education for Congolese. During this forty-year period the church missions thus developed and considerably influenced language policies vis-à-vis education. They called for the use of Kikongo, Kiswahili, Kitetela, Lingala, Lomongo, Tshiluba, and Zande, as well as Kinyarwanda[3] in primary education as informed by the new curriculum of 1948. Under this curriculum French was required as a subject of instruction in most government-subsidized elementary schools and as the medium of instruction from grade four onward through the four years of the secondary school cycle (Polomé 1968; Ndoma 1977). French was

[2] One example of this was the refusal of Congolese in the Rwandan-controlled area to have their secondary school children take a different state examination from the one 'examen d'état' given by the national Ministry of Education in Kinshasa.

[3] Rwanda and Burundi, where Kinyarwanda and Kirundi, respectively, are widely spoken, were annexed to the Congo in 1925 by Belgium as a single administrative entity known as 'Le Congo belge et le Ruanda-Urundi' (Nzongola-Ntalaja 2002).

eventually imposed as the exclusive medium of instruction in all government and sub-sidized schools in 1958. Flemish, the co-official language of Belgium, was introduced in such schools as one of the foreign language choices along with English and German at secondary school level (Bokamba 1976; Yates 1981). After the accession of DRC to political independence on 30 June 1960, the country adopted French as its exclusive official language without any debate in the Parliament. Four of the seven indigenous languages mentioned above, namely Kikongo, Kiswahili, Lingala, and Tshiluba, were recognized as national languages in certain public domains, and continued to be taught as obligatory subjects in primary and secondary schools in their respective regions of dominance (Polomé 1968; Ndoma 1977). They were also offered as subjects in university departments of philology up until the late 1980s.

12.3.2 Pervasive Multilingualism

Since the advent of political independence, language policies in public domains in DRC have remained practically static and the country continues to be characterized by pervasive multilingualism. The DRC's estimated 214 languages, consisting mainly of Bantu and a small number of Nilo-Saharan languages in northern parts of the country, rank it third in Africa in terms of numbers of languages, after Nigeria (521 languages) and Cameroon (286 languages) (*Ethnologue* 2005). This multiplicity of languages and the subsumed cultures naturally raises a number of fundamental questions from a Western perspective, including the basis, if any, upon which nationalism is defined and achieved, how inter-ethnic communication is conducted, and how discourse in public domains is carried out.

The initial creation of the Congo Free State in the nineteenth century from a variety of kingdoms, empires, and chieftaincies formed the multilingual state that we know today as DRC where contact in different spheres of activities both within and across ethnic boundaries has facilitated the spread of selected indigenous languages as 'regional' or 'trade languages'. The six best known of these are: Kikongo, Kiswahili, Lingala, Lomongo, Tshiluba, and Zande.[4] French constitutes a seventh language, the medium of the elite and 'higher domains'. In what follows, the chapter outlines the geographical and functional distribution of these seven major languages in DRC, so as to provide a better contextualization of the place of language in matters of national identity in the country.

Kikongo, the language of the former Kingdom of the Kongo that included parts of northern Angola and southern Congo-Brazzaville, is the dominant lingua franca of the provinces of Bas-Congo and Bandundu in the west of DRC. Kikongo was also the dominant language of Leopoldville (now Kinshasa) up to the late 1920s when it was overtaken by Lingala. It is used in the family domain, in inter-ethnic communication

---

[4] In addition to these six languages, other Congolese languages which were codified were: Alur, Bushi, Ginandza, Ikeleve, Kibemba/Cibemba, Kilega, Kinande, Kiruund, Kisanga, Lingombe, Lokele, Lugbara, Lunda, Mangbetu, Ndembu, Ngbaka, Ngbandi, and Tshokwe/Cokwe (Ndoma 1977).

between non-Kikongo interlocutors, in selected worship services, and local market-places and administration in its region. It also serves as the medium of communication for selected educational programmes on the national radio services, as well as on regional radio programmes for similar functions, including news broadcasting. At the national level, Kikongo is used to a limited extent on the *Radio et Télévision Nationale Congolaise* (RTNC) in Kinshasa for selected broadcast programmes, especially news in translation and various educational programmes. It is further utilized to a limited extent, often in a code-mixed variety with Lingala, in the Congolese popular music known all over the world as 'Soukous' or 'Congolese rumba'. In the area of education, it serves as the medium of instruction in lower primary schooling (up to third grade) in the two provinces, and as a subject of instruction in secondary and tertiary education.

Kiswahili represents the dominant lingua franca of much of the eastern region of DRC: the Orientale, Nord Kivu, Sud Kivu, Maniema, and Katanga provinces. While Lingala competes with Kiswahili in the Orientale Province, and Tshiluba with it in the Katanga Province, Kiswahili still remains the default regional lingua franca for much of non-official communication. Like Kikongo, Kiswahili is used in worship, in broadcasting services locally and regionally, in marketplaces, in local and regional administration, and on RTNC for news in translation and educational programmes. It is also used in a similar fashion to Kikongo in Congolese music. During Laurent Kabila's short presidency it served as the de facto official language of his mixed army of child soldiers (*kadogo*), and Rwandan and Ugandan military personnel. Kiswahili furthermore functions as the medium of instruction in lower primary education in its provinces of dominance, and as a subject of instruction in secondary and tertiary education.

Lingala, which originated in the Equateur Province, is first of all the dominant language of that province, and of the capital city of Kinshasa for which it is the default/unmarked language of daily communication, and second, the competing lingua franca against Kikongo in the Bas-Congo and Bandundu provinces, and Kiswahili in the Orientale province. Like Kikongo and Kiswahili, Lingala is utilized in local and regional administration, church services, broadcasting of news and educational programmes on RTNC, in marketplaces in all (sub-)regions where it is commonly present, and in advertisements on radio and TV. It is also the common medium of soap opera shows and theatrical performances on RTNC in Kinshasa. Additionally, Lingala serves as the medium of instruction in lower primary education in the Equateur province and the federal district of Kinshasa, and as a subject of instruction in secondary and tertiary education.

Unlike Kikongo and Kiswahili, Lingala has many nationwide functions that far exceed even those of the official language (French), with many of these having evolved since the colonial era. Lingala has served as the official language of the Congolese armed forces since 1930 (Polomé 1968; Bokamba 1976), as the official language of the Catholic clergy and worship in the diocese of Kinshasa – the largest diocese in the DRC – since 1966, as the dominant trade language in marketplaces and along the Congo River and many of its tributaries in the western part of DRC as far as Kisangani in the Orientale province, and as the dominant language (at least 70 per cent) of Congolese music. Lingala's roles in the security forces, which include the national police and the Congolese national army, and in Congolese music make it a national medium: it is used and heard practically everywhere in DRC by almost all segments of the population. The colonial and post-colonial policy of stationing battalions of soldiers of the Congolese National Army (ANC) in each province has facilitated and privileged the spread of Lingala into the provinces to the disadvantage of its main competitor: Kiswahili.

Lomongo or *Lonkundo* is a major sub-regional ethnic language of the Equateur province that serves as a lingua franca mainly in two districts in the region: Equateur and Tshuapa. It was once the dominant language of Mbandaka, the capital city of the Equateur province, until it was overtaken by Lingala in the late 1920s. It functions as the medium of communication in worship services in non-urban centres in the two districts, and as the language of selected educational programmes, and of sub-regional trade. Up to the late 1950s missionaries of the Disciples of Christ, one of the major Protestant denominations in DRC, were required to learn Lomongo on their arrival in Mbandaka and before they were sent to their mission posts. The practice was discontinued thereafter as a result of pressure from Lingala as the provincial lingua franca.

Tshiluba is an ethnic and the dominant lingua franca of Kasai Orientale and Kasai Occidentale, as well as the competing lingua franca against Kiswahili in the Katanga province. Like the other three national languages, Tshiluba serves as the lingua franca in local and regional administration, marketplaces, selected local and regional broad-casting programmes, worship services in the two Kasai provinces and parts of Katanga, Congolese popular music, and on RTNC for news in translation and educational programmes. It is also the medium of instruction in lower primary education in the two Kasai provinces, and a subject of instruction in secondary and tertiary education. The expansion of Tshiluba in Katanga during the colonial era was the result of migrant labour in the copper mining industries in major cities such as Lubumbashi, Kolwezi, Likasi, and Kalemie.

Zande is the sixth major ethnic language of DRC and is spoken in the Bas-Uélé District that is situated in the far north of the otherwise Kiswahili- and Lingala-dominated Orientale province. It is used as a sub-regional lingua franca in worship services, marketplaces, and inter-ethnic communication within that district.

Finally, *French*, the exclusive official language since decolonization, is the language of all aspects of administration at the provincial and national levels, the language of international communication, and of education. It is used in worship services, contem-porary religious and popular music, and as the official language of major companies. While the percentage of its speakers as 'a second' language in DRC may be significant (estimated to be between 12 and 15 per cent) and its role in higher public domains critical, it is actually a minority language that is limited to the educated elite. It is the language of official discourse, and hence not accessible as the language of daily communication by the average citizen. Further, unlike the national and sub-regional languages which are learned informally on the street, French is mainly learned formally as a second/foreign language in school. Its frequent poor mastery by both elementary school pupils and teachers has been blamed for the high attrition, wastage rates, and poor academic performance in schools up until the late 1980s (Ndoma 1977; Bokamba 1986).

12.3.3 DRC Language Policy

On the eve of its independence the Congo inherited a language policy that dated back to the 1948 curriculum reform. This advocated the use of regional Congolese languages, including the six regional languages enumerated above, as mediums of instruction in lower primary school (first to third grade), the obligatory teaching of French as a subject from grade two, and the use of French as the medium of instruction from the fourth grade onwards and through university (Bokamba 1976, Yates 1981). This policy applied to all church- or mission-based schools, which were heavily subsidized by the colonial government, but not to the state-sponsored urban schools called 'écoles laiques' that operated under 'le système métropolitain' where French was the exclusive medium of instruction from grade one onwards, starting around 1957 in Kinshasa and 1958 in other cities. The implementation of the general policy was very sporadic, however, largely due to the lack of well-qualified Congolese teachers in small towns and rural community elementary schools. Hence, the regional and national languages (referenced above and in footnote 4) continued to be used for most subjects up to the fifth grade.

While the French-based policy was highly welcome in certain elite quarters as part of a system of education that extended Belgian metropolitan educational programmes to DRC, hence establishing 'equivalency' between the two countries, it also began to encounter opposition from a number of vocal intellectual and political leadership groups at the national level.

The first known indication of this opposition came from Prime Minister Lumumba in a public speech delivered on 9 July 1960 when he stated, in reference to the Africanization of the Congolese National Army (ANC), that:

> he who is today appointed chief commissioner, or commander of the 'Force Publique', even if he does know French, will speak in Swahili or Lingala; we have our own national Flemish.   (van Lierde, 1963: 246).[5]

This statement was not at all surprising as the Prime Minister, who was from Kisangani and also a speaker of Kiswahili, often addressed mass rallies in Lingala during his short political career.

---

[5] Translated from van Lierde's French citation of Lumumba's statement.

Shortly after this in 1962 during the second annual congress of the 'Union Générale des Etudiants Congolais' (UGEC) – a university-level association of Congolese students – there was an explicit call for the replacement of French as official language in the country by an indigenous language. The congress attendees demanded not only that the national government commission a group of education and linguistic experts to study and propose a Congolese national language that should be taught in all secondary schools, but also proposed that this language be accorded the same weight as the teaching of French in elementary and secondary schools.

A third call in apparent support of a change in language policy came four years later, in June 1966, when the Catholic Church of the Congo (then Zaire) overwhelmingly approved Lingala as the Church's official language, and required Lingala in the training of its clergy. This edict was particularly significant and worthy of national attention, because the Catholic Church was the second arm of the colonial state – the Congo then being a predominantly Catholic country as a former Belgian colony – and the largest recipient of government subsidies.

Finally, the same year, the third national conference of directors of national education held in Kinshasa adopted a resolution calling for: (a) the selection and establishment of a national Congolese language that should serve as the medium of instruction throughout the nation, and (b) the teaching of the major Congolese languages in the school system (Bokamba 1976).

It was against this background of interest in the question of national language that President Mobutu somewhat later called on the National University of Zaire's (UNAZA) linguists to carefully consider and propose to the Government a Zairian language that could be adopted as the country's single official national language. Partly at the President's behest, a conference was convened at the Lubumbashi Campus of UNAZA from 22 to 26 May 1974 to address this issue. This was the first conference of its kind in the country since decolonization. The conference achieved two interrelated objectives, but failed to reach a third one. As discussed in Bokamba (1976), it created the National Society of Zairian Linguists, and adopted several language policy proposals of which the first two parts are reproduced below, indicating a high degree of support for national/indigenous languages inspired by the ideology of a return to cultural authenticity promoted by President Mobutu (see section 12.4.3).

The conference proposals were articulated to advance the promotion and teaching of Zairian inter-regional languages in the school system, to use them as mediums of instruction for all subjects up to the eighth grade, and to extend their utilization in this capacity for subjects in social sciences and the humanities, while delaying the teaching of French as a subject from the third grade and restricting its use as a medium of instruction in upper secondary education:

We, the Zairian linguists, meeting here [Lubumbashi] from May 22–26 (1974), considering (1) the importance of the teaching of and in Zairian languages in elementary and

secondary schools; (2) the policy of the return to Zairian authenticity and (3) the present
state of affairs in the area of Zairian languages, make the following proposals:

1. Concerning the elementary school level:

   a) That teaching be carried out in Zairian languages which will serve as the media of
      instruction for all the subjects taught from the first till the sixth grade;

   b) That the Zairian languages begin serving as the media of instruction starting with
      the 1974–1975 academic year, and that the following year [1975–76] they be intro-
      duced in the second grade, and so on progressively until the phasing out of the
      present system (of using French as the medium of instruction);

   c) That the inter-regional language, i.e. the dominant language of the region where
      the school is located, be chosen as the medium of instruction;

   d) That the Zairian language which is used as a medium of instruction from the first
      grade onward be taught as a subject from the third grade onward;

   e) That French be introduced as a subject, but not as the medium of instruction, in the
      third grade and that its teaching be intensified progressively until the second year of
      secondary school so that it can serve as the medium of instruction from the 4th year
      of secondary school.

2. Concerning the secondary school level:

   a) That at the secondary school level all courses be taught in Zairian languages in the
      first and second year;

   b) That a second Zairian language be introduced in the third year of secondary school;
      that this language be taught as a subject but not used as a medium of instruction;
      (and) that it be chosen in terms of its practical importance;

   c) That beginning with the third year of secondary school, the Zairian language that
      is used as the medium of instruction from the first year continue to serve as the
      medium of instruction for certain courses such as social studies, hygiene, compo-
      sition, religion or civics, nutrition, Zairian commerce, correspondence, aesthetics,
      etc.;

   d) That beyond the third year of secondary school certain courses be taught temporar-
      ily in French (cf. point (c) above);

   e) That English be taught from the fourth year of secondary school onward (Bokamba
      1976: 130–1)

These proposals, which were adopted into a language policy by the Mobutu regime,
represented a radical departure from the inherited colonial policy. I will argue below
that the major underlying factors that permitted this development were 'la remise en
question' that began with Lumumba, among others, and President Mobutu's doctrine
of authenticity.

As suggested above, however, the conference stopped short of proposing a specific
official national language for the three main reasons specified in the following statement:

as for the choice of a unique national language, after a [lengthy and heated discussion], the assembly [of Zairian linguists] arrived at the following conclusions: (i) that, at the present time, all the (necessary) conditions are not met for the choice of a unique national language; (ii) that it is therefore premature to make a decision on this matter; [and] (iii) pupils should be given the opportunity to study a second Zairian language of their own choice in order to promote linguistic unity.   (Faik-Nzuji, 1974: 2–3).

These declarations and acts by various constituted national bodies represent the precursors to the heightened Congolese nationalism of the late 1960s to the 1970s to which the chapter now turns. They not only exemplify the extent to which the Congolese people were then interested in the elevation of one of their languages to the status of a national official language, but also testify to the consensus that had emerged by the mid-1970s.

12.4 National Identity

12.4.1 Language and the Construction of National Identity

The existence of a common language shared by the inhabitants of a nation-state is commonly taken to be one of the primary defining factors of nationalism, and is seen in the correspondence between the names of languages and those of countries in many nations in the world: French/France, German/Germany, Japanese/Japan, Russian/Russia, and so on. The perceived connection between the development of a nation and the sharing of a single language also accounts for the reification of language as the link to 'a glorious past', to cultural authenticity, and to 'self-identification' within a given nationality (Fishman 1972; Bokamba 1976). However, the assumption that a nation need speak a common language in order to develop a strong sense of nationalism fails to allow for the clear existence of national identity in multilingual states such as DRC and other similar cases such as India, South Africa, and Switzerland. In order to account for the occurrence of nationalism and national identity in multilingual states, I will assume the following less restrictive definition of nationalism in Fishman (1972: 5):

> [N]ationalism [arises from] . . . the organizationally heightened and elaborated beliefs, attitudes, and behaviors of societies acting on behalf of their avowed ethnocultural self-interest

This allows us to identify a range of salient forces as contributing towards the creation of national identity: language, broader unity, shared cultural authenticity, history, beliefs, social practices, and behaviours vis-à-vis selves and others. How these elements configure in the equation of nationalism seems to depend on their interaction over the course of the history of the nation concerned, and also on the role played by the elite in enforcing and creating appropriate cultural givens. Consider, now, the question of linguistic and ethnic identity in DRC.

12.4.2 Linguistic and Ethnic Identity

DRC, as indicated earlier, is home to over 200 linguistic groups, representing major and minor languages. When asked the question: 'What are you?' or 'What ethnic group are you from?', most Congolese, especially uneducated and rural community inhabitants, identify themselves first by the name of their ethno-linguistic group, as a Lendu, Lokele, Moluba, Mongala, etc. When asked 'What is your nationality?', however, Congolese very seldom identify themselves with their ethnic group. Hence, while linguistic and ethnic identity is invoked for sub-national reasons and ceremonies, and is often exploited for political objectives in the absence of a tradition of political parties, or in attempts to obtain employment in urban centres in the absence of well-established selection and hiring criteria, educated Congolese have since decolonization viewed themselves as Congolese nationals, and not as 'tribespersons' belonging to smaller nation-states. This observation is supported by the fact that no single rebellion of any significance has been proclaimed on behalf of a given ethnic group since 1960, despite the occurrence of ethnic conflict in earlier Congolese history prior to independence. Further, except for certain politically motivated incidents of ethnic cleansing fomented during the Mobutu regime in the Kasai and Katanga provinces, DRC has not experienced post-independence ethnic conflict of the type that has characterized its smaller neighbours to the east, Rwanda and Burundi, where there are just two primary ethnic groups: the Hutus and the Tutsis.

What could be the possible explanation for this accommodative and essentially peaceful coexistence in diversity? I believe the answer lies in a number of forces that are in part mentioned in the definition of nationalism above and subsequent discussion, and include particularly Congolese national consciousness arising from the territorial integrity of DRC, its common history of suffering under colonialism, the struggle for liberation and against subsequent externally driven predatory economic practices, and the deliberate efforts by certain Congolese politicians and clergymen to reinforce a national identity. Having discussed several of these themes earlier in the chapter, section 12.4.3 now highlights the doctrine of authenticity promoted by President Mobutu, and argues that Congolese national consciousness has come to supersede ethnic and linguistic parochialisms in part because of the deliberate guiding actions of some of the country's leaders.

12.4.3 Authenticity and the Choice of National Languages: the Mobutu Era

The doctrine of a 'return to authenticity' is a philosophy which President Mobutu is credited with having introduced in 1967 and enforced through to the late 1980s. As discussed extensively in Bokamba (1976), authenticity was essentially a nationalistic cultural ideology of self-appraisal and reaffirmation of the Congolese people vis-à-vis the external world, especially the West, following almost eighty years of cultural abnegation during the period of colonization. President Mobutu, in a speech delivered at the United Nations' General Assembly in New York City on 4 October 1973, defined it as follows:

> [Authenticity is] the awakening of political consciousness on the part of the Zairian people to return to their own roots, to seek the value systems of their ancestors in order to select judiciously those values that contribute to their harmonious and natural development. It is the refusal of the Zairian people to espouse blindly imported ideologies. It is the affirmation of the Zairian man or of man in short, where he is, and how he is made with his own mental capabilities and social structures.
>
> The return to authenticity is not a narrow nationalism, a blind return to the past, but it is, on the contrary, a tool for peace between nations, a necessary living condition among groupings of people, [and] a platform for cooperation among states. Because, authenticity represents not only the in-depth knowledge of one's own culture, but also a respect for cultural heritage of others.   (Mobutu 1973: 2)

The concept of authenticity emerged as part of a political programme of action known as the Manifesto of N'Sele which outlined three broad objectives for the country; (a) re-establishment of the national government's authority throughout the country and winning the respect of foreign powers; (b) achievement of economic independence, financial stability, and social development; and (c) the promotion of the well-being of every citizen through a programme of social justice with particular emphasis on the upgrading of labour and the labour force (Dubois 1973: 5). The three objectives were to be achieved through the vigorous application of a policy of 'authentic nationalism' (Kangafu-Kutumbagana 1973; Bokamba 1976; Ndaywell è Nziem 1998). Though Mobutu may be credited with the first explicit call for a return to authenticity in 1967, the roots of the move and desire to positively re-emphasize pride in Congolese and African cultural heritage and the importance of this for national unity can be traced back to the late 1950s and early 1960s, as documented in part in the works of Congolese intellectuals such as Mabika-Kalanda (1962), and in the speeches of future prime minister Patrice Lumumba among other thinkers at the time.

Authenticity was warmly embraced by the Congolese people, with some initial vigorous opposition from the Catholic Diocese of Kinshasa (Ndaywel é Nziem 1998), and expressed externally in different ways: removal of Western given names and their replacement with authentic Congolese or other African names, replacement of Western-language city names with their authentic indigenous names (e.g. Léopoldville reverted to its original name Kinshasa, Stanleyville to Kisangani, Elizabethville to Lubumbashi), the wearing of the *abacost*, a modified Nehru-type of suit for men, in place of Western suits, increased wearing of the *mamputa* 'wrap around' garment in place of Western dresses for women, and the braiding of women's hair instead of straightening it to emulate Caucasians. Also, as a result of the authenticity campaign, the ever-popular Congolese music increasingly incorporated traditional dances into its repertoires, and inspired new groups of musicians to combine the traditional dance steps into new and contemporary dance. Newspapers furthermore dropped their French names and took on Lingala names or names in other languages (though French continued to be used for the internal content of newspapers). Additionally, as part of the name-changing aspect of the authenticity campaign, Mobutu also took the step of renaming the actual country as Zaire (though in fact the term Congo was not 'unauthentic' and had a long history of indigenous use).

Overall, authenticity, which was initially resisted in certain intellectual quarters, emerged as a very popular 're-awakening' movement of the masses and elites of all stripes. It was basic, transparent, immediate, and practical to almost everyone, and had something to offer every Congolese citizen. For the intellectual, it was a foundation for a new sense of pride in the nation, its people, their history, and artistic accomplishments (Kangafu-Kutumbagana 1973; Dubois 1973). For the common citizen, it provided a frame of reference and an ideological context for identification with the cultural heritage which the Congolese felt a part of. Authenticity also offered the Congolese a much-needed equilibrium as the country faced the accelerating encroachment of contemporary Western culture in its daily life, and re-awarded prestige to many aspects of indigenous culture that had been long been rejected as 'barbaric' by colonial forces. Finally, in 1967 Zaire needed a rallying cry for uniting the most dynamic elements of the country in the difficult task of nation-building. This was particularly so in view of the mental alienation ('déracinement') from their indigenous culture which Congolese had suffered for almost eighty years of colonialism (Mabika-Kalanda 1962), and in view of the first five years of chaotic independence that they experienced before the ascendance of President Mobutu to power. Zaire in the 1960s and 1970s needed a force that could counter-balance any divisive forces of ethnicity and regionalism that might threaten the country's territorial integrity. The ideology of a return to authenticity or authentic nationalism turned out to be that rallying cry.

Quite generally then, Congolese nationalism can be said to have evolved in large measure as the result of a shared experience of suffering during the colonial period and the important acts of intellectual and political elites aimed at fostering self-esteem and authentic nationalism. While Lumumba's Congolese nationalism, Pan-Africanism, and cultural authenticity were prematurely decapitated by his assassination, and while Mobutu may be ultimately best known for his mismanagement of private companies and the kleptocracy that permeated much of his administration, each of them made, directly or indirectly, a major contribution to Congolese nationalism. Lumumba championed Congolese nationalism, democratic ideals, and the need to build a Congolese nation on its own terms. He translated his political philosophy into reality by addressing political rallies, whenever it was feasible and appropriate, in Kiswahili (in the East) and in Lingala (in the West) during much of his short political career. Mobutu also often addressed mass rallies in Lingala, and both leaders oversaw security forces that used Lingala as their official language. Hence, even though the linguists at the Lubumbashi conference refrained from recommending the adoption of a single indigenous language as the country's official national language, the legitimization of authenticity and the promotion of all four national languages in certain public domains has helped Congolese nationalism emerge with a broad multilingualism symbolized by the four national languages. As noted earlier, this kind of nationalism in plurilingualism may be neither new nor unique, but it is surprising considering the country's chaotic pre-independence history. One might instead have expected deep cleavages along provincial or major linguistic lines, but this is not the case. Indeed, since independence the country has experienced no attempts at secession based on linguistic or ethno-linguistic claims.

12.4.4 National Identity in the post-Mobutu Era

Congolese national identity under plurilingualism not only thrived under Mobutu and survived even his last six and a half years of descent to unpopularity, but also triumphed over the most threatening post-colonial crisis: the regime change invasion of 1996–97 spearheaded by Rwanda and Uganda, and the following open war for natural resources of 1998–2002 carried out by the same countries. In the former movement, an initial intervention in the eastern part of DRC, ostensibly against Hutu guerrillas active in Rwanda, subsequently developed into a general attempt to overthrow Mobutu's dictatorship and brought an army of primarily Kiswahili-speaking troops to the capital, Kinshasa. Not only did this result in a dramatic increase in the Kiswahili-speaking population in Kinshasa, but also the Kiswahilization of key central government positions, and businesses. Kiswahili, instead of Lingala, became the de facto official language of the new Congolese army after Mobutu's forces were routed and Laurent Kabila declared himself the new president of the country on 17 May 1997. During this period there were also other overt signs of efforts by the Kabila regime to introduce a new language policy. For example, in the production of the country's currency, Kiswahili and English words were added to French on the face of the Congolese 5-, 100-, and 500-franc bills, and Lingala, which had appeared on the previous monetary unit, the zaire, was removed. While these acts did not seriously threaten Congolese identity, as Kabila was a recognized Congolese politician who had served in Lumumba's government and engaged in (inconsequential) rebellion against Mobutu for thirty years, there was the feeling that the country was adopting a new and different nationalistic orientation: one directed from the Kiswahili-speaking East.

The most serious threat to Congolese national unity occurred in 1998 when Rwandan officers who had brought Kabila to power but then been dismissed by him re-invaded the country, and during the following two years created proxy Congolese rebellions to pillage the country's natural resources under the cover of so-called civil war. By 2002 these forces had achieved a de facto partitioning of the country into three major regions and separate governments, and the central government simply lost control of most of its northern and eastern provinces. Despite such partitioning of the country and the apparent threat to the continued unity of DRC, such events have actually not negatively affected the perception of plurilingual national identity held by the Congolese. In fact, the current threat posed by what is perceived as a legitimized government of warlords and 'foreigners' has had the opposite effect and heightened Congolese nationalism. This is not surprising, as similar events from history are known to have promoted a stronger sense of patriotism.

12.5 Attitudes Towards Congolese Languages

As can be surmised from the discussion thus far, the Congolese can be seen as true multilinguals who are strongly attached to their languages and the diversity of cultures that they embody. Congolese music, which is produced predominantly in Lingala, is a dominant form of entertainment appreciated throughout the country irrespective of mother-tongue loyalties. The most-enjoyed television shows on RTNC in Kinshasa are soap operas made in Lingala, not French language shows or movies. Elsewhere in the country where other national languages dominate, they are equally well appreciated and used in their acquired domains, often in competition with French. This is particularly true in services of worship which are generally conducted in the national languages in urban centres and in other major sub-regional languages in non-urban communities. It is also true for radio broadcasting, where both French and the national languages are used sequentially, in different programmes. In trade routes along the Congo River and its tributaries and in open markets, the national and sub-regional languages are the unmarked mediums of daily communication.

There is also very little evidence, generally speaking, that the Congolese in the post-independence era feel any linguistic inferiority vis-à-vis French or any other languages of wider communication (LWC). In fact, the Congolese learn and use as many languages as their communicative needs require, often in code-mixed varieties: either one Congolese language mixed with another Congolese language, or a Congolese language mixed with French (Bokamba 1988). What is interesting, in light of these positive attitudes, is that the Congolese, like their counterparts in the so-called English-, French-, and Portuguese-speaking parts of Africa (Swigart 2001; Stroud 2002), have bought into the colonial ideologies that European languages rather than any indigenous languages are the best mediums of post-secondary education, and that to be considered educated one must be instructed in French or some other European language of wider communication (Bokamba 1976). While it is true that French is more marketable in a range of sectors than most of the national languages, even within DRC, the conclusion that it should be the defining criterion of education is a negative attitudinal inheritance from the period of colonial rule.

Except for this acceptance of the myth of the greater suitability of French for higher levels of education, the Congolese are very practical regarding their code repertoires: they are accustomed to using each of their acquired languages according to what sociolinguists term 'the context of situation'. Congolese code-mix and code-switch with ease throughout the day, anywhere and anytime. As a result of these communicative practices which have been deployed for over a century, there are mutual borrowings between Congolese languages, as well as between French and the national languages. The introduction of English as an obligatory foreign language in secondary schools in the late 1950s, and subsequently as a required subject for one year at the university level, has expanded the range of contact further between the Congolese and major Western languages. Furthermore, the advent of both the Kabila regime and globalization have increased the currency of English in urban centres, and hence its contact with the Congolese national languages. This has resulted, to an interesting extent, in a diminution of the value of French as the defining language of high social standing and education.

DRC's stable multilingualism, acceptance of LWCs such as English and French, and its people's positive attitudes towards their national and major languages can also be noted to camouflage two emergent problems: language shift and inter-generational language loss. Though there are so far no empirical studies that document these phenomena extensively among languages in DRC, there is considerable anecdotal evidence from various languages which suggests that there is much ongoing language shift and loss occurring within the country. From the author's personal experience growing up in DRC in the 1950s and in more recent decades observing society at large as well as patterns among extended family members in Kinshasa, it appears that both of these phenomena have affected mainly minority languages primarily used within ethnic groups and in family domains.[6]

Language shift in DRC has been occurring gradually since the establishment of urban centres during the colonial period as a result of immigration from the rural communities. Speakers of certain languages who moved from the countryside and smaller towns to reside in major commercial centres often encountered a speech community dominated by at least one of the national languages: Lingala, Kiswahili, Kikongo, or Tshiluba. The first generation of such urban migrant workers generally learned the dominant local lingua franca, while maintaining their mother tongue. In some cases speakers of one national language had to learn a second one, and over the years began to shift in terms of their code hierarchy with the mother tongue becoming secondary to the lingua franca. This was the case of Kikongo-speakers in the capital who had to learn and use Lingala, which had come to dominate many non-official domains from the late 1920s, and also the case of Tshiluba- and Chibemba-speakers in Lubumbashi who had to learn Kiswahili around the same period. Zande- and Lokele-speakers faced a similar situation in Kisangani with regard to Kiswahili, as did Lomongo-speakers in Mbandaka with Lingala. Lingala-speakers working in

---

[6] In one of the author's extended family groups living in Kinshasa, two of the six children born in Kinshasa do not speak Dzamba, a minority Bantu language related to Lingala and the native language of both parents, in spite of the fact that there are also sizeable Dzamba-speaking communities in Kinshasa. In another family group, all six children born in Kinshasa do not understand nor speak either of the parents' native languages. In both families Lingala has become the main language of daily communication.

Matadi and Boma, in the Bas-Congo Province, also had to learn Kikongo, the dominant language of the two cities and the province at that time.

While first-generation migrants to the cities maintained their mother tongues in those circumstances and exhibited little evidence of language shift, their offspring, as observed in other multilingual settings (Fishman 2004), often exhibited stronger characteristics of language shift. For such speakers, the lingua franca or national language became the dominant language, with the mother or father tongue being largely restricted to the extended family domain and felt to be uncomfortable for use beyond that domain. In linguistic groups with a long tradition of mother-tongue literacy, language shift among second generation migrants may be common, but (full) language loss does not occur so often (cf. Zentella 2004; Silva-Corvalan 2004). In DRC, it appears that both language shift and loss occur in the second generation, especially in major urban centres dominated by one or two of the national languages. The offspring of such speakers, that is the third generation of the family, subsequently exhibit typical inter-generational language loss. A few have passive knowledge of the mother or father tongue, but most have simply failed to acquire it. The lingua franca / national language of their hometown has become their first language, and children may show very little interest in the mother / father tongue when there is a more dominant language used locally and in education. Situations such as this, which are observed in many other African urban centres, represent a serious threat to the preservation of minority languages. However, considered from the particular viewpoint of national integration, minority language shift and loss may at the same time be seen as potentially enhancing Congolese national identity through a reduction in the use of the country's many minority languages and an increase in the use of DRC's national languages.

12.6 Conclusion

As noted in section 12.4.1, the existence of a single language that is spoken by the great majority of citizens of a country is frequently assumed to be an essential prerequisite for the growth and fostering of national identity. A unique shared language, along with territorial boundaries, a common history, and given and constructed shared customs, can be used to emphasize and strengthen sentiments of belonging to a single nation-state. The existence of multiple languages in a single state is accordingly often perceived to be conducive to the proliferation of multiple nationalities, or worse, 'tribalism', within the same territorial boundaries, and a lack of shared tradition and associated culture. As a result, a broadly shared national identity is assumed to be effectively impossible to conceive. To avoid such potential difficulties, many nations have indeed engaged in language rationalization de facto as in the case of the USA (Fishman 2004; Wiley 2004) or de jure as in the case of France (Laitin 2001; Judge 2000).

This chapter has argued that such a monolingual characterization of national identity is in fact erroneous and fails to allow for clear cases of strong nationalism in stable multilingual societies, such as that of DRC. What the example of DRC demonstrates is that while broadly shared language may be a significant component of nationalism, it does not always have to be a necessary or dominant key for the development of nations. Other factors may be equally important in defining national identity, and what the elites of a country may do in 'heightening' such a sense of identity is also critical. The shared history of suffering of the Congolese people during the colonial and post-colonial eras, their common quest for liberation from oppressive rulers, and their pride in the nation's popular music appreciated throughout the continent and beyond, have been the ingredients that the elites have exploited to cement Congolese nationalism – *la congolité*. Thus, while a common language spoken among the masses within specific national boundaries may give the appearance of national unity and therefore possible national identity, that appearance may simply be a mirage, and not the full picture, as the case of now balkanized monolingual Somalia attests. National identity can in fact develop strongly in plurilingual as well as in monolingual nations. Perhaps one day Lingala, the dominant language of Congolese music and most of the Congolese diaspora, may become the single most important symbol of *Congolité*, but that would not seem to be necessary for Congolese national identity to continue to thrive as it currently does.

13

Kenya: Language and the Search for a Coherent National Identity

Chege Githiora

13.1 Introduction

Kenya is only forty-three years old as an independent, republican nation-state. It is a plural society that encompasses within its boundaries a diverse population of ethnic nations.[1] Contemporary Kenya, like other nations of Africa, is engaged in a search for cohesion, unity, and a collective identity as a modern nation. This quest shapes its general policy of cultural and linguistic pluralism that recognizes the rights of all languages and cultures of the communities found within state boundaries. In this type of situation, language plays a central role in defining or mediating the ongoing formations and expressions of social identity. Individuals have complex multiple identities, involving region, language, socio-economic class, gender, and political and economic factors as well as religious and ethnic ones. Kenyan 'national' identity is necessarily a recent phenomenon because the idea of 'Kenya' as a country is a modern construction, invented purely by European imperial and colonial interests. Forged from at least forty-two different ethno-linguistic groups,[2] their members have retained strongly grounded, localized identities which primarily are defined in terms of language, but also through claims to specific physical spaces, external community linkages, economic roles and practices – all within new boundaries and altered ways of life.

Nations in the modern sense are a relatively recent political phenomenon, now at the core of the current world economic order. Anthony Smith (1991) divides nations into those that have developed chiefly from ethnic groups that have modified and

---

[1] The so called 'tribes', a term I find inadequate to describe the complexity of political, economic, and social structures embodied by the term 'nation', and hence avoid in this chapter. It can also be noted that the connotations of backwardness frequently associated with use of the term 'tribe' may serve to conceal the similarity of so-named groups to ethnic groups found in other parts of the world (Barbour and Carmichael 2000: 7).

[2] This is the most widely used working figure, but in the next section I point at some of the issues surrounding demarcation or counting of languages.

extended their ethnic identities to encompass larger populations, and those that have developed within particular states where a common sense of national identity has arisen within the state to encompass a previously diverse population.[3] Kenya seems to belong to the latter category, and language plays an important role in cultivating that sense of national identity among citizens. Over those four decades, a 'national' culture has certainly taken form, that is, a national identity that goes beyond the obvious symbols such as identity cards and birth certificates. Swahili, for example, is widely accepted as the 'national' language, the language of communication among Kenyans of all regional and social backgrounds. It is spoken by more than two-thirds of the population (Heine and Möhlig 1980), and is therefore by far the language known by most Kenyans. It serves as the language of *solidarity* in Kenya because beyond its role as a common language of Kenya's peoples, it also functions to establish among speakers a common ground, a sense of unity, a degree of intimacy and closeness or 'shared fate' (Brown and Gilman 1960). Educational policies implemented at the beginning of the eighties (the '8:4:4' system of education) also imply that Kenyans under the age of 31 years (at time of writing), who have completed primary and secondary education, will have received formal instruction in the language up to high-school level. The ex-colonial language English remains the language of prestige purposes in areas of education, science, big business, law, parliament, better-paid employment, etc.; it is therefore the language of *power*, whose deployment often serves to establish formality and social distance between interlocutors. The asymmetric relationship existing between Swahili and English is reflected by the roles and functions taken up by individuals when selecting to use either language in specific contexts. Given that both serve to varying degrees as lingua francas, Swahili and English serve as pan-ethnic mediums for the projection of identities in Kenya. Both are often used in expressions of nationalism, a function that is encouraged by a state that claims to be engaged in the arduous process of forging a modern, unified country. However, there is no doubt that '*ukabila*' or negative ethnocentricity retains an uneasy shadow over Kenya's national unity. The constant 'fight' against it echoes with frequency in national discourse such as newspaper editorials, letters to the editor, news analysis, government reports, and political commentary from many players in Kenyan society.

13.2 Language in Kenya

13.2.1 An Overview of Language in Kenya

Kenya is a multilingual and multi-ethnic state where about fifty languages and dialects are spoken, according to data sifted from various sources.[4] It has a current population of 33 million citizens distributed thickly in the coastal, central, and western regions of the country, and sparsely in the northeast. The languages of Kenya reflect a diversity of families and sub-families, and mutual cross-linguistic influences.

---

[3] See Barbour and Carmichael (2000).   [4] Including *Ethnologue* 2005.

The Niger-Congo phylum is well represented by about 65 per cent of Kenyans who speak some Bantu language or other (e.g. Swahili, Luyia, Gikuyu, Kamba).[5] The Nilo-Saharan super-family is represented by Nilotic languages, which make up about 30 per cent of the total languages spoken in Kenya (e.g. Masai, Luo, Nandi), and 3 per cent of Kenyans speak a Cushitic (Afro-Asiatic) language (e.g. Somali, Orma, Borana). Minority languages include those spoken by descendants of speakers of languages of the Indo-European family such as Punjabi, Gujarati, Hindi, and English, while a few of the indigenous African languages such as El Molo and Okiek languages are nearly extinct, principally because the speakers of these languages have assimilated into larger communities of Maa, Kalenjin, and Gikuyu speakers (Heine and Möhlig 1980; *Ethnologue* 2005). Area distribution of languages in Kenya makes a striking contrast: the majority Bantu languages are spoken in only about 20 per cent of the national territory, while Nilotic languages occupy about 35 per cent and the Cushitic languages more than 40 per cent of the country's territory.[6]

13.2.2 Languages and Dialects

The usual difficulties of establishing clear boundaries between languages and dialects are also found in Kenya, which is why the estimate of total languages ranges from thirty to sixty, according to different reports. Dialect boundaries are not clearly cut isoglosses, but rather dialect continua, which are further obfuscated when 'culture' or ethnicity – rather than proper linguistic criteria of structure or typology – is used as the basis for demarcating what is language or dialect. This is due to the influence of such factors as social prestige, historic cultural ties, economic linkages, political fluctuations, state boundaries, or mere 'convenience'. The Abaluyia, for example, are said to be speakers of the 'Luyia' language and are considered Kenya's third largest ethnic group, according to the 1969 and 1991 censuses.[7] But in fact, the 'Luyia' people who live in the western province of the country speak a cluster of closely related dialects (estimates range from sixteen to twenty-six, e.g. Masaba, Kabras, Saamia, Bukusu) rather than a single, unified language. There are also many speakers of dialects of the same language who inhabit eastern Uganda and who are generally excluded from

[5] Kenya's Bantu languages are commonly divided into three general groups: western (Luyia, Kuria, etc.), central (Gikuyu, Kamba, etc.) and coastal (Swahili, Digo, Taita, etc.). A major characteristic of Bantu languages is the occurrence of noun classes whereby the head noun or phrase in a sentence 'triggers' verbal agreement on verbs and 'concordial agreement' on its modifiers such as adjectives, to reflect the singular and plural forms accordingly. All Kenyan Bantu languages except Swahili are also tone languages, making use of both lexically and grammatically relevant contrasts in tone.

[6] There is also Kenyan Sign Language for the deaf (KSL), approved by relevant official institutions such as the Kenya National Association of the Deaf. KSL appears mainly unrelated to other countries' sign languages although it has been standardized with slight variations since 1961. It would appear, for example, that the deaf in neighbouring Uganda and Tanzania do not really understand KSL. But those living in different parts of Kenya can understand each other completely even with some dialect differences.

[7] Kenya Bureau of Statistics (KBS), Government Printer. Also known in some literature as 'Luhyia'.

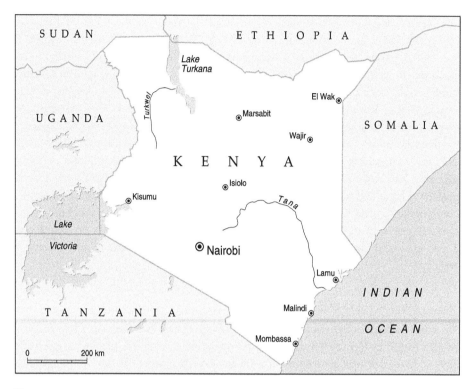

Kenya

studies of 'Kenyan-Luyia' (Agongo 1980). Thus while there is a larger 'Luyia' identity which is based on commonality of language and cultural practices, it is separated by political rather than ethno-linguistic boundaries. One result is a form of linguistic nationalism based on the modern Kenyan and Ugandan states, rather than language itself. Furthermore, there are within the same community inner-group identities based on perceived or real distinctions in the 'culture' of each of the dialects' speakers. These secondary identities may well change according to political fluctuations nationwide, adjusted cultural ties or economic linkages. Kipsigis, Keiyo, and Nandi are grouped together and their internal differences ignored under a single language referred to as Kalenjin. Likewise, the expansive northeastern part of the country is considered 'Somali-speaking' because it is seen as culturally little differentiated. Yet, in addition to the more numerous Somali-speakers, there are a number of distinct Oromo (Cushitic) languages such as Borana, Sakuye, Garreh, and Ajuran. Many Kenyans from the coastal areas may also identify themselves as 'Swahili' because of religious and cultural practices, without letting it be known that their vernacular language is really some other non-Swahili language. Such levels of concentric identities are typical of the majority of Kenyan people. They are to a great extent language-based and a composite of Kenyan national identity.

13.2.3 Minority and Endangered Languages

Swahili, the language that will be discussed further in sections 13.3 and 13.4 below, tends to dominate the study and research about Kenya's languages. But a number of minority languages occupy an important linguistic position in terms of how they inform us about issues of language contact, shift, endangerment, and death. As previously mentioned, about two-thirds of Kenyans are bilingual in Swahili and a mother tongue. However, there is a small, but significant group who have lost competence in their mother tongue, as they speak only English vernacular at home, in school, and socializing. Among the larger groups of speakers (e.g. Luo, Luyia, or Masai), a form of stable bilingualism exists, but for the smaller ethno-linguistic communities, 'marked bilingualism' (Batibo 2005) is a force for total assimilation into the dominant language and culture through the adoption of the lifestyle of the larger, economically better-off communities. Language shift therefore becomes one of the conditions necessary for individuals' acceptance into the larger group by adapting to the assimilating community's value system. In Western industrial societies, this may take the form of changed lifestyles, economic and labour roles in addition to the loss of language of the 'old country'. In Kenya's case, assimilation too causes radical changes of lifestyle such as a shift from fishing to pastoralism as in the case of Elmolo who have assimilated into the larger Masai and Turkana groups. Elmolo are Kenya's most endangered people, who lived on the shores of Lake Turkana in northern Kenya. Their estimated remaining number of speakers ranges from eight to 500.[8] A complete language shift may have taken place (i.e. the languages are nearly extinct) in the case of two Cushitic language-speaking communities – Yaaku and Omotik – whose speakers have abandoned their language in favour of Masai, a Nilotic language. A similar process of cultural and linguistic assimilation also places Okiek – a Nilotic language – on the list of Kenyan near-extinct languages. Another case is that of Suba, a Bantu language that is nearly completely absorbed by the larger, numerically dominant Luo (Nilotic) language.

No significant pidgins have emerged from Kenya; what has been termed 'Cutchie Swahili' ('Asian Swahili') or 'Shamba Swahili' is basically a non-standard Swahili sociolect spoken by Asian traders and European settler farmers respectively. The one acknowledged creole language of Kenya is Nubi (or 'Kinubi', in its Swahili form), a creolized form of Arabic spoken by a small minority of people whose origins date back to the colonial period in what are now northern Uganda and Sudan. The British imperial 'King's African Rifles' (KAR) recruited soldiers and footmen from a variety of such peoples as the Lendu, Aluru, Bakaa, Muru, and Kakwaa. These were engaged to assist in the establishment and administration of the emerging east African colony, and in anti-slavery campaigns. They were settled where their descendants now live in Nairobi city's Kibera quarter, and in a smaller community located a few kilometres

---

[8] Of course such changes of lifestyle can occur internally without language shift, as in the case of southern Masai who practise farming in addition to pastoralism.

from Kisii town in western Kenya (Whitely 1974; Heine and Möhlig 1980).[9] In Kibera, it is clear that while the language is still alive across generations, greatest proficiency is among the elders, and some teenagers and preadolescents have difficulties with even simple tasks such as counting. It certainly is the household language of Nubi families, the language of intimacy among family members and friends. However, proficiency in Swahili is very high among Nubi-speakers who wield it as an important expression of their identification as Kenyans; it is the language of the street, local business, and daily interaction in the larger, non-Nubi community.[10] Kinubi is not used in any of the schools as medium of instruction during the first years of school and there is no known radio programming or any sort of publication in the language.[11] Kinubi may be an endangered language due to the relatively small number of its fluent speakers living in one of the most densely populated quarters in Africa, within a strongly assimilating context of Swahili especially among the young generation.[12]

13.3 Language in Kenya: Sociolinguistic Dimensions

13.3.1 Power vs. Solidarity

Kenya's inception by European powers dates back to the Berlin Conference of 1884 and its subsequent appropriation by Britain as its 'protectorate' in the early years of the twentieth century. In 1910, it was declared a 'colony'. The symmetric boundaries of an entity named 'Kenya' brought together diverse peoples but they also tore apart existing settlements and populations' movements too were frozen within the newly established 'state' boundaries. For example, large portions of some of Kenya's largest ethno-linguistic communities such as Somali, Luo, Luyia, and Masai are also found in the neighbouring countries of Somalia, Ethiopia, Uganda, and Tanzania.

In the emergent British dominion, English language was stamped on the new colony and it fast gained currency since it was clearly identified as the language of power within the new order in which a tiny settler minority backed by colonial administrative machinery spoke in English. But a pragmatism borne of the missionary and colonial agenda recognized Swahili's potentiality and promoted it as the most suitable language for Christian evangelization and basic literacy of Africans, although there was early resistance by some who regarded Swahili as too Qur'anic and therefore

---

[9] Settled by the British government on a 4,000-acre plot which the Nubis called 'Kibra' meaning 'woods' in their language. Due to heavy rural–urban migration of Kenyans, Nubis currently lay claim to a fraction of what is now one of the most densely populated areas of Africa.

[10] The allegiance or identity of members of minority communities who have extended ties or origins outside Kenyan boundaries is often placed under suspicion by authorities. The burden of proof is placed on the individual Nubi, Somali, Swahili, or other such.

[11] There was a now defunct publication of the 'Kibera Lands Committee' called 'The New Dawn'.

[12] 3,000–6,000 of the estimated 10,000 Nubi-speakers of Kenya live in Kibera, whose population is 386,315 living in an area encompassing Kibera, Laini Saba, and Sera Ngombe locations (Source: 1999 Population and Housing Census, Kenya Government Printers, January 2001).

unsuitable for spreading the Christian gospel.[13] The imperial military machinery also used Swahili with its KAR East African Battalion soldiers especially during the interwar years in a deliberate attempt to 'construct a distinct identity in the colony . . . out of the diverse ethno-linguistic backgrounds of the African soldiers' (Mutonya and Parsons 2004). Those practices of the colonial state had the practical effect of solidifying the role of Swahili as a pan-ethnic language of solidarity that threatened to lead to greater political unification of east Africans. As early as 1922, an East African Workers Union had been formed to fight for Africans' and Asians' rights, and against compulsory labour, increased tax, and land alienation (Singh 1969). This early political organization was comprised of people from all regions of Kenya whose chief common language, and the language of mutual political solidarity, was Swahili. Throughout the late forties and fifties, intense political activity ('agitation') defined Kenya, and the anti-colonial message was delivered to Kenyans principally in Swahili as political leaders sought to unite all Kenya's Africans in their demand for independence. The very success of Swahili in giving a single voice to African political dissent led to intervention by the colonial state that feared the consequences of Swahili's expanded role. By 1952, as the anti-colonial movement was breaking into violence, a government commission recommended that Swahili be eliminated from the school and administrative system except where it was the mother tongue, while selected 'tribal vernaculars' would be preserved (the Binn Report of 1952). Within a few years yet another commission (Prator/Hutasoit) ushered in the 'English Medium Approach' to primary instruction by endorsing English as the only language of instruction, a policy that remained unaffected by the first post-independence Kenya Education Commission of 1964 (the 'Ominde Report'; see Chimerah 1998). When this nascent linguistic nationalism was nipped in the bud, one of its repercussions was the stunting of the spread of use of Swahili by Kenyans, and a concomitant emphasis on the use of the languages of their ethnic community. A direct consequence of this was that nationalist ideas and propaganda then had to be expressed by means of Kenya's regional languages, thus drastically limiting the reach of the message. Political pamphlets in Gikuyu, Kamba, Luo, and other languages were many, but their impact was naturally curtailed outside these communities in the rest of Kenya.[14]

13.3.2 English in Kenya

English language remains, of course, a core aspect of Kenya's colonial legacy and therefore is directly involved in questions of national identity. In independent Kenya, English was conceptualized as providing the country's access to the world's technical and scientific information and knowledge, necessary for modernization and economic

[13] Roel (1930), cited in Topan (1992), for example, saw it necessary to 'free Swahili of its Arabic character' in order for the language to be used for Christian evangelization.

[14] For example, Jomo Kenyatta's *Mũiguithania* ('Reconciliator') and Henry Muoria's *Mũmenyereri* ('Guardian'); Bildad Kaggia's *Inooro ria Agĩkũyũ* ('Whetstone of the Gikuyu People'), John Cege's *Wĩyathi* ('Freedom').

development. This notion was, of course, challenged across the border in Tanzania where these objectives would be sought via Swahili. In Kenya, there are constant calls from intellectuals and cultural activists for a more elevated use of Swahili in national curricula (e.g. Chimerah 1998; Mazrui and Mazrui 1998; Mbaabu 1985; Thiong'o 1981) but English continues practically unchallenged in higher education, and therefore in the workplace as well. Many Kenyan graduates would cite inadequate knowledge of Swahili, and the paucity of books, journals, and other literature on science and technology in Kenyan languages, as reasons for the necessity to use English rather than Kenyan languages at the workplace and in education by scientists, engineers, technocrats, and researchers. Thus English in Kenya is not only used in written communication, board-level discussions and such like, but also in everyday communication among educated Kenyans and professionals. Swahili or other Kenyan languages are used in communication within communities or households, in mass politics and popular culture. Generally, Kenyans do not seem to see major contradictions between nationhood and not being proficient in Swahili, at least at the highest levels of speech and reasoning. Among families of higher socio-economic status, English is the vernacular used within the family and interpersonal relationships, and Swahili with the house help, gardener, shopkeeper, or newspaper vendor. The system of education, law, and administration is based on English. Among the best educated, English rather than in Swahili soon becomes dominant (after the four early years of primary school), although a minority attains excellent skills in both languages as well as a mother tongue. Socio-economic stratification is reflected by the differentiated use of language: the higher status groups are more proficient in English than in Swahili; the lower ones have a primary competence in Swahili or other languages, and can only carry out basic communication in English. A minority of economically and politically powerful English speakers of Kenya – native and assimilated – find no anomaly in being nationalistic while having limited competence in the national language, and appear to feel that they can be English-speaking without necessarily failing to be good Kenyans.

13.3.3 Language and Nationalism

The antagonism behind the British colonial administration's policy that promoted English and actively worked against Swahili was clearly understood by Kenyan nationalists. In the immediate post-independence period, Swahili was quickly adopted as the language of expression of national ideals, political aspirations, and optimism about the future, independent Kenya. Similar to the situation in the newly independent states of Latin America in the early nineteenth century (Anderson 1991), the new leadership rallied the people of Kenya around new icons of *uhuru*, freedom, such as the new flag of an independent Commonwealth republic, a national anthem, and patriotic songs. The obvious language that would express a nationalist message of solidarity in political speeches at mass rallies or in public broadcasting in the new Kenya was Swahili. The very first post-independence commission of 1964 saw national unity as the main aim of the new state,[15] though it also noted the need to preserve the cultures and languages of different ethnic groups. The commission called for Swahili to be recognized as the language of national unity while retaining English as the chief medium of instruction. Vernaculars were relegated to a few teaching hours per week and were only taught in the first three years of school. In a 1969 speech in parliament, the founding president, Jomo Kenyatta, declared Swahili a 'national language' and English an 'imperialist' language from which new Kenya should free itself. He went on to urge parliament to institute Swahili as the nation's language of pride and identification. In 1974 he ordered debate in parliament to be carried out in Swahili, a practice that took root and continued for some years, and somehow managed to overcome the circularity of debating in Swahili the content of laws which were written in English, and which would also be amended and published in English. Continuing attempts to institutionalize Swahili as a true national language of Kenya can be further seen in a 1976 commission which submitted the 'Gachathi Report' recommending the examination of Swahili in primary and secondary levels, with the continued use of vernaculars as the medium of instruction in early grades of primary school. However, none of these recommendations and exhortations was able to succeed in entrenching Swahili strongly enough to fully replace the high-status roles of English in business and education. There is continued debate in parliament, in the popular press, and the mass media about whether Swahili can in fact ever replace English as the language of power in higher education, international business, and so on. Some argue that Swahili is not sufficiently developed in scientific or higher education terminology, and that there are not enough books and other teaching materials available in the language. It is furthermore suggested that students need to train in an international language in order to compete in the world of business and in international job markets. The same school of thought argues that former colonial languages such as English remain the most 'neutral' since they come in as 'outsiders' to a politically charged context of ethnic competition and rivalries with each group wishing to promote its own language. Against this, the most powerful and widely accepted argument for Swahili is that it is the best potential unifier for the nation because it is an *African* language that is easily accepted by Kenyans of all ethnic and regional background as a 'neutral' language, devoid of connotations of power as its native speakers constitute an ethnic minority that is neither politically nor economically domineering.

The most important structural change in Kenya's education system as far as language is concerned appeared from the 1981 MacCay report which initiated a modified system of education popularly known as '8:4:4'. This consists of eight years of primary, four of secondary, and four at university, replacing the previous O- and A-level system inherited from the British. Although English would continue to be the medium of instruction, Swahili was made a compulsory and examinable subject at both primary and secondary levels of education. Other indigenous vernaculars retained

---

[15] Kenya Education Commission, 1964. See Chimerah (1998) and Mazrui and Mazrui (1995).

their position of playing a minimal role in the early grades of primary school, but over the years, the pressure to master English for economic advancement and Swahili for its academic value has undermined the vernaculars enough to make their teaching or use in the classroom virtually non-existent in very many cases. Ironically, teachers argue that they prefer to invest the time assigned to vernacular language instruction in improving students' skills in English, the language needed to perform well in national examinations. Nevertheless, it is reasonable to assert that, in a positive way, the '8:4:4' system has given an entire generation of students a greater formal knowledge of Swahili through making it compulsory at the early levels of education. In doing so, the acquisition of a good knowledge of Swahili may contribute positively toward the much-desired goal of national integration.

In mass politics and popular culture Swahili speaks for itself. It is by far the language most commonly used to articulate and illustrate Kenya's popular history and politics, to communicate pan-ethnic messages and evoke nationalist images. The state leadership uses Swahili to reach out to the people, in countrywide political campaigns, to immortalize episodes in the national memory, to create a nationalist ethos and cultivate similar sentiments through Swahili words, coined phrases, and slogans. A few prime examples of slogans known to every Kenyan serve to demonstrate how Swahili is used to engrave politics into popular culture: *Uhuru na Kazi* 'Freedom and Work', a rallying call of the first post-independence government exhorting people to work hard in the spirit of *Harambee* or 'pulling/working together' – self-help – to build schools and hospitals and improve their general welfare; and *Fuata Nyayo*: 'Follow the footsteps', a government slogan of the eighties, a promise by the successor to the founding president not to change the course of the nation after the demise of the latter. Two other, more recent, popular slogans/phrases are: *Yote yawezekana* – 'Everything is possible', and *Unbwogable*, the title of a popular hip-hop song meaning 'unbeatable/unconquerable' in Sheng, the urban Swahili of widespread use especially among the young. The political party that won the most recent general election of 2002 very successfully adopted this last as a campaign slogan. In all, there is little doubt that Swahili is 'the language of the nation' and is favoured as such by the greatest majority of citizens as sample surveys in Nairobi city have clearly demonstrated (Githiora 2002).

In the intellectual arena, linguists, educators, and cultural activists advocate the use of an African language to express national identity and promote integration and to preserve the cultures through adoption of a single language such as Swahili. It is argued that there is a need to avoid alienating the great majority from the minority elite of those educated to high levels in English (approximately 20 per cent), by failing to provide a meaningful education, in an alien language which is far removed from its context (Thiong'o 1981, 1993). It is also stressed that it is pedagogically easier and better to impart knowledge in a language that is well understood by the student (Mazrui and Mazrui 1995; Chimerah 1998). Organizations such as CHAKITA (the National Council of Swahili) actively work with African counterparts such as CHAKAMA (East

African Swahili Council) to further institutionalize Swahili in the educational system by calling for the establishment of Swahili-medium schools, and by campaigning for Swahili to have greater official space in government and politics, and to fully embrace (i.e. formalize) Swahili as the language of government and public policy. The recent inclusion of Swahili as an official language in the country's new constitution is, in good part, a result of lobbying carried out by such groups.

13.4 Swahili and Statehood: Kenya vs. Tanzania

In considering the role of Swahili in Kenya, it is worth making a brief comparison with the situation of Swahili in Tanzania – Kenya and Tanzania both being countries that use Swahili as an official language.[16] Swahili is now formally recognized as the national language of Kenya, *and* as an official language of the country, alongside English. This was enshrined in a constitutional clause in the first major overhaul of the country's constitution since independence (Kenya's Draft Constitution 2004[17]). There is also no doubt that Swahili is the universal lingua franca of Kenya today in small-scale trade and media. In Tanzania, somewhat ironically, although Swahili is the de facto official language of the country, this is actually not formally stated in the country's constitution.

The spread and growth of Swahili in Tanzania can in certain ways be likened to that of standard Italian in Italy during the early half of the twentieth century. In discussing the language situation in Italy, Ruzza (2000: 174) describes how 'with fascism, primary education became universal, diffusing knowledge of standard Italian among peasants and the urban poor', and it is noted that new attention to and pride in standard Italian emerged, accompanying a general resurgence in emphasis on the history and power of the country highlighted by the fascist leadership. In the case of Tanzania, it was anti-imperialism rather than fascist ideology that inspired the founding president of Tanzania, Julius Nyerere, to embark on a 'socialist' path of social and economic development, popularly known by its Swahili form *Ujamaa*. One of the tenets of this model was the complete institutionalization of Swahili language at every level of the new nation's workings: in the free and universal education programme, in politics, government, and administration. A vocal anti-imperialist stance and a people-centred leadership fostered strong nationalist and pan-Africanist sentiments among citizens of the new state, resulting in a widely acknowledged sense of cohesion and

[16] It is commonly suggested that at least 60 million people in east and central Africa speak Swahili on a daily basis as a vernacular or regional lingua franca. In actuality the number may be considerably higher. The total populations of Tanzania and Kenya alone are 30 million each, with at least 95 per cent and 65 per cent competence in each respective country. Smaller but significant proportions speak Swahili on a daily basis in Congo, Rwanda, Burundi, Mozambique, and in the diaspora, principally in the Gulf states, Europe, and the USA.

[17] Article 8.1. 'The national language of the Republic of Kenya is Kiswahili.'
Article 8.2. 'The official languages of Kenya are Kiswahili and English, and all official documents shall be made available in those languages.' (CRKC Adopted Version available at: http://www.eastandard.net/pdf/draft050505.pdf)

national identity that is the envy of all African states up to the present. Nyerere was an ardent proponent of a philosophy that required the Swahili language to reflect a revolutionary, anti-colonial, anti-imperialist zeal; streets were renamed, youth brigades made up of university graduates were dispatched across the nation to teach a nationalist curriculum in Swahili, and the internal migration of people of different mother-tongue backgrounds within the country's borders was much encouraged.[18] Among other effects of such earnest planning and implementation was a linguistically unified nation. Swahili truly became the 'national language' of Tanzania, with two important consequences. First of all, it appropriated Swahili language for the larger nation while dissociating it from the localized ethnic identity of the original native speakers – the 'new Tanzanian' was projected by his use of standard rather than a localized dialect of Swahili.[19] Secondly, fast and widespread adoption of Swahili as the national language eventually led to a massive loss of minority languages of Tanzania (Batibo 2005).

Comparatively, post-independence Kenya's path of national development has been devoid of ideological positioning despite early, vague assertions that it would pursue a national economic policy based on 'African socialism'.[20] However, in actual fact, Kenya's statehood did not waver from the colonial project built around a focus on ethnic and regional interests and control. This position was concretized by a leadership that exercised a 'cautious, conservative nationalism' (Maloba 1989), one that merely sought political independence without changing in any fundamental way colonial structures or Kenya's position within the declining British empire. Beyond the early 1969 pronouncement in favour of Swahili by the founding president, for example, no genuine national plan for the institutionalization of Swahili was pursued. Rather, successive governments have continued to give English a primary role in conducting their business, while reserving Swahili for lower-status functions such as addressing the masses on certain occasions, or at the end of official speeches delivered in English.

The national curriculum also laid as much if not more emphasis on Kenyan vernaculars in both colonial and post-independent Kenya. The first four years of primary education are conducted in the vernacular, with English and Swahili taught as subjects. Beyond primary levels, English becomes the medium of instruction except in Swahili studies at university. Thus the laissez-faire attitude towards language in Kenya is without any specific ideological grounding or cohesion. It has resulted in unregulated, natural development of languages with little conscious or focused planning so that for example, ways of speaking Swahili in Kenya lack uniformity from one region of the country to another, and from one social group of speakers to another, according to local, regional language influences and social status. From this perspective of language, the rural–urban divide also becomes starkly demarcated

---

[18] The encouragement of internal migration from different parts of the country was also a feature of the years of nation-building in Italy during the years of fascist rule (Ruzza 2000).

[19] Massamba goes further, taking the controversial position that in fact, 'Swahili people' (Waswahili) are *all those who live on the east African coast* where Swahili is spoken (2002: 272, my emphasis).

[20] KANU Manifesto for Independence, Social Democracy and Stability. KANU (1960/61. 12).

because of the clear correspondence between linguistic variation on the one hand, and economic and regional imbalances on the other. For the majority of Kenyans, primacy is accorded to English for prestigious purposes and the vernacular is used to encode local solidarity. Swahili retains its ancient role as vehicular language, and is at the same time recognized as the language of a particular ethnic group of people known as 'Waswahili'. As such, it is resisted as a home language or vernacular in many non-ethnically Swahili households, a position that is consistent with ordinary Kenyan attitudes towards language and ethnicity.

Kenya's 'language policy' so far has not gone beyond well-intended declarations and reports by various commissions. The latter lack realistic methods of implementation because they were in large measure populist enunciations of a conservative leadership that found it difficult to dispense with the high-status colonial language, English, in order to pursue a nationalist programme that would give priority to an African language. The lack of seriousness in language planning is evidenced by the lack of any close study of Kenya's sociolinguistic situation which would provide a viable, scientific basis for building on aspirations to stimulate the growth of the country's indigenous languages. In any language-engineering enterprise for example, it would be necessary to clearly understand the different roles that each of the fifty-odd languages and their dialects play in different tasks within the state. All the same, it would seem that certain very general principles do underlie Kenya's language and educational policies. UN declarations, for example, are cited by various Kenyan commissions appointed over the years since the 1950 UN Charter (and subsequent resolutions) on the use of mother tongue, and the role of culture in nation-building:

Art. 17: Every national or ethnic minority or group has the right to preserve its own cultural identity...
Art. 19: Cultural autonomy consists further in an educational system providing instruction on all educational levels in the language of the group...
Art. 20: Linguistic autonomy consists in facilitating the use of the mother tongue before administrative and judicial authorities...

Today, most Kenyans use a Kenyan mother tongue at home, or Swahili as vernacular. There is a vibrant and competitive TV industry, and 'community radios' which air news and entertainment in different Kenyan languages, Swahili, and English. At the same time Kenyan bills, parliamentary debates, laws, and statutes are still drafted in English, but a few parliamentarians who wish to can debate in Swahili. Court interpreters provide translation services into Swahili or any other Kenyan language as required, including Kenyan Sign Language (KSL) for the deaf. Overall competence in either of the two official languages is always difficult to establish, but Heine and Möhlig (1980) report that Kenyans have on average 'a second language competence of 1.01 languages', or in other words, citizens speak at least one other language in addition to their first. The capital city, Nairobi, may be considered a microcosm of Kenya's ethno-linguistic mosaic, a true 'melting pot' of Kenyan cultures and a commercial hub of east Africa. One recent study on multilingualism and language use revealed that the average number of languages spoken by a city resident is three, while 25 per cent of the total sampled population lived in bilingual households (Githiora 2002).

13.5 Kenyan Swahili as Basis of National Identity

The Swahili language that developed to become the common coastal language as early as the thirteenth century has been much influenced by Arabic, and has also incorporated loan words from Hindi, Persian, Portuguese, and English. Its ability to adapt to changing contexts has contributed to its unique position among the languages of east and central Africa. Kiunguja, the dialect spoken in Zanzibar, is known as 'Kiswahili Sanifu' or 'Standard Swahili' and is the variety that is taught in Kenyan schools. But in fact the dialects that most influence Kenyan speakers of Swahili are Kimvita, the Mombasa dialect, and to a lesser extent, Kiamu, spoken on the northern coast island of Lamu. Historically, the former was at the heartland of the origin of the Swahili people and language, while the latter was the highest regarded literary form in which the oldest Swahili manuscripts – written in Arabic script – were found. Whereas the decision to formalize a 'standard' was an ordinary feature in the creation of modern (east African) states, the choice of Kiunguja as 'Kiswahili Sanifu' was met with some resistance among speakers of the other dialects and their supporters. However, the 1933 decision of the Interterritorial Language Committee (ITLC) is widely accepted and the modern written standard is based on this dialect.

Ordinary spoken Kenyan Swahili however contains many localized influences especially during informal interaction, in mass media and culture. Some peculiarities of what are widely seen as non-standard features, 'Kenyan Swahili', are actually idiosyncratic of the northern dialects of the Swahili coast. In more recent times, the urban Swahili mixed code known as 'Sheng' has emerged from Nairobi, the capital city, and spread far among the younger speakers in smaller towns and rural areas of Kenya. Its use affects even traditionally conservative Swahili-speaking speech communities of the coast such as those of Lamu and Pate Islands.[21] This new code adds fuel to the discussion of dialect or regional variations, linguistic innovations, mother-tongue influences, and how such codes affects communication, education, and the desired spread and use of 'Standard Swahili'. There are particular concerns from educators that Sheng interferes with formal learning inside the classroom because students fail to perceive the boundaries between Sheng and Standard Swahili. Ultimately, many youngsters are more fluent in the restricted code than in classroom (Standard) Swahili. Against this criticism, supporters of Sheng argue that it is the code which best reflects modern Kenya because of its readiness to mix the different languages of Kenya.

---

[21] Personal observation, 2005.

13.5.1 Features of Kenyan Swahili

While Swahili itself did not emerge from a single 'nation-state' in the modern sense, each of the current nation-states of east and central Africa has produced a version of Swahili with its own distinctive character and flavour, and 'ways of speaking' that make one or the other nation identifiable as a 'speech community' (Hymes 1974), a literal marking of boundaries between 'us' and 'them' that in itself mirrors national identity. We have seen that the path that each of the two principal Swahili-speaking nations, Kenya and Tanzania, has taken in its state and identity formation has resulted in important distinctions which are evident in the study of language use and practices. Due to ethnic nationalism and a lack of uniform spread and development of Swahili, mother tongue interference (including that of localized dialects of Swahili – 'Swahili vernaculars') is very strong in Kenya. Additionally, a significant proportion of citizens (35 per cent) speak a non-Bantu language. Such facts have linguistic ramifications, for example in terms of these speakers' ease of acquisition and subsequent competence in Swahili, a Bantu language.[22] Such linguistic, regional, and historical factors, as well as political ideologies, have helped shape a distinct form of 'Kenyan Swahili', which has identifiable, characteristic features. Certain markers make it stand in clear distinction to, for example, 'Tanzanian' Swahili, which is characterized by a high degree of uniformity of speech behaviour, competence and near universal use of the language in its national territory. Kenyan Swahili also stands in contrast to 'Congo' Swahili, which has a strong Bantu orientation[23] and more borrowed words from regional languages such as Lingala or Kikongo, and French, the colonizing language of that central African region. These real or at times perceived differences create important markers that can be used to project national identities.

In Kenyan Swahili, for example, the standard Swahili system of agreement is much simplified, with many differences to Standard Swahili being due to mother tongue interference or localized (Swahili) dialect influences. Other aspects of the grammar of Kenyan Swahili that are different from those of Standard Swahili include, for example, the way that relative clauses and location are expressed via free-standing morphemes/words, rather than suffixes. Speakers of Kenyan Swahili generally complain of the difficulty of Standard Swahili, and it irks coastal native speakers that their children do not do well in national Swahili examinations, which obviously are based on a dialect they are not much in contact with except in the classroom. In addition to frequent, widespread distinctions between general Kenyan Swahili and Standard Swahili, young speakers especially in urban areas are now also increasingly coming

---

[22] An empirical study reported in Heine and Möhlig (1980) suggested that minority language speakers who are non-Bantu-speaking actually had higher proportions of speakers competent in Swahili. This is most probably due to the greater pressure exerted on smaller, less economically independent groups to acquire a more widely spoken second language.

[23] For example, Congo Swahili uses Bantu numbers such as *makumi mawili* 'twenty', *makumi matatu* 'thirty', etc., instead of Arabic-derived equivalents of Standard Swahili, *ishirini, thelathini*, etc. There also are many morphosyntactic differences especially with regard to noun class agreements.

under the influence of Sheng, and this growing new non-standard form of Swahili is today perhaps the most salient and distinctive marker of the range of forms of Swahili spoken in Kenya. Nevertheless, Swahili remains truly the single language Kenyans cherish, characterized by its various spoken forms, uneven spread, and varying competencies.

13.6 Conclusion

Swahili was the chief medium for the expression of nationalism when it was used to deliver the anti-colonial message to the people of the emergent nation of Kenya. In the immediate post-independence period (cf. Kenya Education Commission of 1964), Swahili was quickly adopted as the language of expression of national ideals, political aspirations, and optimism about the future of independent Kenya. In his 1969 speech in parliament, founding president Jomo Kenyatta subsequently declared Swahili a 'national language'. However, beyond such early pronouncements in favour of Swahili, no genuine national plan for the institutionalization of Swahili has been pursued. This official attitude (or lack of it), with little or no ideological grounding or cohesion, has resulted in an unregulated, natural development of the language reflected by the uneven ways of speaking Swahili from one region of Kenya to another and from one social group of speakers to another. Successive governments have continued to give English a primary role in conducting their business, while reserving Swahili for lower-status functions such as addressing the masses on certain occasions, or at the end of official speeches delivered in English during the celebration of national holidays. Backed by an inherently conservative political economy, English retains high-status roles that Swahili finds difficult to usurp in higher education, journalism, law, technology, and big business. This is because of the retention of colonial structures that favour a linguistic hierarchy with English at the top and Kenyan languages at the bottom. A deeply entrenched 'psychic disbelief' in African languages also limits their potential in areas of formal communication, knowledge production, and art. This situation continues to thwart the aspirations for Swahili as a fully across-the-board linguistic vehicle for national integration in all domains. Among high-status groups, Swahili use remains low, occurring only in interaction with low-status groups, in its ancient 'vehicular' sense, that is, as means of basic inter-ethnic communication, or for purposes of symbolic solidarity. Swahili in Kenya is at the same time recognized as the language of a particular ethnic group of a people known as 'Waswahili', and is thus resisted as a home language or vernacular in many non-ethnically Swahili households.

English serves to a lesser extent than Swahili as a pan-ethnic medium for the projection of identities in Kenya, and in some expressions of nationalism. Swahili is favoured as the best unifier for the nation because it is an *African* language that is easily accepted by Kenyans of all ethnic and regional backgrounds as the national language, and for communication among Kenyans of all regional and social backgrounds who regard it a 'neutral' language devoid of connotations of power, or political or economic domination. It is also an African language of international recognition and diffusion and has a body of literature and scholarship in which Kenyans take pride. In mass politics and popular culture Swahili speaks for itself, as it is spoken by more than two thirds of the population, and is by far the language most commonly used to articulate and illustrate Kenya's popular history and politics, to communicate pan-ethnic messages and evoke nationalist images. The state leadership uses Swahili to reach out to the people, in countrywide political campaigns, to immortalize episodes in the national memory, to create a nationalist ethos. Important players in Kenyan society, politics, academia, and popular arts and culture continue to make a persuasive case for it to become the de facto national language of Kenya. A clause in the country's new (2004) constitution will soon be ratified, making Swahili a de jure national and official language. The '8:4:4' system of education has given an entire generation of students a greater formal knowledge of Swahili through making it compulsory at the early levels, where previous curricular emphasis was on Kenyan vernaculars, and English. In doing so, the acquisition of a good knowledge of Swahili should contribute positively to national integration, and bring about the full transition of Swahili from 'vehicular' language to a true national language of Kenya.

14

Tanzania: The Development of Swahili as a National and Official Language

Farouk Topan

14.1 Introduction

Tanzania is a multilingual nation of approximately 35 million people (2002 census), of whom nearly a million reside in the semi-autonomous islands of Zanzibar (Unguja and Pemba).[1] As Polomé (1980: 3) has noted, listing the languages of Tanzania 'is a rather difficult task'; prevalent figures are 124 languages (Batibo 2005: 155) and 127 (cited in *Ethnologue* 2005). When Tanganyika achieved its independence from British rule in 1961, at least two positive aspects of its legacy from the former colonial rule were the stability of its national borders (although externally imposed) and the firm acceptance of Swahili, not only as lingua franca, but also as an aspiring national language of the new nation. The linguistic map of the time, and the national aspirations underlying it, were seen as a model for an emerging African country where the scourge of 'tribalism' was largely absent. None of the ethnic communities was significantly large enough to assume a politically dominant position; nor, it seems, was there a wish to do so. This chapter will explore the factors that brought about this situation, including trade, the presence of colonial powers, the proselytizing and educational endeavours of the missionaries, and the attempts of Julius Nyerere (d.1999), the first President of Tanzania, to create a socialist state whose citizens identify themselves first and foremost as 'Tanzanians'. Language, and more specifically, Swahili, played a major facilitating role in these phases.

---

[1] The United Republic of Tanzania, comprising Tanganyika and Zanzibar, came into existence on 26 April 1964 when the leaders of the two countries agreed to form a Union. Of the two countries, Tanganyika was the first to gain independence from the British in December 1961, becoming a Republic a year later. Zanzibar was granted independence in December 1963 (also from the British) but remained a Sultanate with a Busaidi Sultan as its titular ruler; the Sultanate was overthrown in a revolution in January 1964.

14.2 The Spread of Swahili: Pre-colonial and Colonial Periods

Swahili belongs to the Bantu family of languages which share an extensive pool of common lexicon as well as an elaborate noun class system. Swahili is spoken in Eastern Africa and in parts of Central Africa in countries which include Tanzania, Kenya, Rwanda, Burundi, parts of the Congo, the Comoro Islands, southern Somalia, and northern Msumbiji (Mozambique). Links between East Africa and the Arabic-speaking countries over centuries have resulted in a high incidence of Arabic loanwords in Swahili, an occurrence which has sometimes led to the mistaken belief that Swahili is a 'mixed language'.

The spread of Swahili from its home on the coast and the islands into the interior of Tanganyika is divisible into three main phases. The first phase is associated with trade, when caravans, led by Swahili-speaking peoples, established routes to the north, west, and south of the country. The consolidation of the Busaidi Sultanate in Zanzibar, commencing with Said bin Sultan in the early nineteenth century, further developed and institutionalized this commercial enterprise, thus laying the foundation for 'the growth of Swahili as a lingua franca along the trade routes' (Abdulaziz 1980: 140).

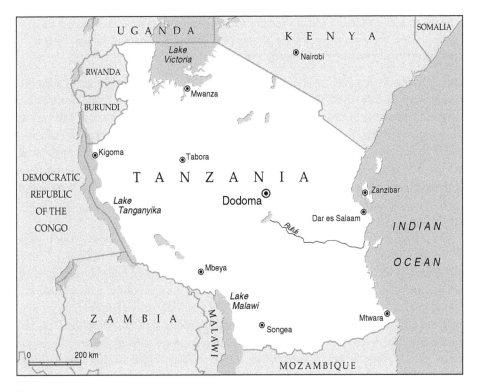

Tanzania

The spread of Swahili in this way, characterized as 'horizontal' by Heine (1977), was spontaneous and non-formal. The method changed to a 'vertical' one in the next two phases when Swahili was taught formally in schools, and its spread became channelled and systematic.

Missionary activities comprised the second phase. Swahili was used as the language of proselytization and of the publications of the church. It had initially been suggested that the use of other local languages was perhaps a better way of reaching out to the people in the area, but the widespread use of Swahili, and the economic advantages of using a single language, generated a consensus in its favour. The German missionary based at Mombasa, Ludwig Krapf, thought it 'practical' to adopt Swahili as it was 'the most cultivated of the dialects in this part of Africa' that is spoken from the equator southwards to the Portuguese settlements of Mozambique. For that reason, 'it should be made to supersede, as much as possible, the minor dialects inland which are spoken by only a small population' (Krapf 1882: xi). The British missionary, Bishop Edward Steere of Zanzibar, had gone much further in his support:

> a point of the greatest importance to our Central African Mission [is] that Swahili should be thoroughly examined and well learnt. For, if the members of the mission can go forth from Zanzibar, or, still better, can leave England already well acquainted with this language, and provided with books and translations adapted to their wants, they will carry with them a key that can unlock the secrets of an immense variety of strange dialects, whose very names are as yet unknown to us.   (Steere 1870: iii)

The only question which exercised the minds of these early missionaries was the choice of the dialect which they should adopt for that purpose. Krapf, and more so his assistant, Rebmann, strongly advocated the use of KiMvita, the dialect of Mombasa, while Steere felt equally strongly in favour of KiUnguja, the dialect spoken in Zanzibar town (Topan 1992: 337–8).[2] KiUnguja finally won the debate when Krapf came round to think of it as 'not without usefulness'. Not only was it spoken by a very large number of people, but it 'also affords to the translator the resource of being able to adopt at will an Arabic word when in difficulty for a proper expression in Kisuahili' (Krapf 1882: xii).

The early missionaries – some of them scholars of Swahili – viewed Arabic as a useful pool from which to draw vocabulary, especially religious terminology. Their successors, however, moved away from this perception the more their familiarity with the societies of mainland Tanganyika increased. KiUnguja then came to be considered, not as an asset, but as a liability since the dialect carried words of Arabic origin that reflected notions associated with Islam. The main exponent of this view, the German missionary Roehl, was keen to 'de-Arabicize' the language used in the translation of the Bible. Thus the Stuttgart Bible of 1930 was published in a Swahili which Roehl

---

[2]   A note on the representation of these languages in English. We follow the convention of using 'Swahili' in this chapter when referring to the language in English but retain the prefix 'ki' when referring to its dialects. 'Swahili' as an adjective is also employed without the prefix 'ki'.

tried to 'Bantuize' as much as possible. Although Roehl's translation was criticized by Canon Broomfield of Zanzibar (1931: 77–85), the Stuttgart edition proved popular among the people of the mainland (Topan 1992: 341).

The third phase, largely concurrent with and supportive of missionary activities, relates to the Colonial period, from the beginning of the 1890s to 1961 when Tanganyika gained its independence. The period, first of German and then British rule, served as both foundational and formative in the spread of Swahili as a lingua franca. Four main areas of development were: administration, education, the media, and scholarship.

After establishing their rule in Tanganyika, the Germans first tried to introduce their own language through administration and education. But when it became clear that German would not be successful, they turned their attention and resources instead to Swahili. An administrative framework was developed gradually at the village level (and beyond) in cooperation with traditional local authorities; a school was established in Tanga, a town on the coast, in 1893 to provide training to Africans to occupy places as junior administrative officials. By 1914, as Whiteley (1969: 60) points out, 'the Administration was able to conduct much of its correspondence with village headmen in Swahili'; indeed, not much attention was likely to be given to letters not written in either Swahili or German. A working knowledge of Swahili was thus a prerequisite for participation in government through the junior civil service.

Reinforcing this situation, and preparing individuals for it, were government and mission schools. In the two decades or so before World War I, the Germans had established three types of schools. There were sixty village primary schools (Nebenschulen) which gave three years of education in Swahili; nine middle schools (Hauptschulen) giving a two-year course in reading, writing and arithmetic; and one high school (Oberschule) in Tanga (mentioned above) which offered clerical, industrial, and teacher training (Cameron and Dodd 1970: 56, cited in Abdulaziz 1980: 140). The backbone of Western education during the early period, however, was the set of mission schools of various denominations (mainly from Germany, Britain, and France) established in different parts of Tanganyika. According to Hildebrandt (1981: 194), the colonial governments 'would not have been able (or perhaps willing) to build all the schools which the missions built between 1878 and 1914'.

The preparation of textbooks for the schools was another activity which helped to spread and entrench the use of Swahili nationally. Although some mission publications were in local languages, these soon gave way to Swahili for economic and pragmatic reasons. Missionaries were also among the first Western scholars to study Swahili and publish their scholarship. The contributions of both Krapf and Steere to Swahili scholarship are significant. Steere's *A Handbook of the Swahili Language* (1870) and Krapf's *A Dictionary of the Suahili Language* (1882) are both pioneering studies of the grammar and lexis of the language, two examples in a long list of publications by missionaries which stretches into the early 1960s. The Oriental Seminar at Berlin held Swahili courses for German officials posted to Tanganyika;

the British later did likewise through the School of Oriental and African Studies in London.

Another important contribution to the spread and consolidation of Swahili during the German period was the publication of newspapers by the Administration and, perhaps more effectively, by the missions. Whiteley (1969: 60) names a few of these, including the first newspapers sponsored by the Universities' Mission to Central Africa, *Msimulizi* ('The Narrator', 1888) and *Habari za Mwezi* ('Monthly News', possibly 1894). A newspaper with a wider circulation, *Kiongozi* 'The Leader' was started in 1905. The British later continued this practice; the most renowned Swahili newspaper during the British period was *Mambo Leo* 'Current Affairs', started in 1923, whose readership was national. Radio also became an important vehicle of language use and dissemination during the later Colonial period.

By the time the governance of Tanganyika passed into British hands after World War I, Swahili had become well entrenched in the country. The main advantage to the British was that they could administer through a single language in education, in the civil service, the police, and the army; thus staffing problems were minimized, and members of the civil services could be transferred from one part of the country to another. Crucially, as Whiteley points out, there was also some evidence that such factors 'engendered a sense of belonging to a unit larger than the tribe, though the situation varied considerably across the country' (1969: 61).

The British, in the main, built upon the system introduced by the Germans and consolidated the development of Swahili in many respects. However, their attempts in three overlapping areas – linguistic, institutional, and educational – have had a lasting effect on the language, impinging ultimately upon the perception of national identity as forged through Swahili. The first of these steps, undertaken in 1930, was the decision to select KiUnguja (the Zanzibari dialect) as 'standard' Swahili. The second, also implemented in the same year, was to set up the Inter-Territorial Language Committee to oversee the process of standardization and development of Swahili. The term 'Inter-Territorial' was important as it signified, even then, the importance of Swahili across national boundaries (viz. Tanganyika, Kenya, Zanzibar, and, to a lesser extent, Uganda). Two aspects of 'standardization' were emphasized in practice: uniformity in the articulation and application of grammar – especially in written Swahili – and uniformity in the orthography of the language.[3] School textbooks, as well as literary manuscripts, had to be reviewed by the Committee. When it was satisfied that the Swahili used was 'correct', the Committee issued an 'imprimatur' of approval which was duly printed at the beginning of the volume. As the Committee consisted mainly of Colonial officials – effective African participation began after the War in 1946 – sentiments against this procedure and, indeed, standardization as such, were voiced

---

[3] The publication of the *Standard Swahili–English Dictionary* by the Committee under the direction of Frederick Johnson (1939) and E.O Ashton's *Swahili Grammar* (1944) 'were landmarks in the process of Swahili standardization' (Blommaert 1999: 88); both books were for years necessary standard works in the repertoire of students of Swahili.

both by Africans and non-Africans.[4] The criticisms reflect, in a sense, the status of Swahili as a language of the people as a whole: it was felt that the people themselves should develop their own language.

The third far-reaching step taken by the British was the introduction of English in the administrative and educational systems in East Africa. In Tanganyika and in Zanzibar, English effectively became the official language during the colonial period. It was not only taught in schools as a subject, but was the medium of instruction from early on in the primary schools through to secondary schools and teachers' colleges. The upper strata of the army, the police, and the judiciary employed English, as did the various legislative organs of government. Promotion and advancement in the administration depended upon one's knowledge of English. Thus, gradually, English came to be perceived as the language of progress, advancement, and social mobility. By the time Julius Nyerere came on the political scene in 1954 – when he founded the Tanganyika African National Union (TANU) – Tanganyika and Zanzibar were officially bilingual countries: Swahili functioned in the wider and popular 'horizontal' areas of communication, while English occupied the upper, and socially strategic 'vertical' areas.

14.3 Towards Independence, and After

From the outset, Nyerere understood well the status, role, and appeal of Swahili among the people. Although he himself belonged to a small ethnic community – the Zanaki – he had a masterful command of Swahili, and used it to its most effective advantage in his oratory. He thus personified the linguistic ideal of a Tanzanian. But apart from a personal love of and skill in the language,[5] Nyerere saw three socio-political advantages in the use of Swahili nationally. The first, and perhaps the most important, was that it united the people. Thus, unlike his counterparts in other countries, he could communicate directly with the people in a language they understood; only three times during the 'struggle for freedom' prior to independence did he ever feel the need to resort to translators. The second advantage flowed from the first: Nyerere firmly believed that the use of Swahili stopped Tanzania from sliding into tribalism. He linked these two aspects in a speech, quoted by Laitin (1992: 91–2), which

---

[4] A member of the Kenya Education Department gives the following views in the Committee's *Bulletin* for 1934:'While, doubtless, all are ready to admit that Swahili, like any other language is bound to develop and grow, in form, idiom and vocabulary, as a result of the impact of the civilisations of the immigrant communities, yet surely the development must come from the Swahili mind, and must not be superimposed on them from without. But that is just what we have tried, and are still trying to do, with the result that we are in the somewhat ludicrous position of teaching Swahilis their own language through the medium of books, many of which are not Swahili in form or content, and whose language has but little resemblance to the spoken tongue' (Whiteley 1969: 85).

[5] Nyerere was an accomplished Swahili poet as well, and the first writer to translate Shakespeare into Swahili (*Julius Caesar* in 1963 and *Merchant of Venice* in 1969, inspiring another scholar, S. S. Mushi, to do likewise with *Macbeth* in 1968 and *The Tempest* in 1969). Blommaert has analysed Nyerere's style and political discourse in a number of works (1990, 1991, and 1999 among others).

Nyerere delivered when he stepped down as Chairman of the Party in 1990; it was part of his reflection and assessment of his period in office (which was virtually from 1954):

> Making Kiswahili Tanzania's language helped us greatly in the battle against tribalism. If every Tanzanian had stuck to using his tribal language or if we had tried to make English the official language of Tanzania, I am pretty sure that would not have created the national unity we currently enjoy. Although I am personally of the opinion that we should continue teaching English in our schools because English is the Kiswahili of the world, we have, however, an enormous duty to continue to promote and enhance Kiswahili. It is a great weapon for our country's unity.

Empowerment of the ordinary individual through language was the third advantage. What mattered most to the nationalists in the pre-independence days was the ability of the individual to participate fully in the political process. Swahili made this possible. Moreover, as Kaniki (1974: 3) points out, Swahili 'made TANU leaders easily acceptable as leaders of Tanganyika rather than of this or that ethnic group'. From the beginning, TANU used Swahili throughout its organization, meetings, rallies, and in its communication with the masses, thus associating the language 'with national identity, integration and development' (Abdulaziz 1980: 146).[6]

After independence, Nyerere vigorously promoted the use of Swahili in various ways. He decreed it the national language, and, as the first President of the new Republic, Nyerere delivered his first address to Parliament in Swahili on 10 December 1962, a step which 'paved the way for a general move away from English' (Legère 2006: 379). In 1967, the Vice-President, Rashidi Kawawa, decreed that Swahili would thenceforward be used wherever possible in government and para-governmental bodies and that English was to be employed only where necessary (Abdulaziz 1980: 146). The same year saw the introduction of two fundamental policies of the Government and Party – the Arusha Declaration and 'Education for Self-reliance' – both of which required the use of Swahili among the masses for their success.

The Arusha Declaration was the anchor-sheet of Nyerere's policy of *ujamaa* ('familyhood' but usually translated as 'African socialism') which was seen as pervading all areas of Tanzanian national life. It enunciated principles of equality, dignity, work ethics, ownership of national resources, a rejection of exploitation of one human being by another, and the creation of a classless society. The Declaration 'was to be the blueprint of the ideological base for Tanzanian nationalism' (Abdulaziz, 1980: 146). One of the ways of implementing the policy of socialism was through the practice of 'villagization', a bringing together of people from various smaller villages into larger communes. Swahili was the common language employed in the villages, and indeed in enunciating, explaining, and discussing *ujamaa* issues throughout the country.[7]

---

[6] TANU merged with the Afro-Shirazi Party of Zanzibar in 1977 to form *Chama cha Mapinduzi* (CCM, the 'Party of Revolution'), thus changing its name from English to Swahili; CCM is the current party of government in both parts of the Union (of Tanganyika and Zanzibar).

[7] Considerable writing exists on Nyerere's *ujamaa* policy and its impact on Tanzania, up to and even after it was gradually abandoned in the mid-1980s; Nyerere's major writings on *ujamaa* are given in Legère

Nyerere himself had, characteristically, spearheaded the campaign, introducing newer and fresher political connotations to ordinary words and phrases. The word for 'straw', *mrija*, for example, acquired the meaning of 'exploitation', associated with the visual image of neo-colonialists in foreign countries sucking away (*kunyonya*) the resources of Tanzania through straws that crossed nations and oceans (this imagery being produced in cartoons in newspapers at the time). The new metaphorical uses of such words and phrases soon caught on and became part of the common language of the late 1960s and 1970s.

Language was also an important instrument of the second nation-building policy, 'Education for Self-reliance', announced in March 1967, just a month after the Arusha Declaration. The idea behind the policy was both pragmatic and visionary, and related to the economic and social conditions of the majority of Tanzanians. It was noted that the colonial system of education which the new nation had inherited placed much emphasis on the importance of secondary and tertiary education, yet only 10 to 15 per cent of primary school children actually got admitted to secondary schools, and the remaining 85 to 90 per cent had to stop at the primary level and 'make do' with whatever skills they possessed in order to earn a living. Through the policy of 'Education for Self-reliance' Nyerere sought not so much to reverse the emphasis, as to make primary education sufficient in itself for the needs of the majority of the school-going population. Pupils would be taught the basic skills needed for life in a predominantly agricultural society that was striving to be socialist. Nyerere explained what he perceived to be the requirements of the people:

> For the majority of our people the thing which matters is that they should be able to read and write fluently in Swahili, that they should have an ability to do arithmetic, and that they should learn something of the history, values, and working of their country and government, and that they should acquire the skills necessary to earn their living. (Nyerere 1967: 24)

Swahili was thus in the vanguard of nation-building, both policies utilizing its services for the betterment of the people. Its status in the late 1960s and early 1970s was 'idealized' in four ways (Blommaert 1999: 69–72). Firstly, it was considered the carrier of African and Tanzanian values and it was 'romantizised' as such. It was linked to 'racial pride, freedom, Ujamaa and anticolonialism' (ibid.: 69). Secondly, it was seen as a symbol of national unity, a language that was 'anti-tribal'. Thirdly, Swahili was perceived as an egalitarian language that belonged to all, that is, 'ethnically unmarked', since its first language speakers did not constitute a dominant (or potentially dominant) group in independent Tanzania, and did not pose a threat to the growth of a fully inclusive Swahili-centred national identity (ibid.: 70). Finally, it was seen as a modern language that was capable of being used in all walks of life by modern Tanzanians.

(2006: 400–2). For a more extensive understanding of the relationship between *ujamaa* and Swahili, see Blommaert (cited earlier, note 5) and Russell (1990); the impact of *ujamaa* in Swahili literature is discussed in Topan (2006a).

While 'the Nyerere factor', as Russell calls it (1990: 366), was important in promoting such perceptions of Swahili, institutions created for its development also played a role in providing tangible materials for its use. The erstwhile Inter-Territorial Language Committee was transformed into the Institute of Swahili Research and became part of the University College of Dar es Salaam in 1964. When the latter became a University in 1970 (with the dissolution of the University of East Africa), the Department of Swahili came into existence with a record intake of first-year students. The Government also set up the National Swahili Council through an act of Parliament in 1967 with the overall aim of promoting and developing the usage of Swahili throughout the United Republic. Besides these academic and government organs, there also existed a number of popular bodies – such as poets' and writers' associations – which participated in the development of Swahili in their own ways.

The contribution of the academic bodies has been significant. The Institute of Swahili Research, for instance – working sometimes in partnership with the Department of Swahili – has produced word-lists, dictionaries (both English–Swahili and Swahili–English), monographs on aspects of Swahili language, linguistics, and literature, and journals. The enormous output of these institutions has not only enriched Swahili studies, particularly in the field of lexicography and Swahili linguistics, but has created fresh terminology and registers of these disciplines in Swahili. A new generation of Swahili scholars and writers have employed such discourse in their training, and now use it with confidence and ease. Perhaps unsurprisingly, scholars of Swahili at the University of Dar es Salaam have been the foremost supporters of the national and cultural use of Swahili in the manner envisaged by Nyerere. F. E. M. K. Senkoro, a scholar of Swahili literature, argues for the existence of a direct link between Tanzanian and Swahili identity, stating the following in his attempts at defining Swahili literature:

> We shall decide that a particular work is or is not Swahili literature on the basis of its projection of and relationship with the culture of the Swahili people. Here the term Swahili does not mean an ethnic group of Swahili people, for such an ethnic group does not exist today. The Swahili people here are the citizens of East and Central Africa in general and not only those who live on the coastline of these countries.   (Senkoro 1988, quoted in translation in Mazrui and Shariff 1993: 90)

There is, thus, a denial of the continued existence of 'core' Swahili peoples of the coast and islands (i.e. 'original' first language speakers who today number at least a million), as well as an appropriation of their language, dispossessing them of it in a significant way.[8]

---

[8] The erosion of an ethnic Swahili identity distinct from Tanzanian national identity has occurred in three areas: first, in terms of locality, an earlier ethnic Swahili identity has been geographically (and ethnically) widened from the coast and the islands to the Tanzanian nation as a whole; second, in terms of language, it is declared that all Tanzanians should speak Swahili as their national language; third, in terms of religion, a 'Swahili' is no longer necessarily also a Muslim. See Eastman (1971), Mazrui and Shariff (1993), Salim (1985), and Topan (2006b) for discussion of these points.

14.4 Swahili and English

Though Swahili was vigorously promoted as Tanganyika's (and then Tanzania's) national language in the period following independence, English also continued to occur prominently as the country's official language. However, the momentum and impetus given to Swahili in the post-independence days, especially after 1967, brought it to the fore, as we have seen, as a viable partner, and increasingly as an alternative, to English in official spheres. One such sphere was, and still is, education. The role of these two languages in education has been a matter of debate in Tanzania for nearly four decades; the central issue over the years has been whether Swahili should replace English as a medium of instruction in secondary schools and beyond in tertiary education.[9]

During the colonial period, Swahili was used as a medium of instruction in the first four years of primary school (standard 1 to 4); English was taught as a subject in standards 3 and 4, and was the medium of instruction from standard 5 to 8 and in secondary schools. Tanzania continued with this policy until 1967 when Swahili was made the medium of instruction throughout the seven years of primary school. This step was perceived in Tanzania's second Five Year Plan (1969–74) as 'part of a larger plan to implement the use of kiSwahili as the medium of instruction throughout the educational system' (Brock-Utne 2005: 56). The rationale for the change was explained in the Plan itself:

> The division between kiSwahili education at primary level and English education at the secondary level will create and perpetuate a linguistic gulf between different groups and will also tend to lend an alien atmosphere to higher education, making it inevitably remote from the problems of the masses of society.   (Brock-Utne 2005: 56)

The Tanzanian Government in 1969 thus had the intention of putting into place educational measures that would remove sociolinguistic inequalities and make education more accessible to the people, a goal that would be in keeping with the precepts of *ujamaa*. To such an end, the Ministry of National Education devised a timetable for a phased introduction of Swahili as a medium of instruction in secondary schools for certain subjects from 1969 to 1973. The timetable, however, was not implemented, except for political science and Swahili as a subject in secondary schools.

The issue came to the fore again after the National Swahili Council reported in 1977 that students in secondary schools found it difficult to learn their subjects through English. A Presidential Commission chaired by the Minister of Education, Jackson Makweta, recommended in 1982 that the medium of instruction in secondary and tertiary education should shift to Swahili. Again, a phased programme was suggested, commencing with Form I in January 1985 and university level in 1991. However, in

[9] There is considerable literature on the debate, both in English and Swahili, representing both sides of the argument. Roy-Campbell (2001) provides a detailed analysis of the situation in Tanzania, especially in chapters 5–7; see also Brock-Utne (2005: 51–87) for a lucid summary of the major phases and events of the debate.

August 1983, Makweta 'was quoted in the press as saying that the expected change of medium was not going to take place' (Brock-Utne 2005: 57).

Various reasons have been put forward by scholars and analysts for the government's change of heart on this issue, reasons which have as much to do with Swahili as with English. For Swahili, the main reasons are said to be the 'inadequacy' of the language to function as a medium of instruction in secondary schools and beyond, shortage of textbooks and resources in translation, shortage of trained teachers, a general state of unpreparedness. Roy-Campbell (2001) has analysed such reasons at length, dealing also with the positive arguments put forward (mainly by politicians and some educationalists) in favour of retaining English. These will not be rehearsed here, but two points are pertinent to our topic as they press upon the perception of a Tanzanian identity. The first, articulated by Nyerere himself, is that Tanzania should be a bilingual country where Swahili and English are used by its citizens, although only a small number (just over 5 per cent) speak the latter. English enables Tanzanians to have access to the outside world, to its knowledge, business, and global culture. Underlying this approach is the attitude, widespread among some politicians, parents, teachers, and students, that English is not only a 'functional' language, especially in science, technology, and knowledge generally, but it is also 'a tool of social progress' (Roy-Campbell 2001: 151). Resulting from such an attitude is the second conclusion: English, because of its benefits for the country, must be maintained in Tanzania.

Nyerere saw the roles of English and Swahili rather differently from the way some of the pro-Swahili nationalists viewed them. To him, the two languages were complementary, and not in competition, and there was consequently no issue of potentially having to replace English, as he stated strongly in 1984:

> English is the Swahili of the world and for that reason must be taught and given the weight it deserves in our country. . . . It is wrong to leave English to die. To reject English is foolishness, not patriotism . . . English will be the medium of instruction in secondary schools and institutions of higher education because if it is left only as a normal subject, it may die.   (cited in Roy-Campbell 2001: 100)

It is thus not surprising that Nyerere rejected the recommendation of the 1982 Presidential Commission on Education to extend Swahili as a language of instruction in post-primary education. Furthermore, he also accepted a proposal from the British Government to strengthen the learning and teaching of English in Tanzanian schools through the English Language Teaching Support Project (1987–91) 'by means of syllabus development, teacher training and the provision of books' (Roy-Campbell 2001: 103)[10]. It was acknowledged that proficiency in English had fallen among secondary

---

[10] Roy-Campbell states that one condition for this project 'laid down by the Overseas Development Agency (ODA) of the British government, the funding agency for the project, was that the Ministry of Education should ensure that English remained the medium of instruction in secondary schools, a condition which the Tanzanian government accepted' (2001: 103). It is a condition which seems to have matched well with Nyerere's own views on the use of English in education.

school children, affecting their understanding of other subjects taught through the medium of English. To Nyerere and those favouring English, the solution lay in improving knowledge of the language; to the pro-Swahili camp (even within the government), the solution was to replace English with Swahili, thus maintaining continuity from the primary school in a language which children speak fluently. The debate has continued in Tanzania (even after the death of Nyerere in 1999), underpinned by considerations of ideology, pedagogy, and practical necessities, both local and global.[11]

14.5 Ethnic Languages

The success of Swahili as a national and official language, promoted by the government, has resulted in its dominance over other indigenous languages. As we have seen, the goal from the outset was to avoid 'tribalism', which also meant not only active adoption of a single national language, but discouragement of the use of other indigenous languages in official or national situations. According to Batibo, Nyerere admitted in a speech in 1984 'that the high-level empowerment of Kiswahili as the national language was likely to affect the other languages in the country. To him, this was an inevitable development, inasmuch as good moves often have side effects that are likely to be adverse' (Batibo 2005: 59). Swahili has encroached gradually but progressively in areas previously occupied by indigenous languages. On the other hand, Nyerere and other leaders have consciously imported into Swahili words and phrases from other languages (two prominent examples being the words *bunge* for 'parliament' and *ikulu*, 'State House').

Although other indigenous languages are not given definite status in the national system as such, their creative and expressive aspects are integrated in school curricular activities. Songs, poems, dances, and other forms of verbal art from the other indigenous languages of Tanzania are taught in schools, though usually through the medium of Swahili. It can also be noted that traditional scholars and academics have written books in Swahili on the customs of their peoples, their history and other aspects of local cultures. On the whole, though, indigenous languages have tended to be pushed sideways by the dominance of Swahili. Batibo (2005: 151–2) categorizes thirty-three of Tanzania's languages as 'highly endangered' and nine as 'extinct or nearly extinct'. The situation, however, 'is currently being checked by certain local developments' (ibid.: 11); we shall return to this below.

---

[11] Brock-Utne reports that in 1997, the Ministry of Education and Culture issued a policy statement signalling its intention to devise 'a special plan to enable the use of kiSwahili as a medium of instruction in education and training at all levels . . .' Following discussions in the press, in seminars and meetings, the then Minister of Education, Joseph Mungai, stated in 2001 that he would not consider replacing English as a language of instruction in secondary schools. Brock-Utne quotes the Minister as saying in a BBC interview in October 2003 that 'he did not see kiSwahili fit to be used at higher levels of education' as a language of instruction, nor did parents want it as such (Brock-Utne 2005: 69).

14.6 Conclusion

Tanzania is one of the few African countries south of the Sahara whose lingua franca is also the national language. The success of Swahili, as we have seen, is due to a variety of factors: the establishment of caravan routes that laid the foundations for Swahili as a lingua franca; the extensive use of Swahili in the administration of the country by the Germans and the British; the use of Swahili by missionaries in their schools and other proselytizing activities; and the intensive promotion of Swahili as a national language by Julius Nyerere, one of whose aims was to create a Tanzanian national identity. Nyerere's efforts could be considered as the culmination of the process that invested Swahili with the status of a national language. For it was in his period that a modern 'nation' came into existence, freed from its colonial governance.

With independence from the British began the real process of 'nation-building' (*kujenga taifa*) for Nyerere, a process committed to the creation of one nation out of various ethnic communities. Laitin (1992: 9), rather more pragmatically, refers to such an endeavour as 'state construction', meaning the establishment of 'effective social control over a bounded territory' where language is employed to construct 'organizations capable of maintaining order in society and extracting resources from society'. Use of the national language, Swahili, has been critical here as a tool in the language rationalization policy of the country following independence; indeed, Laitin (1992: 192) refers to Tanzania as 'the most celebrated case of language rationalization in Africa'.[12] Such a perception, however, needs to be viewed within the context of three developments that have occurred since independence.

The first is in relation to the standardization of Swahili that first began in the 1930s. Whiteley (1969: 94) has observed that Swahili 'was standardized from the outside, as it were,' meaning that most of those who had engaged in the exercise were in fact expatriates. Since independence, as we have noted, institutions in Tanzania concerned with Swahili have tried to redress the balance by working on various aspects of 'standard Swahili' (*Kiswahili sanifu*). However, the perception on the islands is that the type of Swahili which is promoted in Dar es Salaam is no longer KiUnguja proper, the dialect of Zanzibar, but a newer, rather different, 'official' version, nicknamed *Kisanifu*, the 'standardized' dialect. Children who speak the KiUnguja dialect as their first language do not necessarily perform well in standard Swahili. A similar concern with Kenyan children prompted King'ei to study the extent of the acceptability of standard forms by 'non-KiUnguja native Kiswahili speakers' (King'ei 2000: 81–8). One of his observations is that, in Kenya, 'little had been heard in scholarship about the attitude

---

[12] Laitin (1992: 9) defines 'language rationalization' as 'the territorial specification of a common language for purposes of efficient administration and rule', such a policy also implying that 'a citizen needs to have facility in a single language in order to take advantage of a wide range of mobility opportunities in the territory' (ibid.: 9)

of native speakers towards the language' (ibid.: 81).[13] While the same cannot be said of the situation in Tanzania, where there is a good degree of interaction between Swahili institutions in Zanzibar and mainland Tanzania, each segment operates fairly independently. Institutions in Dar es Salaam and elsewhere on mainland Tanzania have had extensive history and experience behind them – for example, the Institute of Swahili Research celebrated its golden jubilee in 2005 – while those in Zanzibar are fairly recent. Both, however, engender commitment towards Swahili and its role in national identity.

The second development, still ongoing, concerns the continuing coexistence of English alongside Swahili in various domains. While the status of Swahili as a national language is beyond question – though there are scholars and politicians who would prefer to see its status enshrined in the Tanzanian Constitution (which, surprisingly, it is not) – the relationship between the two languages as official languages needs further comment. We have discussed above the main aspects of the debate in the field of education where considerable ambiguity surrounds the issue of whether Swahili should replace English as the medium of instruction in secondary and tertiary education. In other areas, however, 'Swahili has expanded at the expense of English' since independence (Batibo 2005: 10). English is today used in secondary and tertiary education (as already noted), in the higher courts (with interpreters where necessary), and international communication. Some official documents, signboards, and road signs are in English, though Batibo attributes the latter two to 'status sentiments rather than communication needs' (ibid.). Newer areas for English now include its use in computer and internet communications, some radio and television stations (especially privately owned), newspapers, and satellite stations. Also, my impression is that a good number of loanwords are today imported from English and phonetically Swahilized; one comes across this trend especially in newspapers and on the radio. It is furthermore not uncommon to hear code-switching among Western-educated individuals. The successful promotion of Swahili as the national language has therefore not resulted in the full disappearance of English from certain official and national-level domains of life in Tanzania.

The third significant aspect of development since independence is in connection with the other indigenous languages of the country. Swahili has now become so well entrenched as the national language that there is no threat to it from other Tanzanian languages. With such an effective national promotion of Swahili, Nyerere's and his government's original aim of eliminating the threat of 'tribalism' from Tanzania has

---

[13] Thus, it is interesting that some KiUnguja and KiMvita speakers share a common sentiment about standard Swahili (probably for different reasons); but to speak of them as being 'against' standard Swahili would be putting too strong an interpretation on their views. Another of their shared views, expressed by Swahili scholars of the coast and the islands, is that much of their Swahili vocabulary is gradually becoming lost as it is not being collected nor recorded systematically, save in the fiction writing of writers from these regions. Even the latter is frequently standardized to meet publishers' demands for standard school texts. In the mid-1970s, a Swahili publishing company, Shungwaya, was set up in Kenya to cater for writers who wished to write in their own dialect; however, it subsequently closed in the mid-1980s.

essentially been achieved. Additionally, given the intermarriages and language shifts that have occurred since independence, the newer generations not only speak Swahili fluently – and increasingly as first-language speakers – but they are now so at ease with their national identity and linguistic situation that they also happily acknowledge the 'ethnic' origins of their parents' languages. In connection with this, Batibo (2005: 11) remarks that various local developments such as 'regional consciousness, decentraliza-tion of administration to the regions and liberalization of the economy' have actually tended to check the slide of local indigenous languages towards endangerment and extinction in recent times.

As has been described during the course of the chapter, a combination of historical and political circumstances have made it possible for Swahili to be invested with the status of (single) national language in Tanzania, and given a crucial role in the forging of national identity, principally at the instigation of Julius Nyerere, the country's first president. Nyerere's charisma and leadership have subsequently sustained that impor-tant status of Swahili in Tanzania for half a century, and the national language has become firmly and successfully embedded in the daily life of the population. As for what the future may hold, here I would like to quote an assessment of the current post-Nyerere situation offered in Laitin (1992) (which is a summary of views received by him from other scholars as well):

> The macro dynamic toward rationalization is not inexorable; it will take considerable political effort by Nyerere's successors to ensure Swahili's integrity and [future] develop-ment as Tanzania's sole official language. But there remains the possibility that Nyerere's rationalization strategy – supported by historical circumstances and assiduous political effort – will succeed and that Swahili will be the only necessary language for communica-tion, education, and occupational mobility throughout Tanzania.   (Laitin 1992: 141; also note 5)

As far as it is possible to predict the future, current patterns suggest that the present strong position of Swahili as the country's national language is unlikely to undergo any change and Tanzanians will increasingly define themselves through the language during the course of the twenty-first century. As an official language, however, my personal belief is that Swahili will continue to share that status with English, and Swahili will continue to have an oscillating relationship with English. One of the basic cultural characteristics of the Swahili in history has been their willingness to accommodate 'the other' with a sense of comfort, confidence and self-assurance. As Tanzania develops over the decades to come, Tanzanians may therefore well show the same continued accommodation with English.

15

The Horn of Africa: Ethiopia, Eritrea, Djibouti, and Somalia

David Appleyard and Martin Orwin

15.1 Introduction

The Horn of Africa is here understood as comprising four countries: Djibouti, Eritrea, Ethiopia, and Somalia. Of these the largest both in terms of landmass and population is Ethiopia, followed by Somalia, Eritrea, and Djibouti in that order. Ethiopia also has the highest overall density of population of the four countries. Whilst all four countries have in part shared histories and some common cultural patterns and influences, owing in large part to their geographical contiguity, the dominant factor that has been central to history and culture alike across the region is the ancient and at times conflicting presence of two world religions, Christianity in the case of highland Ethiopia and Eritrea, and Islam elsewhere. Ethiopia and Eritrea, which historically formed a single entity, have been Christian since the fourth century and the Ethiopian kingdom constituted an expansive political and cultural nucleus in the Ethiopian highlands from even before that time. Islam already entered the Horn from its earliest days in the seventh and eighth centuries AD, and the growth of Islamic states in the southern and eastern parts of the region from the thirteenth century onwards inevitably led to conflict with the Christian kingdom. Islam today is dominant in the east of the Horn and along the Red Sea littoral, in Djibouti and Somalia, and with around 50 per cent of the population of Eritrea. Historically religion rather than language seems to have been the main criterion of identity and adherence to a political entity or state, at least judging from written histories, both chronicles and hagiographies.

The region has had varying experiences of colonialism. Djibouti, Eritrea, and Somalia have had as long a period under colonial rule as most other countries in sub-Saharan Africa. Djibouti was, for instance, under French control from 1862 to 1977, and even after independence French influence has remained strong. Eritrea was an Italian colony from 1890 until 1941, after which it passed first under British and then Ethiopian control. Somalia was formed in 1960 out of the union of two former colonies, British Somaliland in the north, which had been a British protectorate since

1886, and the more populous Italian Somaliland in the south, which originated in 1889 and attained its final extent in 1927. It could be argued that these three countries are creations of their colonial past, insofar as neither Djibouti nor Somalia derive from any historical polity other than the artificial creations of French, British, and Italian Somaliland, and Eritrea arises out of the Italian domination of what was historically part of the Ethiopian kingdom. Ethiopia, on the other hand, had only the briefest experience of foreign domination, from 1935 to 1941, when it was occupied by Italy, and is one of very few African countries that escaped a significant colonial period in its history. Indeed, it has sometimes been said, especially by nationalities within Ethiopia seeking greater autonomy, that Ethiopia herself was a colonial power during the last decades of the nineteenth and into the twentieth century, the period that saw the greatest expansion of the Ethiopian empire.

The Horn of Africa has more recently been beset with considerable unrest and political upheaval, during the last forty years of the twentieth century, first with thirty years of Eritrean separatist struggle culminating in 1991 in the defeat of Ethiopia and, in 1993, the achievement of full independence and separation. Secondly, at around the same time, Somalia, which had achieved independence from its British and Italian colonial masters barely some thirty or so years before, was riven by clan warfare and to all intents and purposes ceased to exist, having broken up into several entities which have not achieved internationally recognized status. The collapse of the Somali state had in part been triggered by a disastrous war with Ethiopia in 1977–78 over the Ogaden region, the south eastern portion of that country inhabited by Somalis. Then, following Eritrean separation from Ethiopia, these two countries engaged in bitter conflict over ill-defined portions of their common frontier. All of these conflicts were to a considerable extent driven by a sense of ethnic identity and the perception that that sense needed formal recognition in the nation-state.

The Horn is amongst the linguistically more complex, or diverse, areas of Africa in terms of the numbers of languages spoken. According to *Ethnologue* (2005), there are 114 languages spoken in the four countries of the region: Djibouti with five (but this includes French, the ex-colonial language, and Standard Arabic), Eritrea with twelve (again including two ex-colonial languages, English and Italian, and also Standard Arabic), Ethiopia with eighty-four (which includes English), and Somalia with thirteen (also including English and Standard Arabic). If we exclude these 'outside' languages of wider communication, there are then just over 100 languages spoken in the Horn. Some languages in the *Ethnologue* lists are spoken in more than one country of the region, for instance, Somali which is spoken not only in Somalia but also in Ethiopia and Djibouti, and Tigrinya which is spoken in Eritrea and Ethiopia. The *Ethnologue* numbers are also slightly inflated owing to the fact that in some instances varieties of what is commonly considered a single language are counted separately. This is the case with Somali, for which five varieties are listed under Somalia alongside the standard language, or with Oromo, another major language of the area, spoken mostly in Ethiopia, but also in Somalia and indeed outside the Horn properly speaking, in

Kenya. However, taking these factors into consideration a total number of just above 100 gives a good idea of the overall situation.

When we actually look at the distribution of languages in the region, however, the highest density of languages occurs in the west and especially the southwest of Ethiopia. This is not just in terms of the number of separate languages, but also in terms of the range of different language families involved. Of course, this makes the Horn much less linguistically diverse than some other African countries or regions, such as Nigeria, or East Africa (Tanzania, Kenya, and Uganda), but more diverse than, say, South Africa, Botswana, Swaziland, and Lesotho combined.

15.2 Ethiopia, including Eritrea before 1993[1]

The states that were to develop into Ethiopia and Eritrea have a long history, going back over two millennia. In the first century BC the kingdom of Aksum, named after its capital city, arose out of the amalgamation of a number of small independent kingdoms or chiefdoms in what is now Eritrea and northern Ethiopia to become a powerful and expansive trading state that dominated both the Horn of Africa and the lands on the opposite shore of the Red Sea before the rise of Islam in the seventh century. Aksum was a literate society, at least insofar as its rulers left inscriptions some of which were written in three languages: Greek as the international language of the period; Sabaic, the principal ancient language of Southern Arabia with which Ethiopia had long had cultural contacts, which evidently still carried some historical prestige in Ethiopia; and Ge'ez, the indigenous language of Aksum itself. With the adoption of Christianity as the religion of the Aksumite kingdom in the fourth decade of the fourth century and the eventual translation into Ge'ez of the Bible and a few other Christian texts probably towards the end of the following century, Ge'ez attained the status of a written language that was to far outlast its life as the spoken language of the region. Over the following centuries, and especially after the loss of Ethiopian control over the Red Sea coast with the spread of Islam and the Arab seizure of the coast, the nucleus of the Christian kingdom moved progressively further south into the Ethiopian highlands, where Ge'ez as the dialect of the Aksum region had presumably not been the spoken language. The areas south of the heartlands of the Aksumite kingdom probably had a mixed population of speakers of Semitic dialects related to Ge'ez, the ancestors of modern languages such as Amharic, and Cushitic languages, principally Agaw or Central Cushitic languages.[2] However, Ge'ez as the language of the Church retained its prestigious role as the sole written medium of the Christian kingdom long after it ceased to be a spoken vernacular, and we can only surmise what

---

[1] Ethiopia and Eritrea historically formed a single state until modern times, and since to that extent they have a considerable shared linguistic history, discussion of language and identity in Eritrea prior to full independence in 1993 is here included under Ethiopia.

[2] See below for a brief account of the languages of Ethiopia.

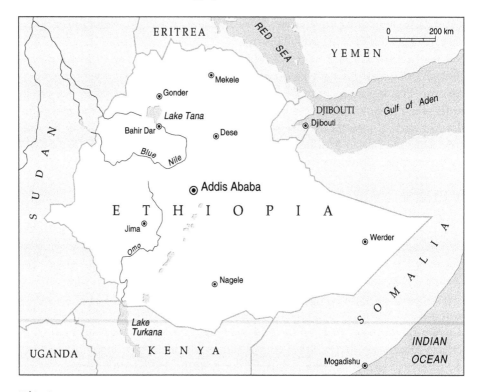

Ethiopia

the various spoken languages were, at least until the first vestiges of Amharic appeared in the fourteenth century.

The languages of Ethiopia belong mostly to the Afro-Asiatic language phylum or super-family, of which three branches are represented: Semitic, Cushitic, and Omotic. The Semitic family, of course, includes a number of languages spoken outside Africa in the Middle East, most notably Arabic and Hebrew. All the Semitic languages of Ethiopia, however, belong to the Ethiopian Semitic branch of the family (also sometimes called Ethiosemitic). The best known and largest members of this branch are Amharic and Tigrinya, with around 17.5 and 4.5 million speakers respectively according to the most recent censuses (*Ethnologue* 2005).[3] Most of the members of the Cushitic family of languages are spoken in the Horn, though one, Beja, is spoken both in Eritrea and outside the Horn properly speaking in the neighbouring parts of the Sudan, and there are some remnant Cushitic languages in Kenya and Tanzania. The best known and again the largest Cushitic languages are Somali and Oromo, with

[3] Ethiopia 1998 census, Eritrea 2001 for Tigrinya in Eritrea. Generally speaking, census figures from the region are not absolutely reliable when it comes to language, and there are in some instances discrepancies between numbers of people (a) identifying themselves as members of a specific ethnic group, e.g. Amhara, and (b) indicating a first-language knowledge of the relevant language, i.e. Amharic. Therefore, the figures given here are approximate.

around 12.5 and at least 17.5 million speakers, respectively.[4] Somali, as was indicated earlier, is spoken in all the countries of the Horn apart from Eritrea, and Oromo is also spoken outside Ethiopia, in Somalia and Kenya. The Omotic languages are spoken entirely in Ethiopia, in the linguistically diverse and complex southwest region of the country. The largest Omotic language is Wolaytta, with somewhat over 1 million speakers.

Aside from Afro-Asiatic languages there are also a number of languages that belong to the Nilo-Saharan super-family or phylum spoken in western Eritrea and western and southwestern Ethiopia. The majority of Nilo-Saharan languages are to be found outside the Horn, of course, especially in Kenya, Uganda, Sudan, Chad, and further west. Indeed, many of the Nilo-Saharan languages of Ethiopia are also spoken or have close relatives in the Sudan, and there are only two Nilo-Saharan languages which are spoken entirely within the Horn, Kunama and Nara, both in Eritrea.

Of the eighty-plus languages of Ethiopia and Eritrea,[5] 36 per cent have between 10,000 and 100,000 speakers, whilst around 28 per cent have fewer than 10,000, of which around thirteen or so have 3,000 or fewer speakers and are in a vulnerable position. Whilst it is unrealistic to give a specific minimum number of speakers before a language can be judged to be endangered, there can be no doubt that the survival of several smaller Ethiopian languages is questionable. Only eight languages in Eritrea and Ethiopia (9.5 per cent of the total) have over a million speakers, using *Ethnologue*'s figures and conflating the three varieties of Oromo into one (see Table 15.1). It should be noted in the table that elsewhere the three Omotic varieties (belonging to the Central Ometo subgroup) Gamo, Gofa, and Dawro have been described as separate languages, and none of them individually has more than 600,000 speakers.

The dominant language of Ethiopia (and thus Eritrea before independence) has historically been Amharic, and even with the far-reaching changes in language policy in Ethiopia since the 1980s, and especially since the change of regime in 1991, Amharic still retains its role as the most widespread, most widely used language, as well as being the working language of the bureaucracy and the national government. It is the main lingua franca of Ethiopia and is together with English the constitutionally recognized

---

[4] The number of speakers of Oromo varies widely from one source to another, up to as many as 30 million. This latter corresponds better with the number of people identifying themselves as Oromo in Ethiopia, not all of whom speak Oromo. *Ethnologue* (2005) gives the number of speakers as around 17.3 million when all varieties are added together; other sources raise this number to between 24 and 25 million. The Ethiopian National Census of 1994, however, recorded the Oromo as the largest nationality with 32.1 per cent of the population, which would have been c. 17,150,000 in 1994, which was more than the 30.2 per cent given for the Amhara (i.e. c. 16,150,000 at the time).

[5] *Ethnologue* (2005) gives 84 living languages, but this includes English and Ethiopian Sign Language. Also, whilst on the one hand some entries encompass several varieties or dialects that elsewhere are listed as separate languages (e.g. 'Säbat Bét Guragé' encompassing the five varieties Chäha, Gura, Muher, Gyéto, and Ezha), on the other hand several dialects of Oromo are entered separately (Boranaa-Arsi-Gujii Oromo, Eastern or Qottu Oromo, and West Central Oromo, which includes Macha or Wallagga Oromo, Wallo Oromo, and Tuulamaa Oromo).

Table 15.1 Major languages of Ethiopia and Eritrea

	No. of Speakers		No. of Speakers
Amharic	17,372,913	Sidamo	1,876,329
Oromo	17,080,000	Afar	1,439,367
Tigrinya	4,424,875	Gamo-Gofa-Dawro	1,236,637
Somali	3,334,113	Wolaytta	1,231,678

official language of the country. It is also the majority language of most urban-dwelling Ethiopians except where Tigrinya is the first language.

The current status and wide distribution of Amharic are in the first instance due to the deliberate amharization policies of previous Ethiopian governments since the end of the nineteenth century. However, the origins of the dominance of Amharic go much further back. Amharic had been the language of the royal court and the dominant political elite in Ethiopia since the rise of the Solomonic dynasty in 1270. The spread of Amharic over an ever-increasing area of the Ethiopian highlands accompanied the successive conquests of various Ethiopian rulers, and was consolidated by the practice adopted first by King Amdä S'eyon[6] in the fourteenth century, and more recently by Emperors Menilek II and Haile Sellassie in the late nineteenth and first half of the twentieth centuries, of settling colonists in the newly absorbed areas. Interestingly, not all these settlers in the new territories were native Amhara, but Amharic was the language used by them, such was its status as the principal Ethiopian lingua franca already.

The Amharas had originated from the area that sometimes bore their name, in what is now central Ethiopia.[7] With their rise to power they assumed the role of the inheritors of the Christian Aksumite tradition, a connection promoted by the legend of a dynastic origin traced through the kings of Aksum to the union of King Solomon and the Queen of Sheba. The ensuing process of amharization entailed not only the adoption of the Amharic language, but also the acceptance of the Ethiopian Orthodox faith such that the two became inseparable, and for some other ethnic groups in Ethiopia today the term for 'Amhara' also means Orthodox Christian. Amharic therefore has a long history as the lingua franca of Christian Ethiopia. Already by 1620, a Portuguese Jesuit visitor to Ethiopia noted that Amharic was widely used as a means of intercommunication between the Ethiopian kingdom's linguistically diverse peoples.

Whilst Ge'ez retained its role as the language of the Church and the primary written language of the kingdom, Amharic became the language of government and was characterized as the 'language of the king', or *lessanä negus* in Ge'ez. There are

---

[6] Ge'ez, Amharic, and Tigrinya names and terms are rendered in a systematic transcription, aside from a handful of names that have a more or less accepted spelling in English, such as Haile Sellassie, Addis Ababa, etc.

[7] The modern region called Amhara covers a much larger area than the ancient region.

however some surviving examples of written Amharic from before the modern period. The oldest surviving pieces are the famous 'Royal Songs'. These were originally oral compositions, panegyrics in praise of Kings Amdä S'eyon, Yeshaq, and Zär'a Ya'eqob, and later Gälawdéwos, and thus variously date from the fourteenth through to the sixteenth centuries, though they were written down at a later date. To these poems can be added further texts of the same genre, such as four short poems in praise of Abalä Krestos, celebrating his feats in the wars against the Oromo at the time of Kings Särs'ä Dengel and Susenyos, that is towards the end of the sixteenth and at the beginning of the seventeenth centuries. It is a matter of speculation, but it is likely that similar, originally oral praise poetry may come to light in future, in the endnotes of Ethiopian manuscripts. Clearly this kind of material must have been frequently composed when the occasion arose. What is fortuitous, however, and of great value for the history of Amharic, is that, for whatever reason, someone chose to write these particular poems down, where hundreds of others would have continued to be transmitted orally and must eventually have been forgotten.

The vestiges of written Amharic are not, however, entirely restricted to secular literature. Stemming from the seventeenth century onwards, and just possibly from the late sixteenth century, we also find some examples of texts in the field of religious polemics, ostensibly composed in response to the missionary activities of the Jesuits in Ethiopia. The latter are known to have prepared materials in Amharic in promotion of the Catholic faith, adopting what was for Ethiopia the novel idea of using the vernacular in religious teaching. The Ethiopian response was to counter these with Orthodox instructional texts written in Amharic, or in a mixture of Ge'ez and Amharic, thus rendering them more readily accessible to the ordinary cleric and his flock. In addition, it seems likely that the Amharic translations of a number of originally Ge'ez treatises on various aspects of the Christian religion were made in this period.

When we look at the type of material in Amharic that was committed to writing before the nineteenth century – panegyric poetry, religious polemics, biblical exegesis, magico-medical and therapeutic texts, and lexical material in traditional grammars, called *säwasew* – we may suspect that a large part of it originated as orally transmitted texts, with the presumed exception of religious polemics and perhaps at least some of the lexical and grammatical material. Even the latter, though, to some extent may well have originated in oral transmission in the context of the traditional church school. Throughout the history of Ethiopian literature up to the nineteenth century, Ge'ez, as the language of the church, as has already been remarked, remained essentially unchallenged in its position as the language of literacy in Christian Ethiopia.

The second half of the nineteenth century, however, saw a resurgence and consolidation of imperial power in Ethiopia after over two centuries of decline, fragmentation, and decentralization of the state into the hands of local rulers and warlords. In some ways, this was in response to challenges offered by renewed contact with

Europe, not only through missionaries, but also travellers, merchants, and official envoys from European governments. In the earlier part of the century, correspondence with European governments had begun to be written in Amharic and not in Ge'ez or Arabic (as the 'international' language of the wider region). Even rulers whose first language was not Amharic, like Säbagades of Tigray, chose to write in Amharic and not his native Tigrinya. It is in this connection highly significant that Téwodros II (ruled 1855–68), who essentially embodied the resurgence of the Ethiopian state, not only conducted his international correspondence in Amharic, but also elected to have his official history[8] written in Amharic, and not Ge'ez like his predecessors. Thereafter, Amharic became the written language of secular business, including an emerging written literature. Even during the reign of the Tigrean emperor, Yohannes IV (ruled 1872–89), whose first language was Tigrinya and for whom Tigrinya was most likely his preferred spoken language, Amharic was established as the language of government. So, by this time, Amharic had developed as the literary and political lingua franca of Ethiopia, 'not confined to its native speakers but . . . a vehicle for the expression of what we may call, for lack of a better term, Abyssinian cultural and political life' (Bahru 2004: 310).

In the twentieth century, the process of amharization, especially in terms of language, moved from being a more or less automatic part of the process of an expanding Ethiopian empire to become deliberate government policy. Emperor Haile Sellassie (ruled 1930–74) continued the centralization policies of his immediate predecessors, particularly after his restoration in 1941 following the Italian 'interlude'. He promoted the expansion of a modern, Western-style education system and the consolidation of a modern military and state bureaucracy with Amharic as the common language across his multi-ethnic empire. Under Haile Sellassie, Amharic was the only Ethiopian language used in education, replacing English in primary schools in 1963. Out of the country's ninety or so living languages only Amharic and Tigrinya were permitted in publishing and broadcasting. Aside from a few rare publications mostly by foreigners, such as Bible translations or catechismal and instructional material by missionaries, or collections of oral literature by scholars, no other Ethiopian languages had at the time been committed to writing, apart of course from Ge'ez. Missionaries were allowed to give some initial instruction through the medium of local languages, which were always other than Amharic as missionary activity was only permitted in areas in which the Ethiopian Orthodox Church was not already well established, but they were required to move on to Amharic once their students' knowledge of the language was deemed sufficient. The de facto dominance of Amharic was further more given legal status in the Revised Constitution of 1955, which stated for the first time that Amharic was the official language of Ethiopia, and as such was to be used in schools, in legal transactions (albeit with the right to have an interpreter), in government business, in the media, and indeed in everything down to banknotes and postage stamps. It is worth

---

[8] There are in fact three chronicles of Téwodros's reign.

mentioning in this connection that during the period from 1952 to 1962, when Eritrea was federated to Ethiopia, Arabic and Tigrinya were the official languages there and both were used in Eritrean schools, but when Eritrea was fully reincorporated into the Ethiopian state in 1962 Amharic was imposed as the medium of instruction (Cooper 1976: 188–9; Bahru 2004: 312).

This language policy was an integral and in many ways an inevitable part of the centralist concept of national integration and the centralized state that the imperial government was creating. In this kind of system tolerance of multilingualism at the state level is typically perceived as conducive to regional or ethnic separatism, and the notion that other languages should be fostered is unthinkable. However, by the mid-1960s and early 1970s various challenges began to be heard in the form of a growing regional and ethno-nationalist awareness and the call for linguistic representation. Two languages in particular benefited from Ethiopia's response: Somali, which became the first Ethiopian language other than Amharic to have a programme on Radio Ethiopia, and Tigrinya, which was given greater freedom in printed media. Some materials in Tigrinya had been published before, but the scale had been small and very much localized. Both of these responses were obviously linked to immediate political pressures, in the first instance as a reaction to unrest in the Somali-inhabited region of Ogaden and the newly emergent independent Somalia, and in the second to growing calls for a return to Eritrean self-determination. Language had now firmly become an integral part of nationalist and ethnic consciousness in Ethiopia.

Calls for the recognition of other ethnicities and other languages were not, however, the only challenge to the ever-increasingly centralized and amharicized Ethiopia of Haile Sellassie. A growing radical voice, mostly from politicized student movements which had adopted a leftist, Marxist stance, led inexorably after 1970 to the events of the Ethiopian revolution of 1974. Even though at first this took the form of a relatively benign military-led coup, the Marxist voice quickly prevailed and became the ideology of the new regime after the seizure of power within a matter of months by junior officers under Mängestu Haylä Maryam and the 'Därg' ('committee' in Amharic). One of the principles of the Marxist ideology espoused by the new government was the right of nationalities to self-determination, albeit after the model of the Soviet Union. The Marxism of the Därg was to a large extent a political veneer rather than a genuine conviction, more 'rhetorical than real' (Bahru 2004: 313), necessitated by the switching of sources of foreign aid from the West headed by the United States, as had been the case under Haile Sellassie, to the Soviet Union and her allies, especially the German Democratic Republic. As far as the recognition of the rights of nationalities went, this meant that there was a great deal of talk but what was done was superficial, and no room was allowed for anything that might jeopardize national and territorial integrity. On the one hand, the Programme of the Revolutionary Government declared 'all necessary effort will be made to free the diversified cultures of Ethiopia from Imperialist culture', and 'no nationality will dominate another one since the history, culture, language and religion of each nationality will have equal recognition'. On the other hand, however, calls for the separation of Eritrea were met with an even heavier iron fist than before, leading to a full-scale war in the north which ended in 1991 in the fall of the Därg.

Nonetheless, noticeable progress was made in the question of language rights when compared with what was permitted under the imperial government. Oromo, which has as many first-language speakers as Amharic, or more according to some authorities, but which had suffered severe repression before, obtained its first weekly newspaper, *Barissa*, published like all newspapers by the Ministry of Information. Limited radio broadcasting in Oromo and Tigrinya was also begun. Taking Amharic as a compulsory part of the school-leaving certificate examinations was stopped. Most importantly of all, however, literacy classes were introduced for regional languages. This began with just Oromo and Tigrinya. Tigrinya, of course, had already been committed to writing, using the same script as Amharic, in the nineteenth century. The number of languages in the literacy campaign was later expanded in stages to fifteen selected languages by 1984, which it was claimed covered over 90 per cent of the country's population. These were Amharic, Oromo, Tigrinya, Wolaytta, Somali, Hadiyya, Kambaata, Gedeo, Tigre, Kunama, Sidamo, Silt'e, Afar, Kafa-Mocha, and Saho. Whilst most of the languages in the list are obvious choices because of their relatively large number of speakers (i.e. over 500,000), Saho has today just over 200,000 speakers, and a language not in the list, Gamo, has almost 600,000. The Mass Literacy Programme was to produce not only literacy-training materials in the various languages, but also other printed media. However, as has been the case elsewhere in Africa, the programme was impeded by the lack of resources, both trained teachers and teaching materials, and, more significantly, learners were not always convinced of the value of acquiring literacy in these languages when Amharic remained so essential to careers and advancement within the country. Amharic was still required to proceed through the education system, and was a *sine qua non* for career progression within business, government, and the military.

Literacy in the selected languages was also taught exclusively through the Ethiopian script, which was held by the regime as a mark of national integrity and national heritage. The Ethiopian script is a syllabary in which the letters represent combinations of thirty-three consonant symbols and seven vowels. As such, it is not as easily adaptable to other phonemic systems as, say, an alphabet would be. It is thus ill-suited to representing most of the languages in the literacy list that have different phonemic systems from Amharic and Tigrinya, especially larger vowel inventories. It was also perceived by some nationalistic and separatist groups, and particularly the Oromo Liberation Front (OLF), as being too closely allied to the Amhara-led regime and was thus rejected along with all things 'Abyssinian'. Accordingly, already in 1974 the OLF chose to adopt a Latin-based alphabet which was being developed and used by exiled groups.

As the two largest languages of the country aside from Amharic, Oromo and Tigrinya occupied and still occupy a special place in the debate about language rights and language use in Ethiopia (and now Eritrea in the case of Tigrinya). Oromos and Tigreans were in the forefront of the demand for the use of their own languages in all the apparatus of modern life in Ethiopia. Language rights were conceived as one of the first and most tangible facets of the recognition of other ethnicities' rights. Tigrinya, as was mentioned above, does have a history as a written language. It is mentioned in some of the oldest European sources on Ethiopia, for example in Job Ludolf's writings of the 1690s, as well as indigenous texts,[9] but there do not seem to be any extant examples of written Tigrinya before the nineteenth century, aside perhaps from a very brief Tigrinya–Turkish and a Tigrinya–Arabic vocabulary, both in a manuscript which has been dated to the seventeenth or eighteenth century. All other instances of early written Tigrinya are securely datable to the nineteenth century. The earliest is the customary law code known as the Statute of Loggo Sarda, presumably originally transmitted orally like other local law codes. A translation of the Gospels was made by Däbtära Matéwos of 'Adwa in the 1830s, though this was not published until 1866. Almost all the other Tigrinya texts published in the nineteenth century were produced as a direct result of European missionary activity, both the Catholic Mission and more particularly the Swedish Evangelical Mission. The closing years of the century, however, saw the production of three original pieces of Tigrinya writing by Fesseha Giyorgis, two of which were published in Rome in 1895 and 1897, respectively, whilst the third, a history of Ethiopia, was not published until 1987. Under the British Mandate, Eritrea had had its first Tigrinya-language newspaper, 'The Eritrean Weekly News' (*Nay Eretra Sämunawi Gazét'a* in Tigrinya) founded in 1942 by the British Information Services, but this ceased when all Eritrean newspapers were banned in 1953 by the imperial government. Oromo, on the other hand, had only been written by missionaries and foreign scholars, usually using the Ethiopian syllabary. Amongst the earliest publications were a handful of European grammars and dictionaries dating from the second half of the nineteenth century, and a spelling book published in 1894 and a translation of the Bible published in Switzerland in 1899, both by Onesimus Nesib. There was no tradition of an indigenously produced written literature. Oromo was and is, however, a major lingua franca in southern parts of Ethiopia, vying with Amharic in this role, used in everyday transactions, especially in the marketplace, by various peoples with different first languages.

---

[9] An especially interesting reference was made by the Italian scholar Carlo Conti Rossini in his introduction to Mauro da Leonessa's Tigrinya Grammar, where he speaks of land contracts from Endä Abba Matta that show 'indications from the 13th century that the Tigrinya language was already formed'. He also mentions an Eritrean monk called Yeshaq who between 1403 and 1450 is said to have written in Tigrinya. What exactly constituted these 'indications' and what any such early Tigrinya material might have been is not now known.

15.3 Ethiopia after 1991

The Tigrean-led government[10] that overthrew Mängestu Haylä Maryam's regime in 1991 instituted an essentially decentralized system, giving unprecedented powers to the country's major ethnic groups and totally reorganizing the administrative map of Ethiopia along broadly ethnic lines. By 1996 the old provinces, some of which had existed in one form or another for centuries, whilst others dated only to the conquests of the late nineteenth and early twentieth centuries, had been scrapped and eleven new 'states' or regions (*kellel* in Amharic) were created, many of which bear names deriving from the principal ethnic groups inhabiting them: Amhara, Oromia, Afar, Benishangul-Gumuz, Somali, and so on. The process of division was instituted in 1994, when Ethiopia became the Federal Democratic Republic of Ethiopia with a two-tiered hierarchy of a central federal government and ethnically based regional states with their own internal government structures. From the point of view of language rights, whilst Amharic remains the working language of the government, the regions and sub-zones have been given the right to chose their own working language and medium of instruction in primary education. Most have chosen the principal language of the region in each case. Amharic is taught as a subject in schools, including where it is not the first language, but a varying mixture of Amharic and English remains the language of instruction at the secondary level, and English retains its position at the tertiary level.

The language policies of the post-1991 government have not, however, been completely without problems. Many parents whose first language is not Amharic or who come from a non-Amhara background still feel that Amharic provides a better opportunity for their children than a local language. Some ethnic groups, such as the Kambaata in the awkwardly named 'Southern Nations, Nationalities and Peoples' Region' (SNNPR), have chosen to keep with Amharic, whilst their neighbours and linguistic close relatives, the Hadiyya, have opted for their own language. In the process of language development, the Ethiopian government has also given nationalities the choice of developing orthographies for their languages in either an Ethiopian script-based format or in a Latin-based one, recalling the controversies that beset Oromo in the 1970s. There have been disastrous moves, too: the SNNPR, which is perhaps the most linguistically diverse of the regions, was more or less obliged to choose Amharic as its working language because of the absence of an obvious local candidate in such a complex area, whilst the various sub-zones have chosen their own local languages. The complexity of the language situation even at this level, however, led to a linguistic experiment that ended in popular unrest, showing all too graphically how language has become a sensitive issue in the new ethnically defined Ethiopia. An attempt was made artificially to coalesce four closely related Omotic languages, Wolaytta, Gamo, Gofa, and Dawro into a single 'pan-dialect' dubbed Wogagoda, an acronym formed

---

[10] This was formed out of the erstwhile Ethiopian People's Revolutionary Democratic Front (EPRDF) which was dominated by the Tigrean People's Liberation Front (TPLF).

from the first syllables of each language's name. After riots and interventions by federal troops this ill-conceived creation had to be withdrawn.[11]

An increasingly important factor in language use in Ethiopia today is, as elsewhere in Africa, the growing rate of urbanization and the move of ever-increasing numbers of people to the towns. Ethiopia remains an essentially rural and agrarian society, but the towns and cities are growing: in 1970 the population of Addis Ababa was estimated at 683,500 but by 1995/6 it had reached around 2,084,000. A series of four studies published in 1976 and headed by Robert L. Cooper concluded that Amharic was the major language used in Ethiopian towns, followed closely by Tigrinya (in the north, in Tigray and Eritrea), and then by Oromo (mostly in the west of the country).[12] Amongst factory workers Amharic and Oromo were the commonest languages, both as first and second languages, though Amharic was used by almost 95 per cent of the non-Amharic first-language speakers. Amongst university students, unsurprisingly, Amharic was the language with both the largest number of first-language speakers and the main or only second language of the others. The study on language use in markets, however, did not reveal an overall lingua franca, which was an unexpected result for the researchers. Markets are of course archetypically multi-ethnic environments in Ethiopia, drawing people in from the countryside within a sometimes considerable radius and in a naturally linguistically complex environment various languages are regularly used. Markets, unlike towns, let alone factories or universities, are an ancient institution in Ethiopia and traders have long been accustomed to speaking at least enough of their customers' language(s) to facilitate business, thus impeding the emergence of a single trade lingua franca. A more recent study of language use amongst school students in Ethiopian towns (Meyer and Richter 2003) also reveals the predominant position of Amharic in the urban environment, 65.2 per cent of the non-Amhara students interviewed being bilingual with Amharic besides their first language, with a further 11 per cent being multilingual with Amharic besides another or other Ethiopian language(s) and their first language. As Bahru (2004: 315) says, there is evidence for what has been characterized as 'linguistic migration' to the towns in search of Amharic. This situation on the ground will only help to reinforce the dominant position of Amharic whatever the politico-linguistic sensitivities and aspirations of other nationalities might indicate. Somewhat tellingly, Bahru (ibid.: 303) recounts the story of the meeting to ratify the charter of the Transitional Government of Ethiopia after the fall of the regime of Mängestu Haylä Maryam in 1991, where the first order of business was to determine the working language of the meeting. Recognizing the difficulty of getting interpreters for all the various first languages of the delegates, the decision was taken to adopt Amharic, which everyone knew, whilst organizations that had brought interpreters would be permitted to use their own languages if they wished. The Eritrean leader chose to speak in Tigrinya, but was visibly dissatisfied

---

[11] Ironically, *Ethnologue* (2005) still regards these as dialects of a single language.
[12] Chapters 11, 13, 15, and 16 in Bender et al. (1976).

by the Amharic translation that his interpreter produced, Bahru says, as he obviously knew the language better than the interpreter. The spokesman of the Oromo OLF spoke in Oromo, but his speech was translated into English, presumably because of the OLF's total rejection of Amharic. The majority of the other delegates and representatives there, however, did not have sufficient English to understand the translation and so could not follow the OLF presentation. This and the various studies quoted above serve to highlight that because of its history Amharic remains to date the most effective and most widely used medium of inter-ethnic communication in Ethiopia. With the course of time, Tigrinya and Oromo as the two other large languages of the country are increasingly challenging that position as languages of wider communication, but their scope is likely to remain within relatively restricted areas, Tigrinya in the north and Oromo in the west and a good part of the south. Other languages, like Afar, Somali, Wolaytta, Sidamo, and so on, are likely to retain even more clearly defined regional importance.

15.4 Eritrea after 1993

There are nine languages spoken in Eritrea: in descending order of numbers of speakers, Tigrinya, Tigre, Saho, Afar, Beja, Kunama, Nara, Bilin, and Rasha'ida Arabic. The first four of these are also spoken in Ethiopia. The Arabic of the Rasha'ida is a Hijazi dialect that was introduced into Eritrea by a small number of immigrants from the coast of the Arabian side of the Red Sea in the nineteenth century. In addition to these indigenous languages, English and Standard Arabic are also recognized as working languages of the country, and there are still a few Italian speakers as a result of Eritrea's colonial experience. Amharic is also spoken to a degree by educated Eritreans as a legacy of the period when the country formed part of Ethiopia. Tigrinya, with approximately 1.2 million speakers in Eritrea according to *Ethnologue* (2005), and Tigre, with around 800,000, are by far the largest languages of the country.[13] Both belong to the Ethiopian Semitic family of languages and are closely related to one another, together forming the northern branch of the family along with Ge'ez. An additional member of this branch, and therefore an additional Eritrean language, may be Dahalik spoken on the Dahlak Islands off the Eritrean coast. At present there is a debate whether this is indeed a separate language or a particularly divergent dialect of Tigre, and it is as such not recognized by the Eritrean government as a separate language in its language programmes. Of the other languages, Saho, Afar, Beja, and Bilin belong to the Cushitic family, and Kunama and Nara form independent branches of the Nilo-Saharan phylum or super-family.

---

[13] There are probably more speakers of Tigrinya in Eritrea than this figure as censuses suggest that Tigrinya speakers form around 50 per cent of the population of Eritrea, which in 1992 was 4,298,269. Similarly, Tigre speakers are said to form around 31 per cent of the population, which would raise the number of speakers to around 1.3 million.

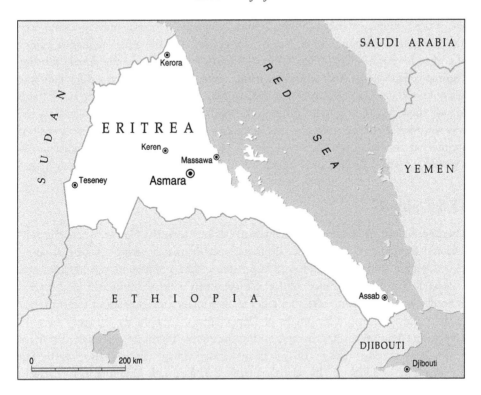

Eritrea

The struggle for Eritrean independence from Ethiopia was initially led by the Eritrean Liberation Front (ELF) and the Eritrean People's Liberation Front (EPLF). The former was dominated by Muslim lowlanders and had adopted a 'pan-Arab' revolutionary identity, and the latter by Christian highlanders with a more Marxist stance, and mostly Tigrinya speakers. The EPLF eventually dominated, also spearheading the fall of the regime of Mängestu Haylä Maryam in northern Ethiopia, and then under Isayyas Afäwärqi secured the formal independence of Eritrea from Ethiopia after the referendum of 1993.

The pre-eminent position of Tigrinya as the principal language of Eritrea was thus secured not only on grounds of numerical superiority. However, just as was the case in Ethiopia, the new Eritrean government readily espoused a programme of recognizing and empowering the different nationalities of the country. The nine languages of Eritrea are all being developed for use in primary education, which has necessitated a programme of standardization, including developing orthographies and teaching materials. Only Tigrinya had been written before, apart from the usual missionary and foreign scholarly materials, and some small-scale productions by expatriate communities, such as a Bilin dictionary and a grammar published in Sweden and Norway, respectively. The Eritrean Ministry of Education adopted the policy of restricting the

use of the Ethiopian syllabary to the Semitic languages Tigrinya and Tigre, and promoted the development of Latin-based orthographies for the other languages, except
of course for Arabic. There was some resistance, however, from the largely Muslim
Tigre speakers who wished, on the one hand, not to use the Ethiopian script which was
felt to be too closely linked with Orthodox Christian culture, and on the other hand
to have their children educated through the medium of Arabic. The familiar concern
was voiced that education in minority languages could be a handicap whereas use of
an international language like Arabic would give students access to the wider world.
Tigrinya, Standard Arabic, and English are used in secondary and tertiary education.

15.5 Djibouti

The Republic of Djibouti (capital Djibouti) lies between the Gulf of Aden, the self-
declared Republic of Somaliland, Ethiopia, and Eritrea, covering an area of some
23,000 square kilometres, and with estimates of the population varying between
c. 500,000 and 800,000. Since 1862 there has been a French presence in the area,
although it was not until 1896 that a decree was made bringing about the existence
of the Côte Française des Somalis et Dependances. In 1946 the territory became
a Territoire Française d'Outre-mer, taking the name Territoire Française des Afars
et des Issas in 1967, and in 1977 it gained independence from France, becoming
the Republic of Djibouti. In terms of language, although Djibouti is a relatively
small country, there is not one major indigenous language, rather two, Somali and
Afar, spoken by roughly half of the indigenous population each. The languages are
related, both being members of the Lowland East Cushitic branch of Afro-Asiatic.
Both groups of speakers share the same religion, Islam, and are predominantly
nomadic pastoralists herding camels and sheep and goats and neither are restricted
to the territory of Djibouti, with the Afars living also in Eritrea and in Ethiopia
and the Somalis in the self-declared Republic of Somaliland, Somalia, Ethiopia, and
Kenya.

Being a major port in the Gulf of Aden, just south of the Red Sea, the capital of
Djibouti is a cosmopolitan place with communities of speakers of other languages.
A large community of Yemeni Arabic speakers live in the city engaged in trade and
business and speak the variety of Arabic from Yemen. The other significant expatriate
community is the French who still have a noticeable presence in the capital and work
in various spheres such as education and the military. In the streets of Djibouti one can
also hear Amharic, Harari, Greek, Hindi, and Tigrinya, although these are spoken by
relatively few people.

When it comes to national language, neither Afar nor Somali functions in this
way. The two national languages are French and Arabic, despite the fact that for
most inhabitants these languages are little used in daily life. This status of national
language is reflected in a number of ways. For example, in the constitution it is
stated that for a person to be eligible for election as a member of the Assemblée

Nationale that person must know how to read and write, and must speak French or Arabic fluently. By Arabic here is meant modern standard literary Arabic rather than a particular colloquial variety. Laws are drafted in these two languages as are communications and official correspondence predominantly, although it seems that French is used a little more than Arabic and that it is more prominent, perhaps due to the fact that most educated adults have had an education in French rather than Arabic.

The other area in which the status of the languages is important is in education. Government-provided education follows the French system although Afar and Somali are used to some extent in the first stages and this can lead to there being predominantly Somali or Afar schools. There are also schools funded by Islamic organizations in which Arabic is the medium of education.

What is interesting about Djibouti is the way in which language and identity are concentrated in such a small country in two distinct languages. There is a sense in which the two indigenous languages and the associated communities are in a greater 'competitive' environment than in countries where there is a greater number of languages, and in order for there not to be any sense of favouring one or the other, neither has been given the status of a national language, such a status being instead accorded to the two foreign-origin languages French and Arabic, which have become prominent in Djibouti for historical and religious reasons.

15.6 Somalia/Somaliland

Turning to the much larger southern neighbour of Djibouti, Somalia is often pointed to as an example of a monoglot state in Africa and can therefore be seen as a rarity on a continent (or indeed in the whole world) where linguistic diversity within countries is the norm. However, to look at Somalia or Somali just from this perspective is to miss important issues which relate to language and identity for the Somali people as a whole. The Somalis inhabit the Horn of Africa east of a line running from southwest Djibouti to the River Tana in Kenya, which encompasses the Republic of Somalia, the self-declared Republic of Somaliland,[14] and parts of Djibouti, Ethiopia, and Kenya. In other words it is not just the case that Somalia is a country in which only Somali is spoken; rather Somali is spoken in four countries, or five according to whether Somaliland is seen as a separate country or not. Much of Somali politics during the 1960s and the 1970s, as was also the case prior to independence, was concerned with addressing this issue of a single people being divided by borders imposed from outside. The way this was handled was a contributory factor to the military coup in 1969 and also led to conflict in 1977–78 with Ethiopia in the Ogaden war which caused great upheaval in the area, the reverberations of which continue today. At the core of the

---

[14] Somaliland claimed independence in 1991 from the rest of Somalia. It is the territory that had been the British Somaliland Protectorate and joined to form Somalia in 1960 when it and the UN Trusteeship of Somalia, administered by Italy, became independent.

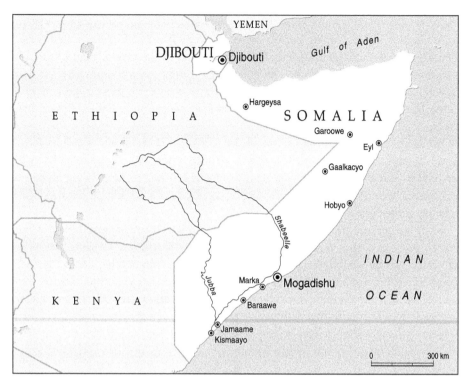

Somalia and Djibouti

common Somali identity traversing official state boundaries was, and still is, the Somali language, along with Islam and a shared socio-economic system based predominantly on nomadic pastoralism.

Somali is a member of the lowland East Cushitic branch of Afro-Asiatic and specifically of a sub-branch known as Omo-Tana which includes also Rendille, Boni, Dhaasenech, and Bayso although all of these languages have far fewer than the estimated 12.5 million Somali speakers.[15] The Somali language can be divided into a number of dialect groups (see, for example, Lamberti 1986: 14–32). The 'Northern' dialects are spoken predominantly by the nomadic pastoralists and, despite the 'Northern' labelling given to the group in English, also in western and southwestern regions of the Somali territories. The Somali name for this dialect group, Af Maxaad Tidhi, which does not link it to any particular geographical region but instead refers to a grammatical difference between this dialect group and others, is probably a better appellation. The Central dialects, comprising the May and Digil dialect groups, are spoken by the sedentary agriculturalists living between the two main rivers, the Jubba and the Shabeelle, in the central portion of the Somali territories. Elsewhere there are the Benaadir dialects, spoken along the southern coast and also some parts of

[15] http://www.ethnologue.com/show_language.asp?code=som

southern-central Somalia, and Ashraaf, a dialect spoken just in Mogadishu and in the region around and to the north of Marka on the coast southwest of Mogadishu. It seems that these mutually intelligible Benaadir dialect groups are closer to the Northern dialects than to the Central dialects. Despite the existence of such dialect differences, however, all Somalis understand what is now referred to as Standard Somali and in general see themselves as speaking one language, although, particularly for the Af May speakers their particular dialect is an important part of their identity within Somali society as a whole.

Looking to the country of Somalia, rather than the territory of the language, which stretches across multiple states, a few minority languages exist alongside Somali there, though the territory of Somaliland has no linguistic minorities. With regard to Cushitic languages, in parts of the southwestern regions there are groups of Oromo speakers and, in the far south, Boni. Along the southern coast of Somalia there are communities speaking northern varieties of the Swahili language complex: KiBajuni is spoken along part of the coastal strip in the region of the lower Jubba and especially in the town of Kismaayo, and Chi-Mwiini is spoken in the town of Baraawe (Brava) and along the adjacent coast and the Bajun Islands where it tends to be referred to as Bajuni. A further Bantu languages, Mushungulu, is spoken along the banks of the Jubba in the vicinity of the town of Jamaame and is regarded as corresponding to the Shambaa language of Tanzania (according to W. I. G. Möhlig, as mentioned in Lamberti 1986: 33).

What is now referred to as Standard Somali in English, the language that is used by major broadcasters such as the BBC World Service and also in much written communication, is based on the Northern dialect group, or Maxaad Tidhi dialects. It developed in this way because these dialects were already being used as a lingua franca prior to broadcasting and mass media. Two things contributed to this: firstly the Maxaad Tidhi dialects were the most widespread, being spoken by nomadic pastoralists who move around many parts of the Somali territories, and secondly the most familiar poetry in the language was that of the nomads – as these poems could quickly spread far, the language in which they were composed came to be heard more widely. One feature of Standard Somali which must be emphasized however is that it is not standardized in any official way and the label 'Standard' seems less the label of a particular variety and more the label of a range of varieties which are generally accepted as being understood by any other speaker of Somali. This allows for some variation in the Standard variety, variations from which speakers of the language can tell the area where a person is likely to be from. For example the verb *yidhi* takes a set of prefixes to mark person in the variety spoken in the northern regions, but in southern regions it is likely that people will conjugate the verb with suffixes, leading to northern *wuu yidhi* 'he said' contrasting with southern *wuu dhahay* 'he said', both variations being understood by all speakers.

Let us now turn to the writing of the Somali language and its status as a national language. The importance of writing Somali became particularly prominent when the inhabitants of both the British Protectorate, corresponding to the north-west of present-day Somalia (the self-declared Republic of Somaliland) and the Italian-administered UN Trusteeship, corresponding to the south of the country, were looking towards independence as a single Somali state governed by Somalis themselves. Although there had been much discussion about devising a standard orthography for the language well before independence, no decision had been made as to which script to adopt, and it was this that hindered the adoption of Somali as an official language on independence in 1960. Since officials of the newly independent Somalia came from both the (former) British- and Italian-governed territories, some had the habit of using Italian for written communication, having been educated through Italian, whereas others used English, as the result of an English-medium education. Whilst it was the case that some of these people also knew Arabic and could communicate in writing through this language, it was nevertheless the case that the European languages continued to be very much used in official communications, leading to the odd situation in which written communications sometimes had to be translated from one European language to the other in order for Somali officials to understand them; and this when these officials would have been able to communicate in speech in Somali with no difficulty. It was not until 1972, when the military regime of Mohamed Siyaad Barre decreed that the Latin alphabet be used to represent Somali, that a writing system was finally officially adopted. The actual story of choosing the script which preceded the 1972 decree involved various issues relating to identity, and so we shall look at it in some detail here.

The earliest known way of writing Somali was with Arabic script. The Arabic language has for a long time been part of Somali life through learning and reading the Qur'an and other religious texts, and various scholars would gain a good knowledge of Arabic through the study of Islamic texts and through travel to centres of learning both in the Horn of Africa and further afield. Such scholars and also those who had the benefit of more extensive religious education were then able to use the language as a means of written communication. It is important to stress here that it was the Arabic language itself that was used in these instances rather than Somali written in the Arabic alphabet. However, the Arabic alphabet was additionally used to render Somali as well in certain instances and a few examples of this have become known, the most famous being a poem by Sheekh Uweys al-Baraawi (published in Cerulli 1964). It is also known that there were written communications in which parts were written in Arabic (language and script) and other parts were written in Somali using the Arabic alphabet. For the vast majority of Somalis, though, written communication was simply not part of their lives. If they wanted to send a message to someone else far away it would normally be done by oral means, giving the message to someone who was travelling in the relevant direction and who would then pass the message on to the receiver or possibly pass it on to someone else who would take it further. Poetry, which is central to Somali culture, was also passed on in this way and types of poetry which poets wanted to be heard more widely would be composed, memorized, and recited verbatim to the extent that there arose a 'definitive text' of the poem (Orwin 2003).

In the middle of the twentieth century, when the sense of a need to write Somali increased considerably, various candidates began to make themselves apparent. These were the Arabic alphabet, the Latin alphabet, and thirdly, the possibility of an indigenous writing system. Arabic script, as we have seen, had been used for Somali to a certain extent prior to this, but not in any systematic or standardized way, and it was with a view to achieving a standardized orthography that various attempts were made to develop a writing system based on Arabic, which could then stand as a candidate for official acceptance.

Curiously the first published attempt at this had actually been made much earlier by a British Indian army captain in 1887 who published his system in the *Indian Antiquary* (King 1887). Later, and at a time when it might more readily be taken up, the famous Somali scholar and poet Muuse Galaal published another system (Muuse 1954). The arguments in favour of adopting the Arabic alphabet were that it was known to many people through their religious education which, even if it was only slight, involved learning to read the Qur'an in Arabic. Also the very fact that the alphabet was the one used in the Qur'an gave it a status higher than the other candidates from a religious perspective and thus from the perspective of the Somalis' identity as Muslims. There was also the sense that using the Arabic alphabet would be an outward sign that the country and its people were more closely associated with the Islamic and the Arabic-speaking world than with the Western world. While these were the pros, the cons related to the fact that the sounds of Somali could not all easily be accommodated by the alphabet as it stood. This was particularly the case with the vowels. Arabic has three letters which represent long vowels and three diacritic marks which represent the three short vowels. In Somali on the other hand there are five long and five short vowels. Although it was possible to develop a script which could easily be rendered in handwriting, it was pointed out that there would have to be modifications to printing machines and typewriters which would have been expensive and time-consuming and likely to remain as a continual problem.

The second candidate for a script was an indigenous invented script. A UNESCO commission in the 1960s set up to help the newly independent state find a writing system looked at no less than ten unique Somali national scripts (Laitin 1977: 87). Of these only one had been used to any significant extent, a script called Osmania developed in the 1920s by Osman Yuusuf Keenadiid. As a way of rendering Somali, Osmania functioned very well and so from a technical linguistic perspective was perfectly sound. A second important argument in support of Osmania was the fact that it was indigenous to the Somalis and as such was regarded as an expression of Somali identity. However, for many people the significant clan aspect of Somali identity also entered the equation here and the script was seen by some not so much as a Somali script but as a script of the particular clan of the inventor, namely the Osman Mahmoud branch of the Majerteen, a Daarood clan group. The other issue which went against adopting Osmania was the practical issue of printing and typing, since the machines and technology needed for using this script would all have had to be newly designed and constructed.

The third candidate for the establishment of a standard Somali orthography was a version of the Latin alphabet. The Latin alphabet lent itself well to writing Somali as it could cope with all the sounds in the language. Furthermore, from the perspective of technology it was very suitable since the machines and typewriters used to produce printed English and Italian were readily available. The major argument against the Latin alphabet related to the Somalis' identity both as Somalis and as Muslims, as the Latin alphabet was seen to have been brought to the territory by European powers. Proponents of the Arabic script for some time used the catchy Arabic phrase *Latin laa diin* 'Latin, no religion' to help raise awareness of their viewpoint.

The issue of devising a script for official use in administration figured much in discussion during the run-up to independence, but due to the strong feelings held by the proponents of each of the three potential candidates, this in turn being associated with different aspects of Somali identity (as Somalis, as Muslims, and as members of particular clans), no decision on the adoption of a particular writing system was made, and it was only in 1972 that the military regime of Mohamed Siyaad Barre finally made a choice and decreed that the Latin alphabet would be used. The specific version chosen was that devised by Shire Jama Ahmed, which was based on others such as that developed by Muuse Galaal and B. W. Andrzejewski in a collaborative project set up by the British authorities in Somaliland in the early 1950s. However, unlike the system devised by the latter, Shire's script involved no diacritics or altering of letter shapes, making it much more straightforward to print and to type. Indeed Shire had already used his Latin alphabet script back in the 1960s to print a series of books of poetry, proverbs, and folktales in Somali.[16]

Once the new script was officially adopted, there was a great sense of optimism about the use of Somali language in written form and it was welcomed by the vast majority of people as a further important step in the development of the language the Somalis still feel so proud of. Since 1972, the script has indeed proven to be very successful, particularly so in recent years with the expansion of information and computer technology such as email and the internet in which Somali can now be used with amazing ease.

Following the actual decision to adopt a Latin alphabet script for Somali, the next pressing issue was how people would learn the new script and also how to make Somali the national language of the country. These issues were handled more or less

---

[16] An important footnote to the writing of Somali is that in recent years there has been a movement to create an orthography for the Af May dialect group of Somali, the Central dialects. This has led to the development of an alphabet, based on the Latin alphabet, by a forum called the Kulung Technical Committee in Toronto and London. To what extent this will lead to the regular use of Af May as a written language remains to be seen.

simultaneously. First, Somali was officially pronounced the national language in 1972, as the script was introduced, and came to replace English, Italian, and Arabic in official spheres, with all government employees being required to learn (and be tested in) written Somali. Wider, nationwide literacy campaigns were then undertaken, first in the major towns and afterwards in the countryside, so as to bring knowledge of the script to the general population. These campaigns were staffed by teachers and students including many from secondary schools who were mobilized and travelled around the country teaching in towns, villages, and in makeshift schools in the countryside to members of the nomad population. This brought the new script to the vast majority of Somalis, and the simplicity of the script combined with the fact that the language was now written essentially as it was pronounced meant that there was much hope that literacy among the population would rise quickly. Such developments also had implications for education, as the early stages of school could now be taught in Somali, allowing more people to take greater advantage of public education. Subsequent political developments in the Horn of Africa, however, unfortunately impeded the progress of the spread of literacy, and though the literacy rate increased significantly in the years following 1972, the Ogaden war with Ethiopia in 1977–8, the occurrence of civil war in Somalia in the late 1980s, and the fragmented situation since 1991 have meant that educational opportunities even at the most basic level have remained minimal for much of the population.[17]

For those who have gained access to education, however, the development of a written form of Somali is certainly a major success story in a part of the world which has had more than its fair share of general difficulties over the last three decades. Being able to write the shared language of the nation allowed people to engage in communication in written form in ways that had not previously been possible, in recent years also making use of Somali on the internet. The new use of Somali in official documents from the 1970s onwards resulted in people seeing their Somali identity realized in an important way which had not been present before in the oral culture of the people and allowed people to understand written documents and forms much more readily.[18] Alongside such progress in Somali language matters, it should be noted that Somalia as a country also continued to maintain a linguistic window on the outside world through the teaching of Arabic and English in schools at different levels, and the learning of these languages is still

[17] The authorities in the self-declared Republic of Somaliland have set up schools, as have those in the autonomous region of Puntland. There are also universities in these parts where, in Somaliland at least, all teaching is in English, apart from Somali literature classes. Elsewhere local people and non-governmental organizations have also set up schools, and international organizations such as the Africa Educational Trust based in London have been active in bringing basic education, particularly literacy and numeracy education, to a greater number of people throughout the Somali territories. In spite of such efforts, however, the literacy rate among Somalis as a whole is still among the lowest in the world.

[18] Either through the direct reading of such documents, or, in the case of non-literate members of the population, through having the content of official documents read out aloud by those who had become literate.

very popular among Somalis today when they are presented with the opportunity for this.[19]

While the declaration of Somali as the country's national language and its replacement of English, Italian, and Arabic in official domains has clearly been a very significant, positive development for the country and its population, leading to Somalia being widely feted as a rare example of an African state which has successfully promoted an indigenous language to national and official functions in place of other, ex-colonial languages, a consideration of language and its relevance for national identity should not lose sight of the fact that Somalia has also sadly been wracked by severe domestic conflict in recent decades and a notable absence of national cohesion. A general point to emerge from an examination of language in Somalia is that dominant monolingualism and the sharing of a single culture and religion are no guarantee that a population will remain bound together with a national loyalty superseding loyalties to other social, regional, or political structures, and even largely homogeneous societies such as that of the Somalis may be torn apart by the strength of other forces. The troubles in Somalia over the last two decades causing fragmentation of the country have occurred despite the Somalis sharing a common national language, in which they all take pride, and despite other commonly shared aspects of culture and religion, indicating that such links, even when strong, may not be enough to ensure the unity of a single ethno-linguistic group in the form of a nation-state. What can nevertheless be hoped for in Somalia / Somaliland is that the ability for all Somalis to communicate with each other through the same language, whether orally or in written form, will be of help in the future re-establishment of peace and reconciliation among the Somali people across the range of territory they currently occupy.

---

[19] The existence of a large Somali diaspora in Europe, the Gulf States, and North America is one of the factors which stimulates the learning of these languages.

16
Zambia: 'One Zambia, One Nation, Many Languages'

Lutz Marten and Nancy C. Kula

16.1 Introduction

This chapter aims to give the reader an idea of the linguistic situation in Zambia, and how language relates to national identity in the Zambian context. Zambia lies in the heart of central Africa and shares borders with the Democratic Republic of the Congo (DRC) to the north, with Tanzania, Malawi, and Mozambique in the east, with Zimbabwe, Botswana, and Namibia in the south, and with Angola in the west. Zambia has no direct access to the sea, but the Zambezi, one of Africa's largest rivers, runs through Zambia for about 1,000 kilometres. Zambia also lies in the centre of the Bantu-speaking area. Historically, Bantu languages became widely spoken in sub-Saharan Africa from around 300 BC, and present-day Zambia's Bantu languages are the result of several linguistic developments which introduced the languages spoken today through gradual processes of migration, language contact, and language shift over the last two millennia. From the late nineteenth century onwards, different European languages were introduced into what is now Zambia through missionary activities, in particular in education, and through colonial governance as a British colony. As a legacy of this period, English plays an important role in the current language situation, a role which was affirmed after independence in 1964, when English became the official language. After the change from a one-party system to multiparty democracy in 1991, emphasis has shifted towards the promotion of Zambia's seven national languages, Bemba, Nyanja, Tonga, Lozi, Lunda, Luvale, and Kaonde, and contemporary Zambia is an explicit example of a multilingual country.

Questions of language and identity have played an important role throughout modern Zambian history, particularly after independence, when the question of the national identity of the new state took centre stage. Language in Zambia is important for national, political, and ethnic identities, for communication, education, and popular culture. The language situation in Zambia is in some respects similar to those in other African countries, but has its specific, local characteristics. In particular, the chapter shows that a specific system of multilingual structures and traditions, which has its roots in the period before contact with Europeans, is constitutive of Zambian linguistic identity.

The chapter is arranged as follows. In section 16.2, we provide background information about the languages, language situation, and use of language in Zambia in different domains. Section 16.3 provides a historical account of language distribution, use, and policies in Zambia and how these are related to the formation and negotiation of different identities. Section 16.4 provides a discussion of the contemporary situation in light of the historic background provided, and addresses specific topics which are important in the Zambian context. Finally, section 16.5 summarizes some of the major points of the chapter in its conclusion.

16.2 Languages and Language Use in Zambia

The seemingly easy question of how many languages are spoken in Zambia is actually not an easy one to answer, and estimates vary from about twenty to over eighty. The reasons for this are, on the one hand, the notoriously difficult question of what is a language as opposed to a dialect, and on the other hand, in the Zambian context,

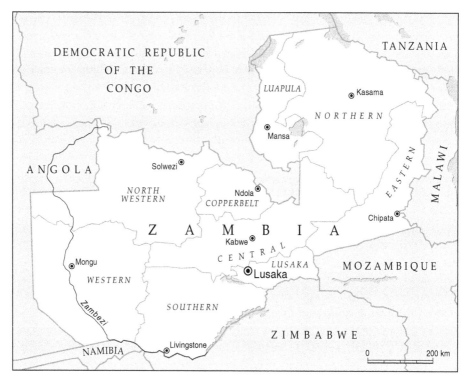

Zambia

the relation between language and tribe (cf. Kashoki 1978). Ethnic identification as tribes, with a chief as leader and focal point, has a long tradition in Zambia and was explicitly manipulated under colonial rule. Today, tribal affiliation is important for both cultural identity and political coalition building (Posner 2005), with the total

Table 16.1 Language groups and dialect clusters of Zambia

Group	Dialect Clusters and Location
A	Aushi, Chishinga, Kabende, Mukulu, Ngumbo, Twa, Unga, Bemba, Bwile, Luunda, Shila, Tabwa (Northern province) Bisa, Kunda (border of Northern and Eastern provinces) Lala, Ambo, Luano, Swaka (Eastern and Central provinces) Lamba, Lima (Copperbelt and Central provinces)
B	Kaonde (North-Western province)
C1	Lozi (Western province)
C2	Kwandi, Kwanga, Mbowe, Mbumi (Western province) Simaa, Imilangu, Mwenyi, Nyengo, Makoma, Liyuwa, Mulonga (Western province) Mashi, Kwandu, Mbukushu (Western province)
D	Lunda, Kosa, Ndembu (North-Western province)
E	Luvale, Luchazi, Mbunda (border of Western and North-Western provinces) Chokwe (North-Western province)
F	Mambwe, Lungu (Northern province) Inamwanga, Iwa, Tambo, Lambya (border of Northern and Eastern provinces)
G	Nyiha, Wandya (border of Northern and Eastern provinces)
H	Nkoya, Lukolwe (or Mbwela), Lushangi, Mashasha (North-Western and border of Western and Southern provinces)
I	Nsenga (Eastern province)
J	Chewa (Nyanja) (Eastern province)
K	Tonga, Toka, Totela, Leya, Subiya, Twa, Shanjo, Fwe (Southern and border of Western and Southern provinces) Ila, Lundwe, Lumbu, Sala (border of Southern and Central provinces) Lenje, Twa (Central province) Soli (Central province)
L	Tumbuka, Fungwe, Senga, Yombe (Eastern province)
M	Goba, Shona (Central province)
N	Chikunda (Central province)
O	Swahili (Northern and Copperbelt provinces)

number of tribes given as seventy-two in both the 1990 and 2000 censuses. However, tribal identity does not correspond directly to linguistic distinctiveness, and there are fewer languages than tribes. In their major survey of language in Zambia, Ohannessian and Kashoki (1978) distinguish eighty-three varieties (excluding European, Indian, and Khoisan languages) which are grouped, based on lexical and grammatical similarity as well as on mutual intelligibility, into twenty-six dialect clusters or 'languages', which in turn are grouped into sixteen groups as represented in Table 16.1, adapted from Ohannessian and Kashoki (1978) (see also Chanda 1996, 2002; Kula 2006; Bickmore 2006).

In addition to these twenty-six clusters of indigenous Bantu languages, the 1978 survey noted European and Asian languages spoken in Zambia, in particular English, which is the official language, as well as Gujarati and, as spoken by less than 1,000 speakers each, Italian, German, Hindu, French, Urdu, and Portuguese. Small communities of Kxoe (San) speakers live in western Zambia, having fled the civil war in neighbouring Angola, numbering approximately 300–400 speakers (Robins et al. 2001).

Table 16.2 Language by numbers of speakers (based on 2000 census)

Language	Use as Predominant Language (%)	Use as Second Language (%)	Language	Use as Predominant Language (%)	Use as Second Language (%)
Bemba	30.1	20.2	English	1.7	26.3
Nyanja	10.7	19.5	Luvale	1.7	1.9
Tonga	10.6	4.4	Lenje	1.4	1.5
Lozi	5.7	5.2	Namwanga	1.3	0.8
Chewa	4.7	2.3	Ngoni	1.2	1.2
Nsenga	3.4	1.6	Mambwe	1.2	0.9
Tumbuka	2.5	1.3	Bisa	1.0	0.4
Lunda	2.2	1.3	Ila	0.8	0.8
Lala	2.0	1.0	Lungu	0.6	0.4
Kaonde	2.0	1.8	Senga	0.6	0.2
Lamba	1.9	1.4			

In terms of language use and numbers of speakers, Zambian languages differ considerably. With respect to these criteria, the main languages of Zambia are Bemba, Nyanja, Tonga, Lozi, and English as shown in Table 16.2, where language use as predominant language (as percentage of the whole population) and as second language (as percentage of those who claim to speak a second language) are given.[1]

---

[1] 8,702,932 was the total number considered as first-language speakers excluding infants and those with speech impairment. 3,385,745 were considered as second-language speakers, making up 34 per cent of the total population. This relatively low number of second-language speakers is probably a reflection of the fact that census data record people's own estimation of their linguistic behaviour and not their actual behaviour.

The data in the Table 16.2 show that Bemba, Nyanja, Tonga, and English are spoken by more than 10 per cent as either first or second language. The table also shows that even a number of the smaller languages are used as second language, and that languages like Luvale and Lenje are spoken by more speakers as second language than as first language, or have as many second-language speakers as first in the case of Ila, even though in all cases they are spoken by less than 2 per cent of the population. This indicates the widespread use of multilingual practices which will be discussed in more detail below. The data in Table 16.2 are based on the level of dialect clusters. However, often language in Zambia is discussed at the group level, rather than at the cluster level, that is, including a number of related varieties. When language use is compared by language groups, the importance of Bemba, Nyanja, Tonga, Lozi, and English becomes even more apparent, as Table 16.3, comparing data over three decades, shows.[2]

Table 16.3 Dialect clusters language use (based on 1980–2000 census)

| Language Group | Percentage of Total Population | | | | | |
| | 1980 | | 1990 | | 2000 | |
	1st lge	2nd lge	1st lge	2nd lge	1st lge	2nd lge
Bemba	39.7	24.4	39.7	27.5	38.5	24.1
Nyanja	19.0	18.0	20.1	25.5	20.6	25.0
Tonga	13.3	7.8	14.8	8.1	13.9	7.7
Lozi	8.0	7.5	7.5	8.4	6.9	6.4
English	4.6	0.8	1.1	17.8	1.7	26.3

As Table 16.3 shows, Bemba (as a language group) is the largest Zambian language spoken as a first language. Nyanja and English have seen the greatest increase in second-language speakers from 1980 to 2000. Bemba, Nyanja, and Tonga are spoken by more than 10 per cent each of the population as first language, comprising together almost 75 per cent of the population. Bemba and Nyanja, together with English, are spoken by more than 70 per cent of second-language speakers. Lozi is spoken both as first and as second language by just under 10 per cent of speakers, while for English, there is a significant difference between use as first language and as second language: in 2000, less than two per cent of Zambians spoke English as first language, but its use among second-language speakers was over 25 per cent. The data in the table also show that the use as second language of the five languages increased in the decade from 1980 to 1990. In contrast, from 1990 to 2000 use as a second language decreased in all cases (even though Nyanja remains fairly stable) except for English which saw a significant increase. While the decrease in 2000 of the Zambian languages

---

[2] The 2000 census recognizes seven language groups (excluding English) that coincide with broad ethnic groups: Bemba, Tonga, North-Western, Barotse (Lozi), Nyanja (or Eastern), Mambwe, and Tumbuka. We present four of these in Table 16.3.

as second languages can be attributed to the increase of English, it is interesting to note that smaller languages that were recorded as having no second-language speakers in 1990 have in 2000 shown figures for second-language speakers. Thus while Bisa, Lungu, and Senga had no second-language speakers in 1990 they recorded 0.4, 0.4, and 0.2 per cent, respectively, in 2000 (see Table 16.2). The picture which emerges from the data is one of a complex and dynamic multilingual situation, where language use changes quite significantly over a comparatively short time-span.

Another important factor in the linguistic situation in Zambia is the social and political status different languages have. English is the official language of Zambia, and the only language so identified in the 1991 Constitution. In addition, seven African languages are designated as national languages: Bemba, Nyanja, Tonga, Lozi, Kaonde, Luvale, and Lunda.[3] English is widely used in the media, in government and business, in education, and in many formal and semi-formal contexts, especially in urban settings. The three major daily newspapers, the *Times of Zambia*, the *Post*, and the *Daily Mail* are all in English, and print media in other languages are restricted to weekly or monthly magazines.[4] Television programmes by the Zambian National Broadcasting Corporation (ZNBC) are predominantly in English, with only short news programmes in the national languages. In addition, programmes on satellite and cable TV, mainly provided in the urban areas by South African broadcasting companies, are in English, or indeed in any of the South African national languages, but not in the languages of Zambia. English is also widely used on the radio, but here the indigenous Zambian languages are also heard, in programmes produced in one of the national languages, covering a range of topics from more serious political and economic issues to more light-hearted 'phone-in' programmes where callers comment live on various issues of general interest.[5] English also plays an important role in education in Zambia. After independence, English became the dominant language at all levels of education, and was used as the medium of instruction throughout, while national languages were taught as subjects. However, this situation has changed more recently, as the use of national languages as languages of instruction in primary schools has been adopted more widely (Carmody 2004). However, at secondary and tertiary level English is still used almost exclusively. As in the media and education, English is the dominant language in government, administration, and business. The majority of government publications, as well as government and official websites, are in English, as is the language of parliament, and the Constitution states that any person wishing

---

[3] Henceforth the terms 'official language' or 'official national language' will be used to refer to English, 'national languages' to the seven nationally recognized African languages, 'Zambian languages' to indigenous Zambian languages (therefore excluding European languages) and 'local languages' to Zambian languages spoken in a specific area.

[4] Notable are *Imbila* (Bemba), *Intanda* (Tonga), *Liseli* (Lozi), *Tsopano* (Nyanja), *Lukanga* (Bemba, Lenje), and *Ngoma* (Kaonde, Lunda, Luvale).

[5] Chanda (1996) reports radio air coverage in hours per week for local languages on the multilingual Radio 1 of ZNBC as: 23 each for Bemba and Tonga, 21 each for Nyanja and Lozi, and 15 each for Kaonde, Luvale, and Lunda.

to stand for parliament has to be fluent in the official language, that is, English. The predominant use of English in the media, government, and education, in addition to the widespread use of English as the language of business and administration, means that knowledge of English is extremely important for finding employment, at least in the 'formal' sector, and English thus has a relatively high social status in Zambia.

The seven Zambian national languages are used alongside English in a number of contexts. We have already mentioned their increasing use in primary education and on the radio. They are also used to disseminate specific government policy or health information (e.g. in cholera alerts). Furthermore, the national languages are the main mediums of wider communication in particular in spoken language and in less formal contexts, although they are also used in the lower ranks of formal administration. Local court proceedings are, for example, conducted in a local national language although the legislating judicial law is in English.[6] Another example is that of police interrogations which are also usually carried out in the local or regional language. Each language has a specific regional base, where it is predominantly used. Bemba is the main language of the Northern, Luapula, Copperbelt, and, to a lesser extent, Central provinces, Nyanja is the main language of the Eastern province as well as of Lusaka (alongside Bemba and English), Tonga of the Southern province, and Lozi of the Western province. Lunda, Luvale, and Kaonde are spoken in the North-Western province which does not have one dominant language (see Map). Throughout all provinces, the national languages play a greater role as languages of wider communication in rural areas, while they are used together with English in urban areas. Looking back at the language use data presented above, we can say that English is an important lingua franca in Zambia as it is not geographically restricted and is used anywhere in the country (albeit more in urban than in rural areas), while Bemba and Nyanja are used by more people than English as a means of communication, even though the majority of them live in the centre, north, and east of the country (cf. Kashoki 1978: 31).

As we have seen above, there are many more languages in Zambia than English and the seven national languages. We have already seen as well that many languages of Zambia in addition to the national languages are spoken both as first and second languages. Often these languages are only spoken in a limited area and by a smaller number of speakers, although, as the data presented above show, this is not always the case. Tumbuka, for example, is used by more speakers than the national languages Lunda, Luvale, and Kaonde. The reason why the latter languages have become national languages has to do with their relative importance in the North-Western province, whereas in the Eastern province, where Tumbuka is spoken, Nyanja is the main language of wider communication, and thus has become a

---

[6] The local court is the lowest court of law in a hierarchy dominated by the magistrate, high, and supreme courts.

national language. As pointed out above, in many cases the relation between ethnic grouping and linguistic grouping is complex, and more detailed work on Zambian languages is necessary to fully understand their distribution and interaction. However, what can be said is that in many parts in Zambia there exists a complex situation of language use, multilingualism and code-switching, where speakers employ a number of different languages in different contexts. For example, speakers may use Nsenga as the home language and local language of communication, but also use Nyanja and English as languages of wider communication. Furthermore, if a Nsenga speaker subsequently takes up a job on the Copperbelt she would in most likelihood add Bemba to her linguistic repertoire, thus choosing between four different languages.

In this section, we have introduced the languages of Zambia, numbers of speakers, and language use in some detail, to show the complexity and the dynamics of the situation, and also the problems of describing linguistic reality in Zambia, for example the choice between calling a variety a dialect or a language, and the difficulties of assessing language use and degree of multilingualism in spoken, informal contexts. In broad outline, though, the language situation in Zambia is well documented and understood: following Ohannessian and Kashoki (1978), we can say that just over thirty languages are spoken in Zambia. English is the official language of the country and is widely used in the public domain. However, in terms of numbers of speakers, Zambia's seven national languages – Bemba, Nyanja, Tonga, Lozi, Lunda, Luvale, Kaonde – are the more important languages of wider communication, and especially the first four account for a large majority of first- and second-language speakers. Zambia is a linguistically complex and dynamic country, with a range of different languages playing different roles in different contexts, and where language plays an important role in the construction and negotiation of social and national identities.

16.3 Historical Settings

Many aspects of the present-day language situation in Zambia are the result of historical developments over a comparatively long time.[7] The basis for today's distribution of languages in Zambia was laid during an extended period of slow processes of migrations and language shift beginning with the earliest introduction of Bantu languages in Zambia from around 300 BC. Subsequent movement of peoples, language contact, local and long-distance trade, colonial rule, and finally independence in 1964 shaped the language situation in the following centuries. It is sometimes assumed that the current language situation is mainly or even exclusively a result of colonial politics. This is certainly true for the introduction of English and its present position

---

[7] The main sources of historical information made use of here are Ehret (1998, 2002), Roberts (1976), Rotberg (1966), and Vansina (1990, 1995).

as one of the main lingua francas. However, we will suggest in this section that several aspects of the language situation of contemporary Zambia can be traced to pre-colonial times and that there is, despite many developments and changes, an element of continuity which characterizes the situation today. It will be suggested that the particular multilingual practices characterizing the language situation in Zambia today have historical roots pre-dating contact with Europeans. This provides an important backdrop for the mutually enhancing relation between multilingualism and national identity which has slowly developed in Zambia since independence. It is thus useful to place the language situation in Zambia today into a historical perspective.

16.3.1 The Language Situation Unfolds: Zambia up to the Eighteenth Century

Virtually all languages spoken in Zambia today belong to the Bantu family, except, of course, the more recent European and Indian languages and the small number of Khoisan languages. Bantu languages began to spread from the area of the Nigeria–Cameroon borderland in west Africa through more or less small processes of migration, language contact, and language shift southwards and eastwards and eventually became spoken in eastern, central, and southern Africa, in an area from just north of the equator all the way to southern Africa (see e.g. Nurse 2006). Archaeological and linguistic evidence suggests that Bantu languages reached Zambia, together with knowledge of iron technology, agriculture, and domestic animals, during the last centuries BC and the first few centuries AD in a gradual process of economic, social, cultural, and linguistic innovation. This was followed by several periods of subsequent change from around the middle of the first millennium during which new technologies and farming methods were introduced together with new Bantu languages which became widespread throughout northern, eastern, and central Zambia. These innovations, among which are distinct pottery designs and iron smelting techniques, did not extend to the far western parts of Zambia, where aspects of cultural continuity can be traced back to the fifth century AD. In broad outline, the linguistic situation in Zambia today results from this period, and was established during the first half of the second millennium. The main centres of innovation during this and subsequent periods often lie to the north, in what is now the southeastern DRC, where the Lunda and Luba states exerted strong influence on Zambia during the sixteenth and seventeenth centuries. Although other links existed, the major periods of contact in particular with southern and western neighbours became relevant only from the eighteenth century onwards. It is regularly said that prior to the arrival of Europeans in central Africa, communities were organized in small groups with little contact beyond each village and without much economic, social, or linguistic development (e.g. Wilson 1941: 11; Mulford 1967: 2; Posner 2005: 57). However, the evidence available suggests that such a characterization is likely to be quite incorrect. In most of what is today Zambia the 'middle ages', from around the turn of the millennium to the 1700s, was a period of trade, interchange, and innovation. In the northeast, a major innovation was in the expansion of millet cultivation by the so-called *citemene* system which involves clearing woodland and using ash as fertilizer. In the south, which is free of tsetse flies, people started to herd cattle. Trade involved salt, iron, and copper. While iron and iron products were useful for tools used in agriculture and food production more generally, the softer copper did not have any specific use and was traded as jewellery in the forms of bangles, crosses, bracelets, and so on. Archaeological records show that salt, iron, and copper works generally produced more than could have been usefully employed locally, and their products are found far from the centres of production, indicating a more or less organized trade network. Copper mining in Kansanshi mine near Solwezi, for example, had started by the fifth century and was part of a trade network which seems to be linked to saltworks in present-day southern DRC and up to Lwena and Ndembu communities in northwestern Zambia and eastern Angola from the 900s onwards (Vansina 2003). Local and regional contact not only involved the exchange of goods, but also new concepts and ideas, linking people across wider regions in which distinct traditions emerge. For pottery design, for example, archaeologists distinguish three main traditions, called Luangwa, Lungwebungu, and Tonga Diaspora, in the northeast, centre, and south of present-day Zambia. Similarly, different regional musical traditions can be distinguished today: along the north, music of the Cokwe/Lunda/Luba/Bemba belt employs harmony in thirds rather than fourths, which is used in most of the rest of Zambia (Baird 2004). This musical tradition cross-cuts more modern cultural regions and thus probably reflects pre-colonial contact. Trade and cultural traditions across these large regions of wider cultural affinity could not result from isolated and static communities, but presuppose ongoing change and innovation in most people's lives and active interchange and contact between different communities and speakers of different languages. In addition to this, probably the strongest evidence for the interactive nature of central Africa's societies during the last two millennia comes from comparative linguistics. When different groups of speakers of a language live in relative isolation from each other, their linguistic varieties will, due to the inevitability of language change, become different over time, and eventually develop into distinct languages. Historical linguists speak of divergence in this case. On the other hand, convergence effects occur when languages become, in certain respects, similar over time. Since any language can and will change in an infinite number of ways, convergence effects can only be explained by contact between the speakers of the languages. The Bantu languages of Zambia are all related and are thus all similar at some level. However, if speakers of early Bantu languages when entering Zambia about 2,000 or so years ago had remained largely in isolation, we would expect a fairly neat division into a number of different languages as a result of linguistic divergence. However, the main large-scale study of Bantu comparison (Bastin et al. 1999) concludes that the Bantu area as a whole is characterized by criss-crossing of local innovation (divergence) and diffusion of innovations by contact (convergence). This also holds true of the Bantu languages of Zambia at the heart of the Bantu area, indeed, it is part of the reason why boundaries between different dialects and languages of Zambia are so hard to draw, as discussed in section 16.2. So, while pre-colonial Zambia arguably saw the development of culturally and linguistically fairly homogeneous societies, for example the Bemba in the north or the Luyana in the west, and while some communities may have entertained fairly little contact with their neighbours, quite generally it seems that many Zambians before the nineteenth century were engaged in one way or the other – for example through trade, marriage, or migration – in interaction with people outside their immediate cultural and linguistic sphere. Although it is true that many important aspects of the language situation in Zambia are a result of much more recent history, which we return to consider in the next section, the basis of today's linguistic distribution, as well as practices of language contact, in itself a form of multilingualism, can be assumed to have been established in a gradual and extended process throughout the last two millennia.

16.3.2 Recent Modifications and Migrations: From the Eighteenth Century to 1964

From the eighteenth century onwards, Zambia's contact with outsiders increased dramatically, through migration movements from the south, the beginning of international trade in ivory, slaves, and guns, colonialism, and industrialization. Linguistically, three main languages became part of the linguistic scene – Kololo, a Sotho language which became known as Lozi; a group of Nguni languages; and English – while the use of languages already present changed through new forms of education and labour movement.

With increasing colonial activity away from the coasts, and rising international demand for gold, ivory, and manpower along trade routes and in large-scale plantations in the new world, Zambia became involved in international trade and many Zambians suffered from slavery, forced labour, and the increasing violence and destabilization brought about by European and local 'traders' outside of official traditional or European control. The main lines of trade and contact ran from the East African coast in the north along old Swahili trade routes, in the south through Mozambique from what was then Portuguese territory, and in the west to Portuguese traders in Angola. However, despite the scale of economic and political changes and human suffering brought about during this period, more lasting effects came later through contact with the south.

In the early part of the nineteenth century Zulu nationalism led to a period of fighting in southern Africa which spilled over into countries much further north. In the aftermath of the *mfecane*, Zulu for 'crushing, scattering', groups of speakers of Southern African Nguni and Sotho languages fled from their original South African homelands northwards and settled among the people they found. In Zambia, groups of displaced Nguni fighters known as Ngoni moved into the Eastern province and into Malawi, while in the west the Kololo, a Sotho-speaking group of people, conquered the Luyi kingdom and changed its linguistic identity in particular. Different groups of Ngoni arrived in southeastern Zambia from the 1840s onwards. They were essentially groups of guerrilla fighters retreating from Zulu armies set to conquer new lands. Their linguistically and culturally heterogeneous structure allowed them to absorb conquered peoples comparatively easily into the elaborate military structures they had developed. After some vicissitudes, they settled among the peoples of the Eastern province, the Chewa, Nsenga, and Tumbuka, and adopted the language of these groups. Thus while many of their customs and cultural traditions, including music, poetry, and ceremonies have high visibility in contemporary Zambia, and frequently contribute to the maintenance of a Ngoni ethnic identity, no Nguni language is actually spoken in Zambia today.

An almost opposite case occurred around the same time in western Zambia when Sotho-speaking Kololo people, similarly *mfecane* victims, crossed the Zambezi at Kazungula at the present-day Botswana–Zambia border point. The Kololo conquered the Luyi kingdom which by that time had been established with fairly well-defined political and administrative structures. Although their rule was ended in the 1860s, their language remained and the Lozi (the Kololo term for Luyi) language of today has close similarities to Sotho, while Luyi is only used as a ceremonial language (Gowlett 1989).

A third influence from the south brought English into the picture. Following colonial expansionist interests, and so as to forestall other Europeans from establishing themselves in the area, Rhodes' British South Africa Company took control of the territory named Northern Rhodesia in 1890. From 1924 to independence, Northern Rhodesia was run by the British Government as a colony, and was part of the Federation of Rhodesia and Nyasaland, comprising Northern and Southern Rhodesia (Zimbabwe) and Nyasaland (Malawi), from 1953 to 1963. British rule on the whole was a dreary affair. With the territory of Zambia initially being mainly taken over to secure strategic interests, the emphasis then turned to exploiting the area as a reservoir of cheap labour and to making profits from the copper mines which initiated large-scale production in the 1930s. For most of the period, it seems to have been a take-the-money-and-run affair and spending on public welfare, health, education, and infrastructure was minute compared to the dividends made from the extraction and sale of copper. Up to the 1920s and beyond education was almost exclusively provided by various mission stations and outposts of the eighteen missionary societies active in the territory (Küster 1999). The missions had a huge impact on the development of African languages and it was partly the activities of the missions which resulted in the growth of modern Zambia's lingua francas, through their use of the African languages as the medium of instruction in the schools they established – sometimes against the wishes of the pupils who preferred English as this provided access to better jobs – and through the introduction of written varieties in the course of Bible translations and early written literature (Carmody 2004). Previously, Bemba, Nyanja, Lozi, and Tonga had been used as languages of wider communication, but now they also came to be used widely in the new systems of formal education. Conversely, in the northwest there was no strong mission activity, and no modern education, and this contributed to the absence of any widely used lingua franca in the area (Posner 2005). A second impact of the colonial rule was large-scale labour movement and the advent of urbanization. While many Zambians had to move south of the border to Southern Rhodesia and South Africa for salaried labour, from the 1930s onwards, copper production on the Copperbelt increased and large numbers of labourers were needed. Partly as a result of company policies, the majority of mineworkers on the Copperbelt were Bemba-speakers from the Northern Province, and thus Bemba became established as the lingua franca in the mines, where a distinct variety, sometimes called 'Town Bemba', developed, reflecting the high degree of language contact in the multilingual situation on the Copperbelt (see Spitulnik 1998). Finally, of course, the introduction of English as the language of politics, administration, and business is a colonial legacy. The number of white settlers in Zambia was never as high as in South Africa or neighbouring Zimbabwe, but still there were a number of English speakers both before and after independence, some of them farmers, but many employed in government, administration, health, and education sectors. Africans learned English in schools, where it was used next to regional languages, and acquired high prestige as it gave access to better paid jobs, first mainly as teachers and later in shops and offices when white collar jobs became available for Africans towards the end of the colonial period. The main growth of English as a lingua franca, however, came only after independence.

Opposition to British colonial rule grew constantly during the twentieth century and was driven by three interrelated aims: full participation of all Zambians in the political process, use of the country's resources for its own people, and political autonomy from both the colonial power and the racist white regime in Southern Rhodesia. Economic participation was especially demanded on the Copperbelt and the collective action in the miners' strikes in 1935 can perhaps be regarded as an early antecedent of Zambian national identity: the striking miners explicitly rejected negotiation through so-called tribal elders, who were appointed by the mining companies to discourage inter-ethnic political consciousness as part of a wider colonial strategy to invent and manipulate tribal identities. The miners used traditional Mbeni dance groups, thought of as 'harmless' by the white administrators, as effective means of communication and coordination between different mines, and posted messages detailing their aims in Bemba, the African language of wider communication on the Copperbelt, which the administration had to have translated (Matongo 1992). The main and final driving force of the independence movement, however, was the Federation with the 'white' South which lasted from 1953 to 1963. While African stakes in colonial Northern Rhodesia were not valued especially highly, many Zambians at the time thought that the state of affairs in the north was better than in the south. Miners in the north had better political organization and their salaries in 1960 were about twice as high as those of mineworkers in the south. Copper was booming, and race relations were, as far as race relations go in colonial contexts, moderately good, and certainly better than under the new Apartheid regime in South Africa, which was eagerly being copied south of the border. There were no pass laws in Northern Rhodesia, and Africans were represented, admittedly through representatives for African affairs appointed by the colonial office, at the Legislative Council. Furthermore, it became clear very quickly that the north was paying more into the federal budget than it got out of it: by 1963 Northern Rhodesia had made a net loss of £97 million and had seen another £260 million of mining profits leave for London, Salisbury, and Johannesburg, with very little of this money coming back into the country. The silver lining of this situation was that it led to the political alliance between black and white Zambians (or at least those who identified with the new independent Zambia), the former outraged in general, the latter outraged by the sell-out of their country, giving rise to the credible and successful implementation of a policy of non-racialism after independence.

On the eve of independence, then, Zambia had gone through almost two centuries of tumultuous events and much of the country had changed. Copper mining had been industrialized and had become the main source of income; the 'line-of-rail', connecting Livingstone in the south with Lusaka and the Copperbelt in the north, had become a major socio-geographical feature; and Zambia had become one of the most urbanized countries in the region. Both inward migration from the south and from Europe, and labour migration of Zambians to Southern Rhodesia, South Africa, the DRC, and Tanzania had brought Zambians into contact with new people, new ideas, and new ways of life. Education had changed from informal traditional acculturation and training to formal schooling, Christianity had become a major religion, and English had been established as the main language for commerce, government, and administration. With all these new developments and changes, it is probably easy to miss the wider continuities. But a number of things did not change dramatically. Copper had been mined for more than a thousand years, sometimes at the very same spots where the modern mines had been built in the twentieth century, although, of course, on a pre-industrialized scale. More significantly, probably most people in Zambia had been in the area for centuries. Chiefs and tribal organization had often been invented and reinterpreted by colonial administrators and anthropologists, based on their own interests and preconceptions. On the other hand, a number of Zambians had been identified as tribes before European contact, and groups like the Bembas and Lozis (or Luyis at the time) had multi-layered structures of allegiance to chiefs and paramount chiefs (the Bemba *Chitimukulu*) or kings (the Lozi *Litunga*) which were often adopted from the political systems of the Luba and Lunda kingdoms to the north. Truly international trade only began with European contact and through Western market forces, but regional trade had been established for centuries, often along well-developed trade routes and through established traders. Though comparatively little is known for sure about language use in pre-colonial Zambia, given the existence of different forms of social organization and different ethnic groups with varying forms of identity, contact through trade and other causes, and the existence of larger regions of cultural affinities, it seems likely that patterns of multilingualism have a long tradition in Zambia, and that the linguistic changes triggered by European contact, that is, the introduction of English and the development of African languages as lingua francas, were absorbed into an established system making use of different languages in different contexts.

16.3.3 Zambia Today: 1964 to the Present

The Republic of Zambia was officially founded on 24 October 1964. Independence celebrations were held at the new Independence Stadium in Lusaka, attended by both old and new political leaders: the Princess Royal and the last Governor, Evelyn Hone, for the outgoing colonial power, and the new president and vice-president, Kenneth Kaunda and Simon Kapwepwe. Proceedings were harmonious; the Colonial Office had been the lesser of two evils compared to Company rule at the beginning of the century, and had given support for Zambia's fight against the Federation and subsequent independence (though this support was perhaps also somewhat lack-lustre). The independence movement was largely conducted as a non-violent civil disobedience campaign, the so-called *Cha-cha-cha* campaign, and the main political party, Kaunda's United National Independence Party (UNIP), had tried to build a large, non-racial, non-ethnic platform. The two main causes which had fuelled the independence movement, the control and distribution of the copper revenues and the fight against the Federation, also became dominant in the early years of the new republic. Increasing copper profits and using the money generated to provide jobs, education, health care, housing, and higher standards of living for all Zambians was the main aim of domestic policies, while foreign policy was determined by the struggle to end colonialism and white rule in Southern Africa. At independence, Zambia had four unfriendly neighbours: the Portuguese colonies Angola and Mozambique, South African-occupied Namibia, and Southern Rhodesia, which after the Unilateral Declaration of Independence in 1965 became Rhodesia under white minority rule and turned from unfriendly to positively hostile. Since virtually all trade links with the outside world at the time ran through Rhodesia, the first few years of independence saw a concerted restructuring programme to find new ways of importing oil, machinery, and most other goods, and of exporting the vital copper which involved air links and the improvement of transport infrastructure to Dar es Salaam in Tanzania and the Benguela railway to Lobito in Angola. Politically, Zambia became, with Tanzania, the most active 'frontline' state, supporting the total liberation of the continent. Many politicians involved in independence movements in southern Africa passed through Lusaka at some stage or other, and many spent many years there; many independence organizations had offices in Zambia, including the South African ANC, and Zambia's role in supporting the eventual liberation of Zimbabwe, Mozambique, Angola, Namibia, and South Africa is an important piece of the history of the region (see e.g. Mbeki 2004).

Zambia's national identity was thus formed essentially on economic and political, especially foreign policy, lines. In addition, the early years of the republic were closely associated with the integrating figure of Kenneth Kaunda and his national philosophy of 'African Humanism' which embodied a number of Christian-informed ethical principles, but was less politically relevant than the *ujamaa* policies in neighbouring Tanzania. Yet, despite these strong points of national identification, 'tribalism' and centrifugal tendencies were seen as a threat to the new country and the establishment of 'national identity' became a paramount task: the national motto adopted after independence was 'One Zambia, One Nation'. It is against this background that English became the national and official language of Zambia, which was based on the view that English would help integrate the different Zambian peoples, while African languages were seen as promoting factionism and tribalism: 'One Zambia, One Nation, One Language' could thus have been the appropriate extension of the national motto at the time. English was also seen as providing the only means for both national and international communication, a view based on the colonially inherited assumption that African languages (and African cultures) are essentially static, backward, isolated, and linked to tribal identities, and thus would not be able to serve as languages of wider communication or affinity – a view which is, as we have shown in the preceding section, clearly contrary to fact (cf. Kashoki 1990).

Fear of tribalism also played a part in the establishment of the 'second republic' in 1972/73, when multiparty democracy was ended and Zambia became a 'one-party participatory democracy'. The move effectively strengthened the ruling UNIP party under Kaunda and removed it (and him) from voter control, but was triggered by the establishment and electoral success of two opposition parties which were seen by Kaunda as tribally based: the African National Congress, associated with Ila and Tonga people of the Southern province, and the United Progressive Party under former vice-president Kapwepwe, which was seen as a Bemba party. Whether the charge of tribalism is in fact true, or whether the two parties could equally be seen as regionally based, and, indeed, whether in either case, this warrants the abolition of political parties, is a different matter (see e.g. Meyns 1995). In any event, UNIP became the only party, and Kaunda sought to have more or less ethnically 'balanced' governments (Posner 2005). During the second republic, conditions in Zambia deteriorated. Political decision making was restricted to UNIP and to the president and often political offices were not seen as representing the interests of society but as lucrative career options. Meanwhile, the economy stalled, inflation rose and foreign debts soared, to about US $7 billion at the end of the 1980s, so that unemployment and economic hardship became the reality for many Zambians. Political and economic dissatisfaction, together with the rapid political changes in Eastern Europe, provided enough motivation for a demand to change the system, and after a period of some unrest, the first multiparty elections of the third republic were held on 31 October 1991. Kaunda stood as presidential candidate of UNIP, was defeated, and power came to the Movement for Multiparty Democracy (MMD), which campaigned with the slogan 'The Hour has Come', under

Frederick Chiluba, the former president of the Zambian Congress of Trade Unions. Whatever else one may think about Kaunda's achievements, to be a president in power and to lose an election and step down gracefully is remarkable in African politics, and this has certainly contributed to Kaunda's renaissance as elder statesman in the 2000s.

Chiluba's main agenda was economic reform and he ran a course of privatization and liberalization of the economy, partly in the fact of heavy protests, which it seems too early to judge. He was re-elected in 1996 and was succeeded as president in 2002 by Levy Mwanawasa, a former vice-president, of the MMD. At the beginning of the millennium Zambia can look back at forty years of independence in which the nation has developed largely peacefully in the absence of major violence, war, or civil unrest. This is all the more remarkable in view of the difficult circumstances in the wider region after independence. Also, today, all of Zambia's neighbours have ended colonialism and there is hope for a democratic and peaceful future in southern Africa. Economically, there is hope as well, as Zambia qualified for full debt cancellation under the Wold Bank's Heavily Indebted Poor Countries Initiative in 2005 which will allow more resources to be invested in human development. However, many areas of public life have declined in the last decades, including school enrolment and health, and it will take some time until levels of the 1970s are reached again. One of the main threats to Zambian well-being at present is the HIV/AIDS pandemic which affects 'all aspects of social and economic growth in the country, weakening the public sector and threatening long-term national development' (WHO 2005).

16.4 Contemporary Themes in Language and Identity in Zambia

As we have shown in the previous section, the establishment of national identity in Zambia occurred first and foremost on the political level, through foreign and domestic policies, and identification with the new president Kaunda. African languages did play a role in the political movements leading up to independence, but only a small one, for example in the miners' strikes in the 1930s, and possibly also through radio broadcasting in African languages from the late 1940s onwards (Roberts 1976: 210). However, the main language of political and official discourse in Zambia became English. Since African languages did not play a significant role in the establishment of national unity (in contrast to, for example, Swahili in Tanzania), there soon ensued a national debate about the role of language in Zambia. As noted earlier, English became the official language and was seen as the only 'non-tribal' alternative available to serve as a vehicle of national unity, an argument often made in post-colonial African language policies. English also became the language of prestige and was linked with modernization and access to international communication. However, this policy was not without its critics. In particular the Zambian linguist Mubanga Kashoki pointed out a number of problems with this approach, in essays mainly dating from the 1970s and collectively published in Kashoki (1990). Kashoki argues that all languages are dynamic systems, and that African languages can be associated with modernity as well as English can. While it is true that English is a major international language, Kashoki points out that the main function of national languages ought to be national communication, and that the demands of international communication can be met by English as second language as is done in many European countries. In terms of national communication, Kashoki argues that African languages – especially Bemba and Nyanja, as established languages of wider communication – serve this function better as they are understood more widely. Finally, Kashoki points out that English is neutral only in a certain sense (i.e. not associated with any ethnic group), but that, especially when used as the only medium in education, it is not neutral, but favours children who already speak English at home, usually those of urban, educated, and well-to-do parents. Having queried the alleged practical advantages of English, Kashoki then asks whether language, and in particular one language, ought to play a role in national identity. Since Zambian national identity has been established politically, the familiar European 'one language, one state' argument applies rather differently: whereas in many countries of western Europe (simplifying somewhat) the use of one language became important for defining the nation-state, the Zambian nation-state was defined without any prior unification of language, so that language, and in particular one language, did not fulfil the integrative role in nation-building in Zambia that it often did in Europe. In view of this, it might be argued that the nation can serve as a feasible political unit in which many languages are spoken, and that national identity is constituted by patterns of multilingualism. Thus, Kashoki concludes, Zambian languages should be developed and be fully employed in the building of the nation and her national identity. In retrospect, Kashoki's position can be seen in many ways as foreshadowing discussions about the role of languages in Zambia from the 1990s onwards.

16.4.1 Changing Perceptions of Zambian Languages

The perception of language, and of Zambian languages in particular, has undergone change in Zambia since the beginning of the third republic. Academic interest in language questions is high and attractively packaged grammatical sketches of Zambian languages can be found in the bookshops of Lusaka's flashy new malls. Government officials now address audiences in regional and sometimes local languages as opposed to English which was the norm some twenty years ago. There is as yet no change in legislation, but in a recent paper Kashoki (2003) has argued – with reference to South Africa and Zimbabwe, but probably equally applicable to Zambia – that legislation ought to acknowledge the country's linguistic diversity and provide for constitutional coding of linguistic rights. Public opinion certainly seems to favour more recognition of Zambia's linguistic heritage and multiplicity. There are a number of reasons for this trend. It is part of a more general, regional, and international trend and mirrors similar discussions in, for example, South Africa. It is related to the change from second to third republic and the MMD's philosophy of plurality, of 'multi' as opposed to 'single', and to the end of centralist forms of societies more widely. It can also be seen as an answer to defining a new sense of national identity. During the 1990s, the main cornerstones of Zambian national identity disappeared: Kaunda's presidency, the frontline status, and economic advancement through nationalization and industrialization. This is now being replaced by a new long tradition, exceptionally long by regional standards, of relative stability, rule of law, and democracy. Democratic language rights fit well into this new mark of identification. A particular interpretation is given by Posner (2005). He proposes that increasing interest in linguistic identity in Zambia is linked to the change of political ground-rules from the second to the third republic, and to voters' basic assumption that they will profit if political power is given to someone in their tribal or linguistic group. In the second republic elections were local, with a choice among different local UNIP candidates, and coalition-building proceeded along tribal lines: too often all candidates belonged to the same, bigger linguistic group. However, with multiparty elections, coalitions have to be large enough to have a reasonable chance of attaining national majorities, and tribal identities are too small to achieve this. Hence, in the third republic, voters build alliances with others of the same language, not tribal group. One has to add to this, though, that culturally, as opposed to politically, tribal identity remains important, and has probably become more important over the last decade, reflecting, like the increased awareness of multilingualism, a trend towards a more pluralistic society. All these different points show that the change in perspective on languages is embedded in a wider change in public conceptions of identity.

16.4.2 Multilingualism

One of the main points of the current discussion is Zambia's multilingualism, which is now seen as an asset, rather than an impediment to national development. However languages are counted, it is clear that, as we have shown above, Zambia is a multilingual country. The majority of Zambians have more than one language in their linguistic repertoire and can choose from among these languages, both for communication and for ethnic and linguistic identities. Furthermore, there are different languages within the boundaries of the state which are used by a large number of speakers in most situations, and different languages are increasingly recognized in public life through legislation and institutions. Multilingualism plays an important role in the construction of contemporary Zambian identity. In urban centres, especially in the capital Lusaka, many Zambians routinely employ three or four languages: English as the language of many official contexts and also as the predominant written language; Bemba and Nyanja as the city's publicly most dominant languages of wider communication which are used in many (and for some speakers in most) informal and semi-formal contexts; and also often a further, different home language within the family (Chisanga 2002). Although the various languages can be associated with different

functional domains as outlined above, actual linguistic reality is frequently characterized by code-switching involving two or more languages. The choice between different
languages available in many Zambian contexts is an important aspect of speakers'
linguistic repertoire and is employed to construct and negotiate social and ethnic
identities. For example, a study reported by Banda (2005) shows how code-switching
between educated Zambian English, colloquial Zambian English, and Nyanja is used
to establish and alter social roles and relationships in the environment of a Lusaka
office. Both the change from and into the different varieties, and the specific structures
made available by the varieties – especially the formal marking of respect in African
languages – are used to negotiate age- and gender-based relations throughout the
discourse. Similarly, Siachitema (1991) shows how language choice is related to the
social relations of discourse participants, and in particular that use of English is more
acceptable when speaking to younger people or people of the same age, while when
addressing older people African languages are seen as expressing more adequately
the respect commonly accorded to older people in African society. Examples of code-
switching involving African languages, principally Nyanja and Bemba, are also found
in contemporary Zambian popular music, which has undergone a recent rejuvenation
and is now widely embraced by all generations. Various artists (e.g. k'millian 2004)
use both languages in the lyrics of their songs, expressing the multilingual reality of
contemporary Lusaka.

Even though urban multilingual situations such as in Lusaka are not the norm, the
use of different languages is widespread throughout the country. In section 16.3.1 we
have suggested that the present-day language situation in Zambia is not so much a
product of the colonial era, as instead based on a dynamic system of multilingualism
which has developed over several centuries. A number of the languages which play a
part in the contemporary set-up have been spoken – in older forms – in the area since
the middle of the last millennium. Others, like Lozi, and indeed English, have entered
the system at a later stage. Throughout much of the country's history, linguistic identity has been expressed and negotiated with reference to several languages fulfilling
different functions, as languages of the home or as languages of wider communication,
as languages of insiders or newcomers. The industrial and political transformations of
the last century have contributed to an expansion of the linguistic system in scale,
but not significantly in kind; even though urban multilingualism in Lusaka or on
the Copperbelt is a new phenomenon, the underlying practices are not. Zambian
linguistic identity is constituted by this specific multilingual system, involving Bemba,
Nyanja, Tonga, Lozi, and English as the main languages of wider communication, all
of which are related to a net of regional, social, and ethnic identities. With respect to
language and national identity, we have argued that Zambia's national identity after
independence was mainly referenced to political and economic events, and that in
contrast to the rise of many European nation-states, language did not play a unifying
role in the establishment of Zambian identity. After initial attempts to put English
into the role of official national language, contemporary Zambia is developing a new

model of language and identity, where nation-building and multilingualism are not only compatible, but where the specific multilingual language practices in Zambia are seen as part of the country's national identity, so that now 'One Zambia, One Nation, Many Languages' would be a more appropriate continuation of the national motto.

16.4.3 Some Practical Consequences

The change in perspective on African languages since the 1990s has also led to more practical consequences, two of which are the use of languages in education, and the effort to harmonize the standardization of cross-border languages. While African languages were used in primary education in mission and government schools under colonial rule, English became the sole language of instruction after independence. Although several studies even in the 1970s have shown that this practice had adverse effects on learning and literacy, as pupils were confronted with a language with which they were not familiar, it was not until 2000 that a nationwide reform began to be implemented, in the Basic School Curriculum Framework. The idea presented in the Framework is to use the seven national languages as mediums of instruction from the first grade, and only gradually introduce English from the second grade on (Carmody 2004; Manchisi 2004). The implementation of this scheme is on a regional basis and is particularly encouraged in rural areas where children have little or no contact with English before formal education.

For cross-border languages, the practical outcome of the increase in positive status of African languages is a new, integrative perspective on languages shared with neighbouring countries, reflected in increased work on this issue. Due to Zambia's artificial boundaries, many Zambian languages are also spoken in neighbouring countries. While this has been known for a long time, it is only in the recent climate of promotion of African languages that this question has been addressed from a linguistic perspective. In particular, as elsewhere in Africa, projects have begun to assess the situation and to propose standardized written versions of languages across the Zambian–Malawian border in the east (papers in Banda 2002), of Lozi across the Namibian–Zambian border in the west (Kashoki et al. 1998), and of Bemba across the border between Zambia and the DRC (Kamwangamalu 1997).

16.4.4 Small Languages

Looking back at the data on language use in Zambia presented in section 16.2, we can now highlight certain of the developments there against the background of the discussion in this section. Of the five main languages in terms of numbers of speakers, Bemba and Nyanja are being used by a large number of second-language speakers as important languages of wider communication in the east, north, and central parts of the country, with Nyanja showing an increase particularly in urban areas. Use of English has also dramatically increased probably owing to general higher levels of formal education. Lozi and Tonga remain widely spoken in the south and the west with a slight dip reflecting wider use of the smaller languages in both areas. The three national languages of the North-Western province remain small in terms of numbers of speakers but fare quite well as a language group with 7.7 per cent and 6.8 per cent of first- and second-language speakers, respectively. Although the increase in numbers in the 'other' category reflects an increased use of smaller languages both as first and second language, the census data do not say very much about the remaining majority of Zambian languages, and more work is needed in this area. Two trends would seem to be likely. On the one hand, increasing use of the national languages could lead to language shift and language loss of smaller languages – Swahili in Tanzania provides a parallel for this. On the other hand, the new emphasis and more positive attitudes towards Zambian languages may lead to the improvement of the situation of the smaller languages. The latter seems to be indicated in some cases. One example of this is provided by Nkoya (van Binsbergen 1994). Nkoya speakers live in the eastern part of the Western province and have historically been dominated by the Lozi. Although Nkoya music forms part of Lozi culture, the group's linguistic and cultural identity is seen as threatened by Lozi domination. However, since the 1990s, Nkoya-speakers have profited from the new political climate, in which government officials publicly acknowledge Nkoya, and plans to use Nkoya in some form of education are more realistic than before. Thus, while official emphasis is being placed on the national languages, and demographic trends indicate relative growth of Bemba and Nyanja, Zambia's new multilingual tradition can work to promote the linguistic identity of smaller languages and linguistic complexity more widely.

16.5 Conclusions

This chapter has discussed the language situation in Zambia with particular attention to questions of language and national identity. After providing an outline of the languages spoken in Zambia and their use, we contextualized the present-day situation historically. Our aim in this was to show generally that Zambian history does not begin with European contact, and more specifically, that patterns of language contact and multilingual practices were most likely established in Zambia long before the 1800s. Indeed we proposed that contemporary multilingualism in Zambia has its historical roots in pre-colonial times, and that during the period of British rule an existing system was simply extended and modified. Another important reason for introducing a historical context was to show how modern Zambian national identity was primarily politically and economically informed, and that language was not an important factor for national identity at independence. In the wake of nationalism and out of fear of centrifugal tendencies, English was made the national language of the new republic, on the assumption that a national language was needed to build national identity. It was only during the 1990s that this perception changed, and more emphasis was placed on the importance of African languages for the construction of Zambia's identity. The main argument we have presented in this chapter is that the particular patterns of multilingualism in Zambia, involving all languages to varying degrees, with specific status for the national languages as major regional languages, and Bemba, English, and Nyanja as languages of trans-regional communication, are jointly constitutive of Zambian contemporary national identity, which is, furthermore, built on a long historical tradition.

17

South Africa: The Rocky Road to Nation Building

Rajend Mesthrie

17.1 Introduction

South Africa is a country which has witnessed spectacular and far-reaching changes from the 1990s until the present, having emerged as a constitutional democracy with equal rights for all races and ethno-linguistic groups only in 1994. Prior to this, the country was subject to two forces of colonization and the assertion of their associated languages, Dutch rule from the mid-seventeenth century and British from the early nineteenth century. It then experienced a twentieth century dominated by increasing racial separation and inequality under the system of apartheid, which took colonial dynamics to an extreme and promulgated a near-complete segregation of people into four main groups: White, Black, Indian, and Coloured. In the colonial period first Dutch and then Dutch and English were imposed as the official languages of the territories within South Africa. The twentieth century saw the rapid rise of Afrikaans as the language of power in the Union of South Africa. This was a form of Dutch which had emerged since early European settlement showing considerable influence from local languages, and which came to be seen and promoted as a central symbol of White Afrikaner nationalism during the course of the twentieth century. Under the domination of apartheid, recognition was given to indigenous African languages, but only in their designated 'homelands', areas within South Africa assigned the status of self-governing territories and demarcated along ethno-linguistic lines, KwaZulu being the homeland established for Zulu-speaking people, KwaNdebele that of Ndebele-speakers, and so on. The Afrikaner government thus supported a Herderian view of *nation–language–culture*, and saw not one nation but many nations in the territory, which would be allowed to 'develop separately' (Alexander 1989). These homelands had little legitimacy in the eyes of the Black population, however, as they were ill-resourced, primarily rural, and sustained the apparent divide-and-rule policy of the White government. The extremism of apartheid finally came to a head in the late 1970s and 1980s, with the country close to civil war and under increasing international pressure and economic sanctions. In 1990 the ruling National Party was consequently led to announce the end of apartheid, paving the way for a multi-ethnic democracy which came into being in 1994.

The most tangible of the changes from apartheid to the post-apartheid era have been the negotiated settlement between previously antagonistic forces, the inception of democracy, a new constitution that counts amongst the more progressive in the world, the empowerment of a new Black[1] middle class, and a switch from a system with two official languages at the national level to one now with eleven, including the nine primary indigenous languages. Less tangible have been practices that attempt to realize the new constitutional ideals and the policies they engendered. Here the successes have been more symbolic than material, and a decade on from the new constitution there is a sense in which a new nation is still very much 'under construction'.[2] Following an overview presentation of the historical background to the present situation in South Africa, this chapter focuses on the major debates around language in the transformed democracy, the extent to which language diversity is a resource or a problem, and the role that language is capable of playing both in education, administration, and the economy, and in the general process of nation-building. The chapter draws on certain Gramscian perspectives (Gramsci 1971) to understand how language has been, and to some extent continues to be, a site of struggle in South Africa, and also uses a more bottom-up sociolinguistic perspective to characterize the linguistic diversity that continues to thrive and certain dilemmas that relate to language choice in education.[3]

17.2 Colonial History and Language Policies

Considering the way in which the linguistic and racial composition of South Africa evolved over time, the most indigenous of the country's various linguistic groups are the people labelled 'Khoesan' (a composite term for the Khoekhoe and San), who originally existed as hunter-gatherers in bands consisting of a few small families.[4] Some Khoesan were also livestock herders. The languages of this ethno-linguistic 'group' were actually not all related, and Traill (2002) argues that three

---

[1] In this chapter I use 'Black' to mean 'Black South African' in a narrow sense that excludes other people of colour ('Coloureds' and 'Indians' e.g.). Political unity amongst these groups is sometimes signalled by the lower-case term 'black'.

[2] I take this phrase from the title of a book on race and culture in modern South Africa (Distiller and Steyn 2004).

[3] This chapter is an updated and much expanded version of the text of the annual Oliver Tambo Memorial Lecture, delivered in October 2004, at the invitation of the Ireland–South Africa Association, previously the Anti-Apartheid Movement.

[4] The Khoesan peoples may in fact have originated further north, with archaeological and linguistic evidence suggesting northern Botswana.

South Africa

distinct families of languages are present within the traditional Khoesan designation.[5] Khoesan and Bantu contacts in southern Africa appear to have been extensive, judging from similarities in religious and medical concepts and folk tales about animals (Parsons 1982).

While the Khoesan were the first inhabitants of the area of South Africa, the great majority of South Africa's population belongs to the Bantu subgroup of the Niger-Kordofanian family. The ultimate origins of the Bantu sub-family lie two to three thousand years ago in what is today the Cameroon–Nigeria region (Williamson and Blench 2000). Iron Age civilization was later brought south of the Zambesi and Limpopo by small numbers of Bantu-speaking farmers who first appeared in the area around 300 AD (Herbert and Bailey 2002: 50). Considerably later than this, a key event in modern South African history was the establishment by the Dutch, the richest European trading nation of the time, of a trading station at the Cape in 1652, a half-way house to the East Indies. Strife soon followed between the Dutch and Khoesan over land and cattle, and the Dutch had to look elsewhere for labour for the new colony.

---

[5] Although two click-using languages of Tanzania (Sandawe and Hadza) are sometimes described as San languages, the affinities have yet to be proven and are in any case unlikely (Güldemann and Vossen 2000).

From 1658 onwards slaves were then imported in large numbers from Madagascar, Mozambique, the East Indies, and India. It is one of the ironies of history that at about the time that large numbers of African slaves were being forcibly exported out of Africa into the New World, the southern tip of Africa was itself stocking up on slaves largely from the east (Armstrong and Worden 1989). The slave population of the Cape which resulted from this process was possibly one of the most diverse in the world in terms of origins, religion, culture, and language. The roots of the large Coloured population of the Western Cape go back to this period, with a multiple ancestry that involves the Khoesan, Asian and African slaves, and the offspring of European and non-European.[6] Meanwhile, the Khoesan themselves became significantly reduced in number due to conflicts with the Dutch and the effects of European diseases, and in particular a smallpox epidemic in 1713. All along relations with the European settlers were not benign and ultimately led to the destruction or radical transformation of Khoekhoe and San society. As a result, today there are no longer any Khoe languages spoken in South Africa, apart from some Nama in the Richtersveld area of the Northern Cape.[7] San languages still survive in Namibia, Botswana and elsewhere, and in ever shrinking numbers in South Africa, where their speakers have largely shifted to Afrikaans, though often retaining a distinctive identity from (White) Afrikaners.

The first purely civilian British population came to South Africa in 1820, two decades after the military and diplomatic establishments that displaced Dutch rule in Cape Town and its environs. The British introduced a policy of Anglicization in the Cape, replacing Dutch with English as the language of government, education, and law (Lanham 1978), which caused much discontent among the Dutch/Afrikaners. Feeling their religion, culture, and language to be under threat, and with their rights to keep slaves eroded with the emancipation of 1834, many Afrikaners trekked further into the interior with the intention of escaping British influence. By this time Afrikaans had evolved as a colloquial variety of Dutch, with certain admixture from other languages.[8] Afrikaans culture, which had evolved out of the Dutch and slave experience in southern Africa, gelled as people moved away from Cape Town.

As for the Bantu-speaking peoples present in the area of South Africa, the period from the 1820s onwards is regarded as one of great flux in the political alignments amongst their various groups. Traditional history recounts the rise to power of Shaka in the establishment of a Zulu empire in Natal. This consolidation of a Zulu unity led to conflicts with other chieftains and a period known as the *mfecane*, an Nguni word for 'great wandering, dispersion of people'. Of particular note is the trek of the

---

[6] 'Coloured' is thus not an equivalent to 'Black' as it is in some societies; rather it denotes a major racial category within apartheid classification, essentially referring to people of multiple ancestry, and continues to carry racial and/or cultural associations.

[7] Nama – still fairly widely spoken in Namibia – is the major surviving Khoe language.

[8] Afrikaans is sometimes described as a creole language. The case is far from closed, though it seems safer to consider it a European-derived language with heavy admixture from Cape Khoe and Malay. For ideologies surrounding Afrikaans see Roberge (1990).

Ndebele people away from Zulu territory to the highveld, and subsequently away from Afrikaner firepower into what is now southwestern Zimbabwe. The 1820s onwards was also the period during which African languages were written down for the first time by Western missionaries, in conjunction with local consultants, producing translations of the Bible. In many areas the dialect which was selected by the missionaries for writing came to have prestige because of this association. The rise of written forms of African languages thus did not follow from the more familiar bases of standardization familiar in the West: urbanization and the prestige associated with certain affluent and socially high-placed groups of speakers. Rather it came about as the result of the external force of missionary influence. This has developed into a modern-day paradox: the standard varieties of African languages are associated with rural areas which are no longer centres of prestige. Younger Blacks of high status are more likely to be urban-wise 'modern' people, who speak English and non-standard urban varieties of African languages, showing extensive borrowing of vocabulary, code-switching, and neologisms.[9] The question can thus be raised whether the standardization of African languages via the mission presses, sermons, and nineteenth-century dictionaries may perhaps have taken place too early to be effective as a norm representing Black social and political aspirations and new possibilities of post-colonial, post-apartheid nationalism.

From the late 1840s onwards a second British settlement took place, this time in Natal, which had been annexed from the Afrikaners by the British in 1843. Although many British children born in Natal learned Zulu, a new pidgin form, Fanakalo, arose in the Eastern Cape and Natal out of contacts between the English, Zulus, and Afrikaners. Fanakalo is a stable pidgin that mainly draws on Zulu for its lexis and English for its grammar. The colonists in Natal needed to find a cheap labour source other than amongst the local Zulus, whose men initially resisted cheap manual labour. The government consequently turned to India as a source of cheap labour, bringing Indian people into Natal in sizeable numbers. The antecedents of the four major racial groups identified as such in apartheid South Africa (Black, White, Coloured and Indian) were thus in place by the end of the nineteenth century.[10]

In the 1850s, the trekking Afrikaners eventually established the republics of the Transvaal and Free State. Although they had chosen to escape British domination, and had installed Dutch as the official language of the republics, the influence of the English language nevertheless remained strong. Rather ironically, Afrikaans was first substantially written down by 'non-Whites' in the Cape, the descendants of Muslim

---

[9] Sometimes in the literature this distinction in forms is referred to in terms of 'deep' and 'light' versions of the African languages, with the former term corresponding to the older rural forms and the latter to more modern urban varieties, imbued with mixing and switching (Slabbert and Finlayson 2000).

[10] It goes without saying that the apartheid state imposed a bureaucratic unity upon each of these groups that ill accorded with the diversity and fluidity existing in the nineteenth and early twentieth centuries.

slaves, who used Arabic script to write religious texts in Afrikaans, especially in the period 1868–1910 (Davids 1990: 1). Working-class and rural Coloured culture is in fact still more associated with Afrikaans than with any other language, being complemented by code-mixing between Afrikaans and English in urban areas (McCormick 2002). Afrikaans started to be cultivated by Whites only later, with the formation of the Genootskap van Regte Afrikaners ('Fellowship of True Afrikaners') in 1876 in Paarl. The organization initially faced opposition from aficionados of Dutch, and were referred to in the Cape Argus of 13 September 1877 as a 'number of jokers near Cape Town' (Davids 1991: 2–3).

In another important development, South Africa in the 1860s came to be affected by the discovery of enormous deposits of diamonds and gold in the northern interior. The scramble to gain possession of this new wealth brought Britain into conflict with the Afrikaner republics and led to the annexation of the Transvaal as a British colony in 1877. Afrikaner nationalism grew strongly in this period with resentment at British rapacity, and two wars were fought over control of the land and its wealth, first in 1881, when the Afrikaners won back the Transvaal, and then later between 1899 and 1902, in what is now called 'the South African War', when they were heavily defeated and much maltreated by the British. Elsewhere in the area, in 1879 a British force invaded Zululand to protect its new Transvaal colony from a supposed Zulu threat, creating an offensive which brought about the final subjection of Black people in the nineteenth century. The late nineteenth century also saw urbanization on a large scale, with a large influx of Europeans of Christian and Jewish faith, and a separate large-scale movement of Black and Khoesan/Coloured people into the rapidly developing mining areas, where they came into contact with Indians, Chinese, and people from many parts of Europe, the U.S., and Australia. In this great Babel, the pidgin Fanakalo which had originated in the eastern Cape and Natal proved to be particularly useful as a means of inter-group communication. It is likely that the gathering of different groups in the mining industry also spawned the beginnings of new mixed, urban varieties of African languages (especially Tsotsitaal) which were set to become more prominent during the twentieth century.

Shortly after the turn of the century, the administration of the conquered Boer republics was taken over by the decorated British statesman Alfred Milner who ruled South Africa from the city of Johannesburg, between 1901 and 1905. One of Milner's aims was to anglicize the Afrikaners and bring them into the fold of the British empire. In attempting to achieve this, a heavy emphasis was placed on English over Dutch in the schools provided by the state for the White population (education of the Black population being left to churches and mission schools and not provided by the colonial government). In the wake of the atrocities of the South African War, Afrikaners strongly resisted Milner's Anglicization policy, and the status of Afrikaans as a bearer of local cultural values and the identity of an Afrikaner nation began to gain clear prominence. Nationalism on a large scale thus came into being among the Afrikaners, fuelled by anti-English sentiment and their sense of difference from the Khoesan and Black people. In the development of Afrikaner nationalism, Afrikaner leaders emphasized their uniqueness in Africa, the uniqueness of their language, and their long ties to the land they inhabited.[11]

The Union of South Africa was subsequently formed in 1910, combining the two former Boer republics and the British colonies of the Cape and Natal into one state. The official languages of the Union were Dutch and English, Afrikaans not being recognized as an official language until 1925, when it replaced Dutch in that capacity. During the early twentieth century, the state oversaw the further dispossession of Black people of their land, and the Land Act of 1913, which set aside most of the country's land for control by Whites, destroyed the economic independence of Black people. Somewhat later on, increasing Afrikaner power in the country led to an extended era of Afrikaner nationalism and its cornerstone, the policy of apartheid, instituted in 1948 following elections won by the (Afrikaner) National Party. This philosophy of racial segregation had serious socio-political consequences in everyday life. The Group Areas act of 1950 uprooted established communities to ensure that the four race groups were kept apart and relocated large numbers of Black, Coloured, and Indian people to designated areas. New 'pass laws' were then introduced to channel and regulate black labourers to where they were needed (industries and White farms), whilst keeping their families in the rural areas. As part of the general redistribution of the Black population, the 1940s saw the rapid growth of Black townships like Moroka, which later formed a central part of Soweto in Johannesburg.[12] Another highly significant aspect of the general separation of the population along racial lines was the partitioning of Blacks into subgroups conceived of as different nations/nationalities (*volke*) and defined in terms of language. In many instances this linguistically based classification process might have exaggerated the importance of differences in speech between groups whose language varieties were actually mutually intelligible and not obviously distinguishable as separate languages (as for example with the Ndebele, Zulus, Xhosas, and Swazis of the Nguni language – Kamwangamalu 2000). Each ethno-linguistic group was assigned to live in one of a set of supposedly independent, self-governed (but also heavily controlled) homelands making up a total of just 13 per cent of the area of South Africa, and special permission was required for travel to other parts of the country.

In regard to schooling of the population during the apartheid era, the Bantu Education Act of 1953 consigned Black people to a second-class education in poorly resourced state schools. At this time, mission schools, which had offered quality education (albeit in small numbers) to Black people, often on non-racial lines,

---

[11] One of the claims of entitlement to the land was that the Dutch had settled in South Africa from the south in the seventeenth century, just as the Bantu were coming in from the north. This chronology is however faulty, as early Bantu settlements in South Africa date back to the third century AD. The claim to original ownership made by Afrikaners also dismisses ownership rights of the authochthonous Khoesan.

[12] Such urban townships were not part of any homeland.

were closed down, forcing young Black children into the state-run schools. Such socio-political arrangements clearly influenced the course of linguistic development in South Africa, in terms of restricting regular access to speakers of other languages and varieties, and the consequent heightening of the boundaries of ethnically marked languages and dialects. Scholars (e.g. Harries 1989; Vail 1989; Makoni 1999) insist that what the apartheid state did was to congeal identities and languages that previously were largely fluid, criss-crossing and overlapping. The dramatic division of the population also resulted in the creation and firming up of distinct dialects of the official languages, Afrikaans and English. The main ethnic varieties of English are till today marked not only by clearly distinguishable accents, but by certain features of syntax as well. Likewise, Afrikaans is still bifurcated along the lines of White and Coloured varieties. In its structuring of language in South African society, apartheid policy consistently attempted to impose a clear linguistic hierarchy on the country, and used the education system to play out the prevailing rivalry between Afrikaans and English. In the 1950s, contrary to its own commission's suggestions, the Department of Bantu Education ruled that English and Afrikaans be introduced as subjects in the first year of schooling (to children who were acquainted with neither language). Whereas the commission had also suggested that only one official language (English or Afrikaans) be a compulsory subject, the Department insisted on both, fearing that if only one language were to be chosen, it would be English. For the same reason both English and Afrikaans were to be used as mediums of instruction in secondary schools (Hartshorne 1995: 310).

In some respects, however questionable the motivation underlying it (and seen by many as a further, linguistic, application of Afrikaner divide-and-rule), the apartheid policy of mother-tongue education for up to eight years of primary school was in itself not unsound, resulting in African languages being the general medium of instruction for Black children until secondary school. The UNESCO document of 1953 entitled 'The use of vernacular languages in education' was, at about this time, stressing the important value of mother-tongue education in the early years of schooling. Problems lay in the way this policy was implemented, however, and the manner in which the wishes of parents were commonly ignored. Vernacular education was accompanied both by inferior resources for the education of Blacks and rigid controls over the content of all parts of education (Hartshorne 1995).

In 1960, under Afrikaner influence, South Africa broke its formal colonial ties with Britain, becoming a fully independent new republic.[13] International opposition to apartheid then led to the expulsion of the new republic from the British Commonwealth in the same year. South Africa subsequently developed as a 'laager' state, devoid of the liberal trends present in Western Europe and of the forces of decolonization that

---

[13] In the referendum amongst Whites that led to republicanism, the vote was 52 per cent for; 47 per cent against. In the province of Natal in which English-speaking Whites predominated over Afrikaners, the majority voted against a Republic (Saunders 1994: 201).

were sweeping through many parts of Africa.[14] Resistance to apartheid, especially as embodied in 'Bantu education', led to the Soweto uprisings of 1976, in which Black students protested against the government's decision to enforce the use of Afrikaans as a medium of education in secondary schools in equal measure with English (the Afrikaans Medium Decree of 1974). The students' joint demonstration on 16 June after several weeks of refusing to attend school was crushed with violence and large numbers of those protesting were shot and killed by police confronting the rally. Following on from this critical event of confrontation with the government, the 1970s and 1980s became a period of intense struggle against White domination, in which young Black and Coloured students regularly played a prominent role. It is worthy of note that the event that ultimately led to the arrival of democracy in the country through the escalation of wider protest it inspired should be linguistic in nature and a rejection of Afrikaans in Black schools. Since that time, although Afrikaans has maintained some value as a lingua franca in urban labour contexts, it is not a language generally looked favourably upon by the Black majority due to its negative associations with apartheid and the Afrikaner-led government responsible for the policies of segregation.[15] By way of contrast, English was a language that positively benefited from the excesses of apartheid rule, almost by default. As it was widely used by the linguistically mixed anti-apartheid political leadership, English became perceived as the language of unity and liberation among the Black population. Although Black schoolchildren also had pride in their home languages, the latter had perhaps become too closely connected with the divide-and-rule policy of apartheid to be considered as languages of educational and economic progress.

As both internal pressure, in the form of civil disorder and violence directed at symbols and representatives of the government, and external pressure imposed though economic sanctions and broad international criticism of apartheid continued to mount to ever-higher levels through the 1980s, the government led by F. W. De Klerk finally saw the real need for significant change in the country, and began to dismantle the architecture of apartheid from 1990 until 1994, when a new constitution guaranteeing equal rights for all races had been promulgated (in 1993), and a new pluralist democracy and multi-ethnic era for South Africa was ceremonially declared on 26 April 1994.

17.3 The Post-apartheid Era and Language Policy

Proper, democratic independence thus came relatively late to South Africa. The republic formed in the 1960s did not usher in a post-colonial democracy. Rather there

---

[14] The term *laager* denotes 'an encampment of wagons lashed together for the protection of people and animals within, and as a barricade from which to fire on attackers; the regular defence of [Afrikaners on trek]' (Branford 1991: 171). The word is used figuratively in South African English to denote a siege mentality or ideologically impenetrable mindset.

[15] In addition to the major policies of separation already referred to, apartheid also enforced the separation of races in hospitals, transportation, public toilets, beaches, cemeteries, parks, and a wide range of other common public-use facilities.

was a continuation of dominance from a European-derived regime, and only in the 1990s did South Africa begin to experience the decolonization that had taken place three to four decades earlier in other ex-European colonies of Africa and Asia. Two consequences arise from this late emancipation: (a) that European-derived languages are well entrenched in the country and (b) that globalization had already emerged in the 1990s as a counterforce to post-colonial emancipation and the possible rise of local economic and cultural forces that would favour local languages over the global.

A period of intense political negotiations led to the first democratic elections of 1994. At the negotiating table were the political parties of the day and a number of resistance movements that had previously been banned. The most prominent of the resistance movements was the African National Congress (ANC), whose leaders included Oliver Tambo, Walter Sisulu, and Nelson and Winnie Mandela. The ANC was a non-racial movement, whose leaders of the 1960s were largely forced into exile. It drew upon activists from all race groups, using English as their de facto lingua franca. Indeed, at one time, the ANC leadership seemed to be headed for a policy preferring English as the only official language. However, language was not a great priority for the ANC in the way it was for parties representing Afrikaner nationalism, whose strong attachment to Afrikaans made the future position of this language an important bargaining chip during negotiations prior to 1994 (Crawhall 1993). At the same time many educators and sociolinguists put their weight behind cultural and linguistic pluralism – empowering the majority of South Africans meant empowering their languages too. A policy with English as the only official language would consequently have been anathema to many Afrikaans speakers. A second possible scenario, having both English and Afrikaans as the official languages of the country, would have given off signals to the majority of the population that little had changed in terms of linguistic power relations. Clearly if English and Afrikaans were to remain as official languages, there was a strong case for certain African languages to be given the same status. The classic dilemma of colonized, multilingual societies emerging into new nationhood then presented itself: which of the African languages should be chosen? The politicians' solution was to opt for all nine of the African languages that had had recognition within the homelands system, and which, collectively, were the mother tongues of as much as 99 per cent of the Black population. The eleven-language policy was thus an eleventh-hour compromise, rather than a submission emanating from any political party, and with this compromise, South Africa came to be a country in which eleven languages have formally been recognized as the official languages of the state.

17.3.1 South Africa's Constitutional Provisions on Language

The country's new constitution, passed in 1996, placed an important emphasis on the link between language, culture, and development in its recognition of eleven

Table 17.1 The home languages of South Africa in 2001: numbers and percentages*

	No. of speakers	%
Nguni languages		
Ndebele	711,818	1.6
Swati	1,194,428	2.6
Xhosa	7,907,154	17.6
Zulu	10,677,306	23.8
Sotho languages		
Pedi	4,208,982	9.3
Sotho	3,555,189	7.9
Tswana	3,677,016	8.2
Other languages		
Tsonga	1,992,207	4.4
Venda	1,021,759	2.2
Afrikaans	5,983,426	13.3
English	3,673,197	8.1
Other	217,297	0.4
TOTAL	44,819,779	99.4

*Note that census statistics for second-language use are not available. It is safe to suggest that English occupies a prominent position here. Other important second languages include Zulu and Afrikaans.

languages for official purposes. In addition to the previous official languages, Afrikaans and English, the nine African languages which were promoted to co-official status are the Nguni group of Xhosa, Zulu, Swati, and Ndebele; the Sotho group of Sotho (previously known as South Sotho), Pedi, and Tswana; and Tsonga and Venda (which fall outside the Sotho and Nguni groupings).[16] As the census figures from 2001 show in Table 17.1, these eleven languages account for the home languages of the vast majority of South Africans.[17]

The text of the Constitution dealing with language (Chapter 1, section 6) touches on many important themes pertaining to nationhood:

Languages
6. (1) The official languages of the Republic are Sepedi, Sesotho, Setswana, siSwati, Tshivenda, Xitsonga, Afrikaans, English, isiNdebele, isiXhosa and isiZulu.

---

[16] Pedi is the language which used to be called 'North Sotho', and Swati is what used to be called 'Swazi'. Though certain authors include language prefixes when referring to the indigenous languages of South Africa (e.g. isiZulu, siSwati, Setswana, Tshivenda, Xitsonga, etc.), I prefer not to use these when writing in English; I acknowledge that others have different preferences in this regard.

[17] Though since 2001, large-scale migrations from neighbouring African countries have decreased the very high percentage of home-language coverage in table 17.1. Languages such as French (from Central and West Africa), Kiswahili (from East Africa), and Shona (from Zimbabwe) have been growing in prominence since the last census count.

(2) Recognising the historically diminished use and status of the indigenous languages of our people, the state must take practical and positive measures to elevate the status and advance the use of these languages.

(3) National and provincial governments may use particular official languages for the purposes of government, taking into account usage, practicality, expense, regional circumstances, and the balance of the needs and preferences of the population as a whole or in respective provinces; provided that no national or provincial government may use only one official language. Municipalities must take into consideration the language usage and preferences of their residents.

(4) National and provincial governments, by legislative and other measures, must regulate and monitor the use by those governments of official languages. Without detracting from the provisions of subsection (2), all official languages must enjoy parity of esteem and must be treated equitably.

(5) The Pan South African Language Board must -

    (a) promote and create conditions for the development and use of

        (i) all official languages

        (ii) the Khoi, Nama and San languages; and

        (iii) sign language

    (b) promote and ensure respect for languages, including German, Greek, Gujarati, Hindi, Portuguese, Tamil, Telugu, Urdu, and others commonly used by communities in South Africa, and Arabic, Hebrew, Sanskrit and others used for religious purposes.

As a vision towards multilingual national unity and language maintenance there is little room for discontent here. However, as the major public sectors are discovering, social change within this broad vision is not so easy to achieve in the short term, especially with a high unemployment rate, a low literacy rate, and global economic pressures.[18] The key question for applied linguists and educators is the extent to which the new constitutional flexibility on language can be put into effective practice. In some respects language policy and practice have been in flux in the post-1994 era, with many sectors still experimenting with the most effective and the least divisive language options. Webb (2002: 40, 56) characterizes the constitutional provisions on language as a mission statement, rather than a policy. Du Plessis (2000: 106) also comments on the absence of a national language policy and legislation resulting from it five years after the inception of the new constitution.[19] Others argue that these proposals constitute a policy, but what was lacking was a plan to put the policy into practice.

---

[18] The *Sunday Times* (10/9/2006, p.1) reports that one in three adult South Africans has not had primary education or not completed primary school. This survey was carried out by a non-governmental literacy organization, READ.

[19] That is, whereas there are eleven official languages, South Africa has no formally recognized national language (or national languages).

Several major language bodies and committees have in fact contributed to policy making and to planning. For example, the NEPI (*National Education Policy Investigation*) was an independent initiative of the early 1990s, designed to give input to any future government on crucial issues relating to education. A subgroup on language provided a booklet whose strength was to suggest options, rather than propose a particular policy (NEPI 1992, edited by Kay McCormick, Zubeida Desai, and Sidney Zotwana).[20] LANGTAG (*Language Task Action Group*) was a short-term initiative of the Department of Arts, Culture, Science and Technology (DACST) in 1996. Its brief was to advise the Minister (then Ben Ngubane) on planning for policy-making within the language guidelines of the new constitution. LANGTAG brought together a broad range of language practitioners, including sociolinguists, enabling comprehensive consultations with different communities and sectors, intensive discussions, and some new research (see the LANGTAG final report of 1996). Its role in shaping subsequent policy frameworks is acknowledged by the Minister Ben Ngubane in his foreword to the National Language Policy Framework of 2002. The *Pan South African Languages Board* (PANSALB) is a permanent body established in terms of the constitution as a pro-active agent for, and watchdog over, linguistic rights. After a slow start, which has attracted a fair amount of criticism (Alexander 2002; Heugh 2000; du Plessis 2000) it is beginning to get organized in areas like lexicography for the African languages and language development in general (Marivate 2000). The Language Services division of DACST is more concerned with practical implementation of the language provisos, though there is overlap between itself and PANSALB which is still being ironed out (Mkhulisi 2000).

Since 1996 there has also been a steady output of policy documents, with accompanying implementation plans. At the national level the most important is the National Language Policy Framework (NLPF) (final draft November 2002), devised by the DACST. The framework binds all government structures to a multilingual mode of operation. It enjoins government committees to agree on a working language, with due regard to the rights of individuals to use another language. It promulgates communication with the public in the preferred language of citizens. Government publications are to respect the reality of functional multilingualism, and publish in all eleven official languages where possible, and in any case in no fewer than six of them. The six designated languages are Tsonga, Venda, Afrikaans, English, an Nguni language, and a Sotho language. The latter two are to be chosen on a rotational basis from, respectively: (a) Xhosa, Zulu, Ndebele, and Swati, and (b) Pedi, Sotho, and Tswana. The policy (known as the Languages Bill) still awaits ratification by parliament. Some scholars have expressed concern at what they see as a considerable delay in this procedure.

---

[20] The editors, in keeping with the ethos of the larger project, are not named in the publication. It is now time to acknowledge their efforts.

17.3.2 Language Practice in the Period 1994 to 2006 and its Critics

In the short term, despite what may be called the 'feel-good rainbowism' of the constitution, it was English which consolidated its position at the expense of other languages.[21] In spite of efforts by the likes of ex-President Mandela to make occasional public speeches in Afrikaans, English came to dominate in parliament, higher education, local government, and institutions such as the police, defence force, and the courts. For Afrikaans, in particular, the loss of status and power was dramatic, if to be expected. The dominance of Afrikaans (and hence an Afrikaner power base) in the army, navy, and police force has been 'reduced to an equality', in Neville Alexander's memorable phrase (personal communication). Such an equality, in fact, holds only with the other nine official languages in their struggle to come to terms with the status, power, and utility of English. Hence a more realistic formulation might well be 'reduced to an inequality'. In the rest of this section I turn to critiques by various stakeholders and intellectuals against this development, and also to some counter-critiques.

The most active organization researching and campaigning for an effective multilingual policy in education and beyond is PRAESA (*Project for Alternative Education in South Africa*), an NGO started by Neville Alexander, now a research unit at the University of Cape Town. A committed activist of long standing, Alexander sees language as an indispensable part of the quest for a just social order, enabling the full participation of South Africans in developing themselves and the country. Part of his contribution has been self-confessedly polemical: Alexander has tried to galvanize ordinary citizens and intellectual and educational leaders into avoiding what he sees as the trap of English monolingualism in public life. At the same time PRAESA is engaged in action research on a range of issues such as literacy in African languages, especially Xhosa; more effective methods of mother-tongue education in African languages; and inculcating multilingualism in schools (Plüddemann et al. 2003). More recently PRAESA members have been involved in investigating language policy as a social practice in South Africa (Alexander and Heugh 1999) and the development of African language terminology (Mahlalela and Heugh 2002). Alexander argues (2002: 122):

> The political class, in general, and black political leaders, in particular, are disposed to the promotion of a unilingual, i.e. English-only, language policy in the public service, even though most of them know that the majority of the 'clients' of the state are unable to access information by these means. This, naturally, has considerable implications for the viability of a democratic dispensation. For this reason, the mobilization of the linguistic communities in support of their language rights is an essential aspect of the consolidation of democracy in the new South Africa. Surprisingly, given the tradition of the liberation struggle, especially the grassroots mobilization of the trade union and community

---

[21] For a while the rainbow was taken as a powerful symbol of unity within diversity for the new nation; it is perhaps unsporting to point out that the metaphor has its limits – neither black, white, nor brown feature in rainbows.

organization sectors in which the use of local languages was a condition for the success of these organizations, the leadership has tended to fall into the same traps as earlier leaders of independence and liberation movements in Africa . . .

More incisively he warns (2002: 122–3):

> Language planning processes in South Africa today have a surrealistic aspect to them as a result of the tension between what the governing elites are obliged to do constitutionally and what they prefer to do based on their interests and the convenience of inertia. On the one hand, there are extremely progressive and radical moves being planned and explored by official commissions, advisory panels and statutory bodies dealing with the language issue. On the other hand there is the never-ending chain of procedural impedimenta used by the bureaucracy in collusion with the political leaders – who, of course, are merely responding to the gentle voice of the voters – to retard and obstruct the implementation of the language policy. In South Africa today, language planners are afforded a ringside seat at one of the most fascinating spectacles involving both political smoke-and-mirrors tricks and scholarly timidity.

The suspicion of smoke-and-mirrors tricks is raised by other researchers too. Theo du Plessis, head of the Unit for Language Facilitation and Empowerment at the University of the Free State, laments the lack of congruence between the declaration of eleven official languages and the increasing dominance of English (2001: 102): 'One receives the impression that, in spite of the constitutional obligations, the official downgrading of Afrikaans outweighs the enhancement of the status of African languages.' Further-more, 'the new decision-makers seem inclined to 'enforce' an English-only policy, primarily in order to diminish the status of Afrikaans' (ibid.: 103).

Webb (2002) makes a strong case for the further development of African languages, citing the benefits of nation-building, economic gains, and educational facilitation. He appeals for real (as opposed to symbolic) empowerment of the African languages. Following on Webb's analysis it is instructive to note the successes in language practice as of 2004:

- Resources are being allocated to the development of African languages.
- Computer terminology is being developed in all official languages.
- Research on speech recognition systems is being undertaken.
- Smaller languages like Venda are becoming visible on television.
- There is a greater presence of African languages at least at an informal level in public institutions, centres for tertiary education, public spaces in cities, etc.
- Musical traditions in a variety of languages continue to grow.
- Tertiary institutions are being called upon to develop greater space for the use of African languages.

These successes do not immediately ensure the equality of African languages with English, but they are an important start on a long and winding road. It should be noted that not even Afrikaans received immediate acceptance once it was declared a language by its aficionados in 1875. Some scholars (Alexander 2002; du Plessis 2001) also appear to underestimate the extent to which English (and other European languages used in government in Africa) is seen as a tool of modernization and political development. English is associated with technology, international links, communications networks within Africa, and the business of politics. Webb, by contrast, tends to underestimate the value of African languages in their speakers' own eyes. Witness his conclusions such as 'these languages have become highly stigmatised, and are perceived as worthless by most of their speakers' (Webb 2002: 13). This appears to be insensitive to the 'covert prestige' (Labov 1972) of vernacular languages (Slabbert and Finlayson 2000). African languages are seen as natural mediums for music, sports, radio broadcasts at a local level, and community life and values. Webb (2002: 12) also suggests that 'Black South Africans have not been able to acquire the necessary proficiency in English to use it effectively as an instrument of meaningful access to education'. Here he comes close to articulating a 'semilingual' position, a term used by Doug Young (Young et al. 2004) – that Black pupils end up learning neither their home language nor English at schools. However, no sociolinguist accepts the idea of semilingualism (a 'half-baked theory' to quote Martin-Jones and Romaine 1985), as all human beings have at least one language that they speak comfortably and fluently. This need not be a standard language, which is what confuses educators, who are more interested in inculcating literacy in a prior-established language than validating the home language that the child brings to school. The potential charge of 'semilingualism' misrepresents the linguistic skills of the highly multilingual, young black population.[22]

In another initiative, Kwesi Prah and Neville Alexander have built strong links with scholars and language practitioners elsewhere in Africa, with the intention of raising the profile of African languages. Both scholars see the process of 'harmonization' as crucial to promulgating these languages in education and public life, and going beyond the fatalist feeling that such languages are too small and fragmented to play a meaningful and economically viable role in formal education. The harmonization project arose out of a proposal by Neville Alexander (1989) (and made earlier by politician Jacob Nhlapo in the 1940s) that a new standard Nguni language be developed from the Nguni 'cluster' of Zulu, Xhosa, Swati, and Ndebele, as well as a new Sotho standard based on North Sotho, South Sotho, and Tswana. This would have the satisfying outcome of having two major African languages (plus the smaller Venda and Tsonga) as candidates for official languages. When linguists expressed strong doubt at the feasibility of such a unification at the spoken level, Alexander stressed the benefits at the written level. Whereas the numerous African language boards set up by the apartheid government had worked in competition with each other, and tried to accentuate differences, even

---

[22] Failure to attain literacy adequately in any language is another issue, and a major impediment to the realization of some of the goals of equality espoused in nation-building.

when deciding on new technical terms, Alexander expressed the hope that in the long term, at least at the level of writing and publishing, the languages within each cluster could be brought together rather than forced apart. Alexander could not have anticipated the virulent reaction to his proposals at conferences from Black academics, who stressed the symbolic and cultural value of individual African languages, which ran counter to any attempts at linguistic engineering. The harmonization proposals were accordingly put on the back burner. Effectively this means that whilst Black intellectuals might be committed to unity as a group, they do not tie it to a unification of their languages (assuming that this were practicable). One current policy compromise, however, indirectly gives support for the harmonization rationale. As noted above, the National Language Policy Framework (2002), which has still to be passed, enjoins government departments to publish documents in all eleven official languages where possible, and in any case in no fewer than six of them. The six languages are Tsonga, Venda, Afrikaans, English, an Nguni language and a Sotho language, the latter two to be chosen on a rotational basis from Xhosa/Zulu/Ndebele/Swati and Pedi/Sotho/Tswana. This accords with the harmonization grouping, except that the standard form of one language is intended to stand for the rest of the group during its terms of rotation.

Amongst some intellectuals there is a feeling that perhaps too much energy is actually spent on language debates and appeals to making languages official and insisting on those rights. Max du Preez, a political journalist of Afrikaans background wrote a trenchant critique in a Cape Town newspaper of what he saw as yet another conference on the status of Afrikaans (in August 2004):

> There is probably no other public issue in South African national life that elicits so much heated drivel, falsehoods, pretentiousness and wasted emotion than the issue of the Afrikaans language. I am bored to the depths of my soul with the Afrikaans debate.
>
> Afrikaans is my mother tongue and I love it passionately. I speak Afrikaans to my brothers and sisters...My children are also Afrikaans-speaking, unlike the children of many of the prominent fighters for Afrikaans, and so are my dogs, my ducks and my chickens. I also only swear in Afrikaans.
>
> ... [M]ost of the conference-goers (almost all well over 40) have a professional stake in Afrikaans: publishers, editors, linguists, academics, politicians, business people and those employed by Afrikaans cultural or language lobby groups. If Afrikaans is on the wane, so will their fortunes.
>
> ... In my opinion Afrikaans is more creative and vibrant now than when it was the language of the oppressor. Afrikaans music really only came alive after the 'alternative' resistance music movement of 1988 and beyond.
>
> ... Enjoy your language, stop whining about it. And most of all stop confusing your language rights with your sense of loss of power, prestige and privilege in the new democracy. (Column 'Maximum Headroom', *Argus* 2 September 2004)

Whilst (like all political journalists) du Preez is overstating his case, his stance is a necessary balance to any academic's account of Afrikaans and language planning in the new era. Du Preez's critics might point to the continuing erosion of Afrikaans as a medium of instruction as schools and universities become more multilingual in their student intake, and to the increased power of English in South Africa. An additional, interesting aspect of du Preez's article is whether the sociolinguistically bottom-up perspective he gives is possibly implicitly shared by speakers and intellectuals from the *other* official language communities. That is, do African intellectuals who are not directly involved in language as a profession also dismiss the voice of those intellectuals who put language (and especially *their* language) above all else? Although one cannot be sure, this might go some way in explaining the stalling tactics of government officials as described by Alexander.

It is now time to turn to the extremities of the language spectrum. It has been noted that the smaller language communities – Tsonga, Venda, Swati, and Ndebele – do not feel as empowered as the constitution suggests they should. A particular area of discontent up till recently was their absence on television channels (Beukman 2000: 142). An alliance of sorts was subsequently formed between these groups against what is seen as the increasing power of the other official African languages (Webb 2002; du Plessis 2000). Perhaps it was pressures from this lobby which resulted in the subsequent introduction of a new range of television programmes, especially sitcoms, in Venda and Tsonga with English subtitles, which now attract a wide viewing audience. On the other hand, the proposals of the National Language Policy Framework relating to the translation of national government documents actually elevate Tsonga and Venda above the other African languages, and place them on an equality with Afrikaans and English as official languages which will always be translated into (as opposed to the Nguni and Sotho groups of official languages, which will have one 'representative' language used for official translation at any point in time). This elevation of smaller languages above more numerous ones raises interesting issues, which will no doubt be debated if and when the Languages Bill comes up before parliament. Members of other, non-official language groups have also written in to PANSALB upon invitation to register their fears and complaints about real and perceived neglect arising out of their non-official status, for example (speakers of) Northern Ndebele, Portuguese, the Khoesan and Indian languages (Beukman 2000: 142). Here we see a misunderstanding of the concept of an official language: people who identify with a language that is not one of the chosen eleven have used the opportunity to express their feeling of exclusion, yet official languages are supposed to be vehicles for practical functions, and not just feelings of identification. In this regard, speakers of Portuguese and the Indian and Khoesan languages have largely undergone language shift and therefore function in everyday life in English or Afrikaans, but at a symbolic level still identify with their ancestral tongues. Amongst the smaller languages, some cases for consideration as additional official languages are stronger than others. For example, if (Southern) Ndebele is official, why not Northern Ndebele? Finally, it can be noted that the presence of Sign Language as a lobby has made the language visible on some television programmes (notably news bulletins), and that its use in education has led to its being informally dubbed as the country's 'twelfth official language'.

At the other extremity, no one disputes the utilitarian value of English. In fact many parents seem to desire as much English for their children as soon as possible. De Klerk (2000) gives an account of parents in the Eastern Cape actively discouraging the mother tongue amongst children who are sent to the former White (now non-racial) schools. This is all the more surprising in view of the fact that these are not 'elite families'. However, this case study might not be typical; it does not appear to apply to the large majority of township dwellers. Alexander (2002: 123) warns against politicians who use the argument of the attraction of English to their own ends: 'They [language planners] are told daily by political "visionaries" that "the people want English", despite survey evidence that points to the fact the people want English *and* their own languages.' There are other scholars, who support English as the unambiguous main language of higher education, the economy, and the media, but not at the expense of the African languages. This view is articulated by Stanley Ridge (2004), who calls for an intermediate position between an overemphasis on English and an overemphasis on multilingualism. Ridge criticizes the policy documents for their unnuanced view of multilingualism and of the individual languages. He argues that a blanket call for multilingualism fails to recognize the different domains in which multilingual speakers deploy individual languages:

> Few applied linguists would question the need for circumspection in planning the place of English, given the enormous power associated with it, and the ways its first and second language users have sometimes edged other languages out, often in the name of modernity and development. However, there is also a clear need to have a realistic sense of the significance English does legitimately have in a certain situation and what it can actually deliver.

One group that is immune from Ridge's qualification is the new middle-class Black youth. Once denied quality education and interaction with White and other English-speaking peers, Black pupils appear to be thriving in the former White schools. Their transition to university also appears to be easier than for Black pupils from the 'township' schools. Although still small, and in a minority in the schools mentioned, the new Black middle-class is a confident and highly visible one, marked by a command of English in grammar and accent that is virtually the same as that of their White peers. There is also a class distinction between this group and their counterparts from the Black townships. Those who emulate their White peers (and also follow some globalized norms of fashion and music) are described as *coconuts* ('black on the outside, white on the inside') or *multis* (short for 'from a multiracial school') and are accused of losing their traditional culture. Conversely, the *multis'* opinion of their young Black critics is not very flattering either. Clearly, South Africa is experiencing the growing diffuseness of a society in which racial and class boundaries are shifting.

17.3.3 Issues around the Medium of Instruction

A sense of the practical and ideological difficulties surrounding nation-building can be seen from the choice of medium of instruction. Here the nation is pulling in different directions. The constitution wisely lays down guidelines towards multilingualism, without specifying the languages and options. Most sociolinguists and applied linguists propose that children who come to school without a knowledge of English should have the benefit of initial mother-tongue education. They also propose an early introduction of English as a subject, since this is clearly the medium that many parents prefer for their children as soon as possible. Parents appear to be distrustful of using African languages as mediums of instruction as they associate this with the disadvantage fostered by apartheid education. Many parents also seem to confuse English as a primary school subject and English as a medium of education. The sociolinguistic position has been supported by government authorities; however in the interests of democracy it is the school governing bodies who decide on the issue. Currently, there is no uniform policy in place.

Schools that once operated via the medium of Afrikaans have had to adjust to changing circumstances, and introduce dual-medium education in English and Afrikaans, since Black pupils prefer English. Peter Plüddemann (personal communication) notes that some formerly Afrikaans-medium schools in the Western Cape undergo a two-step change, firstly from Afrikaans medium to Afrikaans and English then, in time, as the intake of Black pupils increases, the focus changes to the need to inculcate Xhosa. Since this inevitably weakens the position of Afrikaans, governing bodies of certain schools try to limit the number of non-Afrikaans speakers. This has brought some schools into conflict with the provincial government, which promulgates greater racial inclusiveness. One prominent case brought before the courts in 2005 was that of the Western Cape Minister of Education and Others vs. the Governing Body of Mikro Primary School. (The judgement in favour of Mikro school to choose Afrikaans as its medium can be seen at http://www.law.wits.ac.za/sca/summary.php?case_id=13073//xxx).

Equally interesting and complex developments are occurring at the tertiary level. Under apartheid separate universities were created for the different race groups, with unequal distribution of resources. The post-apartheid government has attempted to undo the duplication of resources by merging institutions that are in the same locale. Thus the University of KwaZulu-Natal is the result of a merger between the (formerly Indian) University of Durban-Westville, the (formerly black)[23] University of Natal Medical School, the (formerly White) Edgewood College of Education and the two (White) campuses of the University of Natal, based in Durban and Pietermaritzburg. Whereas the medium of instruction at all these institutions was always English, there are now moves to introduce Zulu as co-medium of instruction (*Sunday Times* 22 May 2006). If the merger itself has been fraught with practical and ideological difficulties,

---

[23] The use of lower case in 'black' here signals the broad sense of 'Blacks, Indians and Coloureds'.

the top-down nature of the envisaged language policy raises fundamental questions about the nature of higher education and its role in an African setting. Proponents of the policy claim to be following constitutional guidelines towards language equity (see clauses 2 and 4 cited above) and to be validating the university's role in a region where Zulu is the majority language. Sceptics on the campus point to the localization of the Zulu language, as opposed to the wide intake of students from the country, the continent, and the world outside. There are also doubts that, though Zulu is a language spoken by many and read by some, it might not be able to carry the full burden of modern scientific knowledge right away. The ensuing years will certainly be interesting ones for the campus and for applied linguistic activity. One comparison frequently made by proponents of African languages in higher education is that if Afrikaans, a relatively small and localized language, could make the transition to science and technology in the early twentieth century, why not Zulu and Venda (see, for example, Alexander 2002; Prah 1995)? The issue is precisely that of political will and ideological belief. Afrikaans did it alone, while denying similar resources to the other developing languages of the country. It is doubtful that the same ideological conditions that promoted Afrikaans in higher education exist today. If Zulu (or any other African language) is to thrive at tertiary level, it will require the same commitment evinced by Afrikaans academics and writers a century ago. At the moment this does not seem to be likely: the calls for greater Africanization and functional multilingualism in the universities are currently accompanied by declining enrolments in departments of African languages, and greater use of English in many domains by all educated South Africans. The young Black middle class (a small but influential group that is set to grow) is appropriating English as its language of aspirations in an increasingly globalized economic and cultural milieu.

For Afrikaans at the tertiary level the dilemmas are rather similar to those at lower levels of education. The five major Afrikaans universities (formerly for Whites only) have had to adjust to post-apartheid realities, and embrace a dual-medium system with English. This often entails duplication of lectures. Currently, Stellenbosch University, the most prestigious of the formerly Afrikaans universities, is divided in its language philosophy. One grouping of traditionalists wishes to keep Afrikaans as the sole medium of instruction, arguing that Afrikaans will come under threat as a language of higher education once English is admitted as a co-medium of instruction. They argue for the need for at least one purely Afrikaans-medium university in the country. Opponents of the philosophy on the campus argue that this would lead to a 'laager' effect and will be negatively perceived as a way of keeping out speakers of African languages (see e.g. the overview in www.educationworldonline.net/eduworld/article.php?).[24]

---

[24] This would not be entirely on racial lines, as the university does attract fair numbers of Afrikaans-speaking Coloured students.

17.3.4 *Standard English and English Standards*

To return to the position of English in relation to nation-building, a preoccupation of the English Academy of South Africa (a non-governmental body) with the issue of standards is of some significance (see Titlestad 1996; Wright 1996). This is in contrast to the other official languages, where the burning issues have been the right of use in education and other public domains and the practical implementation of those rights. An important question with regard to a standard form of English in South Africa is precisely 'whose standard?' This is an old question in English studies going back as far as Noah Webster's observations in 1789 on the relationship between American and British English (Kahane 1982: 230). The English Academy of South Africa's position, articulated in a submission to CODESA (Convention for a Democratic South Africa) in 1992, was that L1 English should be the norm; it went so far as to posit Standard British English as the embodiment of that norm (see Titlestad 1996: 169–70). Whilst it is true that South African English norms derive largely from the south of England, the English Academy's pronouncement lent itself to misconstrual at a crucial time in the first attempts at building a new nation. It seemed to be dismissive of the norms of Black South Africans in particular. There have been recent counter-calls from some academics for a restandardization of English towards Black norms (Wade 1995; Makalela 2004). The latter has in fact proposed the harmonization of the Englishes of South Africa, in what is apparently *not* a parody of the weightier Nhlapo–Alexander position for already standardized African languages. Unfortunately we seem to suffer from too heavy a faith in language planning. In contrast to any attempts to engineer a new English standard, sociolinguistics leads us to expect that a new informal variety of English will eventually arise in a natural and spontaneous way out of the non-racial and multicultural experiences of middle-class children in the schools. This process will be gradual and organic. A slightly more 'careful' version of this variety might then become the formal standard too. It is however, unlikely to veer too far from 'General South African English' norms in broad phonetic and syntactic structure, taking into account again the influence of the media in an era of global technologies.[25] At the same time I would be surprised if this new formal standard did not carry some traces of influence from educated, middle-class South Africans of colour. This position was in fact articulately argued by the writer and critic, Njabulo Ndebele (1987). But it is not one of harmonization in the language planner's sense. Nor does it apply to any significant extent to written grammatical norms, as Ndebele's own prose suggests.

A second issue raised in English Academy circles (e.g. Titlestad 1998) is whether the new policies may have too much confidence in the effective translation of advanced English texts into the indigenous languages and the use of these translations.[26]

---

[25] 'General South African English' is the current linguistic term for the non-stigmatized variety of South African English hitherto characteristic of the White middle-classes. It differs from a southern British middle-class norm and from a stigmatized 'broad' South African English (see Lanham 1978; Lass 2002).

[26] Similarly, Young, van der Vlugt, and Qanya (2004) caution that attempts to translate English scientific terminology even at the primary level sometimes prove too 'deep' for children to understand.

Titlestad argues that scarce financial resources would be better employed in improving the teaching of English at all levels. He sees empowerment following mainly from the acquisition of marketable skills in English. Whereas mother-tongue education for non-English speakers is vital in the primary schools, he believes that the needs of the marketplace (more and more directed by global changes) require an increasing need for better levels of English competence.

17.4 Language and Nationhood – Two Concluding Perspectives

17.4.1 A Gramscian Sociological Perspective

Antonio Gramsci's (1971) well-known proposition holds that in some societies the old order can be seen to be dying, while a new one still struggles to be born. Gramsci argued that language is always used by those in power for hegemonic purposes, and whenever language rises to the fore in public debates, it is a sign of political and social realignments or consolidation. Crawhall (1993) argues that from such a macro-political perspective the eleven-language policy adopted in the 1990s was an initial move to reduce the linguistic power of the previous regime: this largely applied to downgrading Afrikaans, the language formerly associated with the army, navy, and police. The policy has quite clearly increased the power of English and its adherents. Crawhall's analysis suggests that the inculcation of English served to establish a new Black elite whose socio-symbolic repertoire differentiated it from the masses, who were multilingual, but had less command of English, especially of English literacy. One can add another dimension and trend currently in progress: a move to reduce the power of English speakers, who are still prominent in the economy and higher education sectors, by invoking the need for multilingualism involving African languages. For a while there was even the promise of an alliance between two sets of strange bedfellows both espousing multilingualism – Afrikaans language leaders and African language intellectuals. In the new post-apartheid era Afrikaans intellectuals saw the opportunity to fight for their language rights, not on grounds of exclusivity, as previously, but on constitutionally hallowed multilingual terrain against the glottophagic power of English. This attempt at a multilingual power bloc has not borne fruit, however, as African language scholars do not appear to share the Herderian world view of *volk–language–culture*. Mazrui and Mazrui (1998: 8) argue that such linguistic nationalism in Africa, based on the notion of an identity between language, culture, and nation, is rare and to be found only among the Somali and Afrikaners:

> If the Somali and the Afrikaners are the only genuine linguistic nationalists of the Sahara, where does that leave those Black South Africans who are championing greater recognition of indigenous languages? If Black South Africans are like other Blacks on the continent, they are really defending racial dignity rather than linguistic purity or linguistic autonomy. Language becomes just another aspect of the defence of race – and a valid aspect.

This explanation holds not only for the defence of African languages, but for the question of why the colonial language is embraced by African elites. Racial dignity has two linguistic aspects: one the maintenance of African language(s), the other utilization of European languages (pertaining to the continuing use and status of French, Portuguese, and English in parts of Africa). Despite the importance of tradition and despite the rhetorical challenges to colonialism, the colonial languages are inextricably linked to modernity. As previously discussed, here the traditional African languages fare much less favourably, as they are outcomes of standardization by missionaries in rural areas in a bygone era.

In the short term English has made the most gains; but as long as there is inequality of opportunity and achievement, Gramsci's ideas suggest, language will remain a burning issue, fully implicated in the tussles over nationhood and power. We appear to be seeing this at the universities referred to above in section 17.3.3.

17.4.2 A Bottom-up Sociolinguistic Perspective

Spolsky and Shohamy (2001: 357) caution language planners that 'from the point of view of the language user, language is just one aspect of complex social and cultural and economic choices'. Further, as Le Page and Tabouret-Keller (1985) stress, language is a marker and maker of identity: it reveals our personal backgrounds and social aspirations. It thus metaphorically marks where we come from and where we hope 'to be going'. Mazrui and Mazrui (1998: 18) make a significant distinction between 'communalist' and 'ecumenical' languages. The former are coterminous with 'race' or 'tribe' and define people who speak them as belonging to the same community. Arabic and Hausa are such languages. Ecumenical languages transcend these boundaries of racial or ethnic definition. Swahili is the paradigm example, since it does not necessarily confer a 'Mswahili' identity on a speaker. This distinction and potential aspect of South Africa's languages needs to be kept in mind by planners and critics. Almost all the languages of the country (apart from English, possibly) are in Mazrui and Mazrui's terms 'communalist' (a better term might simply be 'community-oriented languages'). They are associated with specific groups, without any single language emerging as a lingua franca. There were indications that Zulu might have been beginning to fulfil that role, with its spread in the Gauteng area. However, the adversative relations between supporters of Inkatha (the traditionalist Zulu cultural party) and the ANC (drawing on all ethnic groups) might have stalled this spread (Buntu Mfenyana, personal communication, 1996). It is little wonder that amongst the youth, especially males, 'alternative' urban codes like Tsotsitaal and Isicamtho, stripped of the 'communalist' associations of the standard languages, have arisen. For educated Black South Africans the repertoire therefore is as follows:

- H (high) code of social and educational aspiration and contacts with people who do not speak an Nguni or Sotho language – English ('ecumenical', High)

- codes of interaction with elders and solidarity within the community – one of many home and community languages ('communalist', neither High nor Low)
- for solidarity with other young Black people (especially amongst males) not sharing one's home language – Tsotsitaal and Isicamtho ('ecumenical', Low)

A South African identity for a vast number of South Africans is conveyed by a balance of these three levels. Too much emphasis upon the traditional African languages in certain contexts appears – ironically – to many people a reminder of the apartheid era with its denial of racial dignity. Too much use of English by Black South Africans is seen (by Blacks) as inappropriate and 'being too White' (Slabbert and Finlayson 2000). English is therefore likely to gain ground as the language of aspirations, but not at the cost of the African languages, which will continue to carry a local, rather than international, intellectual and cultural load. The question is whether the complementarity I, and others, believe in (and which I see in parts of India, for example) can be supported meaningfully by our educational and socio-political actions.

References

Abdulaziz, M. H. (1980), 'The Ecology of Tanzanian National Language Policy', in C. Polomé and C. P. Hill (eds.), *Language in Tanzania* (Oxford: Oxford University Press), 139–75.

Abdulkadir, H. (2000), 'Nigerian Pidgin: an Analytical View', in Molemobile (ed.), 245–53.

Acquah, Justice G. K. (2006), 'Citizenship', in *National Integration, Proceedings 2003* (Accra: Ghana Academy of Arts and Sciences), 39–59.

Adegbija, E. (1994), *Language Attitudes in Sub-Saharan Africa: a Sociolinguistic Overview* (Clevedon: Multilingual Matters).

—— (2000), 'Language attitudes in West Africa', *International Journal of the Sociology of Language* 141: 75–100.

Adegbite, W. (2004), 'Enlightenment and Attitudes of the Nigerian Elite on the Roles of Languages in Nigeria', in Muthwii and Kioko (eds.), 89–100.

Adesanoye, F. A. (1994), 'An Outlook for English in Nigeria', in Asein and Adesanoye (eds.), 86–96.

Agongo, R. M. (1980), 'Linguistic and Attitudinal Factors in the Maintenance of Luyia Group Identity', Ph.D. dissertation, University of Texas at Austin.

Ahmed, J. M. (1960), *The Intellectual Origins of Egyptian Nationalism* (London: Oxford University Press).

Akinwumi, O. (2004), *Crises and Conflicts in Nigeria: a Political History since 1960* (Muenster: Lit Verlag).

Alexander, N. (1989), *Language Policy and National Unity in South Africa/Azania* (Cape Town: Buchu Books).

—— (2002), 'Linguistic Rights, Language Planning and Democracy in Post-Apartheid South Africa', in S. Baker (ed.), *Language Policy: Lessons from Global Models* (Monterey: Monterey Institute of International Studies), 116–29.

—— and Heugh, K. (1999), 'Language Policy in the New South Africa', in A. Zegeye and R. Kriger (eds.), *Cultural Change and Development in Southern Africa*, Culturelink Special Issue 1998–1999 (Zagreb: Institute for International Relations), 9–34.

Alexandre, P. (1968), 'Some Linguistic Problems of Nation Building in Africa', in Fishman, Ferguson and Das Gupta (eds.), 119–27.

Alidou, H., and Jung, I. (2002), 'Education Languages Policies in Francophone Africa: What Have We Learned From Field Experiences?', in S. Baker (ed.), *Language Policy: Lessons from Global Models* (Monterey: Monterey Institute of International Studies), 59–73.

Aljabri, M. A. (1995), *Mas'alat Al huwiyya* (Beirut: Publications of the Center for Arab Unity Studies).

Almandjra, M. (1996), *La décolonisation culturelle* (Marrakesh: Walili).

Al-Sharkawi, M. (2002), 'Socio-Demographic Parameters of the Arabization of Egypt', *Language: Contributions to Arabic Linguistics* 3: 101–42 (Cairo Linguists Group and Arab Research Centre).

Amenumey, D. E. K. (1989), *The Ewe Unification Movement, a Political History* (Accra: Ghana Universities Press).

Amonoo, R. F. (1989), *Language and Nationhood*. J. B. Danquah Memorial Lectures, 22nd Series 2 (Accra: Ghana Academy of Arts and Sciences).

Anderson, B. (1991), *Imagined Communities: Reflections on the Origin and Spread of Nationalism* (New York: Verso).

Andriamirado, S. (1987), *Le Mali aujourd'hui* (Paris: Jeune Afrique).

Ansre, G. (1970), 'Language policy', paper presented at the International Conference on Cultural Diversity and National Understanding within West African Countries, held at Ile Ife, Nigeria.

Anstey, R. (1966), *King Leopold's Legacy* (London: Oxford University Press).

Anyidoho, A. (2004), 'English-only Medium of Instruction?', *Legon Journal of the Humanities* 15: 81–97.

Appel, R., and Muysken, P. (1987), *Language Contact and Bilingualism* (London: Edward Arnold).

Apronti, E. O. (1974), 'Language and National Integration in Ghana', *Legon Journal of the Humanities* 1: 54–60.

Armstrong, J. C., and Worden, N. (1989), 'The Slaves, 1652–1834', in R. Elphick and H. Giliomee (eds.), *The Shaping of South African Society, 1652–3*, 2nd edn. (Cape Town: Maskew Miller Longman), 109–83.

Asante, N. S. K. B. (2006), 'The Constitutional and Legal Framework of National Integration', *National Integration, Proceedings 2003* (Accra: Ghana Academy of Arts and Sciences), 1–27.

Asein, S. O., and Adesanoye, F. A. (1994) (eds.), *Language and Polity* (Ibadan: Sam Bookman).

'Awad, L. (1947), *Plutoland* (Cairo: Matba'at al-Karnak).

——(1993), *Muqaddima fi fiqh al-lugha al-'arabiyya* (Cairo: Dar Sina). (First published in 1980.)

Ayache, A. (1956), *Le Maroc, bilan d'une colonisation* (Paris: Editions sociales).

Babajide, A. (2001), 'Language Attitude Patterns of Nigerians', in Igboanusi (ed.), 1–13.

Badawi, E. S. (1973), *Mustawayaat al-'arabiyya al-mu'asira fii misr* (Cairo: Dar Al- Ma'arif).

Badru, P. (1998), *Imperialism and Ethnic Politics in Nigeria, 1960–96* (Trenton, NJ: Africa World Press).

Bahru, Z. (2004), 'The Changing Fortunes of the Amharic Language: Lingua Franca or Instrument of Domination?', in V. Böll, D. Nosnitsin, T. Rave, W. Smidt, and E. Sokolinskaia (eds.), *Studia Aethiopica. In Honour of Siegbert Uhlig on the Occasion of his 65th Birthday* (Wiesbaden: Harrassowitz Verlag), 303–18.

Baird, M. (2004), 'Music – Muziek', in T. Draisma, E. Kruzinga, and T. Scott (eds.), *Inside Zambia 1964–2004* (The Hague: Cordaid, Wageningen: ICCO, NGDO, and Werkgroup Zambia), 105–15.

Bamgbose, A. (1991), *Language and the Nation* (Edinburgh: Edinburgh University Press).

——(1994), 'Language and Nation Building', in Asein and Adesanoye (eds.), 1–14.

——(2000), 'Language Planning in West Africa', *International Journal of the Sociology of Language* 141: 101–17.

Banda, F. (2002) (ed.), *Language Across Borders* (Cape Town: CASAS).

——(2005), 'Analysing Social Identity in Casual Zambian / English Conversation: A Systemic Functional Linguistic Approach', *Southern African Linguistics and Applied Language Studies* 23: 217–31.

Bangura, A. K. (2006), 'The Krio Language: Diglossic and Political Realities', in Dixon-Fyle and Cole (eds.), 151–66.

Banjo, A. (1981), 'Grammars and Grammarians', Inaugural Lecture, Ibadan, University of Ibadan.

Barbour, S., and Carmichael, C. (2000), *Language and Nationalism in Europe* (Oxford: Oxford University Press).

Barry, A. (1988), 'Langues nationales et développement au Mali', in *Jamana, Revue culturelle malienne* (Bamako) 20: 22–6.

—— (1990), 'Etude du plurilinguisme au Mali: le cas de Djenné', in *Boucle du Niger – approches multidisciplinaires* (Tokyo: Institut de Recherches sur les Langues et Cultures d'Asie et d'Afrique), 2: 183–210.

Bastin, Y., Coupez, A., and Mann, M. (1999), *Continuity and Divergence in the Bantu Languages: Perspectives from a Lexicostatistic Study* (Tervuren: Musée royal d'Afrique Centrale).

Batibo, H. M. (2005), *Language Decline and Death in Africa. Causes, Consequences and Challenges* (Clevedon: Multilingual Matters).

Bell, H. (1970), *Place Names in the Belly of Stones*, Linguistic Monograph Series 20 (Khartoum: Sudan Research Unit, University of Khartoum).

—— (1976), *Language Survey Questionnaire Manual* (Khartoum: Institute of African and Asian Studies, University of Khartoum).

—— (1978–80) (ed.), 'Language Survey of the Sudan', 'Sample of Locality'. Mimeo booklets nos. 1–29 (Khartoum: Institute of African and Asian Studies, University of Khartoum).

—— and Haashim, M. J. (2006), 'Resolution of Ethnolinguistic Conflict: How Languages may Contribute to the Stability of the Sudan', paper presented at the 7th International Sudan Studies conference, April 2006, Bergen.

Bemile, S. K. (2000), 'Promotion of Ghanaian Languages and its Impact on National Unity: the Dagara Case', in C. Lentz and P. Nugent (eds.), *Ethnicity in Ghana, the Limits of Invention* (Basingstoke: MacMillan Press Ltd./New York: St. Martin's Press, Inc), 204–55.

Bender, M. L. (1983) (ed.), *Nilo-Saharan Studies* (East Lansing: Michigan State University, African Studies Center).

—— (2003), *The Nilo-Saharan Languages*, Lincom Handbooks in Linguistics 06 (Munich: Lincom Europa).

—— Bowen, J., Cooper, R., and Ferguson, C. (1976) (eds.), *Language in Ethiopia* (London: Oxford University Press).

Bendor-Samuel, J. (1989) (ed.), *The Niger-Congo Languages* (New York: Lanham, London: University Press of America).

Bentahila, A., and Davies, A. E. (1991), 'Standards for Arabic: One, Two or Many?', *Indian Journal of Applied Linguistics*, 17: 69–88.

Bernus, E. (1992), 'Etre Touareg au Mali', in *Politique africaine*, no. 47: 'Le Mali. La transition' (Paris: Karthala), 23–30.

Beshir, M. O. (1969), *Educational Development in the Sudan, 1898 to 1956* (Oxford: Clarendon Press).

Beukman, J. (2000), 'Towards a Commission for the Promotion and Protection of the Rights of Cultural, Religious and Linguistic Communities', in de Prez and du Plessis (eds.), 138–47.

Bickmore, L. (2006), Languages of Zambia Homepage. Available online at http://www.albany.edu/~lb527/LOZ.html.

Biloa, E. (2003), *La langue française au Cameroun* (Bern: Peter Lang).

—— (2006), *Le français en contact avec l'anglais au Cameroun* (Munich: Lincom Europa).

Binsbergen, W. van (1994), 'Minority Language, Ethnicity and the State in Two African Situations', in R. Fardon and G. Furniss (eds.), *African Languages, Development and the State* (London, New York: Routledge), 142–88.

Bishai, W. B. (1960), 'Notes on the Coptic Substratum in Egyptian Arabic', *Journal of the American Oriental Society*, 80: 225–9.

—— (1963), 'The Transition from Coptic to Arabic', *The Muslim World* 53: 145–50.

Bitja'a Kody, Z. D. (1999), 'Problématique de la cohabitation des langues', in G. M. Zé (ed.), *Le français langue africaine: enjeux et atouts pour la Francophonie* (Paris: Publisud), 80–95.

—— (2003), *Annuaire des langues du Cameroun* (Yaoundé: Éditions du CERDOTOLA).

Blommaert, J. (1990), 'Modern African Political Style: Strategies and Genres in Swahili Political Discourse', *Discourse and Society* 1 (2): 115–31.

—— (1991), 'Some Problems in the Interpretation of Swahili Political Texts', in J. Blommaert (ed.), *Swahili Studies: Essays in Honour of Marcel van Spaandonck* (Ghent:Academia), 109–35.

—— (1999), *State Ideology and Language in Tanzania* (Cologne: Rüdiger Köppe Verlag).

—— (2006), 'Language Policy and National Identity', in T. Ricento (ed.), *An Introduction to Language Policy – Theory and Method* (Oxford: Blackwell Publishing), 238–54.

Boadi, L. K. A. (1976), 'Mother Tongue Education in Ghana', in A. Bamgbose (ed.), *Mother Tongue Education: The West African Experience* (London: Hodder and Stoughton), 83–112.

—— (1994), *Linguistic Barriers to Communication in the Modern World*. The J. B. Danquah Memorial Lectures, 27th series (Accra: Ghana Academy of Arts and Sciences).

Bokamba, E. G. (1976), 'Authenticity and the Choice of a National Language: the Case of Zaire', *Présence Africaine*, 99–100: 104–42.

—— (1986), 'Education and Development in Zaire', in G. Nzongola-Ntalaja (ed.), *The Crisis in Zaire: Myths and Realities* (Trenton, NJ: Africa World Press), 191–218.

—— (1988), 'Code-mixing, Language Variation and Linguistic Theory: Evidence from Bantu Languages', *Lingua* 76: 21–62.

—— (forthcoming), 'Arguments for Multilingual Policies in Public Domains in Africa', to appear in E. A. Anchimbe (ed.), *Linguistic Identity in Postcolonial Multilingual Spaces* (London: Cambridge Scholars Press).

Boukous, A. (1995), *Société, langues et cultures au Maroc* (Rabat: Publications of the Faculty of Letters, Rabat).

Bouquet, C. (2005), *Géopolitique de la Côte d'Ivoire. Le désespoir de Kourouma* (Paris: Armand Colin).

Bouwman, D. (2005), 'Throwing Stones at the Moon: the Role of Arabic in Contemporary Mali', Ph.D. dissertation, School of Asian, African and Amerindian Studies, Leiden, the Netherlands.

Braeckman, C. (2003), *Les nouveaux prédateurs: Politique des puissances en Afrique centrale* (Brussels: Librairie Arthème Fayard).

Branford, J. (with W. Branford) (1991), *A Dictionary of South African English* (Cape Town: Oxford University Press).

Breidlid, A. (2006), 'Educational Discourses in the Sudan: Conflict or Co-existence?', paper presented at the 7th International Sudan Studies conference, April 2006, Bergen, Norway.

Breton, R., and Fohtung, B. (1991), *Atlas administratif des langues nationales du Cameroun* (Yaoundé: CERDOTOLA/CREA, Paris: ACCT).

Brock-Utne, B. (2005), 'The Continued Battle over Kiswahili as the Language of Instruction in Tanzania', in B. Brock-Utne and R. K. Hopson (eds.), *Languages of Instruction for African Emancipation: Focus on Postcolonial Contexts and Considerations* (Dar es Salaam: Mkuki na Nyota Publishers; Cape Town: CASAS), 51–87.

Broomfield, G. W. (1931), 'The Re-Bantuization of the Swahili Language', *Africa* 4: 77–85.

Brown, R., and Gilman, A. (1960), 'Pronouns of Power and Solidarity', in T. Sebeok (ed.), *Style in Language* (Cambridge, MA: MIT Press), 253–76.

Calvet, L.-J. (1992), 'Les langues des marchés au Mali', in L.-J. Calvet (ed.), *Les langues des marchés en Afrique* (Paris: Didier Erudition), 193–218.

Cameron, J., and Dodd, W. A. (1970), *Society, School and Progress in Tanzania* (Oxford: Pergamon Press).

Canut, C. (1996), *Dynamiques linguistiques au Mali* (Paris: Didier Erudition).

—— and G. Dumestre (1993), 'Français, bambara et langues nationales au Mali', in D. de Robillard and M. Beniamino (eds.), *Le français dans l'espace francophone* (Paris: Champion), 1: 219–28.

—— and B. Keita (1994), 'Dynamique linguistique en zone mandingue: attitudes et comportements', in Dumestre (ed.), 89–162.

Carmody, B. (2004), *The Evolution of Education in Zambia* (Lusaka: Bookworld Publishers).

Census Data Base (South Africa) (2001). http://www.statssa.gov.za

Cerulli, E. (1964), *Somalia: scritti vari editi ed inediti III* (Rome: Ministero degli affari esteri).

Chanda, V. M. (1996), 'Les langues en Zambie', in J.-P. Daloz and J. D. Chileshe (eds.), *La Zambie contemporaine* (Paris: Karthala, Nairobi: IFRA), 301–16.

—— (2002), 'Orthography Planning Across Languages and Countries: Some Thoughts and Proposals', in F. Banda (ed.), *Language Across Borders* (Cape Town, CASAS), 27–59.

Charrad, M. (2001), *States and Women's Rights: The Making of Postcolonial Tunisia, Algeria and Morocco* (Berkeley, CA: University of California Press).

Childs, G. T. (2003), *An Introduction to African Languages* (Amsterdam: John Benjamins).

Chimerah, R. (1998), *Kiswahili: Past, Present and Future Horizons* (Nairobi: University of Nairobi Press).

Chinebuah, I. (1977), 'The National Languages in Africa: the Case for Akan in Ghana', *African Languages/Langues Africaines* 3: 60–78.

Chisanga, T. (2002), 'Lusaka Chinyanja and Icibemba', in K. K. Prah (ed.), *Speaking in Unison: the Harmonisation of Southern African Languages* (Cape Town: CASAS), 103–16.

Chrétien, J.-P. and Prunier, G. (1989) (eds.), *Les ethnies ont une histoire* (Paris: Karthala).

Cissé, M. (2005), 'Les politiques linguistiques du Sénégal: entre attentisme et interventionnisme', *Kotoba to Shakai [Language and Society]*, Special Issue on Post-empire and Multilingual Societies in Asia and Africa, 266–313.

Cissé, N. (1992), 'L'Etat malien face au multilinguisme', in *Des langues et des villes. Actes du colloque international, Dakar, 15–17 décembre 1990* (Paris: Didier Erudition), 185–92.

Cole, G. R. (2006), 'Re-thinking the Demographic Make-up of Krio Society', in Dixon-Fyle and Cole (eds.), 33–51.

CONFEMEN (Conférence des ministres de l'éducation des Etats d'expression française) (1986), *Promotion et intégration des langues nationales dans les systèmes éducatifs. Bilan et inventaire* (Paris: Champion).

Conrad, D., and Frank, B. (1995) (eds.), *Status and Identity in West Africa: The Nyamakalaw of Mande* (Bloomington: Indiana University Press).

Constable, D. (1974), 'Bilingualism in the United Republic of Cameroon: Proficiency and Distribution', *Comparative Education* 10:3: 249–53.

Constitution du Mali (1992), in S. M. Ch. Diaby (no date), *Les textes fondamentaux de la IIIe République du Mali* (Bamako).

Cooper, R. L. (1976), 'Government Language Policy', in Bender, Bowen, Cooper, and Ferguson (eds.), *Language in Ethiopia* (London: Oxford University Press), 187–90.

Coury, R. (1982), 'Who "Invented" Egyptian Arab Nationalism? Part 2', *International Journal of Middle Eastern Studies* 14: 459–79.

Crawhall, N. (1993), 'Negotiations and Language Policy Options in South Africa', Cape Town: National Language Project. (Unpublished document.)

Crowder, M. (1962a), *Senegal: A Study in French Assimilation Policy* (London: Oxford University Press).

——(1962b), *The Story of Nigeria* (London: Faber and Faber).

Cruise O'Brien, D. B. (1971), *The Mourides of Senegal: The Political and Economic Organization of an Islamic Brotherhood* (Cambridge: CambridgeUniversity Press).

——(1975), *Saints and Politicians: Essays in the Organization of a Senegalese Peasant Society* (Cambridge: Cambridge University Press).

——(2003), 'The Shadow Politics of Wolofisation: Shuffling Along to Nationhood?', in *Symbolic Confrontations: Muslims Imagining the State in Africa* (New York: Palgrave).

Cunnison, I. (1971), 'Classification by Genealogy: A Problem of the Baqqara Belt', in Y. F. Hasan (ed.), *Sudan in Africa* (Khartoum: Khartoum University Press), 186–96.

Dakubu, M. E. Kropp (1988), *The Languages of Ghana* (London: Kegan Paul Ltd.).

——(1997), *Korle Meets the Sea, a Sociolinguistic History of Accra* (New York: Oxford University Press).

——(2002/3), 'Dealing with the "Multilingualism Problem": Language Policy and the 2000 Population and Housing Census of Ghana', in *Language and Culture in Education and National Development*, Proceedings of the National Seminar organised by the Centre for the Advocacy on Language and Culture, University of Education, Winneba, 1–8.

Davids, A. (1990), 'Words the Slaves Made: a Socio-historical-linguistic Study', *South African Journal of Linguistics* 8(1): 1–24.

De Klerk, V. (2000), 'Language Shift in Grahamstown: a Case Study of Selected Xhosa Speakers', *International Journal of the Sociology of Language* 146: 86–110.

Deng, F. M. (1973), *The Dinka and Their Songs*, Oxford Library of African Literature (Oxford: Clarendon Press).

——and Daly, M. W. (1989), *'Bonds of Silk': The Human Factor in the British Administration of Sudan* (East Lansing: Michigan State University Press).

De Prez, K., and du Plessis, T. (2000) (eds.), *Multilingualism and Government – Belgium, Luxembourg, Switzerland, Former Yugoslavia, South Africa* (Pretoria: van Schaik).

——and Teck, L. (2001) (eds.), *Multilingualism, the Judiciary and Security Services – Belgium, Europe, South Africa, Southern Africa* (Pretoria: van Schaik).

Devisse, J. (1989), 'Islam et ethnies en Afrique', in Chrétien and Prunier (eds.), 103–15.

Diakité, D. (1989), 'Unification étatique et processus ethniques', in Chrétien and Prunier (eds.), 135–48.

——(2000), 'La crise scolaire au Mali', in I. Skattum (ed.), 6–28.

Diop, A.-B. (1981), *La société wolof, tradition et changement: Les systèmes d'inégalité et de domination* (Paris: Karthala).

Diouf, M. (1998), 'The French Colonial Policy of Assimilation and the Civility of the *originaires* of the Four Communes (Senegal): A Nineteenth Century Globalization Project', *Development and Change* 29: 671–96.

Distiller, N., and Steyn, M. (2004), *Under Construction: 'Race' and Identity in South Africa Today* (Sandton, Johannesburg: Heinemann).

Dixon-Fyle, M., and Cole, G. (2006), 'Introduction' in Dixon-Fyle and Cole (eds.), 1–23.

————(2006) (eds.), *New Perspectives on the Sierra Leone Krio* (New York: Peter Lang Publishing, Inc.).

Dombrowsky, K. (1993), 'Théorie et réalité de l'alphabétisation dans la zone Mali-Sud', in Dumestre (ed.), 5–142.

——(1994), 'La situation socio-linguistique du sud du Mali (pays minyanka)', in Dumestre (ed.), 13–88.

Doneux, J. L. (1975), 'Hypothèses pour la comparative des langues atlantiques', *Africana Linguistica* 6: 41–129.

Dreyfus, M., and Juillard, C. (2004), *Le plurilinguisme au Sénégal: Langues et identités en devenir* (Paris: Karthala).

Dubois, V. (1973), 'Zaire under President Sese Seko Mobutu. Part I: The Return to Authenticity', *Fieldstaff Reports*, Vol. XVII, No. 1.

Dumestre, G. (1993) (ed.), *L'alphabétisation fonctionnelle en bambara dans une dynamique de développement. Le cas de la zone cotonnière (Mali-Sud)* (Paris: Didier Erudition).

——(1994a) (ed.), *Stratégies communicatives au Mali: langues régionales, bambara, français* (Paris: Didier Erudition).

——(1994b), 'La dynamique des langues au Mali: le trinôme langues régionales – bambara – français', in G. Dumestre (ed.), 3–12.

——(1997), 'De l'école au Mali', *Nordic Journal of African Studies* 6(2): 31–52.

——(2000), 'De la scolarité souffrante (compléments à "De l'école au Mali")', in Skattum (ed.), 172–86.

——(2003), *Grammaire fondamentale du bambara* (Paris: Karthala).

Du Plessis, T. (2000), 'South Africa: from Two to Eleven Official Languages', in de Prez and du Plessis (eds.), 95–110.

——(2001), 'Democratic Security in Multicultural Societies – the South African Case', in de Prez, du Plessis, and Teck (eds.), 95–105.

Du Preez, M. (2004), 'Maximum Headroom', *Cape Argus*, Cape Town, p. 14.

Eastman, C. M. (1971), 'Who are the Waswahili?', *Africa* 3: 228–36.

Echu, G. (2003) 'Coping with Multilingualism: Trends in the Evolution of Language Policy in Cameroon', *PhiN. Philologie im Netz* 25/2003, 31–46. http://www.fu-berlin.de/phin/phin25/p25i.htm

——(2006), 'Bilinguisme official au Cameroun: du mythe à la réalité', post-scriptum in E. Biloa, 175–87.

Echu, G. (forthcoming) 'The Politics about Cameroon Pidgin English', to appear in *The Carrier Pidgin*.

—— and Grundstrom, A. W. (1999) (eds.), *Official Bilingualism and Linguistic Communication in Cameroon* (New York: Peter Lang).

Ehret, C. (1998), *An African Classical Age: Eastern and Southern Africa in World History, 1000 B.C. to A.D. 400* (Oxford: James Currey).

—— (2001), *A Historical-Comparative Reconstruction of Nilo-Saharan* (Cologne: Rüdiger Köppe Verlag).

—— (2002), *The Civilizations of Africa: A History to 1800* (Oxford: James Currey).

Eid, M. (2002), 'Language is a Choice – Variations in Egyptian Women's Written Discourse', in A. Rouchdy (ed.), *Language Contact and Language Conflict in Arabic – Variations on a Sociolinguistic Theme* (London: RoutledgeCurzon), 203–32.

Eisele, J. (2002), 'Approaching Diglossia – Authorities, Values and Representations', in A. Rouchdy (ed.), *Language Contact and Language Conflict in Arabic – Variations on a Sociolinguistic Theme* (London: Routledge/Curzon), 3–23.

Elbiad, M. (1985), 'A Sociolinguistic Study of the Arabization Process and Its Conditioning Factors in Morocco', Ph.D. dissertation, University of New York at Buffalo.

Elime, W. J. (2000), 'Official Language Bilingualism in the Cameroon Armed Forces: a Case Study of Some Military Personnel in the City of Yaoundé', Postgraduate dissertation, Ecole Normale Supérieure, University of Yaoundé I.

Eliraz, G. (1986), 'Tradition and Change: Egyptian Intellectuals and Linguistic Reforms, 1919–1939', *Asian and African Studies* 20: 233–62.

Elugbe, B. O. (1994), 'National Languages and National Development', in Asein and Adesanoye (eds.), 64–78.

Elzailaee, S. (2006), 'The Failure of the British Colonial Policies in the Nuba Mountains of Central Sudan', paper presented at the 7th International Sudan Studies conference, April 2006, Bergen, Norway.

Ennaji, M. (1988), 'Language Planning in Morocco and Changes in Arabic', *International Journal of the Sociology of Language* 74: 9–39.

—— (1991) (ed.), *Sociolinguistics of the Maghreb*. Special Issue of *International Journal of the Sociology of Language* 87.

—— (1995) (ed.), *Sociolinguistics in Morocco*. Special Issue of *International Journal of the Sociology of Language* 112.

—— (1997) (ed.), *Berber Sociolinguistics*. Special Issue of *International Journal of the Sociology of Language* 123.

—— (1999), 'The Arab World (Maghreb and Near East)', in J. A. Fishman (ed.), *Handbook of Language and Ethnic Identity* (London: Oxford University Press), 382–95.

—— (2002), 'Language Contact, Arabization Policy and Education in Morocco', in A. Rouchdy (ed.), *Language Contact and Language Conflict in Arabic* (London: Routlege/Curzon), 70–88.

—— (2005), *Multilingualism, Cultural Identity and Education in Morocco* (New York: Springer).

Ethnologue: Languages of the World 12th edn. (1991), ed. B. F. Grimes (Dallas, Texas: Summer Institute of Linguistics/SIL).

—— 15th edn. (2005), ed. R. G. Gordon and B. F. Grimes (Dallas, Texas: Summer Institute of Linguistics International). http://www.ethnologue.com

Evans-Pritchard, E. E. (1956), *Nuer Religion* (Oxford: Clarendon Press).

—— (1962 [1948]), 'The Divine Kingship of the Shilluk of the Nilotic Sudan', in *Essays in Social Anthropology* (London: Faber and Faber), 66–86.

—— (1971), *The Azande: History and Political Institutions* (Oxford: Clarendon Press).

Fagerberg-Diallo, S. (2001), 'Constructive Interdependence: the Response of a Senegalese Community to the Question of Why Become Literate', in D. R. Olson and N. Torrance (eds.), *The Making of Literate Societies* (Oxford: Blackwell Publishing), 153–77.

Faik-Nzuji, M. C. (1974), 'Premier seminaire national des linguistes du Zaire', *Habari* 2, No. 7.

Falola, T. (1999), *The History of Nigeria* (London: Greenwood).

Féral, C. de (1993), 'Le français au Cameroun: approximations, vernacularisation et camfranglais', in D. de Robillard and M. Beniamino (eds.), *Le français dans l'espace francophone* (Paris: Champion), 1: 205–18.

Ferguson, C. (1959), 'Diglossia', *Word* 15: 325–40.

—— (1996), 'Epilogue: Diglossia Revisited', in A. Elgibali (ed.), *Understanding Arabic: Essays in Contemporary Arabic Linguistics in Honour of El-Said Badawi*, (Cairo: The American University in Cairo Press), 49–67.

Finegan, E., and Rickford, J. (2004) (eds.), *Language in the USA: Themes for the Twenty-first Century* (Cambridge: Cambridge University Press).

Fishman, J. A. (1968), 'Nationality-Nationalism and Nation-Nationism', in Fishman, Ferguson, and Das Gupta (eds.), 39–51.

—— (1971), 'National Languages and Languages of Wider Communication', in W. H. Whiteley (ed.), 27–56.

—— (1972), *Language and Nationalism: Two Integrative Essays* (Rowley, MA: Newbury House).

—— (1997), 'Language and Ethnicity: A View from Within', in F. Coulmas (ed.), *The Handbook of Sociolinguistics* (Malden: Blackwell), 327–43.

—— (1999) (ed.), *Handbook of Language and Ethnic Identity* (Oxford: Oxford University Press).

—— (2004), 'Multilingualism and non-English Mother Tongues', in Finegan and Rickford (eds.), 115–32.

—— Ferguson, C., and Das Gupta, J. (1968) (eds.), *Language Problems of Developing Nations* (New York: John Wiley).

French, H. (2004), *A Continent for the Taking: The Tragedy and Hope of Africa* (New York: Alfred A. Knopf).

Gabjanda, J. D. (1976), 'An Axiomatic Functionalist Analysis of the Phonology of Yulu', Ph.D. dissertation, University of St. Andrews.

Gal, S., and Irvine, J. T. (1995), 'The Boundaries of Languages and Disciplines: How Ideologies Construct Difference', *Social Research* 62: 996–1001.

Gardi, B. (1989), 'Des "ingénieurs traditionnels" au Mali. Quelques remarques sur les "gens de caste" ', in Chrétien and Prunier (eds.), 91–8.

Gelder, G. van (2004), 'Lost Readers of Cairo', review of Haeri (2003) in *Times Literary Supplement* 30 January 2004, p. 24.

Georis, P., and Agbiano, B. (1965), *Evolution de l'enseignement en République Démocratique du Congo depuis l'indépendance* (Brussels: Edition CEMUBAC).

Gershoni, I., and Jankowski, I. (1986), *Egypt, Islam and the Arabs: The Search for Egyptian Nationalism 1900–1930* (New York and Oxford: Oxford University Press).

Gershoni, I., and Jankowski, I. (1995), *Redefining the Egyptian Nation, 1930–1945* (Cambridge: Cambridge University Press).

Ghana Academy of Arts and Sciences/Friedrich Ebert Stiftung [GAAS/FES] (2005), *Public Forum on Reconciling the Nation* (Accra: Friedrich Ebert Foundation).

Ghana Ministry of Education, Youth and Sports (October 2004), White Paper on the Report of the Education Reform Review Committee (Accra).

Gillespie, W. H. (1955), *The Gold Coast Police 1844–1938* (Accra: Government Printer).

Githiora, C. (2002), 'Sheng: Peer Language, Swahili Dialect or Emerging Creole?', *Journal of African Cultural Studies*, 15(2): 159–81.

Gordon, A. (2003) *Nigeria's Diverse Peoples* (Oxford: ABC).

Government of Ghana (2001), Population and Housing Census 2000 (Accra).

Gowlett, D. F. (1989) 'The Parentage and Development of Lozi', *Journal of African Languages and Linguistics* 11: 127–49.

Gramsci, A. (1971), *Selections from the Prison Notebooks of Antonio Gramsci*, ed. Q. Hoare and G. N. Smith (London: Lawrence and Wishart).

Grandguillaume, G. (1991), 'Arabisation et langues maternelles dans le contexte national au Maghreb', *International Journal of the Sociology of Language* 87: 45–54.

Greenberg, J. (1963), *The Languages of Africa* (Bloomington: Indiana University Press).

Grimes, B. F. (1996), 'Cameroon', in *Ethnologue: The Languages of the World* (Dallas: Summer Institute of Linguistics/SIL).

Guibernau, M. (1996), *Nationalisms: the Nation-state and Nationalism in the Twentieth Century* (Cambridge: Polity Press).

Güldemann, T., and Vossen, R. (2000), 'Khoisan', in Heine and Nurse (eds.), 99–122.

Haeri, N. (1997), *The Sociolinguistic Market of Cair – Gender, Class and Education* (London: Kegan Paul International).

——(2003), *Sacred Language, Ordinary People – Dilemmas of Culture and Politics in Egypt* (New York: Palgrave Macmillan).

Haïdara, M. L. (2005), 'Problématique de l'enseignement des/en langues nationales – le cas du Mali, Ph.D. dissertation, University of Bamako.

Hamid, E. E. (2006), 'The Development of Yulu Language in the Sudan', paper presented at the 7th International Sudan Studies conference, April 2006, Bergen, Norway.

Hannerz, U. (1987), 'The World in Creolisation', *Africa* 57: 546–59.

Harney, E. (2004), *In Senghor's Shadow: Art, Politics, and the Avant-garde in Senegal, 1960–1995* (Durham: Duke University Press).

Harries, P. (1989), 'Exclusion, Classification and Internal Colonialism: the Emergence of Ethnicity among the Tsonga Speakers of South Africa', in L. Vail (ed.), *The Creation of Tribalism in Southern Africa* (London: James Currey), 82–117.

Hartshorne, K. (1995), 'Language Policy in African Education: a Background to the Future', in R. Mesthrie (ed.), *Language and Social History: Studies in South African Sociolinguistics* (Cape Town: David Philip).

Hary, B. (1996), 'The Importance of the Language Continuum in Arabic Multiglossia', in A. Elgibali (ed.), *Understanding Arabic: Essays in Contemporary Arabic Linguistics in Honour of El-Said Badawi*, (Cairo: The American University in Cairo Press), 69–90.

Hattiger, J.-L. (1983), *Le français populaire d'Abidjan : un cas de pidginisation* (Abidjan: Université Nationale de Côte d'Ivoire, Institut de Linguistique Appliquée).

Haycock, B. G. (1971), 'The Place of the Napatan-Meroitic Culture in the History of the Sudan and Africa', in Y. F. Hasan (ed.), *Sudan in Africa* (Khartoum: Khartoum University Press), 26–41.

——(1978), 'The Problem of the Meroitic Language', in R. Thelwall (ed.), *Aspects of Language in the Sudan* (Coleraine: The New University of Ulster), 50–81.

Heine, B. (1968), *Verbreitung und Gliederung der Togorestsprachen* (Berlin: Dietrich Reimer).

——(1977), 'Vertical and Horizontal Communication in Africa', *Afrika Spectrum*, 3: 231–8.

——and Möhlig W. (1980), *The Atlas of the Languages and Dialects of Kenya* (Berlin: Dietrich Reimer Verlag).

——and Nurse, D. (2000) (eds.), *African Languages – an Introduction* (Cambridge: Cambridge University Press).

————(2004) (eds.), *Les langues africaines* (Paris: Karthala).

Herbert, R. K., and Bailey, R. (2002), 'The Bantu Languages: Sociohistorical Perspectives', in Mesthrie (ed.), 50–78.

Heugh, K. (2000), *The Case against Bilingual and Multilingual Education in South Africa*, PRAESA [Project for the Study of Alternative Education in South Africa] Occasional Papers No. 6, University of Cape Town.

Hijazi, A. A.-M. (1979), *Ru'ya hadariyya tabaqiyya li-'urubat misr: dirasa wa-watha'iq* (Beirut: Dar Al-Adab).

Hildebrandt, J. (1981), *History of the Church in Africa. A Survey* (Achimota: Africa Christian Press).

Hochschild, A. (1998), *King Leopold's Ghost: A Story of Greed, Terror, and Heroism in Colonial Africa* (Boston: Houghton Mifflin Company).

Hourani, A. (1983), *Arabic Thought in the Liberal Age – 1789–1939* (Cambridge: Cambridge University Press).

Hussein, T. (1938), *Mustaqbal al-thaqafa fi misr* (Cairo: Matba'at al-Ma'arif).

Hymes, D. (1974), *Foundations in Sociolinguistics: an Ethnographic Approach* (Philadelphia: University of Pennsylvania Press).

Ibrahim, M. H. (1989), 'Communicating in Arabic: Problems and Prospects', in F. Coulmas (ed.), *Language Adaptation* (Cambridge: Cambridge University Press), 39–59.

Idris, H. F. (2006), 'The Status and Use of Arabic and Other Sudanese Languages in Sudan', paper presented at the 7th International Sudan Studies conference, April 2006, Bergen, Norway.

Igboanusi, H. (2001) (ed.), *Language Attitude and Language Conflict in West Africa* (Ibadan: Enicrownfit).

——and Ohia, I. (2001), 'Language Conflict in Nigeria: the Perspective of Linguistic Minorities', in Igboanusi (ed.), 125–42.

——and Peter, L. (2004), 'Oppressing the Oppressed: the Threats of Hausa and English to Nigeria's Minority Languages', *International Journal of the Sociology of Language* 170: 131–40.

————(2005), *Languages in Competition: the Struggle for Supremacy among Nigeria's Major Languages, English and Pidgin* (Frankfurt: Peter Lang).

Institut National de la Statistique, République de Côte d'Ivoire, Bureau Technique Permanent du Recensement (2001), *Premiers résultats définitifs du RGPH-98* (Abidjan: Institut National de la Statistique).

Iruafemi, V. E. (1988), 'Attitudes of Parents towards the Use of Indigenous Languages in the Early Stages of the Education of their Children', Ms., University of Ibadan.

Irvine, J. T. (1993), 'Mastering African Languages: The Politics of Linguistics in Nineteenth Century Senegal', *Social Analysis* 33: 27–46.

——(2006), 'Wolof Communication and Society over Space and Time', keynote address at the International Symposium *Wolof Communication and Society*, Université Gaston Berger de Saint-Louis, Senegal.

——and Gal, S. (2000), 'Language Ideology and Linguistic Differentiation', in P. V. Kroskrity (ed.), *Regimes of Language: Ideologies, Polities, and Identities* (Santa Fe: School of American Research Press/Oxford: James Currey), 35–83.

James, W. (1977), 'The Funj Mystique: Approaches to a Problem of Sudan History', in R. K. Jain (ed.), *Text and Context: The Social Anthropology of Tradition*, ASA Essays 2 (Philadelphia: ISHI), 95–133.

——(1988), *The Listening Ebony: Moral Knowledge, Religion and Power among the Uduk of Sudan*, paperback edn. with new preface, 1999 (Oxford: Clarendon Press).

——(2000), 'The Multiple Voices of Sudanese Airspace', in R. Fardon and G. Furniss (eds.), *African Broadcast Cultures* (Oxford: James Currey), 198–215.

——Baumann, G., and Johnson, D. H. (1996) (eds.), *Juan Maria Schuver's Travels in North East Africa, 1880–83* (London: The Hakluyt Society).

Johnson, D. H. (1994), *Nuer Prophets: A History of Prophecy in the Upper Nile in the Nineteenth and Twentieth Centuries* (Oxford: Clarendon Press).

——(2006), *The Root Causes of Sudan's Civil Wars*, rev. edn. (Oxford: James Currey).

Judge, A. (2000), 'France: One State, One Nation, One Language?' in S. Barbour and C. Carmichael (eds.), *Language and Nationalism in Europe* (Oxford: Oxford University Press), 44–82.

Juillard, C. (1995), *Sociolinguistique urbaine: La vie des langues à Ziguinchor (Sénégal)* (Paris: CNRS Editions).

Kahane, H. (1982), 'American English: from a Colonial Substandard to a Prestige Language', in B. B. Kachru (ed.), *The Other Tongue – English across Cultures* (Oxford: Pergamon).

Kamil, W. (n.d.), *Buhuth fi al-'arabiyya al-mu'asira*. (Cairo: 'Alam al-Kutub).

Kamwangamalu, N. M. (1997), 'Language Frontiers, Language Standardization, and Mother Tongue Education: the Zaire–Zambia Border Area with Reference to the Bemba Cluster', *South African Journal of African Languages* 17: 88–94.

——(2000), 'Apartheid and Ethnicity: Introductory Remarks', *International Journal of the Sociology of Language* 144: 1–6.

Kane, O. (1991), 'L'Enseignement islamique dans les medersas du Mali', in B. Sanankoua and L. Brenner (eds.), *L'Enseignement islamique au Mali* (Bamako: Jamana), 87–104.

Kangafu, K. (1973), *Discours sur l'Authenticité: essai sur le problematique idéologique du Recours à l'Authenticité* (Kinshasa: Les Presses Africaines).

Kaniki, M. H. Y. (1974), 'TANU – The Party of Independence and National Consolidation' in G. Rhumbika (ed.), *Towards Ujamaa* (Nairobi: East African Literature Bureau), 1–30.

Kankwenda, M. J. (2005), *L'économie politique de la prédation au Congo Kinshasa: Des origines à nos jours 1885–2003* (Kinshasa: ICREDES).

Kashoki, M. E. (1978), 'The Language Situation in Zambia', in Ohanessian and Kashoki (eds.), 9–46.

——(1990), *The Factor of Language* (Lusaka: Kenneth Kaunda Foundation).

—— (2003), 'Language Policy Formulation in Multilingual Southern Africa', *Journal of Multilingual and Multicultural Development* 24: 184–94.

—— Katengo, M. E., and Mundia, M. (1998), 'Cross-Border Language Perspectives: Experiences and Lessons from Zambia – Focus on Silozi', in K. Legère (ed.), *Cross-Border Languages* (Windhoek: Gamsberg Macmillan), 168–204.

Kellas, J. G. (1998), *The Politics of Nationalism and Ethnicity* (London: Macmillan Press).

Ki-Zerbo, J. (1978), *Histoire de l'Afrique noire: d'hier à demain* (Paris: Hatier).

King, J. S. (1887), 'Somali as a Written Language', *The Indian Antiquary*, August: 242–3 and October: 285–7.

King'ei, K. (2000), 'Problems of Acceptability of Standard Swahili Forms by Non-Kiunguja Native Kiswahili speakers', in K. Kahigi, Y. Kihore, and M. Mous (eds.), *Lugha za Tanzania. Languages of Tanzania* (Leiden: Research School for Asian, African, and Amerindian Studies (CNWS), Universiteit Leiden), 81–8.

Klein, M. A. (1968), *Islam and Imperialism in Senegal: Sine-Saloum, 1847–1914* (Stanford: Stanford University Press for the Hoover Institution on War, Revolution and Peace).

k'millian (2004), *My Music*, audio CD (Lusaka: Mondo Music).

Knutsen, A. M. (2007), *Variation du français à Abidjan (Côte d'Ivoire). Etude d'un continuum linguistique et social* (Oslo: Université d'Oslo, Acta Humaniora).

Köhler, O. (1970, 1971), 'The Early Study of the Nilotic Languages of the Sudan, 1812–1900', Parts I and II, *Sudan Notes and Records* 51: 85–94, 52: 56–62.

Kokora, P. D. (1983), 'Pourquoi parle-t-on tant de la promotion des langues nationales dans le système éducatif ? Le point de vue de l'Institut de Linguistique Appliquée de l'Université d'Abidjan', in *Cahiers Ivoiriens de Recherche Linguistique* 13: 93–101.

Konaré, A. O. (2005), Preface to *L'état de l'Afrique 2005*, special issue of *Jeune Afrique/L'Intelligent* (Paris: Jeune Afrique).

Konings, P., and Nyamnjoh, F. B. (1997), 'The Anglophone Problem in Cameroon', *Journal of Modern African Studies* 35(2): 207–29.

Kouadio N'Guessan, J. (2001), 'Ecole et langues nationales en Côte d'Ivoire: Dispositions légales et recherches', in R. Chaudenson and L.-J. Calvet (eds.), *Les langues dans l'espace francophone: de la coexistence au partenariat* (Paris: L'Harmattan: Institut de la Francophonie), 177–203.

Kouega, J.-P. (2003), 'Camfranglais: a Novel Slang in Cameroon Schools', *English Today* 19(2): 23–9.

Krapf, J. L. (1882), *A Dictionary of the Suahili Language* (London: Tubner & Co.).

Kula, N. C. (2006), 'Zambia: Language Situation', in K. Brown (ed.), *Encyclopedia of Languages and Linguistics* (Oxford: Elsevier), 13: 744–5.

Küster, S. (1999), *African Education in Colonial Zimbabwe, Zambia and Malawi* (Hamburg: LIT).

Labov, W. (1972), *Sociolinguistic Patterns* (Philadelphia: University of Pennsylvania Press).

Lafage, S. (1982), 'Esquisse des relations interlinguistiques en Côte d'Ivoire', *Bulletin de l'Observatoire du français contemporain en Afrique noire* 3: 9–27.

Laitin, D. (1977), *Politics, Language, and Thought: The Somali Experience* (Chicago: The University of Chicago Press).

—— (1992), *Language Repertoires and State Construction in Africa* (Cambridge: Cambridge University Press).

—— (2001), 'Multilingual States', in R. Mesthrie (ed.), *Concise Encyclopedia of Sociolinguistics* (Amsterdam: Elsevier), 652–57.

Lakhdar Ghazal, A. (1976) (ed.), *Méthodologie générale de l'arabisation de niveau*. (Rabat: IERA).

Lamberti, M. (1986), *Map of Somali Dialects in the Somali Democratic Republic*. With Supplement: *Speech Variation in Somalia with 6 Maps and Foreword by Andrzej Zaborski* (Hamburg: Helmut Buske Verlag).

Landry, R., and Bourhis, R. Y. (1997), 'Linguistic Landscape and Ethnolinguistic Vitality: An Empirical Study', *Journal of Language and Social Psychology* 16: 23–49.

LANGTAG [Language Task Action Group] (1996), *Towards a National Plan for South Africa*. Final Report of the Language Plan Task Group (LANGTAG) (Pretoria: Department of Arts, Culture, Science and Technology).

Lanham, L. (1978), 'South African English', in L. Lanham and K. Prinsloo (eds.), *Language and Communication Studies in South Africa* (Cape Town: Oxford University Press), 138–65.

Lass, R. (2002), 'South African English', in Mesthrie (ed.), 104–26.

Lawrance, B. (2005), 'The History of the Ewe Language and Ewe Language Education', in B. Lawrance (ed.), *The Ewe of Togo and Benin* (Accra: Woeli Publishing Services), 215–29.

Legère, K. (2006), 'J. K. Nyerere of Tanzania and the Empowerment of Swahili', in M. Pütz, J. Fishman, and J. Neff-van Aertselaer (eds.), *Along the Routes to Power: Explorations of Empowerment through Language* (Berlin, New York: Mouton de Gruyter), 373–403.

Le Page, R., and A. Tabouret-Keller (1985), *Acts of Identity* (Cambridge: Cambridge University Press).

Leslie, W. (1983), *Zaire: Continuity and Political Change in an Oppressive State* (Boulder, CO: Westview Press).

Lienhardt, R. G. (1961), *Divinity and Experience: The Religion of the Dinka* (Oxford: Clarendon Press).

van Lierde, J. (1963) (ed.), *La Pensée politique de Patrice Lumumba* (Paris: Présence Africaine).

Luffin, X. (2004), *Kinubi Texts*, Languages of the World/Text Collections 21 (Munich: Lincom Europa).

Mabika-Kalanda, A. (1962), *La remise en question, base de la décolonisation mentale* (Paris: Editions Remarques Africaines).

Madsen, W. (1999), *Genocide and Covert Operations in Africa, 1993–1999* (Lewiston, NY: The Edwin Mellen Press).

Maduka-Durunze, O. (1998), 'Linguistic Pluralism, the National Language Policy, and Problems of Nigerian Nationhood', in O. Okechukwu, A. Akpuru, and S. Emezue (eds.), 71–97.

Mahlalela, B., and Heugh, K. (2002), *Terminology and Schoolbooks in Southern African Languages: Aren't there Any?* PRAESA [Project for the Study of Alternative Education in South Africa] Occasional Papers No. 10, University of Cape Town.

Mahmud, U. A. (1983), *Arabic in the Southern Sudan: History and Spread of a Pidgin-Creole* (Khartoum: FAL Advertising and Print. Co.).

Maho, J. (2001), *African Languages Country by Country: a Reference Guide*, 5th edn. (major revision) (Gothenburg: Department of Oriental and African Languages).

Makalela, L. (2004), 'Making Sense of BSAE for Linguistic Democracy in South Africa', *World Englishes* 23: 355–66.

Makoni, S. (1999), 'Shifting Discourses in Language Studies in South Africa', in K. Prah (ed.), *Knowledge in Black and White* (Cape Town: Centre for Advanced Studies of African Societies, Book Series 2), 143–8.

Maloba, W. (1989), 'Nationalism and Decolonization 1947–1963', in W. R. Ochieng (ed.), *A Modern History of Kenya 1895–1980* (Nairobi: Evans Brothers Ltd.), 173–201.

Manchisi, P. C. (2004), 'The Status of the Indigenous Languages in Institutions of Learning in Zambia: Past, Present and Future', *The African Symposium On-line Journal* 4. Available online at: http://www2.ncsu.edu/ncsu/aern/manpisi.html

Mansour, G. (1993), *Multingualism and Nation Building* (Clevedon: Multilingual Matters).

——(2004), 'A Tale of Two Languages', review of N. Haeri (2003), *Al-Ahram Weekly Monthly Supplement*, issue no. 60: 24.

Marçais, W. (1930–1931), 'La diglossie: un pélérinage aux sources', *Bulletin de la Société Linguistique de Paris* 76(1): 61–98.

Marivate, C. (2000), 'The Mission and Activities of the Pan South African Language Board', in de Prez and du Plessis (eds.), 130–7.

Martin-Jones, M., and Romaine, S. (1985), 'Semilingualism: a Half-baked Theory of Communicative Competence', *Applied Linguistics* 6: 105–17.

Massamba, D. (2002), *Historia ya Kiswahili (50 BK hadi 1500 BK)* (Nairobi: Jomo Kenyatta Foundation).

Matongo, A. B. K. (1992), 'Popular Culture in a Colonial Society: Another Look at Mbeni and Kalela Dances on the Copperbelt 1930–1964', in S. N. Chipungu (ed.), *Guardians of Their Time. Experiences of Zambians Under Colonial Rule 1890–1946* (London, Basingstoke: Macmillan), 180–217.

Mazrui, A., and Mazrui, A. (1995), *Swahili State and Society: The Political Economy of an African Language* (London: James Currey).

——(1998), *The Power of Babel: Language and Governance in the African Experience* (Oxford: James Currey).

——and Shariff, I. N. (1993), *The Swahili: Idiom and Identity of an African People* (Trenton, NJ: Africa World Press).

Mbaabu, I. (1985), *Kiswahili: Past, Present and Future Horizons* (Nairobi: Jomo Kenyatta Foundation).

Mbah Onana, L., and Mbah Onana, M. (1994), 'Le camfranglais' *Diagonales* 32: 29–30.

Mbeki, T. (2004), Toast Remarks by the President of South Africa, Thabo Mbeki, at the State Banquet in his Honour by the President of Zambia, Levy Mwanawasa: Lusaka, Zambia, 23 October 2004, South African Government Information. Available online at http://www.info.gov.za/speeches/2004/04102708451004.htm

McCormick, K. (2002), *Language in Cape Town's District Six* (Oxford: Oxford University Press).

McLaughlin, F. (1995), 'Haalpulaar Identity as a Response to Wolofization', *African Languages and Cultures* 8: 153–68.

——(2001), 'Dakar Wolof and the Configuration of an Urban Identity', *Journal of African Cultural Studies* 14: 153–72.

——(Forthcoming, a), 'The Ascent of Wolof as a Lingua Franca', in C. B. Vigouroux and S. S. Mufwene (eds.), *Globalization and Language Vitality: Perspectives from Black Africa* (London: Continuum Publishers).

——(Forthcoming, b), 'On the origins of urban Wolof: Evidence from Louis Descemet's 1864 phrase book', Ms.

McWilliam, H. O. A., and Kwamena-Poh, M. A. (1975), *The Development of Education in Ghana*, 2nd revised edition (London: Longman Group Limited).

Meinhof, C. (1912), *Die Sprachen der Hamiten* (Hamburg: Friederichsen).

Meldon, J. A. (1913), *English–Arabic Dictionary of Words and Phrases used by the Sudanese in Uganda*, Ms. 53704, School of Oriental and African Studies, University of London.

Mercer, P. (1971), 'Shilluk trade and politics from the mid-seventeenth century to 1861', *Journal of African History* 12: 407–26.

Mesthrie, R. (2002) (ed.), *Language in South Africa* (Cambridge: Cambridge University Press).

Meyer, R., and Richter, R. (2003), *Language Use in Ethiopia from a Network Perspective* (Frankfurt am Main: Peter Lang).

Meyns, P. (1995), *Zambia in der 3. Republik: demokratische Transition und politische Kontinuität* (Hamburg: Institut für Afrika-Kunde).

Miller, C. (2005) (ed.), *Land, Ethnicity and Political Legitimacy in Eastern Sudan: Kassala and Gedaref States* (Cairo: CEDEJ; Khartoum: University of Khartoum Development Studies and Research Centre).

——(2006), 'Language, Identities and Ideologies: A New Era for Sudan?', paper presented at the 7th International Sudan Studies conference, April 2006, Bergen, Norway.

Mitchell, T. F. (1978), 'Educated Spoken Arabic in Egypt and the Levant, with Special Reference to Participle and Tense', *Journal of Linguistics*, 14: 227–58.

——(1986), 'What is Educated Spoken Arabic?', *International Journal of the Sociology of Language*, 61: 7–32.

——(1998), *Colonising Egypt* (Cambridge: Cambridge University Press).

Mkhulisi, N. (2000), 'The National Language Service and the New Language Policy', in de Prez and du Plessis (eds.), 121–9.

Mobutu, S. S. (1973), *Discours du Président de la République à l'Assemblée Générale des Nations Unies, New York, le 4 octobre 1973* (Kinshasa: Département de l'orientation nationale).

Molemobile, V. S. (2000) (ed.), *Nigerianness* (Enugu: Vougasen).

Mouhssine, O. (1995), 'Ambivalence du discours sur l'arabization', *International Journal of the Sociology of Language* 112: 45–61.

Mulford, D. C. (1967), *Zambia: The Politics of Independence 1957–1964* (London: Oxford University Press).

Musa, S. (1947), *al-Balagha al-'asriyya wa-l-lugha al-'arabiyya* (Salama Musa li-l-Nashr wa-l-Tawzi'). (First published 1945.)

Muthwii, M. J., and Kioko, A. N. (2004) (eds.), *New Language Bearings in Africa* (Clevedon: Multilingual Matters).

Mutonya, M., and Parsons, T. (2004), 'KiKAR: A Swahili Variety in Kenya's Colonial Army', *Journal of Language and Linguistics* 25(2): 111–25

Muuse, G. (1954), 'Arabic Script for Somali', *Islamic Quarterly* 1/2: 114–18.

Mwakikagile, G. (2001), *Ethnic Politics in Kenya and Nigeria* (Huntingdon, NY: Nova).

Myers-Scotton, C. (1993), 'Elite Closure as a Powerful Language Strategy: the African Case', *International Journal of the Sociology of Language* 103: 149–63.

Ndaywell è Nziem, I. (1998), *Histoire générale du Congo: De l'héritage ancien à la République Démocratique* (Paris: De Boeck & Larcier, s.a).

Ndebele, N. (1987), 'The English Language and Social Change in South Africa', *English Academy Review* 4: 1–16.

Ndoma, U. (1977), 'Some Aspects of Planning Language Policy in Education in Belgian Congo: 1906–1960', Ph.D. dissertation, Northwestern University, Evanston, IL.

Nelson, H. (1982), *Nigeria: A Country Study* (Washington: U. S. Government Printing Office).

NEPI (National Education Policy Investigation) (1992), *Language* (ed. K. McCormick, Z. Desai, and S. Zotwana) (Cape Town: Oxford University Press).

Ngamassu, D. (1999), 'Le bilinguisme dans l'enseignement extra-scolaire au Cameroun', in Echu and Grundstrom (eds.), 75–83.

Ngbanda, N. H. (2004), *Crimes organisés en Afrique Centrale: Révélations sur les réseux rwandais et occidentaux* (Paris: Editions Duboiris).

Nida, E., and Wonderly, W. (1971), 'Communication Roles of Languages in Multilingual Societies', in Whiteley (ed.), 57–74.

Niedzielski, N., and Preston, D. R. (2000), *Folk Linguistics* (Berlin/New York: Mouton de Gruyter).

Nugent, P. (2000), ' "A few lesser peoples": the Central Togo Minorities and their Ewe Neighbours', in Lentz and Nugent (eds.), *Ethnicity in Ghana, the Limits of Invention* (Basingstoke: MacMillan Press Ltd.; New York: St. Martin's Press, Inc), 162–82.

Nurse, D. (2006), 'Bantu Languages', in K. Brown (ed.), *Encyclopedia of Language and Linguistics* (Oxford: Elsevier), vol. 1, 679–85.

Nyamnjoh, F. (1996), *The Cameroon G.C.E. Crisis: A Test of Anglophone Solidarity* (Limbe: Nooremac Press).

Nyerere, J. K. (1967), *Education for Self-reliance* (Dar es Salaam: Government Printer).

Nzongola-Ntalaja, G. (2002), *The Congo, from Leopold to Kabila: A People's History* (London: Zed Books).

—— (2006), 'The Democratic Transition in DR Congo: The Legacy of the Sovereign National Conference.' Unpublished paper.

Odumuh, T. O. (2000), 'A Look at Mother Tongue Education in Nigeria', in V. S. Molemobile (ed.), 236–44.

O'Fahey, R. S. (1980), *State and Society in Darfur* (London: Hurst).

—— and Spaulding, J. (1974), *Kingdoms of the Sudan* (London: Methuen).

Ogunsiji, A. (2001), 'Utilitarian Dimensions of Language in Nigeria', in Igboanusi (ed.), 152–64.

Ohannessian, S., and Kashoki, M. E. (1978) (eds.), *Language in Zambia* (London: International African Institute).

Okechukwu, O., Akpuru, A., and Emezue, S. (1998) (eds.), *Issues in Contemporary Nigerian History* (Port Harcourt: Educational Books and Investments Ltd.).

Okehie-Offoha, M. U., and Sadiku, M. N. O (1996) (eds.), *Ethnic and Cultural Diversity in Nigeria* (Trenton: Africa World Press).

Okeke, O. (1998), 'Inter-group Relations in Nigeria since 1960', in Okechukwu, Akpuru, and Emezue (eds.), 1–43.

Omamor, A. P. (1994), 'Language planning: Theory and Practice in Some African Countries', in Asein and Adesanoye (eds.), 32–63.

Opheim, M. (1999), 'L'éducation bilingue au Mali: le cas de Dougoukouna, une "école experimentale en bambara", Master's thesis, University of Oslo.

ORTM (*Office de radiodiffusion télévision du Mali*) (2006), www.ortm.net.

Orwin, M. (2003), 'On the Concept of "Definitive Text" in Somali Poetry', *Bulletin of the School of Oriental and African Studies*, 66/3: 334–47.

Osman, S. N. (2006), 'Proverbs and Idiomatic Phrases in Zaghawa Language', paper presented at the 7th International Sudan Studies conference, April 2006, Bergen, Norway.

Owusu-Ansah, A. (2006), 'Indigenous Languages for Ghana', *Daily Graphic*, Monday, June 2006, p. 17.

——and McFarland, D. M. (1995), *Historical Dictionary of Ghana*, 2nd edition (Metuchen/London: The Scarecrow Press Inc.).

Oyebade, A. (2003) (ed.), *The Foundations of Nigeria* (Trenton, NJ: Africa World Press).

——(2003) 'A Retrospect on Colonial Nigeria', in Oyebade (ed.), 15–25.

Oyetade, O. (2001) 'Attitude to Foreign Languages and Indigenous Language Use in Nigeria', in Igboanusi (ed.), 14–29.

Parsons, N. (1982), *A New History of Southern Africa* (London: Macmillan).

Pélissier, P. (1966), *Les paysans du Sénégal: Les civilizations agraires du Cayor à la Casamance* (Saint-Yrieix: Imprimerie Fabrègue).

Perbi, A. (2006), 'Who is a Ghanaian? – a Historical Perspective', in *National Integration, Proceedings 2003* (Accra: Ghana Academy of Arts and Sciences), 29–37.

Persson, A., and Persson, J., with Ahmad Hussein (1979), *Sudanese Colloquial Arabic for Beginners* (High Wycombe: Summer Institute of Linguistics).

—— —— (1991) *Mödö – English Dictionary with Grammar*, Bilingual Dictionaries of Sudan, No. 1 (Nairobi: Summer Institute of Linguistics, Sudan).

Pichl, W. J. (1966), *The Cangin Group: A Language Group in Northern Senegal* (Pittsburgh: Institute of African Affairs, Duquesne University Press).

Platiel, S., and Kaboré, R. (1998) (eds.), *Les langues d'Afrique subsaharienne* (Paris: Ophrys).

Ploog, K. (2002), *Le français à Abidjan. Pour une approche syntaxique du non-standard* (Paris: CNRS Editions).

Plüddemann, P., Braam, D., October, M., and Wababa, Z. (2003), *Dual Medium and Parallel Medium Schooling in the Western Cape: from Default to Design* PRAESA (Project for the Study of Alternative Education in South Africa) Occasional Papers no. 17, University of Cape Town.

Plungian, V., and Tembiné, I. (1994), 'Vers une description sociolinguistique du pays dogon: attitudes linguistiques et problèmes de standardisation', in Dumestre (ed.), 163–96.

Polomé, E. (1968), 'The Choice of Official Languages in the Democratic Republic of the Congo', in Fishman, Ferguson, and Das Gupta (eds.), 295–312.

——(1980), 'The Languages of Tanzania', in E. C. Polomé and C. P. Hill (eds.), *Language in Tanzania* (Oxford: Oxford University Press), 3–25.

Pongo, K. M. (1999), *Transition et conflits politiques au Congo-Kinshasa* (Paris: Editions Karthala).

Posner, D. N. (2005), *Institutions and Ethnic Politics in Africa* (Cambridge: Cambridge University Press).

Prah, K. (1995), *Mother Tongue for Scientific and Technological Development in Africa* (Bonn: German Foundation for International Development).

——(1998) (ed.), *Between Distinction and Extinction* (Johannesburg: Witwatersrand University Press).

Recensement général de la population et de l'habitat (1987), vol. 0, résultats définitifs, tome 1: 'Population, économie, habitat'. (Bamako: Bureau central de recensement, Ministère du Plan, Direction nationale de la statistique et de l'informatique).

Ridge, S. (2004), 'Language Planning in a Rapidly Changing Multilingual Society – the Case of English in South Africa', *Language Problems and Language Policy* 28(2): 199–215.

Rilly, C. (2004), 'The Linguistic Position of Meroitic,' *Arkamani, Sudan Journal of Archaeology and Anthropology* (online journal: see www.arkamani.org/arkamani-library/meroitic/rilly.htm).

Roberge, P. (1990), 'The Ideological Profile of Afrikaans Historical Linguistics', in J. Joseph and T. Taylor (eds.), *Ideologies of Language* (London: Routledge), 131–52.

Roberts, A. (1976), *A History of Zambia* (London: Heinemann).

Robins, S., Madzudzo, E., and Brenzinger, M. (2001), *An Assessment of the Status of the San in South Africa, Angola, Zambia and Zimbabwe* (Windhoek: Legal Assistance Centre).

Roel, K. (1930), 'The Linguistic Situation in East Africa', *Africa* 3: 191–202.

Rossillon, P. (1995) (ed.), *Atlas de la langue française* (Paris: Bordas).

Rotberg, R. I. (1966), *The Rise of Nationalism in Central Africa* (Cambridge, MA: Harvard University Press).

Roy-Campbell, Z. M. (2001), *Empowerment through Language: the African Experience – Tanzania and Beyond* (Trenton, NJ: Africa World Press).

Rubenson, S. (1996), 'The Transition from Coptic to Arabic', *Egypte Monde Arabe*, 27–28 (Centre d'études et de documentation économique, juridique et sociale, CEDEJ): 77–91.

Russell, J. (1990), 'Success as a Source of Conflict in Language-planning: The Tanzanian Case', *Journal of Multilingual and Multicultural Development*, 11(5): 363–75.

Ruzza, C. (2000), 'Language and Nationalism in Italy: Language as a Weak Marker of Identity', in Barbour and Carmichael (eds.), 168–82.

Sadiku, M. (1996), 'The Yoruba', in Okehie-Offoha and Sadiku (eds.), 125–46.

Sadiqi, F. (1991), 'The Spread of English in Morocco', *International Journal of the Sociology of Language* 87: 99–114.

—— (1997), 'The Place of Berber in Morocco', *International Journal of the Sociology of Language* 123: 7–21.

—— (2003), *Women, Gender and Language in Morocco* (Leiden/Boston: Brill Academic Publishers).

—— (to appear), 'The Gendered Use of Arabic and Other Languages in Morocco', in E. Benmamoun (ed.), *Perspectives on Arabic Linguistics* (Amsterdam: John Benjamins).

Salim, A. I. (1985), 'The Elusive "Mswahili": Some Reflections on his Identity and Culture', in J. Maw and D. Parkin (eds.), *Swahili Language and Society* (Wien: Institut für Afrikanistik und Ägyptologie der Universität), 215–27.

Sanderson, L. P., and Sanderson, N. (1981), *Education, Religion and Politics in Southern Sudan 1899–1964* (London: Ithaca Press).

Saunders, C. (1994) (ed.), *An Illustrated Dictionary of South African History* (Johannesburg: Ibis).

Schöpflin, G. (1997), 'The Functions of Myths and a Taxonomy of Myths', in G. Hosking and G. Schöpflin (eds.), *Myths and Nationhood* (London: Hurst), 19–35.

Searing, J. A. (2005), 'Signares and Sailors in Senegal's Atlantic Port Cities: Saint-Louis and Gorée, 1750–1850', paper presented at the Annual Meeting of the African Studies Association, Washington, DC.

Selim, S. (2004), *The Novel and the Rural Imaginary in Egypt, 1880–1985* (New York/London: RoutledgeCurzon).

Sengova, J. (1987), 'The National Language of Sierra Leone: A Decade of Policy Experimentation', *Africa* 57 (4): 519–30.

Sengova, J. (2006), 'Aborigines and Returnees: In Search of Linguistic and Historical Meaning in Delineations of Sierra Leone's Ethnicity and Heritage', in Dixon-Fyle and Cole (eds.), 167–99.

Senkoro, F. E. M. K. (1988), *Ushairi: nadharia na tahakiki* (Dar es Salaam: Dar es Salaam University Press).

Shey, D. Y. (1989), 'The Translation of Some Public Service Examination Questions in Cameroon', Master's degree thesis, University of Yaoundé.

Siachitema, A. (1991), 'The Social Significance of Language Use and Language Choice in a Zambian Urban Setting: An Empirical Study of Three Neighbourhoods in Lusaka', in J. Cheshire (ed.), *English around the World* (Cambridge: Cambridge University Press), 474–90.

Silva-Corvalan, C. (2004), 'Spanish in the Southwest', in Finegan and Rickford (eds.), 205–29.

Silverstein, M. (1996), 'Encountering Language and Languages of Encounter in North American Ethnohistory', *Journal of Linguistic Anthropology* 6: 126–44.

——(1998), 'Contemporary Transformations of Local Linguistic Communities', *Annual Review of Anthropology*, 401–26.

Simard, Y. (1994), 'Les français de Côte d'Ivoire', *Langue française* 104: 20–36.

Simire, G. O. (2004), 'Developing and Promoting Multilingualism in Public Life and Society in Nigeria', in Muthwii and Kioko (eds.), 135–47.

Singh, M. (1969), *History of Kenya's Trade Union Movement to 1952* (Nairobi: East African Publishing House).

Skattum, I. (1994), 'La presse écrite au Mali: un état des lieux', in Dumestre (ed.), 309–60.

——(1997), 'L'éducation bilingue dans un contexte d'oralité et d'exoglossie: théories et réalités du terrain au Mali', *Nordic Journal of African Studies*, 6(2): 74–106.

——(1998), 'Droits de la personne et droits de la collectivité dans la presse écrite au Mali', in *Droits de la personne, droits de la collectivité en Afrique* (Paris, Yaoundé: Eds. Nouvelles du Sud), 67–100.

——(2000a) (ed.), *L'école et les langues nationales au Mali*, Special Issue of *Nordic Journal of African Studies* (Helsinki: Helsinki University Press), vol. 9, no 3.

——(2000b), 'L'apprentissage du français dans un pays "francophone": le cas du Mali', in A. Englebert, M. Pierrard, L. Rosier, and D. van Raemdonck (eds.), *Actes du XXIIe Congrès International de Linguistique et de Philologie Romanes, Bruxelles, 23–29 juillet 1998* (Tübingen: Niemeyer), vol. IX, 331–9.

Slabbert, S., and Finlayson, R. (2000), '"I'm a cleva!": the Linguistic Makeup of Identity in a South African Urban Environment', *International Journal of the Sociology of Language* 144: 119–36.

Smith, A. D. (1991), *National Identity* (Harmondsworth: Penguin).

Smith, I., and Morris, T. A. (2005), *Juba Arabic–English Dictionary*, rev. edn. (Kampala: Fountain Publishers; Oxford: African Books Collective).

Soghayroun, I. el Z. (1981), *The Sudanese Muslim Factor in Uganda* (Khartoum: Khartoum University Press).

Spaulding, J. (1985), *The Heroic Age in Sinnar* (East Lansing: Michigan State University, African Studies Center).

Spencer-Walters, T. (2006), 'Creolization and Kriodom (Re-)Visioning the "Sierra Leone Experiment"', in Dixon-Fyle and Cole (eds.), 223–55.

Spitulnik, D. (1998), 'The Language of the City: Town Bemba as Urban Hybridity', *Journal of Linguistic Anthropology* 8: 30–59.

Spitzer, L. (1974), *The Creoles of Sierra Leone: Responses to Colonialism, 1870–1945* (Madison, WI: The University of Wisconsin Press).

Spolsky, B., and Shohamy, E. (2001), 'Hebrew after a Century of RLS Efforts', in J. Fishman (ed.), *Can Threatened Languages Be Saved?* (Clevedon: Multilingual Matters), 349–62.

Steere, E. (1870), *A Handbook of the Swahili Language as Spoken at Zanzibar* (London: Bell & Daldy).

Steven, G. A. (2006), 'Education during the Civil War and after Civil War, South Sudan', paper presented at the 7th International Sudan Studies conference, April 2006, Bergen, Norway.

Stevenson, R. C. (1971), 'The Significance of the Sudan in Linguistic Research: Past, Present and Future', in Y. F. Hasan (ed.), *Sudan in Africa* (Khartoum: Khartoum University Press), 11–25.

Stroud, C. (2002), 'Framing Bourdieu Socioculturally: Alternative Forms of Linguistic Legitimacy in Postcolonial Mozambique', *Multilingua* 21: 247–73.

Suleiman, Y. (1996), 'Language and Identity in Egyptian Nationalism', in Y. Suleiman (ed.), *Language and Identity in the Middle East and North Africa* (Richmond: Curzon Press), 25–37.

——(2003), *The Arabic Language and National Identity – A Study in Ideology* (Edinburgh: Edinburgh University Press).

——(2004a), *A War of Words – Language and Conflict in the Middle East* (Cambridge: Cambridge University Press).

——(2004b), Review of Haeri (2003), *Journal of Sociolinguistics* 8: 142–6.

——(2006), 'Constructing Language, Constructing National Identities', in T. Omoniyi and G. White (eds.), *Sociolinguistics of Identity* (London: Continuum), 50–71.

Swigart, L. (2001), 'The Limits of Legitimacy: Language Ideology and Shift in Contemporary Senegal', *Journal of Linguistic Anthropology* 10, 1: 90–130.

Tamari, T. (1997), *Les castes de l'Afrique occidentale: Artisans et musiciens endogames* (Nanterre: Société d'Ethnologie).

——(2006), 'The Role of National Languages in Mali's Modernizing Islamic Schools (*Madrasa*)', paper presented at the LEA (Languages and Education in Africa) conference, University of Oslo, 19–22 June.

Thelwall, R. (1971), 'A Linguistic Survey in El Fasher Secondary School', *Sudan Notes and Records* 52: 46–55.

——(1978) (ed.), *Aspects of Language in the Sudan* (Coleraine: The New University of Ulster).

Thiong'o, N. (1981), *Decolonising the Mind: the Politics of Language in African Literature* (Oxford: James Currey; Nairobi: EAEP).

——(1993) *Moving the Centre: The Struggles for Cultural Freedoms* (Oxford: James Currey).

Thyness, H. (2003), 'Facteurs extra-, inter- et intrasystémiques du français au Mali, étudiés à travers les compétences linguistiques des élèves au lycée Abdoul Karim Camara dit Cabral de Ségou', Master's thesis, University of Oslo.

Tice, R. D. (1974), 'Administrative Structure, Ethnicity, and Nation-Building in the Ivory Coast', *Journal of Modern African Studies* 12(2): 211–29.

Titlestad, P. (1996), 'English, the Constitution and South Africa's Language Future', in V. de Klerk (ed.), *Focus on South Africa* (Amsterdam: John Benjamins), 162–73.

——(1998), 'Some Thoughts on English in South Africa at the Present Time', in A. Foley (ed.), *English at the Turn of the Millennium* (Randburg, South Africa: Océ Outsourcing Co.), 33–8.

Todd, L., and Jumbam, M. (1992), 'Kamtok: Anatomy of a Pidgin', *English Today* 8(2): 3–11.

Topan, F. M. (1992), 'Swahili as a Religious Language', *Journal of Religion in Africa* 22(4): 331–49.

——(2006a), 'Why does a Swahili Writer Write? Euphoria, Pain, and Popular Aspirations in Swahili Literature', *Research in African Literatures* 37(3): 103–19.

——(2006b) 'From Coastal to Global: Erosion of the Swahili "Paradox"', in R. Loimeier and R. Seesemann (eds.), *The Global Worlds of the Swahili. Interfaces of Islam, Identity and Spaces in 19th-Century and 20th-Century East Africa* (Berlin: Lit Verlag), 55–66.

Traill, A. (2002), 'The Khoesan Languages', in Mesthrie (ed.), 27–49.

Traoré, M. L. (2006), 'L'utilisation des langues nationales dans le système éducatif malien: historique, défis et perspectives'. Keynote address at the LEA (Languages and Education in Africa) conference, University of Oslo, 19–22 June 2006.

Trimingham, J. S. (1946), *Sudan Colloquial Arabic* (London: Oxford University Press).

Tucker, A. N. (1978), 'The Classification of the Languages of the Sudan', in Thelwall (ed.), 211–21.

——and Bryan, M. A. (1955), *The Non-Bantu Languages of North-Eastern Africa* (London: Oxford University Press for the International African Institute).

————(1966), *Linguistic Analyses: The Non-Bantu Languages of North-Eastern Africa* (London: Oxford University Press for the International African Institute).

Turcotte, D. (1981), *La politique linguistique en Afrique francophone. Une étude comparative de la Côte d'Ivoire et de Madagascar* (Québec: Les Presses d l'Université de Laval).

UNESCO (1974), *Two Studies on Ethnic Group Relations in Africa: Senegal, the United Republic of Tanzania* (Paris: UNESCO).

Vail, L. (1989), 'Introduction: Ethnicity in Southern African History', in L. Vail (ed.), *The Creation of Tribalism in Southern Africa* (London: James Currey), 1–20.

Vaillant, J. (1990), *Black, French, and African: a Life of Léopold Sédar Senghor* (Cambridge, MA: Harvard University Press).

Vanhove, M. (2006), 'The Beja Language Today in Sudan', paper presented at the 7th International Sudan Studies conference, April 2006, Bergen, Norway.

Vansina, J. (1990), *Paths in the Rainforest: Toward a History of Political Tradition in Equatorial Africa* (Oxford: James Currey).

——1995), 'New Linguistic Evidence and "the Bantu Expansion"', *Journal of African History* 36: 173–95.

——(2003), 'Communications Between Angola and East Central Africa Before c. 1700', paper presented at the international symposium *Angola on the Move: Transport Routes, Communication and History*, Berlin, 24–26 September 2003. Available online at http://www.zmo.de/angola/

Verney, P., et al. (1995), *Sudan: Conflict and Minorities*, MRG Report, 95: 3 (London: Minority Rights Group International).

Versteegh, K. (1997). *The Arabic Language* (Edinburgh: Edinburgh University Press).

Vydrine, V. (1994), 'Etude socio-linguistique en pays khassonké', in Dumestre (ed.), 197–280.

Wade, R. (1995), 'A New English for a New South Africa: Restandardisation of South African English', *South African Journal of Linguistics*, Supplement 27: 89–102.

Ward, W. E. F. (1948), *A History of Ghana* (London: George Allen and Unwin Ltd.).

Warschauer, M. (2002), 'Language Choice Online: Globalization and Identity in Egypt', *Journal of Computer-Mediated Communication* 7 : 4, http://jcmc.indiana.edu/vol7/issue4/warschauer.html

Webb, V. (2002), *Language in South Africa – the Role of Language in National Transformation, Reconstruction and Development* (Amsterdam: John Benjamins).

Wendell, C. (1972), *The Evolution of the Egyptian National Image: From its Origins to Ahmad Lutfi al-Sayyid* (Berkeley, CA: University of California Press).

Westermann, D. (1927), *Die westlichen Sudansprachen und ihrer Beziehungen zum Bantu* (Hamburg: Reimer).

Whiteley, W. (1969), *Swahili. The rise of a National Language* (London: Methuen).

——(1971) (ed.), *Language Use and Social Change* (London: Oxford University Press for the International African Institute).

——(1974) (ed.), *Language in Kenya* (Nairobi: Oxford University Press).

WHO (2005), World Health Organization Country Profile Zambia, September 2005. Available online at http://www.who.int/hac/crises/zmb/en/

Wilcocks, William (1893), 'Lima la tujad quwwat al-ikhtira 'lada al-misriyyin al-an?' *Al- Azhar* 6, 1–10.

Wiley, T. G. (2004), 'Language Planning, Language Policy, and the English-Only Movement', in Finegan and Rickford (eds.), 319–38.

Wilks, I. (1993), *Forests of Gold* (Athens: Ohio University Press).

Williams, G. (1994), 'Intelligibility and Language Boundaries among the Cangin Peoples of Senegal', *Journal of West African Languages* 24: 47–67.

Williamson, K., and Blench, R. (2000), 'Niger-Congo', in Heine and Nurse (eds.), 11–42.

Wilson, G. (1941), *An Essay on the Economics of Detribalization in Northern Rhodesia*. The Rhodes–Livingstone Papers, No. 5, Part 1 (Lusaka: Rhodes-Livingstone Institute).

Wioland, F. (1965), *Enquête sur les langues parlées au Sénégal par les élèves de l'enseignement primaire* (Dakar: Centre de Linguistique Appliquée de Dakar).

——and Calvet, M. (1967), 'L'expansion du wolof au Sénégal' *Bulletin de l'IFAN* (Institut Fondamental de l'Afrique Noire) 29: 3–4.

Woods, D. (1988), 'State Action and Class Interests in the Ivory Coast', *African Studies Review*, 31(1): 93–116.

Wright, L. (1996), 'The Standardisation Question in Black South African English', in V. de Klerk (ed.), *Focus on South Africa* (Amsterdam: John Benjamins), 149–62.

Wyse, A. (1989), *The Krio of Sierra Leone: An Interpretive History* (London: C. Hurst & Co. Publishers Ltd.).

Yankah, K. (2004), *Language, the Mass Media and Democracy in Ghana*. Annual Lecture in the Humanities. (Accra: Ghana Academy of Arts and Sciences).

Yates, B. (1981), 'Educating Congolese Abroad: a Historical Note on an African Elite', *The International Journal of African Historical Studies* 14,1: 34–64.

Young, C. M., and Turner, T. (1985), *The Rise and Decline of the Zairian State* (Madison: University of Wisconsin Press).

Young, D., van der Vlugt, J., and Qanya, S. (2004), 'Concept Literacy and Language Use in Teaching and Learning Maths and Science', paper presented at the Southern African Applied Language Studies Association, University of the North, July 2004.

Youssef, A. A. (2003), *From Pharaoh's Lips: Ancient Egyptian Language in the Arabic of Today* (Cairo / New York: The American University in Cairo Press).

Youssi, A. (1995), 'The Moroccan Triglossia: Facts and Implications', *International Journal of the Sociology of Language* 112: 29–43.

Zambia Analytical Report: Census of Population, Housing and Agriculture (1990), Volume 10. Central Statistical Office, Lusaka.

Zambia Analytical Report: Census of Population, Housing and Agriculture (2000), Central Statistical Office, Lusaka.

Zentella, A. C. (2004), 'Spanish in the Northeast', in Finegan and Rickford (eds.), 182–204.

Zroukhi, I. (1999), *Al-dawla fi al-fikr al-'arabi al-hadith: dirasa fikriyya falsafiyya* (Cairo: Dar Al-Fajr li-l-Nashr wa-l-Tawzi').

Index

CPSIA information can be obtained
at www.ICGtesting.com
Printed in the USA
BVHW072203071221
623442BV00006B/91